This Was My England
the story of a childhood

Robert Corfe is a prolific author of books on political science and social issues, and in addition to the present work, he has produced 3 other autobiographical titles under different pseudonyms, viz., *The Girl From East Berlin* *a romantic docu-drama of the East-West divide* (James Furner), an epic novel relating his love affair in the old German capital at the end of the 1950s; *My Conflict With a Soviet Spy* *the story of the Ron Evans spy case* (Eddie Miller), based on his adventures in Scandinavia in the 1960s; and, *Death in Riyadh* *dark secrets in hidden Arabia* (Geoff Carter), based on his experiences as a businessman in the Middle East in the 1980s. He has also been active in different spheres of public life, and in 1987 he founded The Campaign For Industry in promoting home-based productivity. *This Was My England* records the tempestuous first 18 years of his life, and the horrific experiences both at home and at boarding school. It then describes his love for a film star during his teens, and the long-term destructive consequences of this impossible obsession, which led to gestures of suicide and murder. The book is also an interesting social document in that it presents an array of colourful and eccentric characters, and vividly portrays the attitudes and private life of a long past epoch in the 1940s and start of the 50s.

By the same author –

Social Capitalism in theory and practice

Vol. 1
Emergence of the New Majority

Vol. 2
The People's Capitalism

Vol. 3
Prosperity in a stable World

Egalitarianism of the Free Society
and the end of class conflict

The Future of Politics
with the demise of the left/right confrontational system

The Death of Socialism
*the irrelevance of the traditional left & the call for a progressive
politics of universal humanity*

Deism & Social Ethics
the role of religion in the third millennium

Populism Against Progress
and the collapse of aspirational values

Freedom From America
*for safeguarding democracy & the economic & cultural integrity of
peoples*

Land of The Olympians
papers from the enlightened Far North

This Was My England

the story of a childhood

Robert Corfe

Arena Books

First published in 2011 by Arena Books
2nd Impression 2012

Arena Books
6 Southgate Green
Bury St. Edmunds
IP33 2BL

www.arenabooks.co.uk

Corfe, Robert- 1935
This Was My England *the story of a childhood*
    1. Corfe, Robert, 1935 – Childhood and youth. 2. Authors,
    English – 20th century – Biography. 3. Great Britain -
    Social life and customs – 20th century.
    I Title
    941'.084'092-dc22

ISBN-13   978-1-906791- 73-5

BIC categories:- HBTB, JFSP1/2, BGA, JFF, JFSC, HBLW3, BGLA.

Printed and bound by Lightning Source UK

Cover design
by Jason Anscomb

Typeset in
Times New Roman

Prologue

To those who knew them at the time, I believe that both sides of my family presented the most ordinary and stereotypical characteristics of their class – certainly to neighbours, friends, and other casual acquaintances. They led conventional humdrum lives in fulfilling what was expected of them, and they themselves would not like to have been thought of living otherwise. It was always regarded as regrettable to attract public attention, and I remember my father once remarking that it was a "bad day" if ever one's name appeared in the papers – unless of course it was in connection with announcements of birth, marriage or death.

If, then, this book presents the picture of a dysfunctional family, including some of the worse vices or faults of human behaviour, together with an assortment of other supposedly respectable people, who are equally bad or eccentric, then an explanation is called for before embarking on this memoir. The truth, I feel, is to be found in the fact that my family was (and is) no better nor worse than any other average family in this country or elsewhere to be found throughout the four quarters of our planet. Humankind by nature is necessarily individualistic, and hence it follows, is inevitably fallible. Furthermore, there are no absolute standards of morality or behaviour, and each individual puts a different emphasis on what he or she *really* feels is right or wrong.

After seven decades of observation, it seems to me that vice and virtue is equally balanced in each individual amongst the majority, and that whilst some lose out in being held in higher regard because their faults are so visible, whilst better qualities are hidden; there are others more fortunate, because of their likeableness and outward good nature, whose grave defects are concealed except for the rare event on the odd occasion. There may be unfairness in which many are regarded, often for no fault of their own, in the same way there is unfairness in other spheres of existence. Most wish to be seen in a good light, and for this reason they defend themselves, or cover their tracks, by conforming to the standards of their time, but those standards may have no objective basis *per se*, and this is partly demonstrated by the fact that they shift from one generation to another.

But there is also another and more serious question to consider: in most societies and time periods, there are some expectations of right and wrong which do not fit the normal demands of human nature. These usually concern the conventions of human relationships, and in the industrialised world over the past hundred years, there have been huge changes in attitudes and legislation with regard to these matters. These changes have occurred as the inevitable consequences of immense socio-economic pressures in the transformation of society.

It is during this process that domestic life is thrown into turmoil. But for the most part it is hidden from view and is usually only revealed through the pages of fiction. The secret battles which take place behind the net curtains of villages and towns throughout the industrialised world – and even further afield – take the form of bitter conflicts, often giving rise to much unhappiness. And the weapons of the aggrieved, on both sides of a dispute, are always the cry for "morality" versus "freedom." And the resolution of this conflict – but only after a period of time – following social readjustment, are changes to the concepts of morality and freedom in matching new conditions in society.

These radical changes in the ideas of what comprises right or wrong are most clearly demonstrated in hindsight. It is then that we look at our forebears and are appalled at their attitudes and behaviour, but are we therefore to condemn them as bad people? The answer has to be No! They must be judged by the standards of their time, as otherwise we would be unjust to their memory. They may have based their opinions and actions on false premises or prejudice, but if these were the ideas of the time, they could not have acted otherwise. They were, after all, the prisoners of their age.

Every culture and age has its own concept of the *respectable*, which is not so much a system of right or wrong in itself, but rather a set of conventions for behaviour or personal appearance, so that all might present an agreed and accepted image, without in any way betraying their true reality or hidden faults. Respectability is an essential component of society, not only in ensuring smooth everyday relationships, but because of the vulnerability of humankind to so many failings and vices. It serves therefore as an effective disguise, so that each individual may avoid the disdain and criticism of his peers. Everyone is thus made to feel equal and at ease in the company of his friends without the risk of compromising his desired appearance.

In the memoir which follows there is much which may arouse the indignation of the reader. There are several reasons for this. Firstly, it describes events which took place predominantly in the 1940s, or between 1935 and January 1954, and the present world has been transformed out of all recognition since that time. Secondly, as the book which follows is an autobiography, it is necessarily subjective, i.e., it describes the feelings of the author at the time, and this tends to heighten the intensity of unpleasant experiences, whilst casting sometimes a curious light on those which were agreeable. Objective comment on events has sometimes been necessary, in putting them into a contemporary perspective, but this has been kept to a minimum.

If the author has appeared critical of many in this book, or cast them in a bad light, then this may be partly excused – or at least explained - on the grounds he has portrayed himself in the worst light of all. This is not to suggest he has striven to morally abase himself before the world, but merely that he has felt obliged to describe those innermost feelings which arose from the brutality and injustice he incurred in both a home and school environment. If he had failed to do this, then the immense psychological drama of his teenage years, with its dreadful long-term consequences, might simply remain inexplicable. Hence, this memoir has been written in the only way it could, in revealing the unvarnished truth with warts and all.

The question may be asked: what is the meaning of *normality*? In the sense of human behaviour and consciousness, from a purely objective viewpoint, my answer would be that no such thing exists. Normality is nothing more nor less than the striving to achieve the ideal stereotype as it exists in its infinite variations in time and space, and since it can never be wholly achieved in reality because of individual differences in psychological states of mind it therefore remains an unachievable ideal. This is the reality of human nature which divides us from automatons. And those exceptional people who do succeed in achieving the ideal stereotype of their time are often found to be insufferable by their fellow beings.

It may be asked as to why this book was given such a generalised title as, **This Was My England**. There is a sound reason and the title is entirely apt. As I began to write, describing my relatives, their circumstances and anxieties, I soon realised I was delineating the private social history of an age, and to some, the latter might be of greater interest than the life of the author. In any event, the two are inextricably linked, and the development and character of the author could not be properly understood without knowing something about the world in which he was nurtured.

Furthermore, the comments of relatives and others recorded in the book reflect the prejudices of the time, and it is often forgotten that such opinions were commonly held, since succeeding generations would prefer consigning them to oblivion than to publish them for posterity. Most descriptions of the recent past – at least in memoirs or books of popular reminiscence – tend to draw a rosy picture, or present a bland impression of reality, but that is a path I would be loathed to follow. If the truth is to be written, then facts must be stated as they were. In this way I have endeavoured to respect the natural sagacity of readers.

Lastly, I would warn the reader against any thought of complacency in congratulating ourselves in glancing back at an age which may seem shocking in its ignorance or appalling in its cruelty, or otherwise unenlightened on matters we now take for granted. The familiar is always shrouded in a sense of normality, and this tends to be deceptive in undermining our objective perspective of reality. We are always ready to criticize the past or unfamiliar environments, but less ready to question what we *think* we really know. For example, it may be that we face greater social problems at the beginning of the 21st century than ever existed in the 1940s or 50s. Change, when it comes through the reactive pendulum alone, is always suspect, and that has been the predominant pattern of change over the past 60 years.

Legislation may have bettered human relationships in some respects, whilst worsening them in others. Changes in education over the past few decades have entailed sacrificing time for the humanities in place of laying greater emphasis on technology. The outcome is that standards of literacy today (certainly with regard to spelling) are worse than they were in the 1940s. Meanwhile, the decline of the humanities (especially in literature and history) is giving rise to a new form of philistinism which is incompatible with an otherwise highly educated society, in that it leads to a culturally lop-sided knowledge-base for most.

If the interest of this memoir extends beyond the life of the author, then I hope it arouses a curiosity in the nature of change in the sphere of private social life, so that the study of our own age may be approached from a more critical and objective viewpoint. I would not like it thought that I am left with any thoughts of resentment or ill-will against anyone described in this book. Today I would be happy to meet and socialise as an equal with those who at one time might have been described as the "worst of my enemies."

As a final word, it should be mentioned that this memoir was written at the instigation of my younger brother, Russ (or Gavin), following several years of badgering. I am also indebted to him, and also to my youngest brother, Oliver, for reading through the manuscript with regard to identifying inaccuracies, and to gain their assent in the matter of comment or the interpretation of facts. I am exceedingly grateful to both my brothers for their painstaking work in all the above respects. Acknowledgements must also be made to my nephew, Joni Corfe, without whose detailed genealogical researches errors would have been missed, and many useful dates could not have been included. I am even more indebted to him, however, for his painstaking work in preparing the illustrations for this book, often entailing the touching-up, or enlargement and improvement of images from faded and yellowing photographs.

Robert Corfe
May 2011

Contents

CHAPTER 23
I enter the Legal World

An upstairs downstairs world of gossip – The varied staff – A question of class consciousness – How a legal mindset was to be of benefit in the future – My interest in jurisprudence

CHAPTER 24
My Life in the West End

My continuing literary efforts – Theatre going – A Philosophy course – Strange visitors to the office – The Sergeant-Major loses his job – The arrival of Mr. Dawes – The Coronation – Love for a waitress

CHAPTER 25
Old School Friends and Others

The Browns' new residence – A KAS function – Gilbert Harding – Passion for Miss Dainton revived – Attempts at the cure of pipe smoking – End of the PD affair – Assessments for military fitness – Osbourn and his Jewish girl friend – A spiritualist meeting – An evening with Richard Martin – Geoffrey Dunston and our doomed friendship – My grandfather's second marriage

CHAPTER 26
An Ending and a New Beginning

How I ended my employment – A party at KAS – My *Apology* – Final parting – Christmas 1953 – Letters of thanks and good wishes – I join the Army

Epilogue

Illustrations
between pages 170 – 171

Plates – 1

a) Author's paternal grandfather, Ernest William Corfe (1878-1963)
b) Author's paternal grandmother, Ethel Corfe, née Smith (1885-1951)
c) Maternal grandfather, Capt. John Figgins, RN, OBE (1868-1946)
d) Maternal grandmother, Grace Figgins, née Bedbrook (1876-1965)

Plates – 2

a) Great-grandfather, Rear Admiral James Albert Bedbrook (1845-1902)
b) Author's early childhood & later teenage home: 196 Muswell Hill Rd.
c) Author's father, Felix Norman Corfe (1906-1990)
d) Author's mother, Joyce D.P. Corfe, née Figgins (1906-2000)

Plates – 3

a) With paternal grandparents at Ashmount, with l. to r., Uncle Harold
   & father, 1936
b) Author age 2 in London home, 1937
c) With Old Nanny in garden, 1937
d) With maternal grandmother in Melksham, 1937

Plates – 4

a) Easter w/e picnic 1937, w. seated: l. to r. Aunts Anita, Betty, Great-aunt Loo,
   Cousin Maris, Great-aunt Blanche, maternal grandmother, Aunt Pam & mother;
   Standing: Uncles Denys & Vaughan, Great-aunt Gwladys & Great-uncle Percy

b) Whitsun picnic 1937, l. to r. Uncle Dick, Author, mother, cousin Anne, Aunt
   Joan (Brown), cousin Michael & Uncle Harold

Plates – 5

a) In London age 3
b) Sampford Place, Melksham
c) With Ealing Nanny, 1938

Plates – 6

a) Author age 4 at Kingsdown, September 1939
b) On "my land" at back of Sampford Place, 1942
c) Author in background w. cousin Maris & brother, Gavin, in foreground,
   3rd September 1939 at Sampford Place

Plates – 7

a) At Weddon Cross, Somerset, 1943
b) Author with his two younger brothers & Miss Wall at Sampford Place, 1944
c) Hampton Hall, Bathampton, Bath
d) With paternal grandparents, mother & youngest brother, Oliver, 1945
e) G.B.Riddell, Housemaster, Woodbridge Junior School

Illustrations

CHAPTER 1
Two Very Different Families

"Happy families are all alike; every unhappy family is
unhappy in its own way."
Leo Tolstoy, opening words of *Anna Karenina*

On writing an autobiography – My birth – Maternal relatives – Paternal relatives –
Mother – Father – Their early relationship – Their marriage – Tensions between the
two families – My birth gives rise to a family quarrel and long-standing split

When life's work is done and tomorrow holds few prospects for the future, then memories may begin to take on a fresh clarity they had not done for many a year past. The reality of the past can then take on a sharper focus after a life of intense activity and perhaps too hopeful aspirations. This is to be expected, for in the struggle of daily life, it is only the present and the future which really matters. Howsoever the past may inescapably guide and direct our lives, the bustle and absorption of mundane existence ensures that pondering recollections are somehow kept at bay.

But with the onset of age, and the completion of life's task and the prospect of extinction, there is the need for a summing-up, a gathering in of all the loose ends, and a final report to explain if not to justify one's faults or failings, if not to the world at large, then at least to one's personal conscience. And as such a summing-up must be factual and chronological in building a structure from which the conclusions of others may be drawn, rather than comprising meandering reflections on arbitrarily chosen episodes, it must necessarily take on the form of an autobiography.

There are many ways in which an autobiography may be approached. It may be written from the perspective of one's public life, in which event private matters and personal thoughts take on a low profile; or it may be written purely to amuse by passing from one disconnected anecdote to another; or it may set out to portray an idealised self-portrait as one would like to be remembered; or it may recount a life as one would have wished to live; or it may studiously attempt to please one's nearest and dearest, whilst avoiding offence to anyone with whom one may have brushed shoulders throughout the course of life.

The autobiography which follows falls into none of the above categories. Its purpose is to record none other than the deepest and most long-lasting impressions of events and persons as they occurred at the time, shamelessly, and with little regard for my reputation or that of others. There is no way of reaching ultimate truth – if that is ever an imaginable possibility – and neither is it my primary intention, but if an account of one's life is to approximate most closely to the truth, then it is only to be reached through throwing aside all inhibition or sense of self-regard in writing for one's own satisfaction alone. If absolute truth cannot be reached by such an approach, it is certain that absolute honesty can.

If an autobiography is to be truly candid, all sense of pride or status, or need to justify oneself before the world or a higher authority must be brushed aside, as one stands naked and undefended, to be disdained or ridiculed by those who would criticise or moralise according to their temperament. In the following memoir, only occasionally shall I attempt to interpret events if I so choose, preferring to leave the task of interpretation to those professional biographers who are bound to know more about the author than the author knows about himself.

The following therefore sets out to be a *memoir* or *confession* in the sense it is merely a record of memories, in conjunction with care to ascertain the accuracy of facts where documentation exists, and so no academic bookishness is allowed to intervene between immediate impressions and their written transfer to the page. Of course this may give rise to the occasional inaccuracy, but that is a task for those who are better placed than the author to uncover and correct, in revealing to a sometimes prurient readership a revision or re-working of what is believed to be the greater truth.

It needs to be borne in mind that the memory is fallible and liable to play all kinds of tricks, but that is no argument that an autobiography should attempt anything more than a *memoir* from the subjective viewpoint of its author in presenting the impressions of his own personality. If something more is preferred then that must be left to the insight of the professional biographer with his interpretational skills.

*

A life must begin with the author's background, and that means describing the origins of his family's circumstances. I was born at approximately 4.30 pm in the middle of a thunderstorm at 27 Welbeck Street, some ten minutes walk from Oxford Circus, on 23rd August 1935. George V was then King-Emperor, Stanley Baldwin was the Prime Minister, Franklin D. Roosevelt was the President of the USA, and Hitler had been Chancellor of Germany for some 18 months. I was bottle fed because that was most customary amongst the English middle classes in the 1930s. And besides, my mother was repulsed by the idea of breast feeding which she thought "primitive," and soon to be discarded by all classes with the "advance of civilisation." She once told me she disliked anyone to touch her breasts, and disdained as distasteful most kinds of physical contact.

As the eldest son of an eldest son, I was naturally born to be self-important and arrogant, and for the first six years of my life I had a vile temper, whilst being otherwise tortured by all kinds of fears and complexes. The arrogance shows through clearly in those photographs of my early years. On the same day in the same exclusive West End nursing home, a son was born to the wife of the famous actor, Emlyn Williams.

My father's family was very different from my mother's, although both may have held an equal status in different ways. My father's family came from a business background, although at the time of my birth my closest relatives were all professional people, mostly in medicine, but the business mentality was so deeply entrenched that they represented the Protestant work ethic and the spirit of capitalism almost to the point of parody, and they were enriched as a consequence of this far beyond the evidence of their mean expenditure. My mother's family came from a service background, her father, John (Jack) Figgins (1868-1946), having been retired as a Royal Naval captain, and her maternal grandfather, Rear Admiral Bedbrook (1845-1902), had been a leading engineer and ship's architect, and the man who had fought successfully to raise the status of engineers in the Navy through the conferring of military rank in alignment with technical qualifications.

He had begun his career as one of the first midshipmen aboard HMS *Warrior*, Britain's first steel-hulled battleship (now a museum monument in dry dock in Portsmouth, nearby Nelson's flagship, HMS *Victory*), and he ended his career as Chief Inspector of Machinery, and was promoted from the humble title of "Mr." to Rear Admiral. I might add that no serving officer in the history of the Royal Navy did more to enhance the technological repute of those serving below deck, in the democratic struggle to equate skill with status, and in so doing he was a major contributor in ensuring British dominance on the oceans of the world in the decades ahead.

The relatives on both sides of my family were kind and considerate towards me, but I generally preferred the company of my mother's relatives, since although they were poorer financially, my maternal grandparents lived in a mansion in the West country which was richly furnished and surrounded by beautiful gardens. Despite two live-in maids and a gardener, my mother always complained about the "poverty" of her parents, in that they survived on a "miserable naval pension" and a small portfolio of shares. But where there was supposedly poverty, I only saw luxury and good living, and plenty of entertaining, for my grandmother was very sociable and hospitable, and loved laughter and merriment.

My paternal grandfather, Ernest Corfe (1878-1963), was the youngest of six children and brought up in Maidstone, where his family owned a chain of chemist stores which eventually were sold to Timothy Whites early in the 20th century, which in turn in the second half of the same century was acquired by Boots. Shortly after qualifying as a dental surgeon, he volunteered to serve as an Army captain in the Boer War, and was one of the first dental surgeons sent out to South Africa to attend to the appalling condition of the ordinary British soldiers' teeth. I still possess the spurs he wore at that time, for he spent much time on horseback, and he liked to tell stories of his adventures during the course of that War. In 1905 he married my grandmother, Ethel Smith (1885-1951), a great beauty and the daughter of a well-to-do auctioneer in Norfolk. Her father was to meet a horrific death some years later, whilst taking his dog for a walk along the Norfolk coast, when the cliffs gave way, and both man and dog were found dead together on the beach.

My grandmother had one sister, Ruth, who remained a spinster, and two brothers, Sidney and Quentin, both of them eccentric and by profession valuation surveyors, and the latter a favourite great uncle on account of his comical behaviour. My grandparents moved into a newly built Edwardian London suburb, Muswell Hill, where my grandfather set up his dental practice, working 16 hours a day since he also acted as his own mechanic in making dentures. They had four children, Felix (1906-1990), my father, followed by Joan (1907-2006), Maurice (1910-1985), and a late arrival, Harold Martin (1922-1999).

My maternal grandfather, Jack Figgins, was from a far humbler background. His parents were both Scottish but resident in Crewe, Britain's largest railway junction, for my great-grandfather, James Russell Figgins (1841-1908), was a railway engineer who although he rose to a responsible and high managerial position, this did not carry with it any complementary class status in the eyes of southerners. I still remember his large portrait in oils which hung in an ornate gilded frame in my grandparents' dining room. He looked a grand well-dressed Victorian gentleman, grim-visaged, holding the Bible in one hand. My grandfather was, again, one sibling amongst eight others, and as he proved exceptionally bright at school, a distant relative came up with the resources to send him off to the Naval College at Dartmouth, which at that time only comprised a moored sailing vessel.

As a young officer and qualified engineer, my grandfather was ambitious both professionally and socially. On meeting my grandmother, an Admiral's daughter, he was determined to marry her – or so I was told by his future wife. My grandmother was the fourth daughter and one of ten children, several brothers of whom attended St. Paul's School, and one of these struck up a friendship with Walter de la Mare (1873-1956), who later became a noted writer and poet. He soon became a serious suitor to my grandmother, frequently visiting the Bedbrooks' family home in Battersea, and she often told me with pride about her love affair with the great writer, and how they were "destined to be married," but how my grandfather was so insistent in his courtship that she had finally to give way to his wishes, and they were married in 1898, he being older by 6 years.

My great-grandfather, the Admiral, was a man of great humanity with liberal feelings, and probably exerted little influence as to how his children should choose their spouses. My grandmother said she had never known him to strike any of his children except on a single occasion when the youngest son, Cyril, was rude to his mother. My great grandmother, Matilda A. Crocker (1845-1907), came from South Africa and supposedly had a "murky" past which was concealed from the family, the "murkiness" being that she had been born out of wedlock. She, however, was the disciplinarian of the family, responsible for keeping the ten children in order whilst her husband concentrated on naval business in modernising the technology of the Senior Service.

My grandmother was born near the Naval base at Chatham dockyard, where she spent her early happy childhood, and only later did the family move to London. It was commonly said that the Admiral was finally struck down with appendicitis at the same time as Edward VII, and whilst the King survived, my great-grandfather died at the age of 57.

In 1902 my grandparents were fortunate to be stationed and living together in Malta with their 3-year old daughter, Inez, and my grandmother who was a talented singer up to operatic standard, was chosen to sing the leading role of Phoebe Meryll in Gilbert and Sullivan's, *The Yeomen of The Guard* at the Theatre Royal in Valletta. The production was produced by the Malta Amateur Dramatic Society, of which General Sir Francis Grenfell, the Governor of Malta was the President, and Admiral Sir John Fisher, Commander-in-Chief of the Mediterranean, was the Vice-President. The production was a great success and well-received in the local press, and my grandmother received a not inconsiderable fan mail from ordinary admirers – several letters of which have come into my possession. "Grandpa was so proud of me,!" she exclaimed many decades later. She told how some years before visiting Valletta she had dreamed of singing in just such a theatre with its red and white striped décor, and she marvelled at the prescience of such a prediction.

As personalities my maternal grandparents were possibly not ideally suited to one another. My grandmother enjoyed a lively social life and was always at ease in company, whilst my grandfather with his Scottish, and possibly Calvinist background, tended to be dour and serious. He was a man of few words, but with intellectual and literary interests, and with a knack for learning foreign languages. He was fluent in German, acting as an interpreter on foreign exchange visits with the German Imperial Navy, and had a knowledge of Chinese where he was based for three years towards the end of the 19th century. He was certainly a disciplinarian, and often enraged by news reports he read in *The Times*, and I remember an aunt complaining to me that he angrily ordered his guests to stand for the playing of the National anthem on the radio at the end of the day. That was an event which occurred during the early years of the Second World War.

My mother regretted the way my grandmother had treated her husband's relatives whom she openly despised because of their Lancashire accents, and she refused on any occasion to visit her in-laws in the North, and discouraged their visits to the South. My mother, who did not get along with her father, nonetheless wanted to keep up contact with that side of the family, and liked those whom she had met. "That side of the family had such beautiful sky blue eyes," she once explained. There was one brother of my grandfather, Albert (1878-1975), who did visit the home of his successful sibling from time to time. This was an ex-soldier, a tall, shy, kindly bachelor of few words who often took me into the town to buy an ice cream.

My mother had even fonder memories of him a generation earlier, when he would thrust a guinea into her hand, and then rush away without a word until a subsequent visit a year or so later. My mother said he was "teased" or "bullied" by my grandfather when the latter asked why he did not buy himself a house. – "How can I?" replied Albert. "I don't have any money." – "How is it you haven't any money when you have neither a family nor a wife?" My grandfather seemed to have no understanding of the socio-economic and class gap which had developed between the two brothers after a lifetime apart.

The opinion of my mother was that my grandmother was "uninterested" in men to an abnormal degree, and that she found her husband a nuisance around the house when he returned after three years abroad for three months leave before departing once again for another three years. But such was family Naval life at that time! Long absences had to be tolerated. Nonetheless, they did share many of the same opinions, and they did enjoy such social activities as attending public dances on a regular basis.

My mother was the youngest of three children, being born in 1906, and although she went to several private schools, she was poorly educated, and finished her school education at the age of 14. Although she acquired a fair amount of miscellaneous knowledge on music, literature, and the other arts after leaving school, and her conversation tended to be littered with French phrases, she adopted the commonly held prejudice of the uneducated that as soon as one had completed one's formal education, then there was nothing more to be learned, and that all subsequent studies were either absurd or pretentious. She was never tired of ridiculing those – especially if they came from the lower middle classes – who were intent on "self-improvement," and she was contemptuous of professors who supposedly were "egg-heads," "forgetful," "dull," and usually lost for words when they found themselves in good company. Nonetheless, she was fond of reading – invariably modern novels on contemporary domestic life – and she maintained she could never remember a time when she was unable to read.

Her two elder sisters were more fortunate in their education. The eldest sister, Inez, born 1899, for whom I eventually became a favourite nephew, was sent off to a Belgian convent to complete her education and knowledge of French, the result of which was her conversion to lifelong atheism. The middle sister, Joan, born 1903, the most attractive of the three girls, was sent off to an expensive boarding school, at the cost of a benevolent distant relative, the result of which was an overweening snobbery on everything to which snobbishness could be alluded.

As my mother was the "baby" of the family, she remained the favourite of her sisters, but the two elder girls soon developed a hatred for one another which was only ended through death. This hatred arose through a mixture of rivalry and jealousy. Inez was the plainest of the three girls, but probably the most intelligent, but she was soured by a jealous and unforgiving nature. She remained close to my grandmother in helping with domestic chores, and for a time, was almost a substitute mother to the younger siblings. The latter were far more attractive, and on at least one occasion my mother was elected a Carnival Queen, and all three girls were apparently highly-sexed despite their parents, apparently, being the reverse of that.

As my grandfather was stationed in different British ports, when he was not stationed abroad, my mother rarely lived for more than three years in any one place. She was born in Southsea, and at other times lived in Whitley Bay, where she saw the body of a little girl who had been drowned in the sea; and in Scotland, near Glasgow, for which she cherished the happiest memories of her childhood; and finally, just before my grandfather's retirement in 1919, in Littlehampton. As a result of this nomadic existence, she always said she felt at home anywhere in the world, and that she easily made friends, and indeed, she had few prejudices with regard to those she liked or disliked, providing they were only accessible to a friendly approach. She was rarely prepared to moralise as to how people should conduct their lives, providing only they were pleasant and preferably amusing.

My mother's first recollection of her father was as a 3-year old in Southsea. She had never seen him before, and he was returning from a 3-year stint in the Far East. After his carriage, with all his trunks, drew up at their house, following the short journey from his ship moored in

Portsmouth harbour, my mother ran out to kiss her long absent parent, but instead of kissing her father, she threw her arms around the coachman, who was a much more impressive figure, to the amusement of my grandmother and her other daughters.

As became most people at that time, the adults of the family rarely betrayed feelings of extreme upset at personal loss, and my mother retained a passive and equable temperament throughout her life, taking lightly matters of disaster or death. This family characteristic became evident some days following the sinking of the *Titanic* in 1912, when she attended a memorial service with her mother and siblings at a church in Eastleigh, Southampton, when she saw adults crying for the first time. "I only thought children cried," she explained. "I never thought adults were capable of such a thing." The church was packed with soldiers, and she remembered the strong smell of sweat from the assembled troops.

It was in Littlehampton, as a 16-year old where my mother's personal relationship was finally broken with her father. One Autumn day when my grandfather was atop an apple tree in their garden, dropping the fruit into a garden sieve held by my mother standing below, she accidentally dropped the sieve, but my grandfather took it as an intentional act. Angered, he descended from the tree and struck her hard across the face, upon which she let up a loud wailing. My grandmother rushed into the garden, horrified, asking what all the noise was about, intent on calming the situation. My mother never forgave her father, and could seldom be brought to admit he had any good qualities. She often said her father had not done a stroke of work in his life, only ordered others to work for him. It was not until reaching old age that she regretted her attitude, when she kept a silver framed portrait of her father in full uniform in a prominent position in the living room.

Three years after this event occurred my grandfather was finally released from additional voluntary service in the Navy. According to my mother, he did not have the necessary personality to achieve higher rank, and hence there was no possibility for his extending his active career in the Navy, and so at this stage the family set about looking for a permanent home. He considered properties in Essex, Sussex, and Wiltshire, and finally settled on a fine grey stone built mansion constructed in 1837, on the outskirts of the small industrial town of Melksham, situated between Trowbridge and Chippenham, with the river Avon meandering through its centre. He gave the mansion the name of Sampford Place, since he had seen another property in Essex which greatly attracted him with the same name.

As soon as they had settled into their new home with its fine gardens and attractive meadows at the rear of the property, the four women of the household began to seek out a social life for themselves, whilst my grandfather involved himself with the local British Legion. Within a short while they began to entertain a nearby family who were seemingly "respectable," but unknown to themselves, were not admitted as guests of the local gentry. Years later, my Aunt Inez spoke to me about this frightful *faux pas* of her parents – the greatest mistake of their lives – in rushing into a friendship in unknown social territory. This was a colossal disaster, for inadvertently, they had closed all doors to themselves to the people who really mattered in the neighbourhood.

My Aunt Inez soon concluded in her dismay there was no one worth socialising with in the town with its petty tradesmen and dirty manufacturing industry. She was not going to stay in such a place. She had little time to lose – she was already 27 and well beyond the usual marriageable age. Accordingly, she went off to London where she found work, and could live a free life of gaiety and fun. My Aunt Joan, meanwhile, was more fortunate. In the same year the family settled in their new home, she met and married a chemist, Reginald Lawton, working at the huge dairy in Melksham, and both her sisters were bridesmaids at the wedding.

Not long afterwards my mother joined her eldest sister in London, where they lived together in a large lodging house in the West End. Inez took over the responsibility of chaperoning her 19-year old sister, and keeping her out of harm's way, and warning her about all the evil entrapments to be found in the capital. Decades later my mother described with humour the weird and eccentric characters who tenanted this lodging house, which included two middle-aged "pansies," and she impersonated their voice and gestures, as one said to the other after the evening meal, "You wash up and I'll dry," which brought laughter to those who listened to the episode.

As my mother had no formal qualifications she worked as a receptionist and then as a nanny, at one time working for the well-known historian, H.A.L. Fisher and brother of the future Archbishop of Canterbury, and finally she returned to work as a receptionist in Harley Street, at which time she met my father.

*

My father studied both medicine and dental surgery at Guys Hospital, and qualified at the start of the 1930s, and so he had a string of 24 letters behind his name. He had previously been at Highgate School where he played hockey and fives and later tennis and golf – or so it is recorded by those who noted seriously the facts of his life. He was also a member of the School cadets. He had had the most protective upbringing which any child could possibly have endured, and until the day of his marriage had hardly spent a night away from the family home. Shortly after he matriculated from school, my grandfather took him on a short trip to Belgium. This supposedly comprised his great "education for life," and although this country was still referred to as "plucky little Belgium," on account of her resistance to Germany in 1914, my grandfather could nonetheless whisper into his son's ear about the undesirable characteristics of foreigners and their unpleasant habits.

My grandmother was deeply religious, and a member of the Mothers' Union, and churchgoing was regular and taken seriously. Whilst my grandfather had a more relaxed attitude towards religion and sexual morality – he had a number of affairs in his time – he was a conscientious sidesman, and conventional in his theological thinking but without being emotionally committed over doctrinal niceties. The church which the family attended was St. James's in Muswell Hill, and it stands on the highest point of anywhere in London apart from Hampstead and Highgate Village. The family were naturally Anglicans, but my grandmother hung onto this ideal as the defining limit between good and evil.

Although Non-Conformists were barely tolerable – and in Muswell Hill there were churches of every denomination – she had a loathing for Catholics amounting to hatred. They were untrustworthy and liable to treasonable acts, and it was scandalous they were allowed to sit as members of Parliament. What had brought her to think along such lines? Her mind must have been stirred by the school history books of long ago: of Bloody Mary and the burning of the Protestant martyrs; of Phillip II and the Armada sent against England; of Guy Fawkes and the gunpowder plot; of Louis XIV and the threat of a French invasion; of James II and the Glorious Revolution; of Jacobite conspiracies to reverse the Hanoverian succession; and of Lord George Gordon, and the anti-Catholic riots of 1788.

Or it may have been due to the inherited cultural factor of her ancestors having emigrated from Northern Ireland to England early in the 18th century. The family were related to John Thomas Smith, keeper of the prints at the British Museum, and at one time a partner of the sculptor Nollekins, of whom he wrote what is reputedly the most savage biography in the English language, i.e., *Nollekins and his Times* (1828), in retaliation at being excluded as a beneficiary of his will. John Thomas Smith was the son of Nathaniel Smith, two portraits of which (dated 1745) presently hang in my living room. It is just conceivable that such religious prejudices were passed down from generation to generation without any consciousness of maintaining a tradition of ill-intent.

I remember my cousin, Michael, not so many years ago, recollecting how our grandmother would stand behind the living room window on Sunday evenings, glaring across the street in deep disdain, as crowds of Catholics moved along the opposite pavement to mass at the modern church just fifty yards or so down the hill. To her they were evil spirits, owing a greater loyalty to the Pope than the King, and therefore were undeserving of citizenship. Who could have imagined that her youngest and favourite son would eventually – long after her death – marry a Catholic, and that his children would be brought up in that faith?

Although my father had more common sense than to share the rigidly religious views of his mother, he remained strictly conventional on religious questions, whilst being rigid in his approach to most other matters in life. He had little experience of life beyond the conventions of home and school, little imagination, and accepted platitudes and what people said at face value. He was incorruptibly honest in matters of give and take, almost incapable of guile under any circumstances, and consequently blunt and abrasive in his relationships, since he could hardly conceal his feelings which were liable to burst out and cause offence on the most inopportune occasions. My mother once said he had become the joke of the neighbourhood on account of his habit of paying every bill as soon as it dropped through the letter box.

Although he appreciated humour if it was served up on a plate, by a comedian on the radio or the theatre, or through literature such as *Pickwick Papers*, and although he was not above repeating jokes he had heard at Rotary or his Masonic lodge, he was not a humorous man. If he attempted humour, it was usually cruel and at the expense of others – and of course we were obliged to laugh. If he found himself in merry company, such as the family get-togethers at Christmas, which our family often hosted, his merriment was forced and joyless – little more than pretence in imitating those around him. He was too unimaginative to be witty or artistic, or to appreciate the arts in a proper sense, although he did reveal a remarkable knowledge of literature from time to time.

He could – and did recite entire paragraphs from the novels of Dickens and Lord Lytton, usually those at the beginning or end of their books. It always struck me that this was a strange way to teach an appreciation of literature. He had a huge appreciation for Sir Henry Irving and theatrical productions he had seen in childhood, saying that modern actors weren't a patch on the grandiloquent performances of their predecessors. But such opinions may have been more attributable to hearsay than actual experience, bearing in mind that Irving died in 1905, one year before my father's birth.

My mother described him as "nervy," and certainly he was full of fears, and warnings against doing this or that, and he was opposed to adventure or risks of most kinds – except that of the stock exchange which inflicted havoc on his nervous system, for the downturns of the market would frequently put him into the worst of moods. He was also subject to dark moods of depression, often when we were away on holiday, when he would take to his bed feigning illness for days on end, whilst the rest of us played on the beach. He was quite unlike his other siblings, and quite unlike his father, although he may have inherited his depression from my grandmother.

My grandfather had a great sense of humour and loved to relate amusing stories about friends and acquaintances, which although they were at the expense of others, were not marked by the cruelty of those told by my father. He also had a ready wit (whilst my father had none) and would often pick up something I had said and give it a humorous twist. The difference between the two men was that the elder had experienced the wider world, whilst the younger remained the voluntary prisoner of his parents for far too long.

There is one exception in regard to any insensitivity in the above description of my father's character: as a medical student at Guy's he had been sent with others to the East End slums to attend the appalling condition of the poor, and he once described how these were people only dressed in rags, where the children were barefoot, hungry, and horribly diseased. He came out with this story late in life in the 1970s, and it was addressed to a German friend rather than to me, for I had never heard him relate such stories before. The significance to be found in the experience (if not so much in the story itself), I believe, may attribute to his life-long terror of poverty as a social issue, his fear and withering contempt for the downtrodden because of their hopelessness and the ever-present possibility of their revolt. It may account for his right wing views as a defensive response to the prospect of society being overwhelmed and barbarised by a revolutionary proletariat. This, of course, was the age when the privileged intelligentsia in our universities were secretly turning to the cause of Communism, but the existence of widespread poverty and unemployment may just as well have aroused the kind of reactionary conservatism on which my father depended psychologically for the greater part of his life.

As to my father's experience with women before he met my mother, I can only surmise from his occasional outbursts during my teenage years in response to my disappointments in love. He was contemptuous of my even wanting to think about girls, let alone wanting to *associate* with them. He once angrily exclaimed, "You should have nothing to do with women until you're earning £500 a year, and got £500 in the bank. They're just an unnecessary expense." In his eyes, a successful relationship with a woman had nothing to do with experience, or developing the arts of courtship. It was biological and financial, but psychology had nothing to do with it. He could appreciate biology because he was a medical man, but psychology was something suspect and dirty – insolently usurping the role of religion – being the cranky invention of a group of maverick Germans who had illicitly broken away from the proper constraints of the medical profession.

Such views may sound outrageous in the 21st century but they were still common amongst the older generations in the 1950s. In my father's view, a long-term friendship or sexual relationship between a man and a woman was no more complex than that of the amoeba. Therefore, he concluded, if I had any difficulties with a woman, if she was moody or argumentative, I should do what he did, and tell her to "go to hell." If you took any truck from a woman, or gave into her feelings, you were letting yourself into all kinds of trouble. Such was the attitude of my father at the time he met my mother. Such a man could only hope for success with the opposite sex through over-awing or blinding them with the grandeur of his professional qualifications, and the promise of a secure life free from financial anxiety.

*

My mother, meanwhile, had probably had a little more experience of the opposite sex than her future husband by the time they met. For a period she was strongly attached to James de la Mare, a nephew of the writer, Walter de la Mare, and he reciprocated her feelings. He was a man of great charm and personality, whom I met on several formal family occasions, and maintained a life-long employment with a large insurance company. She then had a more serious relationship with a brother of her elder sister's husband, but when he proposed marriage it was on the condition they would go to New Zealand where she would live the life of a farmer's wife. She declined the offer. Her suitor went to New Zealand alone, failed in business, returned a few years later, and eventually died of a heart attack in his 60s. On another occasion she was friendly with a German called, Hess, explaining, "I would clearly have landed myself in the soup if I had married him and found myself in Germany when the War broke out."

She seems otherwise to have had an active social life. When she was in her late 80s she confessed to me that her first sexual experience was on the occasion she was raped by a man she hardly knew behind some bathing huts in Henley-on-Thames, after bathing in the river with a party of friends. Had my father ever known this, bearing in mind his high moral principles, it is doubtful he would ever have married her.

It may therefore be assumed that both my parents, at the time that they met, were therefore naïve with regard to any and every aspect of personal relationships. Their very naivety may have driven them together, for they must have regarded one another as metaphors for ideal qualities rather than as the reality of the personalities they were. My father was obviously a "good catch," and plenty could be said about his "admirable" characteristics to all and sundry. My mother was clearly the "ideal woman," since she was meek, pliable, passive, and obedient, and most significantly, was free of that worst fault to be found in a woman of having the kind of "intelligence" which most irritated a man. Their love affair, if it can be called that, seems to have been rapid, since they were soon engaged and wedding bells were not far off.

However, a serious impediment was soon uncovered and had to be attended to without further ado. Whilst my grandmother was in conversation with her future daughter-in-law, carefully searching out for any secrets she may have hidden away, she discovered to her horror that my mother had never been confirmed. My mother's parents were both non-believers: my grandfather being too much of an intellectual to bother with religion, whilst my grandmother had a very low opinion of the clergy and their hypocrisy, although both occasionally attended church for festive events, and they were always happy to entertain the local pastor for afternoon tea.

The consequence of this discovery was that my mother had to undergo the humiliation of attending religious lessons amongst a party of young people in preparation for her formal reception into the Anglican Church. She was put under the guidance of the Rev. Prebendary E.A. Dunn (1877-1964), of St. James's church, and a good friend of my grandmother. This clergyman, whom I came to know and dislike some years later, for reasons which will become evident later in this memoir, was a large rotund man with a diminutive wife. My mother used to say during the War years that he took all his wife's rations and left her with sparrow feed. He was a well-known churchman in North London, a friend of Dr. Fisher, the Archbishop of Canterbury, and never left his parish in Muswell Hill, since God had appeared to him in a dream telling him not to do so, and this was taken by his respectful congregation as an act of providence. He became most notable for proselytising amongst the large Jewish community in North London and converting them to Christianity.

My mother retained an intense dislike for the Rev. E.A. Dunn because his excess religiosity deprived him of the human touch, and he was remote and unsociable in not bothering to visit his most loyal parishioners. An example of his dogmatic approach was reflected in what my father repeated one day on returning from Evensong, when the Rev. Dunn announced a forthcoming performance of Handel's *Messiah* in the church, adding, "You will not be coming to bathe yourselves in a musical concert, you will be coming to undergo a religious experience." – "Now that would put me off from the start," exclaimed my mother, and that was the reply my father anticipated. All great art, of course, is created on its own terms, and it is certainly not the role of others to *dictate* how it should be appreciated, and even less to identify a divide between artistic technique and the emotional response of the free individual.

At last my parents were married in November 1934, with drums beating and trumpets blowing. In the provincial West country paper, the news report was headed, WILTS SOCIETY WEDDING, and the following formed part of the accompanying text: "The bride wore her bridegroom's present, a pair of diamond earrings, at the wedding of Mr. Felix Norman Corfe, M.R.C.S.. L.R.C.P.,L.D.S.Eng., Muswell Hill, London, eldest son of Mr. Ernest and Mrs. Corfe, Muswell Hill, with Miss Joyce Dulcie Prudence, youngest daughter of Engineer Captain J.W. Figgins, O.B.E., RN, and Mrs. Figgins, of Sampford Place, Melksham, at St. Michael's Church, Melksham, on Saturday. The bride was attired in cream taffeta, and wore her mother's wedding veil. She carried a bouquet of pink roses. She was attended by four bridesmaids, &c. ... Canon Sangster (Vicar) officiated, and the service was choral. Mr. Arlett was at the organ, and the hymns were, 'Lead us, Heavenly Father,' 'O perfect love,' and, 'The Voice that breathed o'er Eden.'" The report was accompanied by full-sized pictures of my grandfather escorting his daughter along the path to the church entrance, and of the bridal party on the steps of Sampford Place.

The following is part of the report taken from another Wiltshire paper: "The large attendance at the church was testimony to the popularity of the bride and her parents, Capt. Figgins being particularly well-known amongst ex-Service men, being a Vice-President of the local Branch of the British Legion. ... as the happy couple left the church to the music of the 'Wedding march' they were showered with confetti and good wishes from their friends who had assembled outside. A reception was held at Sampford Place, the home of the bride's parents, at which there was a large gathering, and later Mr. and Mrs. Corfe left for London, thence to Paris by air liner for their honeymoon, the bride wearing a rust colour suit, brown hat and shoes."

Meanwhile, the local London paper, *The Hornsey Journal*, also reported the wedding at length, the following being an extract from their report: "Mr. Norman Corfe is well known in Muswell Hill, where he has lived all his life. He was educated at Highgate School. He is an active member of the Old Cholmeleions" (his old school association) "and also a member of the Coldfall Tennis Club. Both he and his father are sidesmen at St. James's church."

I am proud to claim my conception occurred in Paris, the world's artistic capital, and hope that in some mysterious way, the rational spirit of France penetrated my parents through impressions and possibly diet, to have been transferred through a combination of genetic and psychological factors (as yet to be scientifically uncovered) to influence my development and future existence. In any event, despite biological inheritance (which became sufficiently evident), I was to develop a personality and traits and aspirations quite different from either of my parents, as will be shown in this memoir. I was not to be influenced by my parents – or so I always liked to think – in any matters of opinion or value, but rather to form my own personality from within through the objectivity of my own reason and common sense. If this was impossible from a psychological aspect, then I certainly became a thoughtful child from an early age, and soon learned to accept few things at their face value.

As I said at the start of this memoir, my parents' families were very different. Whilst on my mother's side they were relaxed with an easy-going charm, as became those with a service background, on my father's side (both the Corfes and the Smiths), tended to be tense, formal, and rigid in their attitudes, as was proper with business people, and if there was little charm, this was replaced with reticence or reserve. It was not long before my maternal grandmother took an intense dislike to her son-in-law on account of his charmless manner and rigid attitude to personal relationships.

An example of this occurred during the early War years when my father dropped a tooth paste glass in the bathroom at Sampford Place. He made a great fuss, apologising for what he had done, and insisted on replacing the glass with an exact copy which he did. I remember my grandmother complaining about this to her daughter in carrying his acknowledgement of regret too far. She felt offended. A guest and close relative should feel at ease in the house, and should not feel the obligation to replace the broken object. My father saw the situation quite differently. He had destroyed an article of value – for all property was sacrosanct – and he felt in honour bound to make up for the loss in no uncertain terms.

Another example of the difference between the two families occurred when I was a teenager, staying with my grandmother and Aunt Inez in Bath. We were in a hurry to get off early one morning, and when my aunt urged me to clean my teeth, I replied, "I don't need to brush my teeth, I've just eaten an apple, and so I can save on the toothpaste." – "Now isn't that a typical Corfe attitude,!" exclaimed my aunt in astonishment to my grandmother. "They have all the money in the world and they still want to save." The Corfes had a notorious reputation for meanness, and hated any kind of expenditure when it could be avoided.

The first serious break in relationships occurred with my birth – which was the cause of the rumpus which followed. My Aunt Inez married in the same year as my parents, being already 35 years of age and desperate to have children. Her husband, a huge man with a domineering appearance and high self-regard was more than 20 years her senior, a qualified architect named Sydie (Bill) Dakers. He was another of those men whom my mother said had "never done a stroke of work in his life," and indeed, the couple remained in straightened financial circumstances until my grandmother bailed them out many years later.

Sydie, or Uncle Bill, was a man who took no nonsense from anybody, and quarrelled with all and sundry. My mother explained that although he was highly talented and artistic, his irascibility kept him out of work, since no one was prepared to put up with his bad temper and arrogance. During his long bachelorhood, he lived in expensive West End lodgings (at one time in the Albany alongside the Royal Academy in Piccadilly), belonged to several of the best London clubs, and spent profusely. He did have charm, was well-read and knowledgeable, was a great conversationalist, and caroused with his drinking friends over whom he dominated as a leading light.

When he met my aunt, she was bowled over by him as a man before whom all other men shrank into insignificance by comparison. As a strong personality with a superior intelligence there was nothing of which he was incapable. As a teenager I was terrified of him, although he always treated me with good humour, and my grandmother insisted I address him as "Sir," which I respectfully did. During the War years he worked as a lecturer at Bristol University, and on one occasion he proudly showed me a cartoon of himself together with a group of other men which had been published in *Punch*.

When they married, it was a quiet civil wedding, as neither wanted to be involved with the church. Since the two married sisters were living in London, it was natural that my parents and Inez and Sydie should meet and socialise together from time to time, but my father soon fell out of favour with the older man. The bone of contention was Ludo. My father won time after time. "He didn't like to lose at Ludo," chuckled my father with understatement many years later. Sydie could never bear to lose at anything – and certainly not to a pipsqueak a generation younger than himself. At first he would move around uneasily on his chair with a darkened brow, but on losing the third round, he would burst out in a temper. My father may not have been entirely blameless, for he was apt to express triumphalism in any kind of competitive situation, although winning at Ludo could hardly be compared with scoring a goal at a cup final. Sydie may well have had some justification for his irritation. "He was always jealous of the younger generation," explained my mother.

Ludo was not really a serious issue and I am sure that Inez was able to alleviate her husband's upset on such occasions, but something far more serious was about to occur. The child for which she desperately hoped was not going to materialise. It soon became apparent she was barren. "She would have been a wonderful mother," reiterated mine on several occasions, "although I'm not quite sure he would have made such a good father." Having come to terms with childlessness, Inez transferred all her interest and affection on the forthcoming child of her youngest sister, with gifts of clothing, etc., for the expected baby, and in the hope of being chosen as a godmother. She seems to have forgotten, however, that a "godmother" has a religious dimension, and that my father would never have allowed a professed atheist to stand in for any of his children. Anyhow that issue did not arise. Shortly before my mother was due to go into the Nursing home in central London for delivery – and she would be away for the average period of ten days – it was arranged that Inez would stay with my father as housekeeper in supervising the maid, and for finalising arrangements for the return of mother and child.

During my mother's absence an almighty row broke out between Aunt Inez and my father which led to a total break in their relationship. Consequently, my father was not to be on speaking terms with his sister-in-law for a period of some 12 years. My mother never discovered the real cause of the quarrel until her dying day, except that I was the subject around which it circulated, as both my father and Aunt Inez resolutely refused to discuss the matter. My analysis of the situation is that it was most likely that my father in his insensitivity, and assumed superiority, had inadvertently said something deeply offensive to his sister-in-law. Perhaps the question of a "godmother" had arisen, and my father, in his candid innocent manner, had mounted his high moral horse. Whatever had occurred must have been shameful and shocking in calling for concealment, as otherwise, either or both parties would eventually have come forward with some kind of explanation.

CHAPTER 2
As a Toddler in London

"Our days, our deeds, all we achieve or are,
Lay folded in our infancy; the things
Of good or ill we choose while yet unborn."

J.T. Trowbridge, *Sonnet: Nativity*

The problem of my name – My cousins – My admiration for their family – My godparents – How my mother ingratiated herself with her in-laws – The unfortunate consequences of this to other relatives – My loathing for Muswell Hill – Haunted by irrational fears – My first love

Not long after my birth, my christening was held at St. James's Church, and I was named Robert Nigel, but only known by the latter. Robert was the choice of my maternal grandfather after a

Scottish relative. In my later teenage years I came to loathe the name of Nigel, and from the time I entered the Army, I insisted on being known as Robert.

Nigel struck me as a name which was effete or effeminate, failing to reflect manliness, or aspirations towards the kind of heroism I admired. What great man had ever been known as Nigel? Sir Walter Scott had written a relatively minor novel, *The Fortunes of Nigel*, about the ruffianly and seamier side of London life during the reign of James I, but what inspiration was that? There was no other noteworthy person in either fact or fiction with the name of Nigel with whom I wished to be associated. During my late pre-pubescent romantic phase, I could not imagine anyone with the name of Nigel swinging a two-edged sword in Knightly combat. Robert was little better, but there was Robert the Bruce or Robert the Devil of Normandy – and then there were many Roberts who had flourished in the arts and literature.

I was, however, happy to be born in the month of August – the month which is named after one of the greatest men who lived: the Emperor Augustus, the man who established an era which was eventually to lead to the longest period of world peace in recorded history. I was also born on the anniversary of the day and the month coinciding with the Emperor's death in AD 14. It was during a period when the arts, literature, and historical scholarship, reached a height of genius which few ages have equalled. Since my teenage years I have regarded this Roman Emperor as a kind of personal deity or guardian angel, whose ideals and qualities most closely matched my hopes for a just and stable world. Perhaps it is no coincidence that August is a warm and sunny month, and since it was the month I entered the world, it remains a constant reminder of the man who sought through practical political means to establish the foundations for eternal peace and prosperity for all peoples irrespective of race, nationality, religion, or the level of their cultural development. The apotheosis he achieved after his demise was never more sell-deserved.

*

My godparents, naturally, were chosen with care. There was my paternal grandfather, who was a safe bet because of his religious principles, and then there was my Uncle Dick, being the husband of my father's sister, Joan. Dick Brown was a tall good-looking businessman, a man of immense charm, witty, good with children, always in control in a social situation, but at the same time self-effacing and ready to admit his faults, and because of this mixture of characteristics, he was universally popular. "No one ever disliked Uncle Dick," said my mother on one occasion. As an entrepreneur, however, he was capable of introducing guile into his charm in driving home a bargain, and on at least one occasion he fell out with my father because of this, and there were other petty matters which occasionally divided the two families.

Joan, my father's sister was the sisterly-love of his life, and as the only daughter of the family, she was joyful and carefree. As Aunt Joan described the situation to me, my father was her "guardian angel," a grimly visaged jealous teenager whenever a boy friend visited the parental home. When such visits occurred, he would sit at the top of the stairs with his chin in his hands, watching or listening to ensure that nothing untoward would occur. Joan responded to this concern with a mixture of amusement and appreciation. Dick and Joan had three children, all of them with great charm and fully endowed with the social graces: Anne, three years older than me, Michael, six months my senior, a great comedian and wit with whom I became very close, and Howard, who used his charm rather than abilities in successfully forwarding his career. The youngest was the same age as my brother, Gavin, and so we four boys and cousins frequently met and played together.

The Browns were great entertainers and not afraid of lavish expenditure. As a family they were in direct contrast to the family of Felix Corfe, which was dull, socially awkward, and on edge with the world since it gave rise to every conceivable fear. In addition the Felix Corfe family was mean-spirited, self-centred, and careful with every penny spent. Nonetheless, the two families met and socialised often, since my Aunt Joan was probably the woman my father loved more than any in his life. It can be no surprise, therefore, that because of the relaxed style of this other family I always envied the Browns, since they seemed so much better than us in so many ways. They were always joyful and happy, and there was always laughter in their house – and most significant of all, there was a spirit of easy-going leisure.

Many decades later my wife was to say that with Michael it was always "two laughs a minute," but our friendship was to be broken for several decades at the start of my 20s – at a period not covered in this memoir. Our closeness was due to our blood relationship rather than the similarity of our temperaments, and tensions inevitably developed between us, the eventual occurrence of which may be anticipated by reading between the lines of those pages towards the close of this book. However, it was due to the tactlessness and careless tongue of my mother that finally brought about the breaking point of our friendship, the consequence of which resulted in the humiliation of being excluded from invitations to formal functions of the family. On expressing my resentment at this treatment to my parents, my father angrily retorted, "the Browns are living above their station and beyond their means. They're a bad example. You should have nothing to do with them." At this response I felt doubly humiliated, since the Browns possessed every quality I wished for, and I was certainly not prepared to accept my father's criticism of their values.

Decades later, long after I had been reconciled with Michael, he admitted he had always been "terrified" of my father. This surprised me for I thought that uninhibited freedom-loving Michael had never been afraid of anybody. This fear may have arisen through the fact that my father never had any compunction about hitting other peoples' children in their own homes if they were "rude," which he thought was not only a right but a duty of responsible adults in correcting "naughty" children. The last occasion on which this occurred (to my knowledge) was in the 1980s whilst my parents were on holiday in Australia, when he struck his grandson, Barnaby, the son of my youngest brother, Oliver. On hearing a distressed crying, my Australian sister-in-law, Julie, the most equable and inoffensive woman, ran angrily into the room, exclaiming to my father, "Did you hit him?" My mother, who was present at the scene and related the story, had the presence of mind to interject with the words, "No, the poor little thing tripped over on the carpet." As the child was a two-year old toddler who had not yet learned to speak, the incident was never revealed and it remained a secret. In expressing her horror over the episode my mother concluded, "I don't know what would have happened if Julie and Oliver had learned the truth."

*

My godmothers were Joan Lawton, my mother's elder sister, who was to take little interest in my existence and to dislike me from an early age; and my Aunt Betty, who was the granddaughter of a famous French chef, M. Menager, whom Edward VII had brought over to England, and appointed as Head Chef at Sandringham. This was a king who enjoyed his food and had a prodigious appetite. Betty was the daughter of Lewis Bedbrook (1877-1962), known as Loots, a favourite brother of my maternal grandmother (whom the latter described as a lively and merry socialite who never aged in his temperament or interests until his dying day in advanced old age) and his French wife, Louise, known as Lou. The latter, and her sister, Marie, were educated and brought up amongst Ladies in Waiting, and other titled people in Court circles, and Lou who died in April 1944, was my mother's favourite aunt. Aunt Betty was a conscientious and generous godmother who always gave worthwhile and valuable presents. Being of French descent, it was not unnatural that she veered towards Anglo-Catholicism, as too did her elder daughter, Maris (three years my senior), and I would not be surprised if both were secretly Roman Catholics.

She also had strong Jacobite leanings, and these were revealed on one occasion after my mother had taken me to see a film about Bonnie Prince Charlie and the uprising of 1745, when she expressed her regret that the Hanoverian, George II, had not been overthrown and the Stuarts restored to the throne, and being insufficiently educated at the time, I was won over to her romantic views. Betty was a close and life-long friend of my mother, until they both died in their 90s, but my mother said her cousin was of a nervous temperament and suffered hypochondria, and when they both worked and lived in London, Betty insisted on travelling with my mother on the tube, since she was afraid to be alone on the underground.

She was married to Vaughan Venables, who was known to the broader Bedbrook family some years before their marriage. As a young man Vaughan had his own car, and after private dances organised by different members of the family, the young ladies hated being paired off by the older generation to be taken home by the future husband of my aunt. This was because Vaughan insisted on fondling any girl he was paired with, and would then go beyond the bounds of propriety until his partner either agreed to satisfy him or else repelled his advances. Of course none of these girls could report back to the older generation, and neither could they refuse to be partnered with the "charming young gentleman" whom their betters put in their charge. I was only to learn this from my mother when in her 80s, after the death of my father, when she revealed a number of untoward stories which would have been forbidden information at an earlier period. As I note later in this memoir, Uncle Vaughan was subsequently to become a war hero in the infantry when he was awarded an MC and attained the rank of major.

*

My mother was always fond of gossip, and there is nothing which more successfully helps to cement new friendships than the communication of gossip – especially if it is malicious or may be given a malicious interpretation. My mother's first introduction to her in-laws had not been entirely propitious, for reasons outlined in the previous chapter, but some months after my birth, an exceptional opportunity arose whereby she might ingratiate herself with my grandmother and thereby be received with greater warmth into the bosom of the Corfe family. The story she was to uncover was to prove a major social disaster for a brother-in-law, and to lead to the severance of a relationship which was never to be renewed. I am not suggesting that my mother set out to be malicious, but only that she wished to further her interests with her in-laws, and that she was either too naïve to anticipate the consequences of her action, or chose to ignore them, or lacked the moral sense to refrain from repeating what could only be harmful to those it concerned.

Shortly after my parents married, my father's younger brother, Maurice, a podgy, good-natured happy-go-lucky man, married his sweetheart, June, who supposedly had a shady past – which none dared to speak of. Maurice was a man who had tried his hand at various occupations – none of them with particular success – including a year in Bremen, where he had learned German, working in a shipping office. At the time he was courting June my father was accompanying his brother in clubs and dance halls. Many years later, my father explained, "he was warned by several men not to associate with 'that girl,' but he took no notice." June was a blonde beauty, witty, charming, generous, and with artistic talents in both singing and painting. Although she spoke with a high-class accent, it was said it was not her proper voice. She either originated from the East End or the Essex Thames side – no one knew exactly about her origins or her family.

On being introduced to the family there were inconsistencies in what she said. Not only was she concealing facts, but she was apparently a consummate liar, but such conclusions could not be admitted to the person concerned for lack of proof. My grandparents were unhappy about the situation but could do nothing about it, and finally, as the couple were determined to tie the knot, they were married. In no time she was pregnant – or so it seemed. As the months passed by, and she became larger and larger, it was apparent she was encountering a particularly difficult pregnancy, for she suffered acute pains, ensuring the sympathy of her in-laws and all those around her.

At last she went into a nursing home and was delivered with a beautiful baby girl named Alvis. Accordingly, friends and relatives arrived with flowers and presents, and congratulations on the happy birth. My mother arrived one day alone at the nursing home for the same purpose, and on departing from her sister-in-law, she got into conversation with one of the nurses – which was typical of her indiscriminate sociability in talking to all and sundry at the drop of a hat, even if it touched on matters which were none of her business. She was astonished to uncover the fact that the baby had not been born in the nursing home and that the mother had never been through a pregnancy.

This was a piece of scandal which was too tempting to suppress, and of course the first person to know was my father. Being the honest person that he was in never concealing the truth, he insisted that this needed to be communicated to his parents without delay. My mother described in detail exactly what had occurred in the nursing home. My grandparents were appalled by this unforgivable deceit, especially in view of all the forethought and ingenuity which had been involved. Consequently, both mother and adopted child were forbidden entry to my grandparents' home, and this also meant exclusion from contact with any extended members of the family. During the War my Uncle Maurice was an occasional visitor to his parents' home, where he appeared in his RAF officer's uniform and a generous moustache as became the flying service, and although he was always alone, he remained his cheerful and good-natured self.

I met June and Alvis for the first time several years after the War, following the death of my grandmother from the King's palsy and a stroke. She died quietly one winter's afternoon whilst sitting by the coal fire in the living room. As my grandfather had a more easy-going and forgiving nature, his daughter-in-law and granddaughter were accepted back into the family circle, and as if to make up for lost time, Maurice and June proved very hospitable, and our family were frequently invited to the various homes they occupied, mostly in Essex, in the post-War period. In later years it surprised me that June never seemed to hold it against my mother for all the upset she had caused the family, but I have since found that those who are little less than honest are often least liable to nurture resentment after an injury has been incurred. In mending matters of the past, and sealing future friendships, the couple probably took the wisest course for their own eventual happiness.

When we grandchildren, that is, the Browns and my younger brother and I were first introduced to Alvis, which occurred at my cousins' home in Totteridge, it felt as if we were meeting a complete stranger. We children were polite, almost deferential, in pulling out different toys from a cupboard to arouse the interest of this long lost cousin, but she seemed distant and quite different from the rest of us. It soon became apparent she existed on a different level from the rest of us, and she was never wholly accepted into the family. I remember her on one occasion disdainfully dismissing the antics of a favourite great uncle, Quentin, when he took us children on a walk around Totteridge. He had been a surveyor and house agent, and remarked on the architecture of the different houses we passed. Alvis thought him a "show off" and "just weird," and when she concluded expressing her disgust, we other children remained silent, for he had always been a respected and much-loved uncle.

On one occasion, on the increasingly rare occurrences when Alvis found herself at larger family gatherings, in her late teenage years, she found herself in the company of Aunt Inez, shortly after the latter had been reconciled with my father. Inez expressed her shock to my parents, saying, "How can a girl like that be so common when she's been brought up in such a good family?" – "Well, we know nothing about her biological past," answered my mother. – "That's right, that's what we call Reversion to Type," said Inez as if suddenly enlightened, seizing on a psychological term she had heard but never properly understood.

The years passed and Alvis married and had two daughters of her own, and they studied ballet and enjoyed the other pursuits of young girls. Whilst Alvis worked in a cigarette factory, her husband ran his own business in recycling pallets. By that time both her parents were dead, and her family were only encountered on grand formal functions when an invitation was felt to be obligatory. I remember on one occasion Alvis boasting about the money she earned in the cigarette factory, which exceeded my earnings as a senior manager, and how successful and prosperous her husband had become in recycling pallets. There was nothing much the rest of us could say in response to these opening conversational gambits, except to nod and remain silent. It was not good form to talk about money in that way and so there was little more to be said. Alvis, and her husband of few words, and their pretty well-dressed daughters, remained social outsiders despite their desperate efforts to ingratiate themselves with the family.

Eventually, on one such celebratory occasion, Alvis was grossly insulted by Aunt Joan, and the family walked out never to be seen or heard of again. Aunt Joan felt she had nothing to lose, since her brother, Maurice, was already dead, and possibly, she was achieving a kind of late revenge for all the upset to her parents which had occurred decades earlier in the mid-1930s. Her youngest son, Howard, who had witnessed the incident, was deeply shaken, exclaiming, "It should never have happened!" Whatever we may have thought in the depths of our heart, we children of the younger generation were always polite and kind towards Alvis and her family, and had no axe to grind with regard to past resentments.

*

Before describing my earliest recollections and impressions, I must first describe the neighbourhood and then the house in which I spent my early years. Muswell Hill was a place I loathed throughout my childhood for what I took to be its ugliness and petty bourgeois values. Whilst on the one hand it became the butt of comedians and social observers for its ultra-respectability, on the other hand, it became the chosen home of public notabilities – especially those in the acting profession, or on radio or TV. It was, therefore, a high status North London suburb, although nothing to compare with Highgate Village or Hampstead – two places for which I formed a deep affection. If one attended the pantomime at the Finsbury Park Hippodrome, for example, the leading comics would usually refer to the "snobs of Muswell Hill," and be assured of laughter and applause. Meanwhile, Arthur Daly, the notorious spiv played by George Cole in the comic TV series, *Minder*, occasionally referred with pride to a "very respectable uncle" who lived in Muswell Hill. The author's critical impressions of the district were therefore already within the public sphere without the need for his having to record his own feelings of the area.

I loathed the pretentiousness of the red brick Edwardian architecture, the wooden decoration over the front porches, and the hideous stained glass set into the leaded front doors. Everything Edwardian was heavy and ugly, and internal furnishings were invariably dark-stained oak. I also hated the place because of its suburban milieu: the identical – or almost identical rows of houses behind their privet or laurel hedges and petty front gardens in quiet streets where nothing of consequence appeared to happen. I concluded, wrongly, that anyone prepared to live in such a place must necessarily be dull and inconsequential – people who had never had a past, and certainly would never have a future. This was a place where nothing changed as one decade followed another.

The most famous building in Muswell Hill was Alexandra Palace, which looked like a ruin before it was built, and was certainly a white elephant before its completion. This nondescript, purposeless, dirty galt brick structure, standing atop a hill in lonesome isolation, looked threatening against the horizon, with its frightening television masts rising from a tower, and the entire pile seemed to be a metaphor for the soullessness and vacuity of Muswell Hill. A cold wind constantly brushed past the building, and only bored hooligans and vandals frequented its surroundings, occasionally breaking a window or spraying graffiti onto the walls.

Until the start of the 21st century that was the picture I held of Muswell Hill and its inhabitants. Early in the present century I was invited to a party in the district, and had to admit the spaciousness of the rooms, the generous open spaces of the hallways, and the solidity of the structures. These were houses which were clearly superior – even aesthetically – to those constructed in the 20s or 30s, and infinitely superior to those which followed later in the century. Before attending the party, I walked along the well-known shopping streets, and was pleased by the quality and variety of the independent retail outlets, and I even discovered a shop stocked with interesting antique Chinese furniture, where I met and talked with a friendly Chinese assistant. Perhaps Muswell Hill was not such a bad place after all. Perhaps it was the associations of unhappy experiences and physical suffering which made me disdain and loathe the place so intensely.

Nonetheless, Muswell Hill had become a very different place since I lived there in the 1930s-40s. The population had trebled since most of the one-family residences had been divided into three flats for three families. Every inch of kerbside was taken up with parked vehicles, since the houses were built before the age of popular car ownership, and so garages were never considered. Buses were the main form of transport to the City or West End, or to Highgate for the underground on the Northern line, although when I first went to work, I took the steam train from Cranley Gardens station, just five minutes from the house, to Finsbury Park and King's Cross. That railway line was removed many decades ago. The area no longer has the stodgy conservatism it once had, and neither is it as quiet or as homogeneous, as its pavements today are packed with those from every conceivable background or place on the planet. There is a more adventurous or innovative air to the place, and politically it is now Lib-Dem or Labour rather than Tory – a transformation which would have shattered the illusions of my grandparents' generation.

The house in which I had been brought up was 196 Muswell Hill Road, close to the centre and not many yards from St. James's church where we worshipped regularly. These were what my father proudly described as his "Professional premises." There was a steep flight of steps and a sloping red-tiled path leading up to the front door. My mother disliked the house, not only because of the difficulty in negotiating a pram up and down the outside steps, but because of the many steep staircases within the house, and what she felt was the bad design of the place. To the right of the steps leading up to the front door was another flight of steps leading down to the door of the coal cellar. Once inside the long hallway which had a decoratively tiled floor in several colours, on the left side was my grandfather's surgery, and on the right side my father's – a much smaller room. When I was about ten years of age, the use of the rooms was reversed, and when my grandfather began to work part-time, he became the junior partner in the practice.

On the left side of the hall, beyond the surgery, was a door leading into the waiting room. This was a large long silent room with a black oak dresser backing onto the wall with the surgery on the other side. The dresser had Toby jugs on its shelves and other ugly pieces of ceramic ware. There was a large brown leather sofa and matching armchairs, and several upright Edwardian chairs with cane seats, and a bookcase loaded with *Punch* annuals dating from the start of the century. Finally, there was a gate-legged table with the latest issues of *Country Life, The Tatler, Punch, The Lady,* and of course, *The Times*, and, *The Financial Times*. The far end of the room looked out onto a patio, and beyond that was a modest garden, most of it lawn.

Returning to the hallway, straight ahead on the left was a swing door leading down some steps, and to the right was the Nurse's (or dental assistant's room), with desk, cupboards and filing cabinets. The Nurse was Miss Gallant, who was employed in the post for some 50 years by both my grandfather and father. She wore the blue uniform and starched collars and cap customary at the time, and was already middle-aged when I knew her. She had once been engaged, but her fiancé was killed in the

First World War, and so as with most women of her generation, she was doomed to a life of spinsterhood. She attended to all the phone calls and the booking of appointments, and the card index in the filing cabinets, etc., in addition to work in the two surgeries. She had a formal businesslike manner, but she was kind and sometimes took us children out to a pantomime or for some other treat. My mother regarded her with slight ridicule because of her fussy and over-conscientious attitude.

Leading to the back door of the house was a dank, dark, stone-floored storage area where gas and oxygen cylinders were kept, and a cupboard where ether and chemicals were stored. There were always strange smells in the place. On one occasion when my father was sorting things around, I picked up a bottle and asked what it contained. "Ether," he replied. – "What does it smell like,?" I asked. – "I'll show you," he replied, and taking a wad of cotton wool, he tipped the bottle onto it, and held the wool over my nose. I experienced an unpleasant shock, and he laughed at my discomfort. "I won't do that again until you need a tooth out," he said. On the right side of the garden, near to the house, was a workshop for the dental mechanic, Mr. Kemp, who was in full-time employment by the practice.

Returning to the house, by the garden door, and straight ahead was a door leading down into the cellar with its whitewashed walls and separate compartments for storing coke and coal. The cellar was where we were to spend many nights in our dressing gowns sitting in deckchairs during the bombing in the years ahead. Returning to the main hallway, on the right hand side and straight ahead were the steep stairs leading up to the first landing. Straight ahead was a toilet on the left, and the bathroom on the right, both looking out onto the back garden. On the right was the kitchen, with a coke burning range for heating the water, a sink near the window overlooking the back garden, a kitchen table, gas oven, and a pulley at the far end of the room where washing was hung to dry.

Ascending another flight of stairs led to the living quarters proper. These rooms were not only hideously decorated but profoundly depressing on the spirit – or so I found them from a very early age. My parents had decided to be fashionable – or certainly my mother – and being fashionable in the context of furnishings (or certainly when following post-19th century design), invariably means following what aesthetically is ephemeral and tawdry. My parents therefore had a slavish appreciation of everything which was up-to-date in the 1930s, something which was not replicated, I am glad to say, by my other relatives. The Browns, for example, lived in a house more elegantly and conservatively decorated, that is, imitation Chippendale and Regency style wallpaper, etc., which although unexciting artistically, was at least not unpleasing to the eye.

The architecture of the house was good imitation Tudor – that is, the external beams were twisted and warped, so giving the false impression of having been exposed to centuries of inclement weather. The only thing which I loathed in their house was the chime of the walnut grandmother clock on the sideboard in the dining room, with its high-pitched modern sound having none of the redolence or grandeur of an ancient grandfather clock. The chime of this clock at once alerted one to the fact that everything in the house was indeed imitation, and reminded one that this was not a long-established residence, but the home of those belonging to the nouveau riche.

As became the 1930s, there were no hanging pictures, and so the walls were bare and boring, covered with cream coloured wallpaper with a mottled surface. Framed family portraits stood on shelves and mantelpieces, and the furniture was probably chosen by my mother, for although my father had neatness to a fault, he had little aesthetic sense. Most of the furniture, including the tea trolley (which is now in my possession) was light coloured oak bought from Heals, and there was plain wall-to-wall carpeting in the three rooms which may be designated the first floor. These rooms were, left to right, the dining room and lounge, with windows looking onto the main road, and my parents' bedroom with a window facing onto the back garden.

The latter was twin-bedded as my mother was averse to double beds, and very late in life she admitted disliking sex except for the specific purpose of procreation. She told me this in a humorous tone of voice in her late 80s, but she was otherwise liberal in her sexual attitudes and appreciated the sexual needs of others. My father, although supposedly strongly sexed, and he enjoyed the favours of other women during his married life, probably took little offence at my mother's reserve in this respect. I have reached this conclusion from various remarks he made when I was a 16-year old, during painfully formal sessions, when I had to sit down and be told about "the birds and the bees." On one of these embarrassing sessions (during which I learned little of any significance I did not already know) he explained that the "male" derives pleasure from sexual intercourse but not the "female" unless she had a "degenerate character." Nice women passively accepted intercourse as a moral obligation to their husbands. I was then warned against consorting with prostitutes, or loose women, or any who found pleasure in the sexual act. As to whether my father actually believed this nonsense or not – or continued to believe it after a certain period of his life – I was never to discover. In view of his actual success with women during his mature life (i.e. beyond the age of 40), I have my doubts. He probably perpetuated these myths to keep me away from *all* women, and such a view will be substantiated later in this memoir.

On the landing of this first floor, a frightening African carving of an evil-looking face was suspended on the wall between the entrance to the dining room and lounge. It was aptly known as the Devil. It was one of the monstrosities my grandfather had brought back from South Africa at the start of the century. Another flight of steep stairs led up to a mezzanine floor where my father's dressing room was situated at the back of the house. This doubled up as the dreaded punishment room. It always had an unpleasant smell of mothballs. In a tallboy my father kept his precious collection of bow ties, cuff links, collars and studs; in a wardrobe he had a large collection of suits and blazers for all occasions, overcoats for differing weather conditions; and in another cupboard he had a wonderful collection of exotic waistcoats. There was also a shoe cupboard with a vast collection of shoes of every conceivable kind – all in immaculate condition.

Clothes were my father's most precious possessions of which he was inordinately proud. He was always a snappy dresser, and since he had the time and space to quietly look through his collection every morning, he rarely wore the same tie or jacket for several days in succession. As I always disdained dandyism as the vanity of those who sought to compensate for other deficiencies, I never learned to take an interest in clothes, and tended to despise those who did. I chose my clothes for warmth and utility, and was only prepared for such expenditure when they fell apart, and my parents never encouraged me to dress with elegance. In later life it needed my wife and daughters to drag me to the outfitters to make an essential purchase.

On the linoleum floor of the dressing room was a blue and orange woollen mat lovingly woven by my father whilst a student at Guy's. It bore the hospital's coat of arms. It was on this mat that my younger brother and I were placed, and our necks bent forward for the bare-bottomed thrashings with a specially selected cane purchased for the purpose from the local ironmonger.

Another flight of stairs led to the top landing. On the far left were two large doors leading into the roof space. I never entered this area but it was used for storing trunks and cases. There were three rooms on the top landing: on the left the maid's room with a low ceiling and squat window looking out to the road, and a marble topped wash stand with a jug and bowl, for the maids were not allowed to use the bathroom; then the nursery, a large room with bars over the windows, also looking out onto the front; and a back room, painted dark green, also with a sloping ceiling in alignment with the roof, usually reserved for the nanny. This room, mysteriously, for a reason I never discovered, always exuded an unpleasant smell reminiscent of liquorice. On a shelf was a picture of three horses' heads, which gave me nightmares during those periods when I slept in the room. There was also a green fluorescent figure which in the dark gave out a ghostly light.

*

My mother described me as a nervous hysterical child, full of irrational fears, and terrified by flies and other flying insects. My earliest memories are of sitting in a high chair eating the baby food Bemax, and I can still smell and taste the cereal after all that time. It was eaten from a high-sided plate decorated with three yellow chicks, and it is recorded that my first spoken words were not "Mamma" or "Papa," but "bore, bore," meaning "more," and I have seldom been fastidious over food. At that time it was considered advisable to underfeed rather than overfeed babies, and a certain greed, over-acquisitiveness, or aggression may have developed from this feeding system. I am not regretting this regime, for underfeeding may indeed lead to a healthier life in later years than allowing a child to eat its fill, bearing in mind the factors which have led to the obesity and serious health risks encountered by the younger generation today.

I next remember sitting on the nursery floor, all alone, looking out onto the landing and the descending stairs beyond, and hearing a hammering which gradually became nearer and nearer. Eventually, a monstrous dark figure appeared below the stairs, an ancient and disfigured old man with a greasy dirty flat cap, a huge brush-like moustache, and threatening metal spikes protruding from his mouth. I screamed in terror at this frightful spectre. He ignored me, but took the spikes from his mouth, and hammered them into the floor carpet. It was Jake, the handyman, and even when it was explained who he was, I always remained afraid when he visited the house.

My next recollection is of sitting in my pram in Muswell Hill, and being confronted by old men with long beards, sometimes with waxed moustaches, pince-nez, or trilbys, and always with starched collars with rounded corners. These ancient Victorians viewed me with admiration, and their eyes glinted with a sensuous expression. I stared back at them fascinated. I became obsessed by the appearance of these old men, and on one occasion my mother said I had caused her acute embarrassment, when I exclaimed, "He looks so old, he's going to fall down dead!" Their psychological effect was curious, for when I lay in bed with a pleasurable erection, it was always the faces of these old men which I found sexually arousing. In later life I could never imagine how such perverse feelings and thoughts could have occurred in this way.

When I was a toddler, my nanny took me to Waterlow Park, probably one of the most beautiful of the smaller North London parks, situated below Highgate Village. Whilst my nanny was seated on a park bench talking to a mother with several children, I saw a pretty little blonde girl in a pink dress, a year or two older than me, and I was suddenly overcome with a deep affection for her. I chased her down the grassy bank and then up again, but she refused to respond to my gestures of affection, and either I may have frightened her or perhaps she just took me for a "silly boy." Shortly afterwards the nanny put me back into the pushchair and we left the park, and I felt deeply sad at parting from my first love.

The following episode took place when I was just two years old, and this is proven by the fact that Old Nanny, who was a temp and features in the story, appears in a photograph with me in the garden in the Summer of 1937. She was giving me a bath one evening when I said I wanted a pee, and requested to be taken to the toilet. "You can use the bath," she said. To me this seemed somehow wrong, besides being unclean, but she insisted. As I stood in the bath she held my penis as I pissed into the bathwater, and her behaviour seemed strange at the time. She was an old woman dressed like a nun, with a veil and a long black dress to her ankles.

At the age of three my mother bought a French bulldog, Beau, so that I might become more accustomed to animals, and lose my fear of those dogs I encountered in the street and of all other living things which moved on legs. We already had a tabby cat called George, but he led his own life and took no notice of me. Beau was a black and white dog with pointed ears and disagreeable expression. He was bought as a puppy but grew up to be hypersensitive, nervous, and then aggressive. Perhaps there was something in the household environment which rubbed off on his character. He was said to fight with all other dogs and I did not get on with him. On one occasion he even jumped out of a high window, although he survived the feat. My mother finally dismissed him as dysfunctional and "mad" in failing to fit in with our family life, and so he was eventually given away to new owners.

The following story was told to me by my mother, but I have no recollection of the incident. I was a demanding child and often fell into furious rages if my wishes were not satisfied. One day whilst in Archway Road my mother bought me a Dinky toy. As we progressed along the road we passed another shop where I saw another Dinky toy I liked better. I was told that I already had a new toy and should be content with that. Thereupon I fell into a frenzy and hurled my new toy into the middle of the road. To punish me, my mother stopped by the kerbside to await the crushing of the object by a passing vehicle, and when this occurred, I screamed disconsolately at my tragic loss.

When I was three years old (and there is a witness to vouch for the date accuracy of this story) I found myself ascending in a crowded lift in Selfridges. I was with my cousin, Carol, ten years older than me, who recollected the episode clearly, and my mother, and we were meeting other relatives for tea on one of the upper floors. A young woman in a green costume took out a cigarette and ignited her lighter, but her hand burst out in flames and she began screaming. She shook her hand, but for some reason the lighter stuck to her fingers. The elderly lift attendant, in his magnificent green uniform and epaulettes, knocked the lighter onto the floor, and the fire was immediately extinguished. I was not frightened by the event but curious at what happened.

The following event I remember with crystal clarity as if it was yesterday. It was dark and late at night, and my parents had gone out to a function. I needed to get up for a pee, and the nanny began to lead me downstairs to the toilet. As we stood on the landing outside my father's dressing room, looking down to the first floor, I was suddenly overcome by a feeling of profound depression at the silence, emptiness, and loneliness of the house. Through the darkness in the lounge I espied the glimmering chromium plated ashtray atop its two-foot column and the weighted base where the ash and cigarette ends were dropped. I was struck by the ugliness of this 1930s artefact and how it oppressed the soul.

During these early years I was haunted by terrible nightmares. One recurring dream was of being chased by lions down dark tunnels until finally I was trapped on both sides when I awoke. Another dream was of hurtling along, to my great terror, at great speed in a noisy underground carriage, as my mother lay outstretched on one of the seats, with hideously contorted Clytemnestra-like features, pointed nose, deep sunken eyes, blood red lips and a snow-white pallid complexion, as she laughed triumphantly at my fear.

My younger brother, Gavin Russell, was born on 16th May 1938. He was supposed to be a girl – or that was the overwhelming wish of my father, for he was long known to love little girls whilst loathing boys – or at least, other people's boys. He was not born in a famous West End nursing home, as I had been, but in a more modest home in Alexandra Park road at the other side of Muswell Hill. I clearly remember being taken along by my father to visit my mother, and standing in the room where my mother and brother were accommodated, but I did not register what followed as it was related many years later. My father was handed the wrapped baby, and after making a pretence for some moments of being pleased with the bundle, he handed it back to my mother, exclaiming, "I don't want it. You can have it back," and my mother was hurt by the gesture but felt she could say nothing in reply.

My brother was never forgiven for being born a boy, and my father never hid his dislike for his second son. Although I incurred more thrashings than my brother, I believe that he was more damaged by my father's attitude. As a first-born, and despite all my faults, I was still expected to have a destiny of some significance, but my brother remained an irrelevance because of the disappointment of his birth. The overhanging shadow of my father's power haunted him for years after his death at the age of 83 in 1990. My brother was cursed with nightmares of the reappearance of our father proclaiming his living status, and returning from an inexplicable absence to attend to his financial affairs, and claw back what had wrongly been passed onto his heirs. I, on the other hand, accepted my father's death and was relieved at his going. I saw him in his coffin and knew he was dead, and as he lay there, pallid with a wax-like complexion, it seemed as if his features had been transformed into those of his mother, who had died 40 years before. My brother, on the contrary, could not face the horrific obligation of paying his respects in this way in visiting the Chapel of Rest.

On only one occasion was I subsequently haunted by a dream of my father. I found myself in the lounge at 196 Muswell Hill Road, and I was vomiting undigested soft bread rolls, and pulling them out of my mouth as they were thrust up into my gullet. My father began to rush about with a sense of determined purpose. "What are you going to do?" I asked apprehensively. He made no answer and I could see he intended to make none as he resolutely pursued his dreadful task. He took up an enamel tray, placing surgical knives and other instruments into the containers. I repeated my question louder and more desperately, but I need not have done so. Already I knew his intentions. He was to cut open my stomach, and remove its contents. He took up a syringe and drew in liquid from a phial, all the while remaining stubbornly silent. Then, with a sudden gesture, he thrust the needle through my jacket into my upper arm. At that point I did something which I never did in real life – or would never dare to do – I fell into a defiant rage, snatching the syringe out of my arm and throwing it across the room, before waking up to a world of sanity.

The dream reflected his behaviour in real life whilst I was a small child. He would never answer questions or explain his actions if engaged in some medical task, as he felt this was an imposition on his professional status, beyond the comprehension of the lay person – and certainly of a child. This is illustrated by an episode when I had bad colds and earache when he forcefully stuffed cotton wool into my ears, rather in the way a dentist would stuff material into a tooth to be filled. The outcome was unfortunate for I became stone deaf – or so said my mother. The doctor then had to be called to the house, and I remember his visit and my fear at having to have my ears syringed. I watched in horror as the doctor drew out his instruments and began to assemble the syringe, and in my naivety, I asked him if he could perform his task whilst I stood at one end of the room whilst he stood at the other – in other words if my ears could be hosed out at a distance, rather as a fireman extinguishes a fire. He made no answer, and when he performed the operation I suffered excruciating pain. The outcome was that the cotton wool was successfully flushed out, and I regained my hearing to the full. It is strange that such an experience should give rise to a nightmare some 50 years after the event.

CHAPTER 3
A Sanctuary from War

"There was a time when meadow, grove,
and stream,
The earth, and every common sight,
To me did seem
Apparelled in celestial light."

William Wordsworth, *Intimations of Immortality*

My maternal grandparents' West country home – A life of freedom – My bad temper – An Old Dame's school – A perverse curiosity – My mother's broken promises "not to tell" – Days on the farm – Why I resolved never to attend school – Social life at Sampford Place, and my mother's relatives

Within 16 months of my brother's birth war clouds were looming, and my father was as fearful of the prospect of war as he was of many things. On the invasion of Poland on 1st September 1939, and hearing on the grapevine through friends in his several exclusive associations, that Britain had limited defence capability, and that London might be flattened within days, he decided to evacuate his family to his parents-in-law's house without further ado. Accordingly, as with thousands of others who were fortunate to be placed in a similar situation with relatives in the provinces, the car was packed and we left for Wiltshire two days before Neville Chamberlain made his historic declaration. The journey was broken, apparently, by a halfway stopover at a hotel where my brother, Gavin, slept in a drawer as there was no cot available.

The arrival in Melksham was the start of a new life, and what I have always regarded as the happiest period of my existence. It was a time of innocence whilst I romped in my Garden of Eden. To me, Sampford Place was the epitome of civilised social life and the aesthetically perfect home, although such an optimistic view may not have been shared by all the adults crowded into the house during those early War years. By today's standards the house was packed with invaluable early and mid-Victorian furniture and many other knick-knacks of the period. But by the standards of 1939, such items were considered as neither valuable nor as antiques, since strictly speaking they were then less than a hundred years old. My mother only regarded furniture of the Regency period or earlier as being of worthwhile value.

My grandparents' furniture was judged as little better than "rubbish" since much of it had been bought from Mrs. Townsend's scrap yard just off the town square. But my grandmother had an eye for the beautiful, and by today's standards, almost every item in my grandparents' house would be valued in hundreds if not thousands of pounds by a contemporary auctioneer. In that era, dominated by the intellectual fallacies of the Bloomsbury set, everything Victorian was despised or ridiculed in the 20th century's barbaric reaction against the values of the previous two centuries, and the outbreak of the Second World War was in some way the retribution for the philistinism of that ghastly century. The furniture and bric-a-brac which my grandparents purchased had been chosen with care and aesthetic discretion, and then arranged in the different rooms with a sense of proportion and design, and it did not matter if different periods were mixed, or stools or screens were added from the Orient.

It is necessary to describe the house and its surroundings. A low grey stone wall bordered the front of the house, with an area of lawn alongside the public pavement, and a large lawn area between the wall and the house. A gravel driveway ran from the handsome cast iron gates (soon to be removed as scrap for the War effort) beneath a stone archway to the front of the house to the left, and also towards a pair of huge oak gates leading into a courtyard at the right of the building. Beyond these gates was a garage for two or three vehicles, and to the right, several stables used for storage. Further to the right you mounted several steps and entered through a wrought iron gate into the Kitchen garden, where all kinds of fruit and vegetables were grown. During the following years members of the Home Guard would attend the garden, often carrying pieces of wood cut into the shape of rifles.

To the left of this garden was a stone wall dividing a piece of grass wasteland from a ditch and farmer's fields beyond. This wasteland which stretched along the back of the house I considered my own, and I spent much time digging up turf and moving it from place to place. On the right side of the Kitchen garden was a long greenhouse backing onto a high stone wall which concealed the property from the street. In the greenhouse sweet grapes and peaches grew down from the glass ceiling, and many other products were grown on side shelves. There were two deep wells at either end of the greenhouse. Until this day, whenever I taste peaches of a particular quality, I am reminded of my grandfather's greenhouse.

Beyond the house to the left was a giant yew, and at the side of the house another large lawn, where croquet was played, and sometimes a dartboard was fixed to the trunk of the tree. This was the area where large parties were often held, for it was out of public view, and during the War years, the house was always filled with guests. To the left of this lawn, bordering the property was a high wall with espalier plums and other fruits. The entire garden was a paradise, and during the Summer I spent my time picking and eating fruit as I chose.

Entering the house by the main door, there was a long hallway attractively painted in dark green. A carpet which once covered the floor of this hallway is now in the entrance hall of my own house. To the immediate right on entering the house was my grandfather's study. This was lined with books in glass-fronted cabinets. There was a large desk, and later during the War, the floor was usually strewn with huge diagrams of battleships on which he was working for the Admiralty. No one was allowed to disturb him in the study which during the day was the only place he was likely to be if he was not working in the garden.

On the left of the hall was a door leading into the sitting room. This was the room where the wireless was situated, a large mahogany piece of furniture. As there was no electricity in the house, there were 12-volt batteries behind the wireless and a confusion of wires connecting them to the equipment. Two or three times a week my grandfather would go down to the electrical shop to get the batteries re-charged. Gas lamps fixed to wall brackets were the light source in the house, giving a softer glow than the offensive glare of an electric light bulb. At Christmas time, especially, there was a far more romantic and exciting atmosphere in the half light and shadows of gaslight than in electric light where everything was displayed without mystery, for electricity gave an equal value to everything on which it cast its light. During the day I liked to go around the house and touch the mantles of the gas lamps and see them burst, for which I was soundly thrashed with a slipper on one occasion by my father.

In the winter when wooden shutters were barred across the windows, and a coal fire burned gently beneath the mantelpiece, we sat around the wireless listening to the latest news, or to music, or to a play on the Home Service. The women would be knitting, and the men stroking the various dogs which inhabited the house from time to time, and occasionally there would be conversation. When Russia came into the War in 1941, I remember my grandfather saying what wonderful people the Russians were and how small children were teaching their grandparents to read and write in a country where most were still illiterate. When I was tired in the evening, I liked to be stroked like a dog, and sat at the feet of great aunts and great uncles for the pleasure of enjoying this sensation.

I remember my grandfather had a volume of *Teach Yourself Chinese*, when in the evening he was brushing up his knowledge of a language he had learned long ago. He described the Chinese as the politest people in the world. He was a very humane man, and although part of a fighting force, my mother said that surprisingly he could not tolerate the sight of blood. I do remember him expressing his disapproval of bull fighting, not merely because of cruelty to bulls but because horses too were killed in the general mêlée of the bullring. I remember him saying that Britain was the best country in the world in which to live because of its mild weather, and because we did not have to live in fear of earthquakes, as did so many peoples, when entire cities were destroyed and thousands lost their lives. His favourite book, according to my mother, was *Pepys Diary*.

The sitting room led onward to the Drawing room, a much larger chamber used in summer or whenever there were many guests in the house. This room had a grand piano, and windows looking out to the street at one end, and French windows leading onto a flight of descending steps at the back of the house. I remember on one occasion when a barn owl had nested beneath these steps. Both these rooms had an assortment of comfy armchairs, upright chairs, stools, footstools, screens inlaid with mother of pearl, Chinese tables, etc. On the walls were innumerable Chinese prints, other pictures and engravings, and on the mantelpieces, side tables and shelves, there were Chinese vases and many ivory pieces intricately carved, and on the floors were Oriental carpets and rugs.

Returning to the hall and proceeding ahead from the direction of the front door, there was on the left a small pantry where the crockery and extra cutlery was stored. To the right was a long tunnel leading to a kind of cloakroom and side door out of the building. There were two water closets (so marked) side by side in this area, a washbasin, and opposite, a door leading into the School room. During air raids, which were infrequent, the tunnel was used as a shelter until the all-clear. German bombers were only likely to pass on their way to Bristol which was heavily bombed. The School room was renamed the Play room, and was also set up as a movable surgery, so allowing my father extra petrol coupons for more frequent weekend trips between London and Melksham.

Returning to the main hallway, further down on the left was the entrance to the dining room. This was a magnificent room with French windows leading out to the side of the building, and also onto a verandah at the back. On the left wall on entering the dining room hung the life size portrait of my great-grandfather, described in the first chapter of this book. Below this oil painting was a spinet loaded with silverware, candelabra, dishes, etc. In front of this was a long table seating up to 20 or so persons. A different set of crockery was used for different periods of the day: orange for breakfast (in meeting the rising sun); the blue Willow pattern for lunch, tea, and dinner; and a special set when visitors were entertained. My grandfather sat in an armchair at the head of the table, and the rest of us sat on heavy upright rosewood chairs.

There was a side table where the larger dishes of food were laid out and I remember the magnificent joints of pre-War ham, and no such meat has tasted the like again through the corruption of post-War food with all kinds of unpleasant additives in the name of "modernisation." Those who have never tasted pre-War food can never hope to enjoy the greatest delight of *haute cuisine*. I remember being surprised at my grandfather taking salt with his porridge at breakfast, and never sugar or milk which he despised. He preferred to eat oats the Scottish way as he had always done in his youth.

Leaving the dining room, on the left was a broad staircase with shallows stairs, which swept round in a magnificent half circle in reaching the first floor, and there were decorative iron banisters supporting a rosewood handrail. Beyond the staircase on the ground floor was a narrow passage leading into the kitchen, but if you crossed the hallway from the dining room, you reached the service area, the floor being laid with flag stones. To the right was the pantry or cool room with slate shelves for storage and a mesh window to let in air but keep out insects.

Leaving the pantry, to the right was a small passage leading to the enclosed courtyard, described above, but opposite the pantry was the entrance to the scullery with sink and shelving for the storage of cooking implements. On the left in the scullery, was a door which opened to the servants' staircase, and straight ahead led into the huge kitchen with windows opposite overlooking fields and letting in plenty of light. Against the wall on the left was a range of five wood and coal burning ovens, for there was no gas cooker. On the walls of this room hung photos of battleships, but not those in which my grandfather had served, as to display such pictures was regarded as "bad form."

On the right side of the kitchen was a door leading into the washroom, where all clothes and linen were attended to. There was a copper cauldron set into a brick structure, below which a wood burning fire could be lit for boiling water. In those days there was no such thing as washing powder – or none that I knew of – and so soda crystals were used for this purpose. In the summer when I became bitten by insects, mostly harvesters, I would dip the soda lumps into warm water and rub them over the bites, so the skin was covered in a white chalky substance.

There was a mangle in the washroom and also a pump set over a sink. The cauldron, naturally, had to be filled manually by carrying buckets of water over from the pump. The walls of the washroom were whitewashed, and beyond the room were some steps leading down into the garage where my grandfather's ancient car was kept, with its yellowing windows and pleasant smell of old leather. My grandfather was supposedly a reckless driver, and my mother would never allow him to take us children out in the car.

In the winter the house was centrally heated with a coke burning boiler situated outside in the courtyard near the pantry window. My grandfather attended to this chore, and I remember the long iron implements he used for raking out cinders and ash, and the huge shovel for feeding the fire above.

Returning to the house and mounting the staircase, straight ahead was a large framed print of highland cattle in a Scottish landscape. I found the long-horned cattle a rather frightening image – so different from the well-groomed clean-faced English cattle I shortly came to know so well. At the top of the staircase, a long hallway, with rooms leading off left and right, led to the front of the house with the bathroom at the far end. The bathroom had a pleasant soapy smell, and the water was heated by a geyser. Whilst being bathed one evening in Christmas 1939, I first heard a party of carol singers singing, *Away in the Manger*, for the first time, and during my childhood years, it remained a favourite carol.

The first room at the right was my grandmother's bedroom, a large chamber which looked over the roof of the verandah leading from the dining room. Honey suckle grew over this roof, and so during the summer the room was suffused with a fine sweet scent. I always liked entering the room as my grandmother was fond of scents, and there was usually the strong smell of aux de Cologne. Beside this room was my grandfather's bedroom, much smaller but with his own washbasin, and a strop for sharpening his razor, for he did not use a safety razor.

Opposite his room was the Bamboo room, so-called because all the furniture, apart from the bed, was made of bamboo and wicker. Some years later this became my bedroom. In a drawer beneath the wardrobe was my grandfather's full dress naval hat with plumes. Opposite my grandmother's bedroom was a passageway which curved round to the left, leading to a small hallway with a door to the servants' staircase and several rooms leading off. Here was the nursery where I slept with the nanny, and nearby was the sick room.

Not long after we arrived at Sampford Place a woman from the Council arrived with an armful of gasmasks, and we all assembled in what was still called the School room, to be fitted or shown how these protective devices were used. To me this was a bit of fun, and I was proud of this new possession, but my brother, being a baby, had a special gasmask into which his entire body was zipped, with a cellophane window to look out of, and he screamed in terror in being placed into this enclosed container.

My memories of life at Melksham are almost entirely happy, although this does not mean I did not have my moments of discontent when I fell into a rage. I was very possessive and hated anyone touching my things, and on one occasion when my tricycle was parked in the passageway leading to the kitchen, I accused the maids of having moved it several yards forward in my absence. They were intimidated, and my grandmother came out of the kitchen to find out what all the fuss was about, and she supported the maids in saying no one had moved my tricycle. I stamped my feet and raged all the more but cannot remember how the matter was finally settled.

During the summer, it must have been 1940 when I was five, everyone was wandering around in dark glasses, and I too wanted to be in the fashion. My grandmother kindly offered to "lend" me my grandfather's dark glasses as he was not using them then, but I had no understanding of the word "lend," or the concept of borrowing. I only understood the concepts of ownership and non-ownership. Some days later my grandmother said that grandpa wanted his dark glasses back. She was standing in the kitchen and I was facing her in the entrance from the scullery. I was outraged at this request which seemed a gross injustice, the breaking of a contract, and an attempt at theft. After a short altercation, I snatched the spectacles off my face, throwing them onto the flagstones, before stamping on them to final destruction, as my grandmother looked on aghast.

On another occasion, after breakfast, I was impatient to get out into the garden and onto my piece of land alongside the ditch, and tried to exit the house by the French windows in the dining room leading onto the verandah. As I could not open the doors, I called for help, and as no one came to assist me in good time, I lost my temper and kicked in the window. The crashing of glass soon brought my grandmother onto the scene who called my mother. I was lucky to escape without cuts.

It was surprising my grandmother was fond of me despite all my faults, but she was, for my mother said she genuinely "disliked boys," and was usually only interested in her female grandchildren. She apparently ignored my cousin, Mervyn, nine years my senior and Aunt Joan's son, and my mother felt sorry for him because of this, and took him under her wing. When my grandfather died, his dress sword was passed on to me as an heirloom and not to Mervyn, and this caused an upset with his mother. Mervyn was a year younger than his sister Carol, and both were always cheerful and bright, laughing and full of fun. Why should my grandmother bother with me, an often irritable and naughty child,? my mother wondered.

We must have attended church rather often at that time, most probably at my father's behest, since apparently I was soon impressed by the preaching of the clergyman, for back in Sampford Place I formed the habit of mounting a chair, as a pulpit in the drawing room, and preaching sermons to my relatives. The words were incoherent, but all the oratorical gestures were correct in driving home a message to the congregation, and this greatly amused those who witnessed these performances. I have no recollection of these episodes, but my cousin Carol reminded me about them decades later.

During the first Christmas in 1939, we were assembled in the drawing room after dinner in the middle of the day, when we were visited by Father Christmas who entered through the French windows carrying a huge sack of presents. It was my Uncle Reg (Aunt Joan's husband) who played the part, but sartorially correct and with a realistic beard. My brother, Gavin, who was then about 18 months, was so terrified by this strange phantom which apparently emerged from nowhere to alarm the throng of relatives with a sack of gifts, that he screamed inconsolably, and was in no mood to engage in the Christmas spirit.

Not long after the outbreak of War, as we were gathering in the dining room for lunch, Miss Beesley, an elderly lodger in the house, announced she had just come from Melksham railway station, where she saw a party of little Belgian children, all wrapped in their winter coats, but with their hands chopped off. "Is there no savagery these Germans are incapable of,?" she concluded. I cannot remember any of my relatives remarking on this story. Perhaps they knew she was lying, or inventing an exaggerated drama out of some foreign children she had seen at the station. In any event, the story was too close to the invented fictions of the First World War to be believable. Naturally, as a 4-year old I accepted her story as the gospel truth, and believed the Germans to be the wickedest people on earth. Shortly thereafter I got to know her even more horrible sister very much better.

She managed an Old Dame's school in the town, and I was sent there to learn basic arithmetic and the alphabet. About five of us attended the school for three hours every morning, when we sat round a table fumbling with bakelite letters or solving simple puzzles. There were silent periods, during which we had to sit with folded arms and not fidget on our chairs, and children's prayers which had to be learned by heart. Miss Beesley was the only teacher, although a younger person sometimes came round to take us for a walk to interesting places such as the railway goods yard or to look at factory buildings from the outside. We always walked in a crocodile holding hands.

Miss Beesley was usually disagreeable and threatening, although it was only her great niece who was the direct object of her anger. If she failed to achieve some difficult task, her great aunt threatened to make her sick in front of the other children, upon which the pretty little girl with long brown hair burst into tears and began sobbing loudly. The rest of us sat round the table silently, intimidated, but never the victims of actual punishment, and so we had nothing to complain of.

When I woke in the morning it was often to the sound of goods trains shunting in the sidings by the railway station, and I enjoyed the strong smell of tar which came from that direction. I had several nannies during this period: there was Melksham Nanny, who came from Ealing, and for a short period there was a local girl, from whom I caught lice, and when this was discovered, she was sacked, and no other local girl was entrusted to be employed again. My head was treated with paraffin and I never caught lice again. As I lay in bed, I remember Melksham Nanny dressing in the half light, and I saw her pudenda, which was the only time during my childhood when I saw the nakedness of a woman, and I noticed her applying a menstrual cloth as she pulled up her underwear.

During this period I was often given mechanical or clockwork toys but I regarded them in quite another light from most children. I soon tired of winding up clockwork mechanisms and seeing vehicles or dolls cross the playroom floor. Instead I was aroused by how these mechanisms actually worked, and with this in mind, I was soon driven to break them open with any implement at hand and look inside. My mother said I was so absorbed by staring at and contemplating these toys as I held them in my hand, that she was convinced I would later become a "car mechanic."

This was a silly assumption, and she might have come to a better conclusion had she realised this activity may have been a metaphor for quite another quality. Might I not have been seen as an aspiring thinker or scientist? But such abstract associations were not likely to occur to my mother who was far too practical and earth-bound in her thinking. One day my great Aunt Lou, who drove around in a green Austin 7, and was the daughter of Edward VII's famous chef, gave me an alarm clock with the idea it would teach me to tell the time. I immediately stuck matchsticks into the back and tried to force it apart, and she was most distressed that I had damaged her gift. I was later to learn that the clock was anyway already broken, and she had only given it to me to twirl around the hour and minute hands.

As I spent most of my time amongst grown-ups in my grandparents' house, I too wanted to give the impression of being an adult. Accordingly, I would sometimes take a book, sit beside a relative in the drawing room, and pretend to read although I could not understand a word. However, in turning over the pages from time to time, I flattered myself that I too behaved like an adult.

We remained for approximately two years in Melksham before finally returning to London, although this period was broken with occasional visits to the London home. As my father at this time was working for two or three days a week in London and other hospitals as far away as Staines and Slough, in attending to the jaws of the war-wounded after they had been off-loaded from the long Red Cross trains, we never seemed adversely restricted in regard to petrol. I always found it depressing returning to London, and it was with dismay when I sighted the first London bus stop sign, or saw the first red London bus, and realised that there was no more beautiful countryside to see as we drove through miles of boring and ugly urban housing before finally reaching Muswell Hill. Arriving home was always an anti-climax.

On one occasion I was brought from London to Melksham by train by the nanny. As we stood on the platform at Swindon, waiting for the connection to Melksham, there were crowds of American servicemen, in addition to several parties of evacuee children together with their minders. The servicemen turned to one another exclaiming, "Look at those poor little kids. What can we do for them?" There were several sweet shops on the platforms and in their windows were stacked huge tins of chocolates and other confectionary, but these delights were not for English people with their restricted allowances. They were things to be seen but not possessed – merely remembrances of a better time with a world at peace.

A party of Americans went into one of these shops, emerging moments later holding tins of chocolates. The lids were ripped off, and without a word, the servicemen began stuffing handfuls of sweets into the coats of the children's pockets. When they came to me, I must have reacted with a gesture of apprehension, for one of the servicemen exclaimed, "Don't be afraid. I'm only giving you some candies." Clearly I was not accustomed to such unusual gestures of charity. This must have been in 1941 or 42, some months after the bombing of Pearl Harbour, by which time I was 6 or 7 years of age.

My father came down to Sampford Place either weekly or fortnightly. If I had done something seriously wrong my mother always used the ultimate threat of telling my father. This brought immediate contrition and pleading. I remember pleading on my knees before my mother in her bedroom not to tell my father about my latest misdemeanour for I knew it would always lead to a thrashing. At last she was persuaded and promised to keep her word, but she betrayed me anyway, and so I had the thrashing, and at that period of my life it was usually with a leather slipper on bare buttocks. She could never be trusted to keep her word, and I can only excuse this with the explanation that she was closely cross-questioned and put under pressure to list all my misdeeds of the previous week.

One Sunday after lunch (I think when the maids had a day off) we guests cleared the dining table and took everything into the scullery. I carried the salt cellar and followed my father. My father told me to "put the salt in the sink," and for a joke – which I thought was very funny at the time – I emptied the salt cellar into the sink. My father did not see the comic side of this – or the intended wit, and so I was taken away to one of the more distant bedrooms and given a thrashing.

One Sunday afternoon when my nanny was taking me for a walk and we were passing along the high street, crowded with pedestrians on a stroll, we witnessed a break-in. Four Irishmen were passing along the pavement on the other side of the road, one of them carrying a bottle. You could tell they were Irish by their ruffled un-brushed hair – and what followed was so deranged that no other race could be credited with having committed such an act. Their leader smashed the glass door of Strattons, the leading grocer of the town, with his bottle, and unbolting the door within, the four walked inside. Moments later they re-emerged, each hugging several bottles of spirit against his breast, but they walked straight into the arms of an astonished passing constable who arrested them on the spot, before dozens of witnesses in the street. Back home it was explained there were many Irish navvies in Melksham employed in road building and repairs.

*

I was given freedom to wander around as I liked, but I was told not to play with the shoeless guttersnipes who lived on the other side of the railway bridge, but before I was five years old, I found myself at the Keens' farm on the road leading out of the town, about half a mile from Sampford Place. There was little danger of walking there alone, since there were no roads to cross. My first visit was early one evening when I walked into one of the two long cowsheds, and watched the milking. "What's your name,?" asked several at once. I gave an answer, and they came back with the reply, "Angel? That's a strange name," for I had not spoken clearly. I needed to repeat my name "Nigel" several times before they understood.

For a day or two I had some difficulty in comprehending their strong West country accent, and whenever I returned after an absence in London, it was always one or two days before my ear was fully attuned to understanding their dialect. It was not long before I insisted spending all day on the farm every day, although I returned for lunch, except on special occasions when I was obliged to stay at home. It was fortunate that the Keens were to take a liking to me. There was old Thomas Keen and his endearing wife and some seven sons, all working on the farm. I spent most of the time with the eldest, Eric, but there was Roy, and also, Geoff, the youngest, whom I remember well.

It was the drama of farm life which most impressed me, for no day was the same, and always there was a crisis to deal with, such as a sick cow, or a pig which needed to be attended to on the difficult birth of a litter. After the milk had been passed through the filters and coolers in the dairy, the churns were loaded and then hauled onto the cart, and I would drive with one of the farm hands with the horse and cart to the collection point in the town at the great dairy alongside the river Avon. Then there was the time spent on the tractor, driving to a distant field and ploughing, or sowing seeds, etc., and I enjoyed the smell of the diesel as I stood or sat alongside or in front of the driver.

If I arrived early in the morning, I found the family sitting around a large table in their kitchen in the grey stone house, and I was astonished by the huge and luxurious breakfasts they enjoyed, with two fried eggs each, plenty of bacon, mushrooms, sausages, tomatoes, etc. By that time eggs were already rationed and an occasional luxury for ordinary townsfolk. Of course the farmers had already been up many hours by then, milking the cows – all done by hand – and carrying the pales of milk on yokes from the cowsheds to the dairy, and so they were hungry and deserved a full breakfast.

Thomas Keen, the elderly father, was a disciplinarian with his sons, and I remember him talking to them in a rough manner as he gave instructions. I was afraid of him and with good reason, and only occasionally did he hobble around the farm on his walking stick in carrying out an inspection. My chief remembrance of him was in the kitchen and dining area, with its flagstone floor, where he sat with a leather bound money box on his lap which he kept locked until expenses needed to be paid, when it was opened with a key drawn from his pocket, and doled out cash for one purpose or another, always after an altercation in double-checking as to how the money was to be spent. He was clearly an astute businessman, and although the farm at that time was leased, 60 years later, in speaking with his grandson, I learned that he subsequently bought smallholdings for several of his sons, besides adding fields to the main property, which became his freehold at the end of the War.

His wife was a kind motherly woman and one afternoon she gave me the job of removing weeds from the little fishpond in the garden. I took up the task with over-enthusiasm, for I removed the lilies and other plants too, and when the old man came into the garden and saw what I had done, he fell into a rage and chased me off the property. However, I was back at the farm the following day, and so I could not have taken his gesture with too much concern.

It was a mixed farm and the cattle were of all colours and different appearances, and all retained their horns, and in stabling where several horses were kept, there was a small Dexter cow which was kept apart from the rest of the herd. There were different breeds of pigs, and chickens wandered everywhere, and several fields away from the farm, in an isolated sty, there was a young boar. Sometimes I played with a niece in the garden, but mostly I chose to stay with the farm workers and attend them on their tasks. Occasionally I cut grass on my land behind Sampford Place, stuffed it into a sack and fed it to the cows in their shed at milking time.

On walking along the footpath to the farm I met a simple man with whom I got into conversation, and sometimes we sat on a seat and conversed awhile. He was about 40 years old and always carried a collection of children's comics and he liked to point out to me the "pretty pictures." I cannot remember anything else that either of us said, but my grandmother explained he had "fallen out of his pram" and knocked his head as a baby, and that was how he became a harmless simpleton. On one occasion when returning from the farm, I saw a party of gypsies passing along the road with their colourfully painted horse drawn carriages. As I had heard that gypsies kidnapped small children when they had the opportunity, I hid in a ditch until they were out of sight.

Harvest time was the most exciting season of the year, for although there was a harvesting machine to cut the crops and thresh the grain, there was a demand for extra labour, and so there was a great hustle and bustle about the farm. I spent all day in the fields, mostly on the huge horse drawn wagons onto which the square bales were loaded. Meanwhile, several men with shot guns hovered around at the edges of the field in readiness to shoot any rabbits which appeared. My body was soon covered with insect bites which developed into irritating red lumps to which I applied soda crystals as soon as I reached home.

One day, Eric, the eldest son obtained his own landholding, situated about three miles away, and on one occasion he took me along to see the new property. He was not there all the time, and so I began to spend more time with one of the younger sons, Roy, who was bespectacled and not as strong as the others. One day he found that one of the cats had had kittens in the hay at the back of the cowshed. "We can't have that," he said, "there'll be too many cats around," and he casually took up each kitten in turn and hurled it against the brick wall.

I was not shocked, for I accepted everything as an inevitable part of farm life. I had often seen chickens killed, either through ringing their necks or thrusting a penknife down their throats. They were then strung up by their legs against a wall to flap around until they bled dry. When I told my grandmother about the kittens, however, she was appalled, saying that that was a "monstrous thing to do," but my understanding and sympathy nonetheless remained with Roy, for he had given a perfectly rational explanation for the deed. Several years later he died of an illness.

Geoff, the youngest son, was another I often accompanied around the farm. When we were in the fields one day, I noticed he cleared his nose by holding a nostril and snorting through the other. When I asked why he did not carry a handkerchief, he laughed, saying he had better things to carry in his pockets. On another day I noticed his hands were cut with barbed wire, and I suggested he should have them bandaged, or at least, put on a plaster. He explained there was no time for that when there was work to be done, and that the bleeding would soon stop of its own accord. Geoff was the only farmhand amongst the Keens who was conscripted for military service and he went into the infantry.

I saw him home from leave on several occasions in his army uniform, and then he was absent for several years in the Far East. Early in the 21st century, after his death, I was told by his son that he was befriended by a brigadier and that he contemplated a life-long career in the army, but he was persuaded against such a course by old Thomas Keen who said that by so doing he would be denying his own inheritance to land. I remember the day when Geoff finally returned from the Army, shortly before he was officially demobbed. Eventually he was to inherit the entire property.

Over the next few years, as I grew bigger, not merely content with watching the tasks of others, I exerted myself with energy, intent on real work. The other workers sometimes chided me for this, saying, "Don't strain yourself – this isn't for you to do," to which I replied, "I'm quite strong enough for this work." I remember on one occasion several of them asking me what I wanted to do when I grew up, to which I responded, "I want to be a farmer." – "This isn't the work for a grandson of Capt. Figgins," came the reply. "When you grow up you'll be a general or an archbishop perhaps." The discussion was not resumed. I knew nothing about the lives of generals or archbishops, but I did know about farming, and that was the only career I wanted.

My mother tended to be vaguely disdainful about the Keens, saying they were "only tenant farmers." On one occasion she was even more dismissive when I mentioned the church they attended, saying, "people like us don't go to that church." Seriously apprehensive about the friends who were my constant companions, I tentatively asked, "Does that mean they're like Catholics or Jews?" – "Oh, nothing like that," reassured my mother in reply. On reminding my mother that I wanted to be a farmer, and would consider no other occupation, she assented to my wishes, but added, "If you work on a farm, you want to work for gentleman farmers." I did not understand what she meant by "gentleman farmers," but as this was clearly intended as a disdainful reference to the Keens, I dropped the subject.

On several occasions I brought in the cows for milking myself, and they were usually three or four fields away from the farm buildings. As I opened the gates between fields to allow the eighty or so head of cattle to pass through, several would stop and stare, as if to say, "Who the hell are you, and what right have you to bring us in for milking?" If they seemed too cheeky or lagged behind the others, a shout or the wave of a stick soon sent them on their way, and showed them who was master.

*

In Melksham I had several childhood illnesses, such as whooping cough and measles, and when I was put to bed I was attended to by an elderly doctor in a black suit carrying a Gladstone bag with its essential instruments. My grandmother held him in high regard as a "charming gentleman," but my father dismissed him as little more than a "quack" who had qualified in the 1880s and never read a medical tract since that time. He was, however, a big noise in the town, and I remember when a dead calf had been found in a ditch, he issued an order forbidding anyone to bathe in nearby streams.

When my nanny took me for walks, we often passed by a Secondary school, and sometimes we heard the screams of a child being punished. "What's happening inside?" I asked the nanny who could see inside the windows whilst I could not as I was far too short. – "A boy's being caned," she replied. – "Where's he being caned?" I asked. – "On the top of the head," she replied. This seemed a strange place to cane a child, but I accepted her explanation. During the weekends my father also took me for walks, and lectured me on my behaviour. He emphasised that when I went to a proper school I should work hard and absorb everything I was taught.

If I was "naughty" I would be caned, and if I did badly in my studies, I would not get a good job, and so would work in a factory all my life, where I would be tied to a machine and whipped by overseers. By this time I had already been introduced to Dickens through a richly illustrated children's book re-telling many of his tales. I knew all about David Copperfield and how he was soundly thrashed by his step-father, Mr. Murdstone; and far worse, I knew about the horrors of Dothebys Hall, and the brutality of the one-eyed schoolmaster, Wackford Squeers. With these impressions firmly planted – and the realities of school life seemed confirmed by both my nanny and my father – I formed a firm resolution, and that was to *never* go to school.

My grandmother meanwhile introduced me to one of her favourite books, *Shock-headed Peter (Struwwelpeter)*, which I found amusing but not shocking. After all, Harriet deserved to be burned to a cinder because she had been told not to play with matches; if a boy sucked his thumbs and a tailor came along and cut them off, then I supposed it was deserved; if a rabbit turned a gun on a huntsman, then the latter was hardly in a position to complain of injustice; and if boys laughed at black boys in the streets because of the colour of their skin, they deserved to be soaked in inkwells and made black themselves for their unkindness to others. Besides, the rhyming verse of Heinrich Hoffmann (even in translation) gave a lightness of touch to these charming moral tales making them of no offence to any child, although stupid adults in the second half of the 20th century were to condemn them as psychologically harmful.

My mother, meanwhile, read me the stories and verses of A.A. Milne – many of the latter of which I learned by heart – in addition to reading me the tales of Hans Christian Andersen, the brothers Grimm, and a book of Russian fairy stories. I still remember vividly the illustrations in this latter book, particularly that of a merry boy with golden locks charging down a snow-covered hill on a toboggan and almost knocking aside an old woman and upsetting her basket of oranges. Such a boy, I felt, was experiencing the highest delight of sensual pleasure in defying all convention or the dictates of others.

Sometimes I bought – or had bought for me – various finds I uncovered at Mrs. Townsend's entrancing and dusty junk market. Once it was a heavy black ceramic head of Mickey Mouse with a round hole at the base suggesting it might at one time have formed part of a larger figure. I had not had it many weeks when I tumbled down the staircase at Sampford Place and it broke into fragments to my great dismay.

Another time I bought what suited me as a walking stick with its mother of pearl knob, and I felt very smart and quite an adult walking around the house with it. When the parish clergyman, Canon Sangster, came to tea one afternoon and as we sat in the playroom, the stick was handed to him to ascertain its original use. He examined it carefully, and concluded it had been made for thrusting gunpowder down the muzzle of a small sporting gun, and this seemed to add value to the object which was certainly an antique.

The object of most value which I bought from Mrs. Townsend – or at least, was to give me most pleasure over the following years – was an annual of the *Magazine of Art*, I think for the year 1888. It was full of haunting and inspiring pictures which were to leave a permanent imprint on my mind. There was no "impressionist rubbish" or anything reflecting the conventionally acceptable styles of modern art of the 20th century. The pictures (all produced in black and white) had the clarity of the Pre-Raphaelites, or the Romanticism beloved in the 19th century. I recollect two pictures by Arnold Böcklin, one entitled, *Meersidyll*, of a beautiful naked woman in the sea embracing a sea monster in the form of a serpent but with a human head, and another of a white long-necked dragon just emerging from a cave amongst mountainous scenery, with several small human figures in the foreground, seemingly threatened by this destructive form.

Another illustration was of an elderly gentleman walking along a forest path at dusk, in a mysterious environment of threat amongst the darkening trees. Another picture was of a handsome knight in armour replacing his sword into its scabbard. A beautiful long-haired maiden stood close by, enraptured by her hero, whilst the bloodied corpse of the rival lay at the feet of the victor. These were conversation pieces which stirred the imagination long after they had been seen.

When I was taken to the town, I was fascinated by the tall factory chimneys and especially by the different formations at their head. Whilst their height and dominance over the town represented power, the smoke pouring into the sky represented activity. One such chimney, I noticed, had the appearance of a circumcised penis – or at least a penis for at that time I knew nothing about circumcision, although most of the Corfe family were circumcised for medical reasons.

Once when I was out with my nanny and we were crossing the railway bridge, a convoy of lorries loaded with noisy men drove by. "Who are those people?" I asked. – "Italian prisoners of war," came the answer. I turned around to the passing vehicles and determined to show my disapproval, I growled and made an ugly face, putting my thumb to my nose in a rude and frightening gesture, and when this was met by laughter, I felt dismayed and humiliated.

In the playroom we kept a pet bird in a cage, but after several weeks it died, it was said from poor quality birdfeed. Shortly thereafter I found a large brown slug on the doorstep to the side door by the playroom, and I wanted to keep this as a pet in replacing the bird. My mother was horrified by the suggestion, and salt was dropped over the slug in destroying it.

I then found a toad nearby the stables and kept this as a pet in a wooden box to which I added grass and moss for comfort. For food, I went around the house swatting flies and feeding the toad from my hand. My toad seemed very contented, but after some weeks it disappeared. When I enquired about this, my mother said that Aunt Joan had secretly removed the toad and let it free, as she thought it cruel it should be kept in a box. I thought it mean that no one had bothered to tell me this.

One Friday evening, my father arrived with a small smooth-haired black dachshund puppy sitting on the front passenger seat. This was a present for my mother, and it was given the name of Woomzie. Such a gift could never have been given at the start of the First World War, for

Dachsunds, a favourite pet of the Kaiser, were then being stoned in the streets. It helps to demonstrate the differing and more fatalistic attitude towards a state of world war which had since developed. From then onwards my mother was never without a dog until shortly before my parents moved into sheltered accommodation many decades later. She subscribed to several dog magazines and read numerous books about dogs.

My Aunt Inez was more professionally committed to dogs than my mother, and later she became a judge at Crufts, an annual event my mother was to attend as a helper for many years and where she made a number of friends. At the time of which I am writing Inez had joined the WRENS, and was already an officer, but she was always accompanied by her pair of black Scotties – a breed on which she became an expert. I therefore became used to dogs at Sampford Place.

Every fortnight a uniformed official arrived from the Admiralty office in Bath to deliver huge diagrams in cardboard rolls to deliver to my grandfather whilst collecting others. These diagrams which were plans of battleships or engine parts, were spread about the study floor, and my grandfather spent his days formulating or checking mathematical calculations. When I mentioned this to my mother many years later, she quickly responded that, "that was a lot of nonsense! They only called round to keep him quiet." Such an opinion was clearly wrong for the War Department would never have wasted its time in "keeping people quiet" in such circumstances. It was far too busy for that. My grandfather was obviously engaged in essential work for the War effort.

Within a short distance of Sampford Place was a mansion which had lately been let to an elderly German Jewish refugee with limited knowledge of the English language. He was a man of broad intellectual interests and my grandfather was a frequent visitor to the house at a time when such people were regarded by the majority with a mixture of suspicion and dislike. They would converse in German, but every time my grandfather returned from the house, he would complain about that "bloody German" and his "wrong ideas," but such arguments did not seem to upset their underlying friendship. It is possible, of course, that my grandfather wanted to convey the impression that their relationship was worse than it was in reality, bearing in mind that the company of this man and his family was shunned by most English people – including my other relatives. Years later, my mother remarked that her father was "very good" to those people in view of the War situation and that they belonged to "the enemy."

Within a year of staying at Sampford Place I fell under the delusion that Winston Churchill was a close family relative. There were two reasons for this: firstly, he was a source of constant conversation and effusive appreciation, and the phrases, "What will Churchill think about this?" or "What will he do about that?" frequently re-occurred. I was unable to appreciate as a 5-year old that distant news events were being discussed. Secondly, my grandmother kept a large framed portrait of Churchill in a decorative silver frame on the grand piano amongst photographs of relatives. Why, then, should the picture of a stranger be displayed in this way?

For extended periods, Aunt Betty and her two daughters, Maris and Susan, stayed with us at Sampford Place. Her husband, Vaughan, was in the Army, and as I observed in an earlier chapter, he was eventually promoted to the rank of major and won the MC. Maris was three years my senior, and Susan was the same age as my brother. I often played with Maris on my plot of land at the back of the house, and I remember we dug a hole and made mud pies. One day as we were playing outside, she asked if I could show her my "Wee-wee." I agreed on the provision she showed me hers.

She took my hand, and we ran into the house and up the stairs to the Bamboo room which was then my bedroom. We hid behind an arras in a corner of the room, and I pulled down my trousers and we got on our haunches. She was fascinated and touched my private parts. When I asked her to lower her knickers, she did so, and I wanted to pursue my curiosity, but it was not to be. At that moment she panicked, for she thought she heard someone approaching, and she quickly pulled up her underwear, and that was the end of the episode. We hurriedly left the room and never made any such contact again, or afterwards referred to what we had done.

When decades later I spoke to Betty about the "wonderful days" at Melksham, she expressed a contrary view. They were not "wonderful days," she said. It was the middle of a war, and a lot of disparate people were crowded together and had to get along as best they could. My grandfather tended to be dictatorial, and they were only there to get away from the bombing in London. She recollected an incident (as recorded in an earlier chapter) when my grandfather reprimanded his relatives at the end of the day for not standing for the National Anthem when it was played on the radio before shutdown. He apparently expected them to behave as his brother officers would have done in the Ward room. For some months four young Army officers were billeted in the house, and they ate with us at meal times, and years later my mother said that all four had been killed in action not long after leaving Sampford Place.

Other aunts who visited occasionally were Gwladys and her daughter Anita. Gwladys was my grandmother's youngest sibling, apart from Cyril. Cyril, according to my mother, was a weak character with "no personality." I had seen a picture of him dressed in full Scottish regalia. When hardly out of his teens, he ran off to Canada and was never seen or heard of again. Some decades later, an elder sister, Blanche, contacted the authorities in Canada to trace his whereabouts. He was tracked down, but the message came back that he did not want any contact with the family, and so no one knew what became of him.

Gwladys, meanwhile, was to become the poor relative of the family. As a little girl attending Queen Victoria's Golden Jubilee in 1887, when the Prince of Wales passed by in his carriage, she cried out loud, "Look, there goes daddy!" for the future Edward VII was so similar in appearance to her father, Admiral Bedbrook. In 1910 she was engaged to a man called Blackett-Jones, who worked for BP. Her eldest brother, Albert, who took on responsibility as head of the family after the death of his father, took a dim view of his sister marrying into such a low status occupation as the "oil industry." What future could there be in that? When Gwladys married he sent her a cheque for 50 guineas with a covering letter saying he would have sent her double that amount if she had married the man of his choice. Gwladys returned the wedding present to her brother in justified anger at the insult. She may have felt there was some kind of reckoning several years later, when her big-spending brother went through the bankruptcy courts, whilst his cocaine addicted wife deserted him for another man.

Gwladys future was not to be fortunate. Her husband was on a business trip to Mexico during the Revolution of 1912, and as he was boarding a ship for the return voyage, he was shot dead by Mexican rebels. At that time she was pregnant with her only child, Anita. She was devastated, and deeply embittered by the tragedy, and it was said she never cut her hair after her husband's death. As her only income was a widow's pension from BP, she lived with her daughter in mean circumstances, and eventually Anita was to qualify as a domestic science teacher. The tragedy of Anita's life was that her mother kept her jealously on a tight leash for her own support, rarely allowing her away from home, and frustrating any inclinations she may have had for developing friendships with the opposite sex.

Although she was good-looking and strove to be well-educated and informed about the world, she was ridiculed by other relatives in the family, perhaps mainly because she tended to be a pedant in compensating for her poverty. My mother was particularly contemptuous of this younger cousin by 6 years because of her educational aspirations – but then my mother despised anyone who placed the value of education above personality or the ability to amuse. Nonetheless, Anita was chosen to be the godmother of my brother, Gavin, and she proved conscientious and generous in this role, often inviting him to the home of the two aunts, or visiting London and taking him to suitable theatrical performances.

She took my brother and me to an early performance of Agatha Christie's *The Mousetrap*, when it was still in its first year.

At Sampford Place I found Aunt Gwladys forbidding and strict, and I remember her glaring at me across the tureens and dishes, with the words that, "Little boys shouldn't talk at the dinner table." Many decades later, she held a 90th birthday celebration at the YWCA in Gt. Russell street, and James de la Mare (the son of Lettie Bedbrook and a nephew of the author) acted as a master of ceremonies, and after the formal lunch, when delivering a eulogy, he read a letter from BP announcing she was the longest standing widow to receive a pension from the company.

As we moved around in groups after lunch, I got into conversation with my great aunt, mentioning the War-time days in Melksham, when she burst out with the words, "The trouble with Grace was that she was lazy," which I thought a bit rich considering that she and her daughter had often been guests at Sampford Place. My grandmother, on the contrary, was always active and certainly a superb cook, as I found in the post-War years, and she was always full of life and enjoyed hosting parties. Perhaps the personalities of the two sisters were incompatible, for my grandmother always referred to her as an "embittered woman" who had never recovered from the death of her husband. Gwladys lived to be 99, inhabiting houses with her daughter (which according to my brother) never seemed to be heated, even in the coldest Winter weather, first in Marlborough, and later, after Anita's retirement from teaching, their move to Margate.

It might be apt at this stage of the memoir to mention my brother's godfather, Denys, for he was another member of the Bedbrook family. Denys was described by my mother as the nicest and most good-natured man she had ever known. He was always pleasant, understanding and modest, and this was surprising (so said my mother) in view of his appalling childhood. He was the only child of Bert, my grandmother's eldest sibling, and his cocaine-addicted wife. On the break-up of Bert's marriage, Denys was contemptuously rejected by his mother and they never met again. "How could any mother reject such a beautiful child?" exclaimed my mother, for he was only four or five at the time. Consequently, Denys was often lodged with my grandmother for extended periods – my grandfather being usually overseas – for Bert was unable (or unwilling) to take on the responsibility or costs of maintaining his son.

As Denys was several years younger than my mother, she tended to take him under her wing. Bert visited the family from time to time, and my mother remembered him as a huge high-spirited man with a remarkable bearskin overcoat and always with a cigar. Although he was unprepared to look after his only child, he was joyful with the children and so a popular uncle. Although he was a bankrupt, he exuded an air of affluence and could easily have been mistaken for a millionaire. When Denys was not staying in my grandparents' home he was passed around to other relatives for safe keeping and upbringing. "How could he have developed into such a well-adjusted adult after such a chaotic childhood?" marvelled my mother.

During the War years Denys joined the Navy but he remained in the ranks, and was sent on the dangerous missions to Mermansk. After the War he married his cousin, Pam, daughter of Blanche, a younger sister of my grandmother, and they eventually had two children, a boy and girl. My parents attended their wedding in Bath, and at the reception held afterwards at the bride's parent's home, Hampton Hall, my father was amused to see a large framed photograph prominently displayed on the grand piano of Pam's first Wedding. Before the War she had loved a man who was already sick, and although her parents had urged her to refrain from marriage, she could not be persuaded. Within 18 months her husband had died of consumption.

Denys went into business on his own account, and later went into partnership with Vaughan Venables (my godmother Betty's husband) who had an importing timber business which was on the slide and saved in the nick of time through the acumen of its new partner. When Denys died towards the end of the 20th century and I attended his funeral, I learned he had been an active member of the Russia Club, and another member of this ex-Servicemen's association who delivered the eulogy, described in vivid terms the privations and dangers of those delivering supplies to our Russian allies in Murmansk, and of how so many British sailors had been torpedoed in the North Atlantic and Arctic waters.

During the halcyon days in Melksham my grandmother had already impressed me with her philosophy of history. We were living in disturbing times when everything was in a state of upset. Things were much better when Queen Victoria was alive. We were secure, and people lived by more civilised values. "We laughed so much in those days, and we had such fun," said my grandmother. People were not like that any more. The modern generation were serious about things which were none of their business, and not serious about those things which really mattered, such as good manners and how to please and charm one's relatives and friends.

And in Queen Victoria's time it would have been impossible for a "mere decorator" who worked on building sites to become the ruler of a great European power. During the War years that was the most scornful remark I ever heard about Hitler from any of my relatives. At least the Kaiser had been born within a high status family, and then become "wicked" when overcome by madness, but Hitler was evil from the day of his birth because of his humble origins. It was the inability to accept one's given status in life which led to the conflict and unhappiness of the age – or so my grandmother insisted.

CHAPTER 4
Return to the Bombing

"There is only one virtue, pugnacity; only one vice, pacifism.
That is the essential condition of war."

Bernard Shaw, *Heartbreak House*, Preface

Am sent to a Convent school – Early infatuations – Ashmount and my father's relatives – Early disdain for the church environment – Biblical versus classical values – A cane is purchased – Its use as a punishment weapon – The bombing at night

After approximately two years in Melksham it became apparent that my father had overestimated the prospects of the bombing of London, and so we thought it sufficiently safe to return to the capital just at the time when the bombing began. I was sorry to return to Muswell Hill, not because of the War – for that was hardly noticeable to a child for what it really was – but because I lost my freedom and felt like a caged bird.

In London I could wander around the house and garden, but no further afield as I had done before. My chosen existence at home was to wind up the gramophone in the lounge, and whilst playing 3 ½ minute 10" 78 rpm records, run round in circles to the music. That was about the limit for my physical recreation. The records which I played were the popular tunes of the period, such as *Night and Day*, and various foxtrots and waltzes. It was the latter which I liked best, and I have ever since retained a weakness for over-appreciating the waltz melody.

My possessive instinct was always strong and possibly this was strengthened by the attitude of my father. I requested and obtained things from my father, but there was confusion as to whether they were actually given or only lent, and when he subsequently asked for the return of such things as garden tools, flowers pots, and all kinds of odds and ends, I was disappointed and hurt by what I felt was the unreliability or alienability of possession. I was therefore moved to ask, "But can I have this as my very very own?" – "What do you mean by your 'very very own'?" he retorted. – "I mean forever." – "No one has anything forever. When we die we lose everything, and can take nothing to heaven." This idea hurt me. "But can I keep it as long as I live?" I asked. – "It probably won't last as long as you live," replied my father, and through this use of clever dialectic, he was always able to retrieve anything he had given.

As I was now 6 years old, it was time for me to start at a proper school, and I soon found I was in no position to carry out my earlier resolution in *never* going to school. At first it was difficult to find a suitable institution, but finally it was decided to send me to the local Convent school in Pages Lane which accepted boys in the primary class, and so I could not be there for more than a year. Most the teachers were nuns but my class teacher was a young lay person for whom I soon formed an attachment. I also formed a liking for a pretty long-haired brunette beside whom I insisted on sitting at the twinned desks, but this was not allowed, as our exact places were allocated to us. "You're not allowed here," the little girl said to me once. – "But I like you," I responded. – "You must do what teacher says," said the girl in such a confident grown up voice that I loved her all the more.

When the girl looked embarrassed and blushed, I asked, "Do you ever cry?" – "Once in a blue moon," she replied in a sophisticated tone, and this was the first time I heard that idiom. "I want to see you cry," I said. – "I can't cry for you," she replied, and I was deeply hurt by this rejection, and by this time the teacher would call me back to my proper desk.

It was in this school that I learned the 12 times tables, for we had to recite them often as a class until we knew them by heart. I was mildly naughty, and on one occasion was told to stand outside the classroom door, but when I did so, I peeped in through the small glass panel and made funny faces which brought laughter from the class. One of the younger nuns took a liking to me, and I remember her burying me beneath her long black dress and pressing me against her legs, all the while laughing at these antics which were witnessed by other children in the playground. We Protestants were not allowed to attend Mass, held several times a week, but I remember peeping into the chapel and noting the beauty of the altar with all its lights, and how different it was from that of St. James's church.

One day we were herded into the school hall to watch a road safety film arranged by the Ministry of Transport. It was a film with cartoon characters and it ended with Donald Duck foolishly running out into the road and being run over by a bus. One of my classmates, a boy, began crying loudly, and had to be consoled by the nuns, and I felt him very stupid to be so upset by the death of a mere duck. After all, I had witnessed many chickens fare a worse fate than that.

Whilst my passion cooled for the little brunette, for my love was clearly not to be reciprocated, my obsession with the class teacher became all the more ardent. My infatuation was to be manifested in a rather unusual way, for once at home I wanted to dress up in women's clothing to approximate the appearance of my teacher as closely as I could. I persuaded my mother to lend me several dresses for which she had no further use, and then I applied lipstick and powder, and a pair of high heeled shoes, and began hobbling around the house as best I could pretending to be a lady. I do not think my father approved of this cross-dressing, for although he said nothing, and certainly did not forbid it, he glanced at me with some misgiving.

One day as I was descending the top staircase, carrying a piece of flex in one hand, I tripped in my high heeled shoes, and came tumbling head over heels down the stairs as my parents looked on in horror from the landing below. I was unhurt although shaken, but my father forbad me to wander around the house in high heels again, and some weeks later I tired of dressing up in women's clothing. It was about this time that my mother took me to a dancing school for small children, but apparently, I was so ill-disciplined that I had to be withdrawn. However, I have no recollection of being taken to these lessons.

Visits to my grandparents at Ashmount, their house at the other side of Muswell Hill in Colney Hatch lane were frequent. Ashmount was built to an architect's design laid down by my grandfather. Although in appearance, with its ground floor Elizabethan style windows, the house looked older than the original Corfe residence, it was of course, a more recently built property. My mother thought it the most uncomfortable and badly designed house she had ever entered. It was everlastingly cold, and a passage at the right side of the house, which ran through the building from back to front, endured a permanent Arctic gale. Viewed from the roadway or the long garden leading to the front, the house conveyed an impression of Gothic gloom.

Once inside, it was dark and the most hideously furnished home I ever encountered. Everywhere were Zulu spears, javelins, shields and masks suspended from the walls – enough to fit out a company of Zulu warriors. These had been brought back from South Africa at the start of the century. There were cartridge shells used as ashtrays and hollowed out elephants' feet used as waste paper baskets. Hand grenades stood about on dark-stained oak furniture as ornaments, and I imagined if their pins were withdrawn then the house would be blown to bits, although I now suppose they must have been de-fused before their availability as valued pieces of furnishing. In the living room, high up on a shelf encircling most the room at picture rail height, were more conventional china ornaments and statuettes. These came from the Smith side of the family. There were also several coloured Morland prints.

In a huge fireplace with a grey stone surround, burned a miserable fire, which my grandmother urged my grandfather to attend to moments before it went out, usually with the words, "Ernest, poke the fire," and this was done with a sword-bayonet after two or three lumps of coal were generously added to the dying embers. There were comfortable armchairs and a sofa and several dark wooden chairs of a rustic design. Coloured glass swirls comprised the upper part of the high windows, but thick stone pilasters partitioned the windows which consequently let in little light.

The dining room at the back was a much lighter room, with a magnificent dining table, a bookcase with the standard classics, and delightful silver ornaments and figurines on the broad window sill by the door leading into a fair-sized garden for a London suburb. On the walls hung 18th century ancestral prints from the Smith side of the family. As the youngest son of a large family my grandfather had clearly not inherited many heirlooms.

The stone floored kitchen and scullery, where the maid had to spend her time was a miserable place. The only natural light came from a glass panel set into the ceiling, whilst the aforesaid Arctic passageway ran through the entire complex to keep it chilly and uncomfortable. In the gloomy hallways on the upper floors I was frightened by the strange African masks which looked down threateningly at me from the high walls. I rarely left the ground floor although I did stay for a day or two with my grandparents once or twice. The upper floors had a maze of rooms, and everywhere there was wall-to-wall carpeting which was unusual at the time.

On several occasions I went to the very top of the house beneath the roof, with my brother and cousins, Michael and Howard Brown, where we played with Uncle Harold's magnificent clockwork Hornby train set. Harold had already been conscripted by this time and was serving in the Tank Regiment. I remember on one occasion we were supervised in this play area by Roger, who was about fifteen years my senior and the son of Sidney, my grandmother's brother. Roger was a family member whom we seldom saw, and he was to lead a strange life. His mother died when he was very young and the housekeeper became her substitute.

He had an elder sister who died tragically alone at the age of 12 of scarlet fever whilst away at boarding school – a probable indication (as clarified in a later chapter) of the appalling schools to which the father was prepared to deposit his children. Sidney was said to be immensely rich, in contrast to his brother Quentin who became little better than a pauper in his old age, although both shared the same profession as surveyors. Although Sidney was rarely seen by his great nephews, he was generous in that he gave us the Letts Schoolboys Diary for Christmas throughout our boyhood years. When he died in the mid-1960s, he left his housekeeper penniless, although they had lived together for the greater part of their lives, and this was regarded by the family as a great omission despite the fact their relationship was never formalised. Roger inherited his father's wealth and was serving in a foreign police force at the time. He then disappeared and was never seen or heard of again.

My paternal grandparents were hospitable, but on a more modest scale than my mother's family, but I do remember that interesting guests from faraway places were sometimes invited for tea. When Uncle Maurice was on leave, he visited in his officers RAF uniform, always jolly and full of life, although of course, his wife and adopted daughter were forbidden to visit the house. Eventually he was posted to North Africa from where he sent back reassuring letters. I remember my grandfather cheerfully telling us that, "Maurice is having a wonderful life. He does nothing all day except loll under the shade of banana trees as a man of leisure." This, of course, could not have reflected the real truth. It is a fact that fighting airmen, as with those in the other armed services, spend 95% of their time doing little which is worth recording, or just waiting around, but the other 5% is spent being shot to pieces.

If my grandmother seemed to express little concern for her younger son, her solicitude for her favourite and youngest child, Harold, was total. In her anxiety, she often said she prayed for his safety all day long: praying from the time she awoke until her final prayer by the bedside at night. "He never leaves my thoughts," she exclaimed. She put all her trust in God, and she knew that God was on Britain's side, just as he had been in the First World War. In her eyes, the proof of this was the miraculous appearance of the Angel of Mons.

This aroused my curiosity and I asked about this "Angel," and she entered into a vivid description of how a light lit up over the battlefield, and a guardian Angel held a protecting shield over British troops as they gained a glorious victory. I was impressed by the story at the time, but of course, years later I was to discover that this was a nonsensical myth, for the historical truth was that the advance was temporary and that hundreds of thousands on both sides were to be slaughtered before the end of the war.

My grandfather had interesting tales to tell about his own experiences in the Boer War. There are two which come to mind. On one occasion when retiring for the night, he drew back the bedclothes to discover a black mamba laid across the length of the bed with its head under the pillow. It must have got into the room through a grill in the window. He called his black servant to remove and kill the offending serpent. On another occasion he was left alone to guard an ammunition dump, when after some hours, a party of Boers galloped up on their horses from all four directions out of nowhere, pointing their rifles at the young captain. My grandfather had no option but to surrender the ammunition, and never seems to have been reprimanded for the incident.

Perhaps a more senior officer was to find himself in trouble for only allocating a single soldier to guard the valuable hoard.

The Browns were naturally frequent visitors at my grandparents, and my grandmother especially was very good to all her grandchildren. Occasionally, she baked her own bread which was delicious, and she often served dripping sandwiches which we children loved, and in summer she would take us out for picnics in the nearby woods. Uncle Dick was not conscripted into the armed services because of his deafness, a hereditary defect of the Brown family, and so he remained in some kind of independent business. At one stage during the War the business found itself in trouble with the authorities, and there were prosecutions. There was much concerned talk and anxiety over the matter at my grandparents' place, until eventually Dick's partner was sent to prison whilst my uncle was exonerated. Before the War he had even been in business with Maurice in an ice cream venture.

As may be imagined, religion was a frequent topic of discussion at my grandparents' house. An issue which I raised on one occasion, as a 7-year old, was that of immortality. My grandfather began to explain the theological theory, but the discussion was soon transmuted into the physical. The body died but the spirit remained. What's the spirit? I asked. It's the essential part of the personality – a kind of indefinable substance. How does it get to Heaven? It flies there with wings, interposed my grandmother. What kind of wings? See-through wings – very much like those of a fly. How does the spirit leave the body? It's believed to leave through the mouth. And what does the spirit look like? It's diaphanous – you can see through it, just like those pictures in your fairy tale story books. I then moved over the discussion to that of fairies by expressing scepticism as to their real existence. Fairies do *really* exist at the bottom of gardens although they're rarely seen, insisted my grandmother with sincerity.

There's no doubt about their real existence, they've been scientifically proven, added my grandfather, and he cited the evidence of the actual photographs of fairies taken at night, the validity of which were confirmed by the great detective writer, Sir Arthur Conan O'Doyle. And the author of the Sherlock Holmes stories, with all his investigative skills, could hardly be wrong on such a matter. By the end of the discussion I was prepared to half believe in the existence of fairies whilst remaining sceptical of the afterlife. I then formed in my own mind the most futile resolution I had ever made in my life: I resolved to maintain my physical existence for all eternity as the best guarantee of immortality.

Attendance at Morning Service at St. James's Church was a regular Sunday event, and although my mother had no religious feelings, she was duly observant and ensured that my brother and I behaved with propriety.

The maid, of course, meanwhile prepared the Sunday joint. The Rev. Prebendary E.A. Dunn, had a charismatic rather than a rational approach to religion, which I saw through from an early age, and it soon filled me with disgust.

When he stood in the pulpit and waived his arm towards the East window, exclaiming, "How can we doubt the existence of God with this glorious sunshine lighting up the world?" the gesture just struck me as banal and childish. This was firstly, because the weather was a matter of chance, and changed from day to day; and secondly, the demonstration in itself did not prove the existence of the deity. By his own argument, were we therefore justified in having a lesser belief in God when the weather was depressing? His words were clearly intended to deceive and that is why they gave rise to disgust.

Another example of his twisted reasoning may be cited in his attempt to demonstrate the over-powering faith in Jesus even amongst the most depraved sectors of society. He told the story of a ruffianly merchant seaman and declared atheist who had been in and out of prison, and could never complete a sentence without an oath of some kind. On being confronted by this person, he produced a crucifix, commanding him to spit at the image. The fact that this man was unable to submit to the clergyman's request supposedly proved his underlying goodness and faith in God. In reality, of course, it demonstrated nothing of the sort. The man's response had nothing to do with religious belief or non-belief, but merely reflected a sense of propriety in maintaining a sense of common decency. It might also be added that the indecent request was anyway insulting in itself.

It was not long before I formed an intense dislike for the Bible, although of course, I could not express such thoughts to any other person. Throughout my childhood I maintained all the proprieties, and outwardly I remained conventional and conservative, in this way ensuring an agreeable appearance to all those with whom I came into contact. In an adult this could be interpreted as hypocrisy, but in a child it was excusable as simple obedience. To me, the Bible was all about killing your enemies without mercy, and causing bloodshed and mayhem at every opportunity, because that is what I heard from the Lessons read from the lectern every Sunday.

"When the Lord thy God shall bring thee into the land whither thou goest to possess it, and hath cast out many nations before thee, the Hittites, the Girgashites, and the Amorites, and the Canaanites, and the Perizzites, and the Hivites, and the Jebusites, seven nations greater and mightier than thou; And then the Lord thy God shall deliver them before thee; thou shalt smite them, *and* utterly destroy them; thou shalt make no covenant with them, nor shew mercy unto them" (*Deuterenomy*, 7 1-2).

These were the passages which were read from the lectern, and these were the passages which were taken as the text for sermons delivered from the pulpit.

Kings and rulers seemed a scurvy lot, since they were always falling into rages and killing messengers who brought bad tidings. I felt sorry for the messengers, since firstly, they were only telling the truth, and secondly, merely carrying out their paid duties. Was truth-telling therefore a criminal act? This was the moral conveyed by the Bible when its messengers came to such a sticky end. The Bible seemed full of vengeance dressed up as Righteousness which in reality was Wickedness, and full of God's chosen who were put in high places before indulging themselves in monstrous infamy. The stories were crude, drawn in black and white, with no place for shades of grey which would have reflected the real truth of the human condition. But who was I to contradict what was supposedly Holy or the Gospel truth? The Christian church had its own way of pulling its weight in the War effort, and it did not present a pretty picture!

It may be that I was taking these church services, with their questionable preaching, too seriously, for when the well-dressed congregation gathered up their brollies and gloves and prayer books to leave the building, there was an exchange of friendly smiles, and an air of civilised normality seemed to return, despite all the horrors and calls to vengeance to which we had been exposed for the last hour and a quarter. By the time we reached the church door, there was even laughter and joking – my grandmother amongst them – as we shook the Vicar's and Curate's hands. - "I like your hat, Mrs. Smith!" – "Little May's looking very rosy today!" and suchlike meaningless pleasantries were offered or exchanged. By the time the crowd had reached beyond the church doors, there were noisy conversational groups, and only we immaculately dressed children stood silent, with solemn or expressionless faces, before all moved off to their nearby homes.

I was left feeling stiff and uncomfortable, with a tinge of embarrassment, as were perhaps most of the children who had attended the service. Did anyone believe a word of what had been said inside the building? Had anyone really listened or made any rational sense of the Readings? What was the mood of those who had endured an hour of genuflections, hymn singing, repetitive prayers, and listening to violence-inspired readings, and a sermon which made nonsense if analysed for its reasoning content? Was the cheerfulness of the departing congregation due to spiritual enhancement, or due to sheer relief at having once again completed one's weekly bounden duty? I believe that those who were leaving the building already had the taste of roast lamb and mint sauce on their tongue rather than the words of the Almighty.

My impressions then and now was that this church-going was a self-satisfying social bonding process in confirming established values, but it comprised a large measure of hypocrisy or religious pretence. It was an obligatory undertaking in the natural course of events, in the same way that apes pick fleas from one another's fur, or bees formed into a swarm. And such religiosity (if such it could be called) was all the more necessary in a war which entailed a struggle for survival. Whilst the sermons of this particular clergyman may be left aside without further comment, the Lessons may be taken as a kind of metaphor in justifying our side in the intractable conflict of war.

If, therefore, I felt sceptical, dismissive, or cynical even, about the weekly Christian worship, it was not because I was intrinsically irreligious, but on the contrary serious and thoughtful about religious matters. I may have conveyed the impression of accepting most things at their face value, but in my own mind this was never so. I was open to idealistic thinking, and this included religion of a certain kind, but not if it was based on irrationality or mysticism, for then, in my own mind, it amounted to the obscenity of deceit.

When decades later I was asked if I had a religious sense, I replied in the affirmative. I was never an agnostic and certainly not an atheist. However, then as now, I have always rejected religion based on Revelation as not only inescapably false, but worse than that, as an offence to the one and only Deity. I have therefore discovered my true spiritual identity in Deism, which whilst positing the existence of God, repudiates all the meaningless mumbo-jumbo of conventional theology. I do not wish to quarrel with the beliefs of mainstream faiths, and am tolerant towards others, and perfectly happy – even proud to call myself an Anglican.

If this sounds contradictory the explanation is to be found in the fact that I regard and value the churches not as religious bodies *per se*, but rather from the sociological aspect of social bonding mechanisms. Furthermore, I believe that if 90% of people in the civilised developed world, claiming to be religious, examined with honesty their true beliefs – or were cross-examined with thoroughness – they would be revealed as Deists with opinions closely resembling my own.

My mother's dislike of the Rev. E.A. Dunn, stemmed only partly from the fact of his tunnelled-vision religiosity, and primarily from the fact of his unsociability in failing to visit parishioners. She compared him unfavourably with the Rev. Canon Sangster who was always happy to visit and converse with my grandparents who were non-churchgoers and even atheists. But Canon Sangster was a humane man with wider interests and a greater understanding of the world.

After church my grandparents often came to our home for an hour or so for a glass of Sherry, before returning to lunch. The conversation usually turned on the outrageous or comical hats which had been worn, and by whom, or those who had been present or not present at the Service, and other personal oddities which had been noted about other Muswell Hill residents. There was much laughter, usually generated by my grandfather, who loved to describe the foibles or eccentricities of others – sometimes his patients. I remember him telling us about a lady having a tooth extraction whilst under a general anaesthetic, when to his alarm her wig slipped off and the difficulty he and his nurse encountered in trying to replace it in its correct position in such a way that the patient would never suspect the mishap after coming to. Such stories threw us into fits of laughter.

To ensure I developed into a good Christian, there was a period of a year or so, when after bedtime my father read to me nightly from the Bible. The stories were usually violent, horrific, or purely stupid, such as the selection process for recruiting an army when crowds of volunteers were asked to drink from a lakeside. Those who lay flat on the ground were conscripted, whilst those who knelt by the water were rejected for military service on the grounds of their carelessness in that an enemy from behind might push them into the water. It struck me there were as many ways of being stupid as there were of being clever, and that such a narrow-minded test of intelligence for military ability was quite misplaced, and could only have been devised by someone with an idiotic imagination.

Of course I never questioned anything which was read to me, but just sat passively in bed as was expected of me. Almost everything read to me was from the *Old Testament*, for apart from the fact it contained the best stories, it was naturally the favoured War-time part of the Bible. Jesus did not seem to have much time for "girding one's loins," or brandishing weapons of war, or crying out for vengeance. My father may even have sensed my distaste for these Bible stories, although he never expressed the suspicion explicitly, for on one occasion he dropped the remark that the *New Testament* was "quite different." Nonetheless, he continued to read from the first section of the book.

Some years later, as a teenager, I came to read the *Eclogues* and *Georgics* or *The Art of Husbandry* of Virgil, and was immediately entranced by these wonderful poems. They revealed a world and a people with whom I could closely identify. Having spent so much time on a farm, and been impressed by the work and drama which this entailed, the poems of Virgil took on a vividness and reality quite missing from anything to be found in the Bible. Here was life as it really existed, with its energy and purposeful existence, with all its idyllic beauty in a sunshine clime. How much more civilised, well-balanced, orderly, and human were the Romans with their workaday lives by comparison with those tempestuous peoples of the Near East!

A little later I was introduced to the Greek poet Hesiod, and was equally impressed by his *Works and Days*, and the peaceful but meaningful picture he drew of Greek village life in the 8th century before our era. It was these writers which I found spiritually uplifting, not the bombastic barbarities of the Bible. It was the peaceful ideals of the classical world which would save civilisation, not the crazy ravings of those who glorified war.

Whilst the Bible interpreted work as a curse inflicted on man through original sin, the classical world, through Hesiod and Virgil, taught that *productive* work was a joy and a natural part of the human condition. What kind of morality or sense was to be found in the curse of work? Its subconscious influence could only contribute towards the tending of idleness, cutting corners, using others to do one's work, the tendency towards usury, or the exploitation of an underclass. It certainly implied an anti-business ethic – or the type of labour entailing the use of hand or muscle.

One could, perhaps, escape the curse of work through money-changing or usury, but that was hardly the path towards creating the ethical society. The Biblical curse of work had certainly been a bane in influencing the development of socialist thought. Firstly, it turned its back entirely on the psychological motivations of productivity and labour; and secondly, it gave rise to endless nonsensical utopias where leisure as *purposefulness* displaced the need to work as meaningful. How much more intelligent and *real* was the classical world in projecting work as part of the natural order in fulfilling both the physical and *spiritual* needs of ordinary humankind.

*

It was at this time that my father carefully sought out and purchased a cane from the local ironmongers. I remember him returning to the house with it in a cheerful mood. He proudly showed it to my brother and me, and in a half-joking manner it was humorously named Mr. Make-'em. – "Mr. Make-'em is the gentleman who'll ensure you'll be good in the future," announced my father cheerfully. We children said nothing. The cane was suspended horizontally over the hideous pink-tinted art deco mirror over the fireplace in the lounge, so that it would always be in view as a reminder of punishment to come. It was shown to visitors who were expected to acknowledge that this was a well-disciplined household.

Over the following years canings were delivered at random intervals and in totally unexpected circumstances. They were always bare-bottomed, and my brother and I suffered excruciating pain, and we invariably yelled the house down. Being deeply religious, my father naturally believed in original sin. His religiosity was such that at one time he seriously considered entering the church. When I asked my mother as to why he had not done so, she replied that money was the deciding factor on realising "that dentistry was more rewarding than being a bishop." From then onwards the greater part of his religiosity (in so far as it was genuine) was probably sublimated through his commitment to Freemasonry, with all its ritual and the obligatory learning of supposedly sacred texts. His core belief was that all children were born intrinsically wicked, and that wickedness could only be removed through thrashing in exactly the same way as dust is beaten from a carpet.

As a teenager I came to the conclusion – or calculated – I had been caned on eight separate occasions, although I cannot now recollect the circumstances of each punishment episode. They were all for trivial offences, and sometimes at the slightest irritation, he would announce, "You've been adding up for a caning. You haven't had one for a long time, and so now it's got to be done."

On one occasion we were thrashed for making a noise early one Sunday morning when my parents were trying to sleep. On another occasion I was thrashed for idly throwing a piece of pointed metal at a two foot square piece of plasterboard standing in the garden verandah. I had taken the piece of plasterboard to be a piece of waste material or a left-over cut from a larger sheet. My father, however, must have attached a higher value to the object, for when he saw it was full of holes, he fell into a rage and I was caned accordingly.

Sometimes we pleaded with our mother to intercede on our behalf, but she never defended us. On occasions when we were thrashed because we had been "adding up for it," I believe the cause of the annoyance stemmed from factors which had nothing to do with indiscipline. We were most probably punished because of the downturn of the stock market on that particular day, as nothing irritated him so much as the daily listings in the *Financial Times*. He read the paper every morning at the breakfast table, and would remark to my mother that this or that stock had taken a tumble when it was not supposed to – as if she had the slightest understanding of such matters.

Each caning was turned into a formal occasion and this added to its horror, for spontaneous punishment, instigated by instinctive anger is always felt more lightly or taken as more justifiable by a child. The ritual of formal punishment, on the other hand, has all the delay and torturous anticipation of pain. The entire process becomes sadistic, often tinged by a degree of hypocrisy.

The canings were usually preceded by a homily – invariably unconvincing – to justify the punishment, and how long we had gone without punishment, and how our parents had had to suffer our constant wrongdoing as a result of this. We were then taken into our father's dressing room and the door was closed. As the elder of the two, I was the first to be beaten. I had to unbutton my braces and then lower my trousers, at which point I hesitated. I was then asked to lower my pants. My father then raised my shirt before pressing down my neck. I heard the swish of the cane, and then with all his strength, he would deliver six of the best.

After one such episode at the following meal time he told us that our yelling was "unmanly" and would never be tolerated at school. If we cried out, we would be beaten all the more, and if we continued to make a noise, the beating would continue until we were silent. I resolved at that point – yet again – never to attend another school. To emphasise the need to refrain from yelling, he pointed out that "being good at school" was not necessarily a safeguard against a caning. He then elaborated on the group canings he had experienced at Highgate. These occurred when the perpetrator of a crime could not be identified.

On one occasion a boy had broken up a master's valuable fountain pen and placed it in his desk, and when the crime was discovered no one would own up. In those circumstances the entire class had to be formed up in a queue. Each boy was then called up to the master's desk, when he had to remove his trousers and underwear before receiving the thrashing which the class deserved. I had a vision of 16-year old schoolboys quietly lining up to take their punishment without complaint or noise, before calmly returning to their desks, but years later I was forced to ask myself as to whether such a thing could *actually* have happened to that age group.

Often, at other times, when no punishment was contemplated, my father would talk in a joking or humorous fashion about naked bottoms and how they were designed for thrashing, or the cat and nine tails as used in the Army, or comical tales about unpopular schoolmasters who became the victims of practical jokes, and how they were avenged on their tricksters through the use of the cane. These were stories at which we were supposed to laugh. On a more serious note, in turning to the great villains of history, such as the Kaiser or Hitler, it was suggested they would never have dared embroil themselves in such wickedness as a war with England if they had been soundly flogged in childhood. A child which has not been flogged is a spoilt child which will be nasty for the rest of its life. In this way we were somehow successfully instilled with a sense of guilt at the idea of having never been flogged if such had been the case.

*

By this time the bombing of London had begun in earnest. On innumerable occasions I remember being awoken from a deep sleep in the middle of the night and carried down the five flights of stairs in a blanket to the musty cellar. At that time my brother and I slept on the top floor in the green room with the unpleasant liquorice smell usually reserved for the nanny. At that time Highgate Nanny – for none were known by their proper names but only by the places from which they came – lived out, and came in daily early in the morning.

As my father was an Air Raid Warden, he was often out on roster duty. There were red buckets of sand about the house, together with fire extinguishers, although I don't know how these could possibly have been put to use if there had been a direct hit. They were merely there as a gesture to give moral support. A common occurrence to which we were exposed were collapsing ceilings. This could occur at any time in any room in the house. No protective cautions with regard to this were taken apart from a sheet of plywood placed over my youngest brother's cot when he was born in 1944. Collapsing ceilings were events which occurred for several years after the War, and although they caused little damage, it was always a shock and there was the mess of broken plaster to clear up afterwards.

It was exciting to hear the air raid warnings, and sometimes we glimpsed the huge beams of the searchlights exploring the skies from the bedroom window before we were carried downstairs. We children were never afraid of the dangers overhead. As we sat in deckchairs, in the damp cellar near the coal and coke bunkers, wrapped in blankets, we tried to sleep if we were not kept awake by the boom from the anti-aircraft batteries, or the sound of planes overhead. Sometimes we heard the sound of a particular kind of aircraft with its higher pitched engine, and we were assured, "that's not a bomber – just a German spy plane overhead. It'll be driven out of London and then shot down."

Sometimes Miss Gallant, the dental nurse, stayed overnight in the house. In her office an iron shelter like a table had been erected in a corner of the room, with a bed beneath the table top, and wire mesh screens on the sides. During air raids, however, she always joined us in the cellar as it was regarded safer there. When the all-clear sounded, we children climbed to the top of the house and put ourselves to bed when we slept immediately. Many years later my mother exclaimed, "I don't know how many hundreds of times your father and I carried you children down all those horrible stairs to the cellar."

CHAPTER 5
To the West country Again

"Childhood has no forebodings."

George Eliot, *The Mill on The Floss*, Bk. 1, Ch. 9.

My brother and I are sent to the parish school – Life in wartime Melksham – Visits to relatives in Bath – Summer holidays in the War years

With the increased intensity of the bombing it was thought better we return to Melksham for our better safety, and of course, I was thrilled with the move, but it was to be for a duration of not more than six to nine months. How happy I was to escape to the Keens' farm, and stand once more as a sudden surprise before the farm workers, as they sat on their milking stools bent over the undersides of the cattle to the sound of liquid squirting into pails. They seemed no less pleased to see me than I to see them. "Where have you come from?" they asked. It was a day or two before my ear was fully attuned to understanding everything they said, but I was already fully at home with the tasks and routine of the farm.

However, I was not able to spend as much time as I would have liked on the farm, since it was thought that getting me into a school was a higher priority. I remember being taken along to a private school outside Melksham where play formed a significant part of the educational process, and when I was shown the various classrooms, I felt that this would suit my requirements, as there was a relaxed and friendly environment and the teachers seemed quite humane. However, it was not to be, probably because of transport difficulties in reaching the location. It was finally decided to send my brother and me to the local parish school of St. Michael's, and the admission arrangements were left to my father.

As this was a free school, open to all and sundry, my father was clearly under the impression that the majority of its working class pupils must be vicious little savages. I was taken along by my father to the headmaster's private home in another part of town, where the details of my acceptance and admittance – and that of my brother – could be discussed in a more discreet environment. As we sat in the headmaster's study, my father pointedly emphasised his social and professional status, and that my brother and I would be "very special pupils." Even at that age I was overcome with a feeling of awkwardness at this assumption of "superiority," but the headmaster patiently listened to everything said without batting an eyelid, and then reassured my father that both of us would be safe and well cared for.

There then came a point in the conversation when my father said he wanted a "confidential word" and my brother and I had to leave the room and stand outside the door. When we were re-admitted, the headmaster explained to us in a benevolent tone, that if either of us was bullied, or threatened, or subjected to any rude or impolite behaviour from any of the other pupils we were *immediately* to report such incidents to the teacher so that the offenders could be punished. Did we understand that? Gavin and I said that we did. This, of course, was the most foolish piece of advice which could have been given, and it subsequently led to several acts of gross injustice. Before leaving, the headmaster opened a drawer in his desk and handed me a Roman coin from the reign of Constantine the Great (still in my possession) which he had found whilst digging in his garden. I do not know why he gave me this gift. Perhaps he thought it was a privilege I should join his school as a pupil.

My time at the school was entirely positive. I never incurred any punishment, and some years later, I told myself I had learned more at that school as a pre-teenager than at any other school I attended. I advanced well in arithmetic and reading, and first learned about the ancient Homeric stories of Odysseus and the Cyclops, and Achilles, the Wooden Horse, and the Fall of Troy, all of which captured my imagination. I mixed well with the other pupils as an equal, and there was full acceptance on both sides without any consciousness of class, regional, or other differences.

There may have been rough and tumble in the playground, but I never discerned bullying towards anyone during my time at the school. There was an occasion when two senior boys quarrelled and decided to settle their differences through fisticuffs, but first they moved the smaller children away from the area for their own safety, before engaging in a fight according to the Queensbury Rules, until blood had been drawn from their noses. One boy said his father had sent home the ear of a Japanese soldier he had cut off on the battlefield. We eagerly asked him to bring the ear to school so we could look at it closely, but he never did.

The most serious breaches of discipline seemed to arise from absenteeism, and sometimes the police would bring shame-faced truants into our classroom, whilst at other times they would bring along householders who were asked to identify boys who had broken windows or stolen apples from gardens.

My brother, on the other hand, who was still quite young and chubby at this time, was not the perfect pupil. On going into the dining hall for lunch, on one occasion, I was surprised to see him standing in the corner as a punishment for some misdemeanour, when he turned round and smiled at me mischievously, but I never learned the cause of his offence. As soon as I arrived at the school, the class teacher took me aside and asked me to report any disrespectful behaviour I might encounter, and this was repeated on several occasions. Consequently, I felt myself under some kind of obligation, and straining all my imaginative ingenuity, I succeeded in reporting – or inventing with some kind of rational explanation – a number of petty incidences. I did not seem to compromise myself with my peers, for I was never confronted for "sneaking," and I can only conclude that either they never knew about my reporting behind their backs, or else the teacher failed to take any subsequent action in the first place.

Eventually, the class teacher must have become tired of my fault-finding, for she told me not to "sneak" any more, and I obeyed her request and never offended in that way again. There was an episode, however, of which I shall always feel ashamed. One day as the school was lined-up and the pupils had to run to their separate classrooms in a line at intervals, a much older boy spat in my direction as he passed by. On reporting this, the matter was taken very seriously, and when his class were summoned for an identity parade, I pointed him out, and he was taken away and caned. I thought then and I still think today that the boy had no intention of spitting *at* me. His spittle fell at my feet, but his act of spitting had no malicious or personal intent, for spitting in the street was customary at that time, and it was pure coincidence that he did so whilst passing by me.

There was another incident of the time of which I was made to feel guilty although I was not properly blameworthy. There was a family called Garrett with whom my grandparents and mother maintained a lifelong friendship. The wife, Madeleine, who became the godmother of my youngest brother, Oliver, was the sister of a famous London eye surgeon by the name of King (who also happened to be Sir Winston Churchill's eye specialist) and her handsome husband was a clerk at a local bank. When my mother first met him through some bank transaction, and made a complimentary remark to my grandmother, the latter replied jokingly, "You can't have him, he's already married." He had earlier been struck down by infantile paralysis although he was still able to cycle to work, although later his condition worsened and he was to spend the last 50 years of his life in a wheelchair.

At this time they had one son, Simon, a toddler who often played with me on my plot of land behind Sampford Place. One day we were walking atop the wall bordering the kitchen garden towards one another when I lost my balance, and to protect myself, I pushed against him, and he fell off into a compost heap. Naturally he began crying loudly at this mishap. To disengage myself from the incident, I ran off in the opposite direction and involved myself in some other activity.

Later in the day I was confronted by my mother for "pushing Simon off the wall," which I denied, although I was curious as to how such information had been communicated, for I was under the impression that Simon had not yet learned to talk. Clearly he was sufficiently coherent to convey these facts to his mother. Eventually I explained I had lost my balance and had no intention of pushing him off the wall, but my mother continued to blame me as I was responsible for looking after a smaller child.

Simon grew to be a large rotund and charming man with a strong artistic instinct, and on the few occasions we met, he was always friendly and never referred to my having once pushed him off a wall. However, he was hypersensitive, and haunted by all kinds of fears, one being that whilst living in a flat near Regents Park, he developed a phobia about being attacked by escaping animals from the Zoo. He worked as a senior executive for an advertising company and remained a lifelong bachelor. After his death from AIDS around the age of 50, I told his younger sister, Julia, who was a god-daughter of my father and the Manager of the Theatre Royal in Bath, about the accident I had in knocking her brother off the wall. She immediately burst out with the words, "We always wondered why he was so full of complexes, and now we know the reason why." I think that perhaps Julie was jumping to false conclusions, or desperate for an explanation for her brother's life-long psychological problems, for his illness and death was a great upset to the family. I imparted this piece of information at my father's funeral in May 1990.

*

One day Gavin and I found ourselves in my grandfather's study, standing before his desk as he was busy. After a moment's silence, my brother came out with the words. "Mummy says you don't like us." I thought that a tactless thing to say, but after a pause, my grandfather responded thoughtfully, "I don't think that's really true." He then put his hand into his pocket and drew out a couple of coins, giving us a penny each, saying, "Now go and buy yourselves an ice cream." We were delighted to receive the money, but following my brother's example, we dropped the pennies into our vests and let them fall out below our trouser legs. "Now don't play the ass," reprimanded our grandfather, and it was the first time I had heard that expression.

*

It was about this time that electricity was installed in the house, and all the gas light fittings were removed and piled up in the playroom. Whilst passing by outside with the nanny and looking into the window, I enquired, "What's in there?" – "Just odds and ends," she replied and that was the first time I had heard that expression.

In the thick winter snow I built a snowman in the front garden, which I regarded as my own valuable possession, and then one day a group of Italian prisoners of War began throwing snowballs at it from the street, which I found very upsetting. Italian prisoners of War were now allowed to wander the streets freely, where they were noisy and always seemed to be enjoying themselves. They worked in factories in the town, disliked the career of soldiering, were ready to surrender at the slightest pretext, and were glad to be out of the War. Some were probably now enjoying a better standard of life than they had ever done in the southern parts of their own country. By the time my grandmother was ready to shoo the Italians away, they had already gone, but they were always gathering in groups outside our house during the lunch hour or in the evenings to talk or laugh. Occasionally I saw German prisoners of War, who were treated quite differently from the Italians. They were marched through the town, always under armed guard, with their hands clasped either behind their necks or over their heads.

On several occasions we visited my grandmother's younger sister, Blanche (1881-1969), who lived in Hampton Hall, Bathampton. Although my mother was contemptuous of the house in which they lived as an "ugly Victorian" residence of no architectural merit, it was by far the most impressive home of any of my relatives, and a visit to Hampton Hall was enjoyed as one of my greatest pleasures. The hospitable environment was always lively, and it was filled with noisy and cheerful guests, mostly great aunts and great uncles.

We drove there by car, with petrol coupons saved for the purpose, and I always experienced excitement on arriving at the City of Bath – probably the most beautiful residential city on our planet – and I still experience the same feeling of exultation to this day when passing by the huge 18th century grey and yellow stone elegant apartment blocks with their tall windows and fine entrances. Everything about the city expressed the rationality and harmony of civilisation at its best. At the centre of the town were the Roman Baths – *Aquae Sulis*, the Latin name of the city – and it was through the classical ideals of Rome that the great 18th century architects constructed the city. From the mountainsides around were (and are) magnificent vistas of the great Crescents overlooking the hills in the opposite direction.

Hampon Hall was situated high up on a hill at the southern side of the town. It was entered via a wrought iron gate between a high grey wall which together with evergreens hid entirely what was to be revealed within. At the other side of the gate were several flights of steep steps leading down to the front of the house which was entered through a Conservatory. Inside the front door was a dark hallway guarded by two suits of Dutch armour at the entrance, whilst on every inch of wall space were suspended pistols, crossed swords, medieval spears, 16th century halberds, and all manner of other weaponry. There was also a Japanese clock with an arrow descending in a straight line as it marked off the sections of the day.

To the right was the spacious drawing room, with a grand piano and a variety of mid-Victorian furniture, and around the sides of the room were stuffed birds, foxes, and other exotic mammals, all under glass cases in protecting them from dust. On the walls hung Italian paintings from every period, mixed with prints, tapestries, and other hanging pictures. On little tables, shelves, and indescribable pieces of Oriental furniture stood hundreds of antique ornaments and knick-knacks of every conceivable description. The high French windows, which did not let in much light, because of the steep gradient of the front garden, led into another conservatory from which wafted the damp heat and pleasant odour of tropical plants. The room was enlivened by the charming conversation and laughter of numerous relatives, the great aunts and uncles all of whom were already adults whilst Queen Victoria was still alive, and therefore had enjoyed the privilege of living in a world of political security and cultured leisure which the 20th century could never hope to regain.

Amongst these interesting Bedbrook relatives was Edith Leverton (1868-1955), who was widowed young and penurious, and then led an independent and hard-working life in earning her own living. She worked with the Duchess of Norfolk in Arundel and Littlehampton, in helping to found what became known as the Child Welfare Centres. She was extrovert, confident, and domineering, and wrote and produced plays – mostly for children to perform, and she rode a tricycle around her home town of Littlehampton. Then there was Violet, or Lettie de la Mare (1874-1962), who was married to James, the brother of the noted poet and novelist, Walter de la Mare; Loots, the great womaniser, and my grandmother's favourite brother, who was a year younger than her; Albert, the eldest brother (1871-1940), a man of great charm and aura of prosperity, an engineer by profession, but frequently in financial difficulties; and May Clark (1872-1940), described by my mother as "a dear little soul with a rotten husband," amongst other friends, relatives, and companions.

Returning to the hall and straight ahead was the dining room, with its dark stained Jacobean furniture, high-backed chairs around a long rectangular table, a dresser at one end of the room and a large bookcase at the other, lined with leather bound multi-volume standard works, such as Campbell's *Lives of the Lord Chancellors*, Archibald Alison's, *History of Europe*, Smiles, *Lives of the Engineers*, Lodge's, *Portraits*, and Walpole's, *Anecdotes of Painting in England*, which I still recollect after this long distance in time. The windows looked out into the back garden with its almost perpendicular descent into the valley below, and across to the mountainous height of the hills at the other side with their handsome Georgian crescents and other apartment blocks.

Leaving the dining room, and turning to the right was a passageway leading to a music room with a radiogram and hundreds of classical 78 rpm records, and several other rooms; and another long passage way leading to one of the finest lavatories I have ever seen. The boxed-in toilet had a mahogany seat with a beautifully decorated bowl beneath, and behind this unit was a church gothic stained glass window depicting the grand Coronation of King Edward VII, and it was fascinating to identify the great Royal personalities and other dignitaries present in the Abbey.

On the upper floors were numberless rooms, all richly furnished, and in the hallways were stuffed stag's and boar's heads, and more weapons – all of them different, and in one room was a display of 365 antique watches displayed in glass cases. Beside this room was Uncle Percy's work room, where he repaired watches and attended to other mechanical implements. In the cellar – or what was supposedly below ground level – were games rooms: in one there were two snooker tables, and in another dart boards, and in a third, a table tennis table.

As the back garden was too steep to walk down, there were cast iron stairs suspended about a foot above ground level which led down to an orchard. Before reaching the orchard, there was terracing for the cultivation of fruit and vegetables. At the bottom of the garden, a quarter of a mile away, was the canal, and beyond that the main London to Bristol railway.

Uncle Percy, according to Aunt Blanche, was descended from a Lord Mayor of London in the reign of Elizabeth I - the family name being Willcox. His father had been a prominent civil engineer and had designed and built the house himself, having been born in 1839 and died in 1929. He was also a talented water-colourist and a member of the Bristol Sketching Club, and over a lifetime had filled a number of huge albums with his paintings, each containing an average of 200 pictures. He travelled widely in Spain, Italy, Switzerland, Germany, France, and the Netherlands, taking his easel and paints wherever he went in recording his impressions of the scenery.

By a stroke of luck I came into possession of one of these albums marked Volume V, containing paintings from the 1890s until 1918 – each picture having been named and dated, although some were purely imaginary and marked "Nowhere." When in extreme old age in the mid-1960s, Blanche and Percy moved into smaller accommodation, which happened to be a nursing home in The Circus (on the other side of town), they sold or disposed of most their possessions, and Aunt Blanche threw the albums into a dustbin as rubbish. It was Aunt Inez who rescued Volume V and gave it to me knowing my appreciation of art. Years later I extracted many of the paintings from the album, framed them, and today they decorate the hallways and living rooms of my house. I gave several of the paintings to my daughters, and auctioned what remained in the album at Sothebys in the 1980s for which I received £9,000.

In their younger days Blanche and Percy lived in Balham (London) and sometimes my mother stayed with the couple and their two daughters, Pam and Doreen. Both these girls were musical and the latter was to marry a man who became an organist at Bath Abbey for many years – Mr. E.W. Maynard. Percy was a civil servant who rode a bike to work at Westminster, and was another of those men whom my mother described as "never having done a stroke of work in his life." This must have been quite untrue for he was highly educated and would not have been engaged in menial employment.

When I last saw him when bedridden in the nursing home in The Circus, I mentioned I had just returned from Germany. He sat thoughtfully for a moment and then said he didn't like Germany and the custom of duelling which he thought was "perverse." He had studied in Heidelberg in the 1890s, and a German friend had been foolishly killed in a dual whilst he was there, and there was a great hubbub when the police were involved and he was questioned. However, as an Englishman he did not fall under serious suspicion and was released. Although duelling was well-established amongst student fraternities, it was still illegal. Whilst the authorities turned a half blind eye to the custom, if there was a death or serious injury, the law soon fell into action. Uncle Percy must have been an Administrative civil servant to maintain the life-style which he did, but as has always been customary in the service, a low public profile is usually kept.

Towards the end of the 20th century, when both my mother and her cousin Pam were widows, in their late 80s, and therefore felt free to speak about taboo topics concerning their earlier lives, the latter told the former that she and her sister, as young girls, were obliged to bounce up and down on their father's lap, which they found an unpleasant experience. My mother explained that her cousin implied her father derived sexual pleasure from this activity, and it surprised me that such a good-natured and unassuming man as Uncle Percy should indulge himself in such a way.

*

During the War years my father was still able to take us on annual holidays to the seaside. When Gavin was a toddler we went to Burnham-on-Sea, and one day on the beach when he destroyed my sandcastle, I hit him with a spade. My father immediately took me back to the hotel where I was beaten with a slipper. When I told my brother about the episode (which he could not recollect) many decades later, he merely remarked that my father had no understanding of children. In 1936 I had been taken to Mundsley, and in 1937 I visited Portishead, where I was photographed with my cousin, Maris, and we had a longer holiday in Swanage. In 1938 we were in Minehead, and probably in Bognor in 1940 or '41.

On one occasion, early in the War, we went to Weston-super-Mare, and it was a pleasant surprise when I met my maternal grandmother in the foyer of the hotel, for she had come to join us for the rest of the holiday. It was during this time that I first saw clowns for the first time, when they performed on the promenade. As their faces and hands were covered in thick grease paint, and their red bulbous noses were not of human proportions, and as their white hats seemed to be sealed onto their heads as part of their anatomy, I took them to be a different species from ordinary human beings. I could never imagine they were men in fancy dress, and their behaviour, in my young eyes, indicated that they did not behave like normal human beings.

In 1943 I celebrated my eighth birthday in Weddon Cross, Somerset – the only non-seaside holiday we ever took. Here we stayed on a farm where I learned to ride a pony, and every morning I took a gentle trot around the country lanes accompanied by a young riding teacher. I remember we visited the pub daily and played skittles, and I became accustomed to my first alcoholic tipple, cider. The only other alcoholic drink I enjoyed between then and my teenage years was Stone's Ginger wine at Christmas, which despite its relatively high alcohol content was at that time nonetheless regarded as a children's drink – or it became so as it tended to be disdained by adults. For my eighth birthday I was given a mock Army uniform, comprising a cardboard front which could be strapped on, a peaked cap and a sword, all of which boosted my ego in giving me a tremendous sense of status when I marched before the other guests staying at the farm.

Whilst we were on this holiday my father noted that one of the other male guests was going off to the telephone in the village at odd hours, supposedly to phone his stockbroker. As this seemed suspicious behaviour, my father contacted the police and the man was discreetly investigated, but he was discovered in reality to be doing what he said. There was much spy mania in the country at the time, and considerable publicity urging the public to report anything which seemed unusual to the authorities.

CHAPTER 6
School and Life in London

"The chief wonder of education is that it does not ruin
everybody concerned in it, teachers and taught."

Henry Adams, *Education of*, p. 55.

At Norfolk House – School friends – Home life – Jane, the maid – The birth of Oliver
and the employment of Miss Wall – How I came to judge my father – The neighbours
– The influence of Arthur Mee – Nightmares and sleepwalking

On returning to London after this second extended evacuation to
the West country, I discovered that the Baird public house in
Fortis Green Road had been flattened by a direct hit, and much
nearer home, St. James's church had been struck by an incendiary, and
the roof burned off – an incident which I did not find unduly
disappointing. Church services were consequently transferred to the
Athenaeum opposite the Odeon cinema where they were held for several
years until temporary repairs had been made.

My education, of course, had somehow to be resumed, and I was
sent to Norfolk House preparatory school. As a 7-year old I was placed in
the most junior class in the school, situated at the top of the building, and
I remember arriving as a new pupil together with the son of Ronald
Shiner (1903-1966), a famous comedian and actor of the time. He was
brought along by his nanny, and he was proudly armed with a cap pistol
which he began shooting at other children. The elderly woman teacher in
charge immediately said she was having no guns in her class, and that the
offending weapon must be removed from its owner and taken home.
Ronald Shiner's son would have none of this, and he put up a struggle
with the nanny, and began screaming at the idea of losing his valued toy.
At the time I was aghast that such a child could be so undisciplined on his
first day at school, and although I experienced a tinge of embarrassment,
I also admired his courage. He was clearly a more rebellious child than
me. We soon struck up a friendship and when he formed a gang in the
playground, I became his second in command.

The teacher was strict and sometimes disagreeable, but she often
called upon our sympathy because of the bad state of her health. She
suffered from indigestion and stomach pains – or so she told us – and she
hoped that none of us would have to suffer later in life as she did. She
said the secret of a healthy stomach was to chew your food properly, and
if you did that every day of our life, you should avoid stomach pains.
Several times a day, she drew a spoon and a bottle containing a delicious
looking deep-pink medicine out of her desk, with great ceremony,

announcing she was now going to follow her doctor's orders. The class sat silent, looking on entranced, licking their lips, as she took her medicine before putting it away again. – "Please, Miss, can we have some?" was a request which was sometimes made. "No," she replied, "you must be ill first, and then only the doctor allows it."

Much time was spent in teaching us respect for flowers and plants, and flower-gathering outside the school was encouraged. When a boy was caught plucking petals, he was reprimanded and asked how he would like it if his ears were pulled off, to which he gave the mistress a look of astonishment. "Oh yes, flowers feel pain just like you do," she assured. We were also taught to believe in fairies. "Fairies live at the bottom of my garden," we were told, "and my friends and I watch them every night, but if they see you they disappear, and so you have to hide behind the net curtains with the light off in the room. They come out of the trees and holes in the ground at midnight, and dance round in a circle. They're beautifully graceful and transparent, and all of us who see the fairies love them. But if you want to see the fairies, you have to believe in them, as otherwise they're invisible."

The school was divided into the four Houses of Wellington, Nelson, Clive and Wolfe, and run by an elderly and irascible couple, Mr. and Mrs. Standfast. Mr. Standfast was a thin man with bi-focals, and he administered the school canings, and assembly for the register and morning prayers were held in a large ground floor room where he also had his class. Whilst he had a certain gravitas, his wife seemed permanently angry and threatening with one pupil or another. The school accepted girls in the induction class, and there was a long-haired brunette for whom I formed an affection, but she did not respond to my advances, and soon I was placed in a higher class. I enjoyed reading and the stories we studied were taken from Arthurian and other Celtic legends, and the books were well illustrated in appealing to our imagination. We often sat at twinned desks, in cold or stuffy classrooms heated by a gas fire, and sometimes two teachers assisted together.

There was one particular boy in the class to which I graduated who was constantly mischievous and noisy, and Mrs. Standfast exclaimed angrily to the class teacher, "He's a proper little Nazi." This epithet was attached to anyone noisier or more unruly than the norm. For much of the day, from mid-morning onwards, there was always the smell of over-boiled cabbage, for the kitchen was on the same floor as my new classroom, and for lunch we moved over to another classroom where the desks were re-arranged in a rectangle around the room.

I enjoyed the lunches on most days, especially the baked potatoes with cheese, and several of the teachers sat with us, and after the meal, before going into the playground, we were asked to spell out words which were then written out on the blackboard, whilst other pupils were asked to ascertain the correctness of the spelling. There was a middle-aged French mistress, with minimal command of English, who sat with us for lunch, and she was held in a kind of awe or special respect by the other teachers because she was a refugee who had narrowly escaped capture by the German invaders.

We had group singing lessons in the so-called music room, which formed part of the assembly room partitioned off, given by a man in a threadbare jacket and trousers with a mouth full of rotten teeth. But he was good-natured and seemed to enjoy his work, and led us in the singing of traditional songs most of which were American. There was also an elderly, short, bald-headed thick-set, and gold framed bespectacled Latin master, who looked the part, and attended St. James's church, called Mr. Goode. He was a good-natured bachelor, always pulling our legs in a silly sort of way, and my father regarded him with mild ridicule, pondering as to whether he had ever had "a girl friend in his younger days," and the very notion struck him as amusing.

One day one of the senior boys, a 12-year old called Brocklehurst, whose father owned a furniture store in the Broadway, Muswell Hill, took the headmaster's cane out of his desk, cut it up with a penknife, and replaced the pieces. I witnessed him do this during a lunch break. We never discovered what Mr. Standfast thought of this episode since he never brought it to the attention of the school. He quietly replaced the cane with another.

There was another classroom on the ground floor with a small library and back copies of the *National Geographic*, and here we were allowed to sit, if we so chose, for the greater part of the lunch hour if the weather was inclement. I greatly enjoyed perusing through the geographical magazines and books on history, and there was one of particular fascination illustrating methods of torture and execution, such as the Boot, the rack, cutting a man in two by means of a rope drawn through the legs, breaking on the wheel, and flaying alive. Most of these methods were used in either England or Scotland. It was not until two or three years later that I learned about the many more diverse modes of torture employed by the Spanish Inquisition. Such things are always of interest to small boys, and do not unduly shock them as they do adults.

Although I never incurred punishment at this school, for by this time I was obedient to authority, I did incur an accident which inflicted extreme physical pain. I was running around the playground when my foot caught in a crevice on the concrete surface, and I was thrown forward and then pulled back like an elastic band, wrenching my ankle out of place. As I was still in intense pain and the foot badly swollen by the time I hobbled back to the classroom, it became evident to the teachers that something was gravely wrong. Initially they had told me to "pull myself together", but when they saw I could no longer walk, Mrs. Standfast arranged for one of the kitchen staff to wheel me home in a push chair.

On arriving home my father was appalled and concerned, but I was shocked by the way he ignored the kindness and task of the woman who brought me back. Hardly looking at her, she was peremptorily dismissed without a tip or a proper "thank you," and I was brought inside. I, of course, had no anxiety about my own condition once the pain had abated. The following day I was taken to a hospital in Staines, being one of the places where my father worked, and I was X-rayed and found to have a fractured left foot. I was then attended to by a Mr. Stevens, who put my leg into plaster where it remained for several weeks, and when the plaster of Paris was eventually removed my skin was green and blue. The surgeon must have taken a liking to me for he kindly gave my father the sum of £5 as a contribution towards my savings to be used in adulthood. About three years later Mr. Stevens died of a heart attack.

Whilst at the school I formed an attachment for a much older and bigger boy called, Entwhistle, with short curly black hair. We fooled around in the playground, and he let me pull his hair, and in the evenings I sometimes telephoned him. He later left the school and went up to Highgate when we lost touch.

There was a classmate with whom I became friendly, called Suffolk, who lived in Woodland Gardens, just off Muswell Hill Road, not too distant from where I lived, and one Saturday afternoon in winter I was invited round for tea. He lived alone in the house with his mother who had recently been widowed through the War. There was an atmosphere of gloom in the house, and both mother and son conveyed an impression of loneliness and depression. I had clearly been invited to brighten up a Saturday afternoon, and whilst the boy seemed reserved and awkward, his mother made a great effort to see we were entertained and kept up a running conversation. When we sat down to tea, and there was an unbroken silence between the three of us, and Suffolk's mother feigned a smile in attempting to raise our spirits, I became so depressed that I broke into tears, and minutes later I requested to be taken home.

Almost as soon as we arrived back from Melksham, my father indulged in a daily ritual at breakfast which continued without break for several years. He would ask, "What do you want to do when you grow up?" to which I invariably answered, "I want to be a farmer." – "You don't want to be a farmer," he would say, "you want to be a doctor." There was only a break of about three months when I decided otherwise. This was following my broken leg, when my father witnessed my leg being bound in plaster, before telling me in detail what occurred in other surgical wards and the operating theatre. He succeeded in arousing my imagination with descriptions of skills entailed in amputating limbs and binding up the stumps, and the high status of men engaged in such a profession.

As soon as I could walk again, he took me to the medical museum in Guy's Hospital, where I was regaled with a much broader range of medical conditions: 16th century paintings of beautiful women with huge tumours on their backsides; foetuses in glass jars in various stages of development; bodies deformed by rickets, elephantiasis, and other diseases; and life-size wax figures pock-marked with the third stage of syphilis. In answer to my questioning, he explained that medical people, because of the privilege which special knowledge endowed, were often able to escape the horrific fate to which more ordinary people were so often exposed.

Despite such efforts to engage my interest in the medical profession, my enthusiasm was short-lived before again returning to my insisting on an agricultural career. My attraction to the medical profession was therefore no more than a passing phase. Cutting or drilling into living bodies required a particular kind of personality and ability, and although I have always respected – even been awed by the orthodox medical profession (albeit not entirely without reservations) I was never again to be drawn to it as an occupation. The medical career as a vocation was possibly not encouraged by the occasional horror stories my father read out at the breakfast table from the *British Medical* Journal.

This together with the *British Dental* Journal was the serious reading material which occupied much of his leisure time for many hours during the week. I remember one such story of an old man who fainted whilst on the toilet, collapsing onto a bottle which disappeared up his rectum. Surgeons were then involved in a difficult operation to extract the bottle without breaking the glass. From that day to this I have always conscientiously moved toilet brushes or plungers away from the toilet seat in the event of my encountering a similar accident. Later, in my teenage years, I often glanced through the *BMJ* out of morbid curiosity at the more unpleasant illustrations.

Whilst my mother assented to the idea of my working for "gentlemen farmers" (whatever that was supposed to mean), my paternal grandfather supported the idea of my farming in Africa. "After the War, there's going to be a great future for the White man in Africa," he exclaimed with confidence. "There's enough land for everyone in East and South Africa, and for the real pioneer, there're millions of square miles of jungle to be cleared and tamed in Central Africa for agricultural purposes."

During these years my mother often took me and Woomzie, the dachshund, for walks in Highgate Wood, with its tall grimy dark tree trunks and ugly black soil. There was nothing countrified by this area which was owned by the Corporation of London, and some years later, Sydie (Aunt Inez's husband) whom I came to know as Uncle Bill, expressed the same opinion of these and nearby woods. His father, apparently, had been the architect who designed and built the parade of shops with their flats above, situated opposite Woodland Rise and backing onto the Wood.

In the middle of the Wood, nearby where the Northern line underground surfaced, was a sports ground, and on one occasion when a barrage balloon was being launched, a WAAF caught her foot in the cabling and was drawn up screaming into the air. There was much rushing about by a dozen or so others involved in the launching, and fortunately, she was brought down safely unharmed. There were several Victorian drinking fountains in the Wood, surmounted by red granite obelisks, with lead cups on chains, from which I drank occasionally.

As we walked along the asphalt paths we often stopped to chat with acquaintances or friends with similar type dogs, and I remember we often encountered an elderly distinguished-looking Russian aristocrat, Count Obolensky, who was also a patient of my father. He was friendly and courteous and had a black smooth-haired dachshund just like ours. My parents knew several families of White Russians who had settled in Muswell Hill. My mother described the older generation of their womenfolk as being miserable, wrapped-up in shawls and unable to speak English.

A favourite hobby at school was collecting pieces of shrapnel in the street, and sometimes exchanging them for stamps or other valuables. My life at home, I felt, was one of confinement compared with the freedom I had enjoyed in Melksham. It was at this time that I first became attracted to the idea of writing books, but initially, this did not take the form of creativity. We had a small book about London with a picture of a Beefeater on its front cloth cover, and I opened this and began copying out the chapter about the Tower. I saw this as "writing a book," which of course it was not, but it occupied my time, and could have helped improve my spelling and grammar.

Shortly thereafter I began writing a series of one-page stories under the general title of *The Book of Dan*, and later, in a duplicate memorandum book, an imaginary historical novel entitled, *In 1780 A Good King John*, all about war with Germany, with plenty of pillage, robbery, and killing. The book was illustrated and reached nine short chapters before I gave it up, and began writing other more worthwhile pieces, amongst which was a detective story, the hero of which was very laid back, and seemed to spend much of his time eating and drinking. I then wrote a novel about the Elizabethan period, called, *A Hero John Hipper*, with plenty of piracy against the Spanish and a fair share of destruction and death. One day my mother drew out a map, which she laid on a table, and pointing out all the red-marked land masses and islands, she exclaimed, "All this belongs to us, and this is what Hitler wants to take away from us." As a small child, I took the Empire to be a very personal possession.

At this time we had a middle-aged maid called Jane who came from Ipswich, who was considered an excellent cook – especially in baking cakes, but she was regarded as "dirty" and not always efficient in other household duties. Her relations with the "Master" and "Mistress" of the house, as she referred to my parents, were not always cordial, and on several occasions she either gave in her notice or was sacked, but she always returned, either because she got on worse elsewhere, or because domestic service was not in such demand as before the War.

She had a friend next door called, May, who was also a maid, and sometimes Jane talked to her out of the kitchen window as the former stood in the neighbour's garden hanging out washing. She was reprimanded by my mother when caught in this "undignified behaviour," and told to fetch scuttles of coke or coal up from the cellar and not waste time. Jane and May went to the "flicks" together at least once a week, and this was their only entertainment. As with most domestics, she must have been desperately lonely, for as she sat in the kitchen alone in the evenings, as the family spent their time in the lounge listening to the wireless, she spoke to herself.

My father thought this very eccentric and highly amusing, and would quietly go down the flight of stairs and listen at the kitchen door, before returning to repeat what she said, and making us laugh. She not only delivered monologues but duologues, so that her list of complaints against the Master and Mistress was answered by a sympathetic listener who advised her as to what she should do. This was her self-entertainment, or the sublimation of her resentment, before retiring to the top of the house to her draughty bedroom with its marble washstand and jug of cold water for washing.

Towards the end of 1943 my mother became pregnant for the third time, and in June 1944 she gave birth to her last child and my youngest brother, Oliver. In preparation for this event, my parents employed a woman of about 60 to look after the new child. She was never known as a conventional nanny, for her duties were too diversified, and she was only ever referred to as Miss Wall – and we never discovered her first name. She had spent the greater part of her life looking after the children of a diplomatic family and so she had travelled worldwide, including Canada,

Australia, and Malaya. My mother said she had learned nothing about foreign countries except that which directly touched her work. For example: in Canada, "baby" could never be left outside in the pram in winter because of wild bears; whilst in Kuala Lumpur she could never get the nappies dried on the line because of the humidity.

As a daily she loyally stayed and worked for the family for over twenty years, having become totally attached to her duties in looking after my youngest brother whom she adored, until her tragic death when her nightdress caught ablaze whilst warming herself by the gas fire. This occurred in the mid-1960s. She survived some days and then died of her burns in the hospital with my mother at her bedside – the name of "Oliver" (who was now in Australia) being on her lips during her final delirium. During her first months of employment she worked together with Jane on general household duties, but with the arrival of the baby, she was his constant attendant, and was brought down to Melksham when we visited my maternal grandparents. She lived in Wood Green with a sister, and had other relatives in the area, and although she was friendly and good to children, she tended to be coy and reserved about her past.

Every week my father drove to Cotterells in Charlotte street in the West End to purchase and fetch his dental supplies, and sometimes for a treat, during holidays, he took me on these weekly outings. He also needed to visit his hairdresser in Selfridges, and for about 40 years there was one particular barber – and no other – whom he insisted on cutting his hair. He was always particular about his appearance and never cut his finger nails with scissors, using a file instead which he generally attended to at the table after meals.

One day whilst in the West End together, my father said, "Let's go to the theatre tonight – there's a good show with Will Hay." I was enthralled by the proposal and readily agreed, but at once I reflected: what am I to think of this man? These constant mood swings between elation and depression, or generosity and callousness, or gestures of friendship and horrific canings and punishments in unpredictable circumstances, presented no proper opportunity for a final value judgement on this person.

Then, without even having heard the word "Utilitarianism" or the names of its proponents, Bentham or James or John Stuart Mill, I asked myself the simple question: do I suffer more pleasure or pain at the hands of this man,? and I immediately came to the conclusion that pain weighed down the scales. From this conclusion I coldly deduced that I should and actually *did* dislike my father, and I never changed my opinion from that day to this. It was therefore not through an act of cruelty or injustice that I consciously came to dislike my father, but through an act of kindness and generosity of spirit.

In a world of good and evil, and of inextricable psychological complexity in human relationships, I was soon made to realise the nonsense of commonplace morality in casting blame or praise on the behaviour of human beings. All humans were imperfect, but in quite different ways, and hence their division into the categories of good and bad were no more than subjective and hence ultimately false. What did matter, however, was the pleasure or pain which human beings imposed on those around them, and I have gone through life using this criterion in the knowledge that resorting to "higher" or artificial codes of morality is not only presumptuous in view of the wide variation in assessing values, but totally impracticable for anyone aspiring to be a world citizen, rather than merely remaining a citizen of the narrow community in which he is nurtured.

As a world citizen I was to be successful in retaining the understanding and long-term friendships with peoples of many nationalities and races across the globe, but that would not have been possible unless I had succeeded in cutting the umbilical cord of my upbringing and the values that this entailed. None of my other relatives of my generation were to achieve this freedom or generosity of spirit, and so consequently, they remained the prisoners of their prejudices and the stuffy restrictions of their immediate environment. My guide in life in *human relationships* has therefore constantly been utilitarian, for only in this way is it possible to develop an appreciation and later a love for those from very different backgrounds.

Some years ago I noted that Oscar Wilde had said somewhere that parents who inflict cruelty on their children are never forgiven. I was shocked by this statement when I heard it, but almost immediately recognised its underlying truth. I am not suggesting I *hated* my father – although that may have been the case with my younger brother (certainly during a part of his life) – but merely that I regarded him with cold disdain on rational grounds. If I could never forgive, in later life, I was prepared to forget his tyranny and cruel punishments, and if I was secretly to loathe him to his dying day, I was nonetheless able to respect him for his professional and financial success and for his integrity in other matters.

When some years later, as a teenager, I told my mother how I came to judge and dislike my father, she was shocked, merely replying, "That's not normal." In my view, then and now, the judgement which I formed was entirely normal – if not inevitable. Something hypocritical may also be seen in my mother's reaction, bearing in mind her relationship with her own father from the age of sixteen. At least I was never to speak ill of my father to anyone throughout the course of my life, although on occasion I was to remark without comment on the canings I had received, but I never made disparaging remarks about my father remotely comparable to those my mother made about my grandfather. On the night I formulated my final judgement on my father, we attended a variety show in a packed theatre, standing at the back of the stalls, and I remember laughing so loudly at the antics of Will Hay, that several people turned round in their seats with a disapproving look.

One night whilst my younger brother and I were sleeping in the dining room for some reason, in the middle of the night, he experienced a strange vision when three black-garbed women walked to my bedside and seemed to cast a blessing or some kind of spell over my sleeping figure. He seemed much impressed by this inexplicable occurrence, and the following morning and subsequently, he interpreted this as the endowment of celestial good fortune by the fates or angelic beings.

The house to the right of ours was occupied by a family called the Camps, and although they had a maid (May, the friend of our Jane) and the father of the household must therefore have been in reasonably paid employment, they were not of sufficient standing to be invited socially to the house. However, they had two attractive daughters, and one day my younger brother was caught making tongue contact with the younger daughter through a hole in the garden fence in a laughing kind of way. My parents were horrified for the elder daughter was known to have consumption, and later she was sent away to a sanatorium for a long period of treatment. This occurred at a time when tuberculosis was still a deadly disease, and was safeguarded as a shameful secret – to a degree hardly less so than syphilis. Nonetheless, the presence of tuberculosis could never be concealed entirely, and gossip soon spread the word.

The guests who visited our house –apart from relatives – were usually middle-aged, for example, there were the Ashtons who lived to the left side of our house. I invariably asked my mother what occupations these people had, and she generally answered, "Oh, they do nothing at all," and from this I gained the impression that leisure was the normal state of existence, whilst those who worked were in the minority – which certainly had a grain of truth *at that time* until the outbreak of War.

During these years my hair was cut at Barnes, a barbers in Fortis Green Road. The proprietor was an elderly man with gold-framed spectacles and a waxed moustache dyed ginger, and he dressed in a long old-fashioned frock coat like those worn by the clerks in Coutts bank until about twenty years ago. His middle-aged assistant had a "gammy" leg, as my mother described it, and he limped badly. Both the barbers were conversational and conservative in their views – although they never attempted to make conversation with children. My mother gave them their instructions and they carried on with the job. I was often made to feel uncomfortable by the conversation of the barbers with their apparently disgruntled patrons. The talk was all about how the world was going to the dogs, and particularly about the shocking behaviour of young people and the jitterbugging craze. Modern youth had never been as bad as they were today, and the barbers added fuel to the fire by relaying stories from the papers about looting from bomb sites, etc.

Frequently I was taken by my mother to the West End, sometimes to shop and then to meet friends or relatives at the smart tea room in Selfridges with its heavy silver plated cutlery, and waitresses in their starched uniforms; and if there was time, I was taken to the one-hour cinema show in Charing Cross Road, to see cartoons, documentaries and the weekly newsreel – and most entertaining of all, the Three Stooges, which always gave rise to great laughter. On other days I was taken to a museum, but this usually proved a "drag" to my mother. My interest in the exhibits exceeded what was expected of an ordinary schoolboy, for I tended to ask "unanswerable" questions. Fascinated, I would lag behind, intent on understanding things which were above my age. Years later I was told by my mother that I was "the most boring child she had ever known." A visit to a museum was for entertainment in passing the time, not for education. School and school alone fulfilled the latter function – and that was her view of life.

Uncle Quentin and Aunt Sybel visited occasionally from their home in Mundsley, Norfolk. They had a huge red American car – far more impressive than that owned by my other relatives – despite their straightened circumstances. I remember when they departed from us on one occasion, and I was already in bed, he wanted to present me with a sixpence. For this purpose, he took up a fire shovel (with its long handle) and kept by the entrance to the loft, and presented me with his gift at the end of the shovel. This ridiculous act of pomposity and exaggerated bowing gave rise to great laughter.

My grandparents at this time divided up the 10-volume set of Arthur Mee's *Children's Encyclopaedia* between the Browns' children and my brother and me. The encyclopaedias had originally been bought for my father and his siblings. These books were the best educational gift we had ever received, for until this day, no children's encyclopaedia has ever been published which matches the high standard of information and imaginative stimulus in capturing the attention and interest of young people. Packed with high quality illustrations, puzzles and articles on science, history, literatures, etc., it presents a universal education in understanding life and culture – and more significantly, the motivation to learn more.

My first introduction to all the truly great British and world writers, and all the significant episodes of history, etc., were absorbed through daily readings from these books. As this edition of the encyclopaedias was published before the outbreak of the so-called Great War, there was a fair and balanced appreciation of all European countries, and I remember flattering references to the "German Emperor" who was intent on raising the educational level of his people and ensuring their best welfare and high standards of living. My younger brother, Gavin, who later became a teacher, and is now in his 70s, still retains a volume of this encyclopaedia by his bedside for perusal before sleep.

What was the secret of this book in capturing the imagination of children and imprinting on their minds a huge corpus of unforgettable knowledge? The answer may be found in two factors: firstly, a strong moral sense in interpreting facts; and secondly, a healthy patriotism, for both these elements gave meaning to the facts recorded. This, of course, is in sharp contrast to the barren and worthless children's encyclopaedias on the market today, with the relativism of their post-modernist approach, whereby values are cast aside in a bland world where facts are minimised as of little significance. In such a dull landscape, therefore, what motivation is left to aid the retention of the memory? The earlier editions of Arthur Mee's major work are superior to those editions which followed in the 1920s and beyond, since the latter began to be spoilt by the increasing ideological divisions and doubts of the post 1918 world.

During this period, when I was eight and nine years old, I suffered horrific nightmares. On one occasion, on finding myself in bed late at night, in my parents' bedroom, facing the window, a huge white ghostly hand emerged from below the horizon, fingers appearing foremost, until the hand curved threateningly towards me as if to crush me in its grasp. I awoke in a sweat. On another occasion, whilst lying in bed in the nanny's room on the top floor, Miss Wall entered, announcing I had a visitor. A hideous old man, bent almost double, with long arms and fingernails six inches long entered, and Miss Wall casually announced before departing, that he had come to scratch my back. The awful spectre climbed under my bed, and digging his nails into the top of my shoulders began to slowly scratch them down my body until reaching my feet. I was paralysed, not merely by fear, but as if a poison had entered my body and prevented even the twitching of a muscle. Again, I awoke in a sweat as if my constitution had been shaken to its core and my heart had stopped.

After being taken to see Walt Disney's *Snow White and the Seven Dwarfs* (produced in 1937), I had nightmares every day for a week afterwards. It was the transformation scene of the beautiful Queen and stepmother into an ugly witch which generated such horror. Could beauty really be transformed into such ugliness, and was a mother and woman of beauty really capable of contemplating and committing such evil? Apparently, yes! This was something to threaten any boy or girl at any time in any place. More seriously, at the age of nine I began to sleepwalk. On several occasions, in the middle of the night, I left my bed, descended four flights of stairs, walked to the front door and opened it. On reaching the steps down to the street I was picked up by my father and put back to bed.

Shortly before reaching the age of nine, thoughts were given to my further education, and in facilitating this from a "professional standpoint," it was thought advisable to send me to an Educational Psychologist. Accordingly, in Spring 1944 I was sent to the Orchard Wing of Westfield College (being the Tavistock clinic premises) in Hampstead. They subsequently sent the following undated "Private and Confidential" letter to my father, which he solemnly read out to the family, expressing his disapproval at my limited abilities, over the breakfast table:-

"Nigel Corfe was tested on May 2nd 1944 at the age of 8 years 8 months. He was given the 1937 revision of the Stanford Binet test and proved to have a mental age of 8 years 2 months, an intelligence quotient of 94. Though broadly speaking this places him in the group possessing just average ability, it must be accepted that this is considerably below the average in general intelligence for those who would normally pass through secondary or public school. It would be unfair to the boy to expect him to reach school certificate standard.

"Nigel passed all the tests at the 7 year level, failed in the content of memory and verbal absurdity tests at his own age level, but higher than that passed on paper cutting test and word naming test. The last showed breadth of interest and easy progress of association.

"On his second visit, Nigel was given a group of 7 performance tests. The results were very variable and the median result (i.e. the one having as many results below as above) was 8 years 6 months. On the most important series, taken separately, Kochs Blocks Designs, the result was the average for 10 years 5 months.

"Nigel's reading, though only at the 6 year level approximately is healthy but he would profit by daily individual encouraging help.

"Nigel gave the best of co-operation. He was slow and thoughtful and both sensitive and sensible. He would be likely to develop most happily and fully if placed in the country in a small school that makes active use of a country environment."

I was horrified by the letter but said nothing, and felt terribly humiliated that this should have been read out in the presence of my brother. These Binet tests have, of course, long since been discredited, but even then I was appalled by the dogmatism and deterministic attitude of the report which made no allowance for later development or change, and the measurement of ability according to years and months –

irrespective of the criteria used – is clearly absurd in view of the wide variation in individual differences. My father carefully filed the letter away amongst other precious documents in his desk, but about a year later, I searched through his papers and retrieved the offending report, hiding it away amongst my own belongings, determined it would never be used against me on any future occasion.

A possible result of this report was that my father spent some time in the evenings over a period of months tutoring me in English and maths. During the day – at any time – sometimes whilst making my way into or out of the house, he would emerge from the surgery and ask me to spell a word or give an answer taken from the twelve times tables. He always chose words which were frequently misspelled, e.g., Harass, Embarrass, Receive, etc. This tutoring and constant testing was certainly most helpful, for I quickly retained all the twelve times tables not only by heart (which is not so difficult), but the calculations when asked for out of their correct order, which is quite another exercise. I must also thank him for ensuring that I soon became a good speller beyond my schoolboy age.

CHAPTER 7
The Inferno of Boarding School

> "'My children,' said an old man to his boys, scared by a
> figure in the dark entry, - 'my children, you will never
> see anything worse than yourselves.'"

Emerson, *Essays, First Series: Spiritual Laws*

Preparations for boarding school – I am deposited – Secret theft and violent robbery – The dyspeptic Matron – First day ceremonial and the Headmaster – Ritual torture – Poor standards of teaching – My clash with the Divinity master – A general election looms – Compulsive gangsterism – An end of term blasphemous concert is enjoyed by all

In view of the continued bombing it was thought that for my better safety I should be sent away to a boarding school in the provinces. When asked my opinion on this proposal I accepted it with alacrity. Anything to get away from London, and if this meant living in the countryside, so much the better! The next question arose as to which school I should be sent. Eton was suggested, but it was thought by various members of the family that I was not sufficiently academic. That privilege was to be reserved for two of my cousins, the elder sons of my father's youngest brother, Harold – but that was to occur many years ahead.

It was then suggested I should be sent to Woodbridge which, Roger, great Uncle Sidney's son, had attended some years before. If its academic record was not so great, it still had a good reputation for getting its leavers into good army regiments and into valued civil service posts throughout the Empire. The motto of the school was, *Pro Deo Rege Patria* (For God, Monarch and Country), and so its values seemed to be in the right place, and when my paternal grandfather was consulted, he thought an affirmative decision could not be far wrong.

Ernest Corfe thought it would toughen me up in preparing me for the wider world. He believed in manliness, and that this was best achieved through contradicting the utilitarian ideal. That is, he believed that pain, whether received or given, was always beneficial to the character, whilst pleasure of any kind, was harmful to character building. Whilst unpleasant tasting food as with unpleasant medicine is always good for the constitution, what was pleasant to the palate was bound in some way to be harmful to health. The same applied to any kind of intellectual or physical activity. In demonstrating his belief, he once had a tooth extracted without anaesthetic, as he wanted to experience the degree of suffering incurred by those patients who refrained from pain-killers on religious or other grounds. Pain was therefore the criterion in assessing the good, whilst pleasure was regarded as both socially and individually harmful.

In the light of careful family discussion, and my enthusiastic assent, the decision was therefore made to send me to Woodbridge. No entry examination or even an interview was required. My parents, however, visited the school, and were shown around the junior quarters, and some time later, my mother remarked on what she felt were the "primitive" living conditions and "basic" washing facilities. The preparations were considerable and sacrifices had to be made by several close relatives. I needed two grey suits, besides shirts, ties, caps and socks, all to a uniform specification. These needed many coupons and my grandparents in addition to my parents generously contributed their clothing rations for the purpose. My elation increased with every day which brought me closer to the new school. A tuck box was bought and this was filled with sweets and other culinary delights.

At last the great day arrived and I was chirpy and optimistic on leaving home. I could never have foretold that I was to jump from the frying pan into the fire. My father drove me to the school, and what would now be hardly more than a two hour drive at that time in spring 1945 took the greater part of the day in driving at no more than 40 mph through innumerable towns and villages until eventually reaching East Suffolk. There were also long delays caused by military convoys carrying supplies and personnel to various destinations – primarily to the East Anglian airfields for the bombing of Germany. After some hours as we drove along the narrow "A" roads in the countryside, my father began to warn and lecture me on "clean living" and the importance of avoiding association with those boys with "unclean habits" using "undesirable language."

He said I would probably meet boys who were quite ignorant about the facts of life, and that I might be told that babies came from beneath "gooseberry bushes" which was a common belief amongst uninformed people. Such stories I should ignore as based on myth. Babies resulted from the union between men and women, and this was through a purely biological process, explained my father, without going into any more details. I reacted awkwardly but assented to everything he said. I already knew all about the "birds and the bees," which I had picked up in the playground at Norfolk House and elsewhere, and I had never met anyone who believed in absurd myths about "gooseberry bushes." What I had learned in the playground was factual and accurate, and I did not need any prudish adults to elaborate further. And as for keeping apart from boys who talked "smut," that would have been quite impracticable. As soon as I arrived at Woodbridge I was to find that "filth" was the normal talk to the exclusion of almost anything else.

The total ignorance of middle class adults on the thinking and character of pre-pubescent boys has always amazed me. An idealised and sentimental view of this age group, most probably transferred by women to their menfolk, is that little boys are little less than angels, quite incapable of impure thoughts and all the corruption and vices of the adult world. As they view their "little darlings," in their white surplices, singing hymns in the candlelit chancel, they cannot imagine that butter could melt in their mouths. The real truth, however, is quite the opposite for unknown to their "mummies" and "daddies," the thoughts of these young people are resistant to any suggestion of godliness or religion, whilst references to sexual aberrations are never far from their innocent lips.

For a hundred years or more the popular press, of course, has been too ready to report on the corruption of choirboys by priests or pastors, but little is suggested about the corruption of the latter by the provocative gestures of the charges for whom they are supposedly responsible. My father had undoubtedly fallen under the delusion with regard to the innocence of the young, and this would seem to contradict his belief in the wickedness of children, and the need for constant thrashings in a carpet-cleaning sort of way. But his view of the wickedness of children had nothing to do with their hidden sexuality. At least they were innocent of that! His view of wickedness stemmed from original sin – something completely abstract and nebulous and inexplicable.

At last we arrived at Woodbridge and booked into the Crown Hotel for the night. After lunch the following day, my father and I sat in the hotel lounge by the log fire, and were entertained by an ex-prefect of Woodbridge School, who was denouncing in a comical fashion to all who would listen, his anger at a male hairdresser having ruined his girl friend's hair. Walking up and down the room to loud laughter from other patrons with their afternoon tipple, he exclaimed, "Tomorrow I'm going to break every beastly little bone in his beastly little body." If this is a foretaste of the kind of humour I'm going to hear at Woodbridge School, I thought, then I'm going to enjoy myself. It might have been preferable if I had given greater weight to the vengeance and cruelty behind his words rather than accept the humour at its face value.

Later that afternoon we arrived at School House, the Junior residence, to be greeted by the Housemaster, Mr. G.B. (or Capt.) Riddell, MA, born 1891, who eventually became the longest serving master at the School. He had supposedly had "half his stomach shot away" during the First World War, and because of this, he was nicknamed "Rubberguts." He was a short thick-set man with a bald head and a permanent grin. If the grin was taken as a sign of benevolence then it was as deceptive as the crocodile's smile. He had a smooth shiny skin as if six layers of French polish had been rubbed into his face and scalp. He was a confirmed bachelor, and known for his hobby of taking photographs of "good-looking boys," and his fondness for being photographed alongside them.

By profession he was a Maths master, and as will be suggested from an episode described below, this exacting discipline had probably erased from him any idea as to the possible value of creativity of any kind – or at least its desirability in schoolboys. He had been awarded the Military Cross in the Great War, and he was one of those wartime officers who liked to maintain the usage of their rank in civilian life. His fondness for military life perhaps exceeded that desirable in a schoolmaster responsible for the general education of the young, for he is recorded to have said on standing down from the OTC in 1930, "I have believed in the corps intensely, and I believe it is through the corps, more than through any other school organisation, that a boy learns that the highest ideal at which he can aim is that of service; and finds that through service he has learnt leadership, and in some ways become part of the school and a builder of its traditions." [*]

At first we had a short tour around the building and as we came down the stone staircase towards the cloakroom and toilets, which were pointed out, my father to my embarrassment added, "You'll find he's very regular." Why did he have to say that? I asked myself, and what

---

[*] Carol & Michael Weaver, *When Duty Calls: The Cadets at Woodbridge School 1908-2009*, published by the Old Woobridgians, 2009, p.34.

interest could that be to anyone else? The House Master ignored the comment and took us to his private study for tea. As the tea cups clattered on saucers, and niceties were exchanged, and the Housemaster continued to grin politely, in the quiet genteel environment, I could never have anticipated the horrors which lay ahead.

An hour later my father departed, and I was left alone, as the first arrival, in the gloomy surroundings of the Junior House school building. As clouds gathered overhead, my loneliness was exacerbated by the silence of the seemingly empty building, and for the first time I felt a sense of evil in the very brickwork of the looming structure. Somewhat later other boys were deposited by parents who quickly drove away from the grounds, and by 5.0 pm I and several other first-timers were surrounded by a hostile crowd of boys of all shapes, sizes and ages ranging from 9 to 13. We were regarded with suspicion and curious attention, and someone called out the words, "New bugs," in a tone of disdain, whilst others spat on the ground in a gesture of contempt. I felt intimidated, for I had never encountered such a situation before.

We were then bluntly asked our names, from what part of the country we came, and what our fathers did for a living, but there was no indication of friendship in their voices. It was as if we were being cross-examined as newly captured enemy prisoners of war. At that moment, foolishly, and under my breath, but insufficiently quiet not to be overheard, I exclaimed the words, "I must be mad!" meaning that I had badly misjudged my optimism in looking forward to the school. My words were immediately taken up by a boy called Williams, who cried, "He says he's mad! He must be mad!" and at once, three or four fists were struck into my ribs.

The Junior House boarded about forty pupils. All the rooms were unheated, the floors bare boards, and in the combined living, dining, and games area (where table tennis and billiard tables could be set up), there were only forms without backs for seating. The only part of the building containing chairs for pupils were in the dormitories, where each pupil had his own for hanging clothes at night. There was no running water, and cold water for washing was brought into the dormitories in the mornings and evenings in buckets by the duty service boy. The dormitories were out of bounds except for certain hours of the day, and those in the most junior class, as myself, had a compulsory rest after lunch.

The blackout blinds, comprising heavy cardboard, helped to some extent in keeping out the cold during freezing nights. It was forbidden to make holes in them, but nonetheless we carved out peep-holes, and sometimes watched squadrons of heavy bombers passing through the sky, late at night, toward their mission of destruction in Germany. The roar from their engines as they slowly passed over the school never failed to awaken us. My arrival at the school occurred shortly before the end of the War in Europe, but I nonetheless remember clearly all the evidence of an ongoing state of war.

There was a tuck box room where we kept our most valuable possessions in sturdy wooden cases, usually secured with heavy locks. This room was supposed to be under special protection against theft, and the junior boys never entered the room alone to open their boxes, for fear of being accused of theft of some object or other from another's tuck box. The period immediately following lunch was the usual time for juniors to go to the tuck box room to retrieve special possessions. It was a known fact, however, that the prefects entered the tuck box room at will, forced open the boxes of other boys and stole their possessions – especially chocolate and other foodstuffs. My tuck box was frequently rifled, and before my second term at the school, I had a second lock fitted, but not even this proved a sufficient deterrent.

Usually the prefects resorted to less subtle methods, preferring violent robbery to the more difficult and irritating process of picking locks. On one occasion, for example, Roger, as mentioned, an old boy of the school, took me out for the afternoon and gave me a set of stamps. That evening, I tried to conceal the fact as best I could, but I was seen with the packet of stamps, and as I carried it together with my album from the dormitory to the dining hall, three prefects jumped out from their room, punched me in the face, pushing me down the concrete staircase, whilst one walked off laughing with the stamps.

On another occasion, I was attacked by the head boy, who ran down the stairs behind me, blindfolded my eyes with his hands, and ordered me to give him what I carried. On that occasion I lost a two ounce bar of chocolate. Robbery was an everyday occurrence, and something which had to be passively accepted as a natural part of school life. The prefects were, in practice, the highest authority in the management of the school. To lodge a complaint with the staff would have been unthinkable for it would have been tantamount to treason.

The most systematic thefts occurred following the weekly pocket money parades. We all had different amounts as contributed by our parents – I had ninepence a week – and these sums were doled out by the House Master as he sat at his study desk, with a money box and register of the pupils' accounts. No one was supposed to know what his peers were receiving – or chose to conceal the fact – but a boy called Saunders, would crouch down outside the study door, peeping through the hinged opening, and espy what each boy received. As soon as the boy emerged from the study, he would be punched and his pocket money grabbed.

It astonished me that these brazen thefts, which took place within feet of where the House Master sat, were never discovered, and that they continued unabated week after week and month after month. Perhaps, on the other hand, the act of thieving was well-known to the masters, and if they believed in the educational theories of ancient Sparta (which was not unlikely), then it was something to be encouraged.

"Fags" were chosen by the prefects themselves from boys they liked most, and fagging often involved sexual abuse. I was fortunate never to be chosen for fagging, although I naturally attended to the duty services of the dormitory as arranged by a roster system. Water carrying into the prefects' room was the most dreaded task, but as occupants of this junior dormitory, we were exempted this duty. All other dormitories had to undertake this task as decided by a roster, and water carriers were expected to climb into the prefects' beds as an obligatory part of their duty. I remember one fag in an adjoining dormitory whimpering almost nightly at the thought of having to carry water into the prefects' room the following morning, and at the buggery he had to endure in satisfying the lust of the prefect to whom he was a bondsman.

In the living hall we had pigeon holes for keeping text books and other possessions, but it was naturally unwise to keep anything of value there. The boys' entrance hall to the building was also the changing room. My first meal in school was Sunday night supper, and meals were always preceded by grace, invariably officiated over by the matron or the House Master's sister. The matron officiated on this occasion, and we drank a diluted form of tea from heavy mugs, and ate with almost rusty cutlery. The temperament of the matron was at once revealed when she constantly scolded different boys for eating too fast – a vice which obsessed her mind. She would pick on a boy, and castigating him in a contemptuous tone, would speak as follows, "You just wait until you reach my age – your stomach will torture your body for all hours of the day and night, and you'll regret you ever ate so quickly in your youth. You can eat now how you like – but you'll be punished for it later –mark my words!" Peanut butter on bread was our staple diet for the evening meal.

At the end of every meal, she piled two table-spoonfuls of white powder into her mug of tea, which she then proceeded to drink in aiding her own digestion. She hated Americans, and when being taken to the doctor one morning in a taxi because of a skin complaint, we noticed lipstick had been added to the Queen Victoria statue in the market square. "It's those American vermin again," she remarked to the driver. The doctor diagnosed my skin complaint as due to eating "too many tomatoes," and to my astonishment, I was reprimanded by the matron for this, for I had no recollection of *ever* having eaten tomatoes at the school. On another occasion she made a fuss over a local incident when an American tank had driven over an ancient wooden bridge, with the result that both tank and bridge collapsed into the river beneath. We schoolboys tended to like Americans as they had a reputation of being kind to children.

The school comprised many buildings in 45 acres of grounds. The main and largest building was the Senior House, being the living quarters for the older boys. This was a Victorian structure. Then there was the oldest part of the school, dating back to the 16th century built around a cloistered quadrangle, surrounded by newer blocks for other classrooms, and last but not least, the ugly but modest chapel. In the Junior House, our lives revolved around the ringing of a bell, for early rising, for breakfast, for luncheon, for supper, and for bed. There was only one bathroom in the building for the use of the boys. Baths came once a month, and were officiated over by the matron who examined our bodies for cleanliness, sores, rashes, etc. Baths were regarded as an extra (and perhaps unnecessary) luxury, and hot water was provided by the geyser, but our personal cleanliness was supposed to be maintained by a cold soapy flannel rubbed over our bodies in the dormitories.

Our inner cleanliness was also attended to, and occasionally we were lined up and had our breaths smelt by the matron. "You stink,!" she would exclaim, "laxative tonight,!" and when the time came, a white vile tasting liquid would be poured down our throats. The toilets were almost the filthiest I have seen anywhere: frequently blocked, whilst the unwashed walls were scrawled with obscene drawings and initials from human excrement.

My first morning at the school was an impressive event. We new "bugs" were herded into the gallery of the main school hall, so we could view clearly the entire ceremonial. After all the boys had taken their places, the masters filed slowly down the aisle in pairs, dressed in the mortar-boards and black gowns, some carrying their canes as symbols of authority, to the singing of the school song. There were prayers, hymn singing and the calling of a register, and I and other new bugs – there were only 3 or 4 of us in total - were appropriately awed by the ceremonial. I was entered on the leather bound School's Admission Register as a paying pupil No. 2419. At that time Boarding fees were £24.00 per term, and there were less than 200 pupils in the entire school, as compared with today's total exceeding 900 scholars, with fees of £7,336.00 per term in 2010.

A few days after my arrival at the school, I was taken to be "interviewed" by the Headmaster, the Revd. Dudley Symon. I was taken to his study by the Head boy, who seemed a pleasant enough chap, and proudly pointed out the quad and other parts of the old building, and gently warned that I might find the Headmaster a little "daunting" but that I shouldn't worry too much as he "wouldn't eat me." I was ushered into a dark room and instructed to stand on a small carpet, before a lectern behind which stood the Headmaster on a low platform. We were left alone in the room, and I was dwarfed by the tall, elderly, thickly-bespectacled man with clerical collar, in a long black gown reaching to his ankles, for he was a doctor of divinity, and this was an exclusively church of England school.

He spoke, what appeared to me, in a slow pompous tone about the significance of my starting out on a new road in life, using long Latin words which I did not understand, and concluded by reading a few verses from the Bible. He never glanced at me, or at the wall behind me, or at anything in particular – in fact my presence seemed to bring no personal recognition whatsoever. I was never to be confronted by the Headmaster again.

New bugs had to undergo a course of ritual torture and special tests of character, and this together with casual bullying, occupied most of the free time and much of the breaks for long periods of time. We were shut up in a box which then was stoned; we were rolled down a hill in a cask; our faces were rubbed into ants' nests; we were tied down onto the ground whilst our trousers were filled with ant-soil; we were held against trees by our legs and arms, and punched in the face and stomach; we were subjected to genital tortures or forms of assault, as shoe blacking of the private parts, and most popular of all, we were held over a bonfire and exposed to heat – our trousers and underwear having first been removed.

On one occasion I was forced to walk around the inside of a sandpit with a sheer two hundred foot drop – a terrifying experience as the track I was following crumbled in my path and the sand was too hard to thrust my fingers into the wall to find a grip. I was fortunate in not being subjected to genital tortures and on no occasion was I raped, but I was subjected to several ritual tortures that were to leave me with lifelong injuries as described below.

As far as I was concerned, the academic qualities of the school proved to be zilch, although the form mistress, Miss Watmough, had a helpful and kindly disposition, and I remember enquiring of her about New Zealand, and from the illustrations in the classroom, I thought it would be a nice country to settle in. During the two terms of attendance, I learned practically nothing of value. Our places in the classroom were fixed by the form teacher, and since I was a new bug, I sat near the back of the room. The French mistress could not speak a word of English – or at least, she spoke no English – and although I was fond of the idea of learning a foreign language, on not one occasion was I called upon to read from the text book or to recite declensions of verbs. In the first form we did no homework, and language learning was entirely oral. I remember the French teacher gabbling away at a great pace, and occasionally writing a few sentences on the blackboard, whilst the class seemed hardly to listen or participate in the proceedings.

Latin was even more incompetently taught, but it was under the direction of one of the most highly respected masters in the school, Mr. A.D. Elliot (born 1882), someone whom we were urged to revere from the depths of our heart, as belonging almost to the stonework and oldest traditions of the school. I remember him as being very ancient and decrepit although he was only 63 at the time. He would sit behind the desk, grunt out orders to various boys in the front two rows to decline a verb or translate a sentence, whilst the rest of the class was ignored, and left to throw ink-blots and paper darts and pass messages from desk to desk. Sometimes he would call out the name of a boy who was not in the class, and a pupil would rise and loudly proclaim (for Mr. Elliot was as deaf as a post), "Excuse me, Sir, but he's in the fourth form, not the first." On other occasions he would forget what class we were, or what lesson had last been studied, and any progress or learning he appeared to instil was practically negligible.

At the end of the first term, this senile old man, was due for final retirement after a service of many years at the school. A book was passed round for everyone to sign, and we were asked to contribute our pocket money for a general collection towards a parting gift, and this I refused to do as I only received ninepence a week. "But what am I going to put beside your name?" asked one of the Senior prefects who held the book. – "I'm sorry, I haven't any money," I pleaded. "You'll have to put noughtpence beside my name." Most pupils gave a penny, but those who wanted to convey a more honourable or generous impression of their appreciation of the school, gave twopence or even threepence.

The following term this ancient Latin master was succeeded by a brutal man with a beaky nose, Mr. Buiseret, nicknamed "Beeswax," who unfairly accused the class of being lazy and backward in its grasp of the language. This man had a daughter, and she rode daily passed the school to and from her own place of learning, and some of us boarders from the Junior House occasionally threw mud or stones at her as she passed by on her bicycle, as somehow we had been nurtured to despise the female sex, and would anyway have thrown stones and dirt at any girl whom we saw passing in the roadway. She always wore a black gym-suit over a white undergarment.

To our astonishment, one day our new Latin master picked out a boy in the class of whom he said that his daughter had recognised as one of her persecutors. How the master was able to identify this boy from a second hand description beggars belief – perhaps he had exceptional features for easy recognition – but in any event, he happened to be one of the most frequent stone throwers. "I'm going to give you six of the best," cried the master, "and never shall any of you again attack my daughter."

He took the boy into a box room adjoining the classroom, but after the first blow, the cane broke into two, and I shall never forget the look of humiliation and frustrated rage on the master's face, as he emerged from the box room with the ridiculous remains of his punishment stick.

During the second term, another young teacher joined the school to teach us maths, on whom we constantly played jokes, and tried to make his life as unpleasant as possible.

The most irascible teacher in the school was perhaps the divinity master, the Rev. John Herbert Edmonds (born 1916), a small thin man of about 30, with a pallid complexion, and liable to outbursts of self-pity. He was also the school Curate, and in chapel, when he was magnificently dressed in colourful vestments and a shapely black cap, he was transformed into an impressive awe-inspiring priest. He gave Holy Communion to the masters and Senior prefects, and conducted the prayers and ritual of the service with all the circumscribed pomp required. In prayer, he would clutch his hands until his knuckles showed white, and his resounding voice pleading for the "mercy and grace of God," conveyed sincerity deep in its conviction.

It was said his irascibility arose partly through his failure to arouse the affection of the Senior House matron, of whom it was said that she preferred the Senior prefects. On a number of occasions, we saw the divinity master and matron sitting quietly together on the lawn at the top of the valley before the Senior House, and we junior boys used often to joke about the failure of their sexual relationship, in addition to much more smutty talk on the same topic.

The teaching of divinity was treated as a serious subject, that is, doctrines were taken and explained as supposedly demonstrable dogma through geometrical diagrams on the blackboard. One day when the divinity master was in an especially irascible temper, he stormed into the room abruptly announcing he would prove the "irrefutable" existence of God. He proceeded to painstakingly draw a complex diagram on the blackboard. Four different colours of chalk were used, and ten minutes taken up before the diagram was completed. In the centre was a triangle representing the Holy Trinity, over this was drawn a half circle, which it was explained represented the indivisibility of God, and from the half circle were drawn a number of rays representing the life-giving qualities of God, and inside the triangle was drawn a red circle, representing the warmth of his heart.

"God is like the sun," concluded the Curate. "He is ever-present, even when hidden behind dark clouds, and his rays can enter the gloomiest rooms, providing the windows remain un-curtained. – Any questions,?" he added nervously turning the chalk between his fingers.

To my early years, and little experience in exploring abstract ideas of a religious nature, there was something illogical, contrived, confused, and even deceitful in these absurd diagrams, analogies and explanations. I was not intentionally recalcitrant but in all humility I raised my hand, and on being called to speak, I stood up and asked: "But Sir, what do those green half circles inside the Indivisibility of God represent?" The response was unexpected. "Damn you, you fool – can't you understand?" replied the young divine in an outburst of anger, and he snapped the chalk between his fingers, and stormed out of the room not to return for the rest of the lesson. We were deserted in the classroom in a state of embarrassed confusion.

When he lost control on another occasion, towards the end of the Spring term, it was on quite another matter, and he stormed at us as follows: "It's all right for *you* at the end of the term. You can return to your rich homes enjoying eight weeks of pampered luxury – served on hand and foot by your affectionate mammas and papas! But oh no, that's not for us! We have to remain here for you brats, slaving away to prepare the work for next term's curriculum. There's no holiday for *us*!"

We junior boys were confined to the grounds, except for one Saturday afternoon in the month, when we could go to the town and spend the money we had saved, usually buying certain kinds of non-rationed sweets, as sherbet sugar, or mineral drinks and other odds and ends. Some boys bought chewing gum from the Yanks, who were stationed in great numbers nearby. Chewing gum was a novelty in England at the time, it had never been on sale in the shops, and it was forbidden to bring it within the precincts of the school. Nonetheless, a packet of chewing gum had a high exchange value in the school: it would be passed from the mouth of one boy to another, it would be concealed somewhere to dry, and would then be taken out and chewed again some days later. Naturally, any chewing gum found was confiscated, and if a boy persisted in the habit, he was caned. Despite this, my father once brought me chewing gum amongst a selection of other confectionary, and fortunately, it was never discovered.

Once a boy bought a bottle of HP brown sauce and a loaf of bread, and on arriving back in the living hall that afternoon, he began to eat the bread and drink the sauce from the bottle. He was caught in the act by the matron who angrily warned him that "worms" had been found in this particular brand, and that was enough to persuade him to throw the bottle away.

In May that year, the War ended in Europe, and on VE day, we were given a holiday and coloured cardboard disks and streamers, that we threw into the air outside the Junior House. It was a great day, but one of the disks I threw had the misfortune to land on a prefect's head, and I was beaten up as a punishment – for accidents of that kind were inexcusable.

During the first half term holiday, my parents came down to visit, and I stayed with them over the weekend at the Crown Hotel. In a tone which was rather too solemn (but nonetheless reflected their concern) they explained that a great event would shortly occur to decide the future of Britain. I knew little of politics at the time, and they said that in two months a general election would be held, and the adult population were going to cast a vote as to who they wanted to govern the country. The outcome would either mean the continuation of "normal" government and national security, or else, its replacement with a government intent on the abolition of property and the loss of India. Worst of all, Churchill might be forced to resign. In view of my maternal grandmother's silver-framed portrait of Churchill, and of all the myths I had absorbed regarding his defence of the realm, I accepted the prospect of a changed administration as truly alarming.

It subsequently proved fortunate I learned the names of the two main political parties, for some weeks later, as the election campaign intensified, the prefects of the Junior House lined us up outside the building after the bell had gone for supper one evening, and asked as we entered the doorway: "Conservative or Labour?" Most of us still knew little about politics, and some hesitated in giving a clear answer, and the prefects shook us by the lapels, crying, "Go on, say either Conservative or Labour!" Just in front of me, a boy pronounced the word, "Labour," perhaps because it was the easier to pronounce, and the prefects at once pushed him aside, crying, "We'll deal with you after supper, you traitor."

During the meal, the word spread that So-and-so was a "Labourite," and supper could not end soon enough, for there was lusting to have his blood, and hatred was rising to fever pitch. Half an hour later, a yelling boy was carried to a nearby field, followed by the entire House, and in furious indignation, the words were barked out, "Labourite traitor!" – "I don't understand, I don't understand!" cried the youth. – "You soon will," laughed another. – "You're Labour – you said so – you dirty traitor!" retorted one of the prefects.

As soon as he was far enough from the building, he was punched from all directions, until he fell to the ground, where he was kicked in the ribs and face. One boy began jumping on his chest and stomach, and the culprit brought up his supper.

Such gestures did not change the course of history, for in July that year, and to the surprise of the country, and perhaps most of all, to the victors, the Labour party was returned to power with a landslide. An environment of depression submerged the school, and I remember at the beginning of the following term, when going into chapel, overhearing a snippet of conversation amongst a group of Senior prefects, who usually waited outside until the entry of the juniors. "You know what this means, it means we've lost the ruddy War," bemoaned one prefect dolefully to another.

Other spare time activities comprised smutty talk and picking up all the accompanying jargon, making wood carvings in a hut in front of the Junior House, playing hide-and-seek, and learning indecent songs in preparation for an end of term concert arranged by the prefects of the House. The time engaged in these activities was small, however, compared with that of fighting, bullying, and undergoing ritual torture. There was an inexplicable tension and anxiety which never seemed to cease, and a neurotic need for fault finding which led to constant conflict. Fights were frequently precipitated through the most absurd and extempore excuses. A boy would suddenly cry, "Belts against braces," or, "Blue eyes against brown eyes," or, "Normans against Saxons," and gangs would instinctively be formed at a moment's notice, followed by angry punches and shouts.

Despite this, I had enough time to write a short novel, and this I read to a group of boys who seemed to enjoy the story, but when the House Master learned of this "surreptitious" creative activity, he discouraged it by publicly ridiculing me in front of the House. The book was an imaginary war thriller, but writing was considered "beneath the dignity" of a Public schoolboy. Some days later I found the manuscript in my locker covered with urine and faeces and so I was obliged to throw it away.

The end of term concert, arranged exclusively by the pupils of the Junior House for their own entertainment, was undertaken with the assent of the House Master, although the details of the programme were naturally kept secret from the teaching staff. The concert was held in the cramped quarters of the woodwork hut, and most of us participated in skits or the singing of indecent or blasphemous songs. It was a carefully arranged and enjoyable affair, and the entire show kept us laughing throughout. There was a mock clergyman who delivered a dirty sermon, a free rendering of the Lord's Prayer, hymns re-written with four-letter words, and paraphrases of well-known Biblical passages. I and another boy sang a many-versed song about a Biblical character who lay naked on her stomach blowing a trumpet from her bottom, for which we were loudly applauded. It was one of the few enjoyable days I experienced at the school.

CHAPTER 8
The Sadistic Head Boy

"Cruelty ever proceeds from a vile mind, and often from
a cowardly heart."

Sir John Harrington, *Orlando Furioso*, Bk. xxxvi, Notes.

The Housemaster's appointee – Brutality encouraged by the housemaster's sister –
The reluctant lover – The traitor and his punishment – My fight with Tuffield – His
gunpowder accident – The Viking ghost – Class war in the school grounds – The
consequences of an early morning quarrel

At the beginning of the second term a new Head boy and set of
prefects were appointed by the House Master for the Junior
House. I had hardly noticed the existence of the new Head boy
the previous term, for so self-effacing was his presence at that time, but
through sadistic cruelty he soon made his mark, and life was made a
living hell for the majority. And in this he was openly encouraged by the
sister of the House Master. "Don't be soft on them. Be hard all the time,"
I remember her exhorting him in front of us one afternoon – and not even
the prefects escaped his pathological outbursts of rage. From then
onwards, gratuitous violence and the drawing of blood became the main
preoccupation of the bullies of the Junior House, and the mere bullying
and ritual torture and arbitrary robbery of the previous term paled in
comparison with what followed now.

The new Head boy was a small pallid person with homosexual
tendencies, called Davey, and I would never hope in my life to encounter
such sadism and brutality again. As we watched him read the Lesson
during the Sunday morning or Evening chapel service, as he often did in
turn with the prefects of the Senior House, one could never imagine he
would harm a fly. His chief lover was not a fag but a reluctant prefect
colleague, of whom it was said that he dragged nightly into his bed. On
one occasion when the prefect resisted these unwelcome advances, the
entire House was called upon to carry him to a nearby field where he was
beaten up and his genitals covered with shoe polish and ant soil.

At other times, an appearance of enforced friendship existed
between these two, and the reluctant prefect and Head boy would
peacefully play together at table tennis or billiards – but there was always
danger around the next corner. On one occasion, after a game of billiards,
the prefect put down his cue, and foolishly remarked in a casual tone,
"Well, it seems as if I've won." This was too much for the Head boy, for
no one was allowed to freely defeat a senior, in sports or otherwise, and
the latter responded at the top of his voice in alerting everyone present,

"Oh no you didn't! You cheated, you rat!" and began chasing the prefect around the billiard table. The prefect was beaten across the head and shoulders until the cue snapped into two, and the unfortunate victim was then punched in the face and ribs.

On bored Sunday afternoons a group of prefects would sit on the bench against the window with their flies open and produce erections before measuring the length of their penises which then became a subject of boasting throughout the House. The boy with the longest penis was Saunders – a notorious thief and bully.

Violent robbery increased inevitably this term, and as there was a craze for stamp collecting, this often took the form of prefects robbing the juniors of their collections. One day whilst fixing stamps into my album, the Head boy sat down opposite me, snatched the book away, and went through its pages from beginning to end, taking out all the stamps he did not possess, exclaiming, "Thank you, that's mine!" as he removed them. As my collection was modest, he only stole a dozen or so stamps from the entire album.

On other occasions, a payment of stamps could be made in lieu of granting sexual favours, or avoiding ritual torture and beatings-up, but one had to possess an exceptionally fine collection, offering complete sets of stamps, before this was viable. The prefect lover of the Head boy was said to have lost more than half his collection to the latter in lieu of being raped over a specified period of time, and I well remember on a number of occasions, him crying in grief as he tore out from his large album, one by one, a complete set of stamps, as the Head boy yelled at him, banging his fist on the table, "More, more!"

Some of us wrote to our parents complaining of this ongoing gross brutality and theft. I remember beginning one of my letters: "Dear Mummy and Daddy. I hate my new school." This of course was "treason," but it was our only possible gesture of protest, for none would even have dreamed of questioning the authority of those in charge. My complaining and tales of woe were ignored by my parents, and in their letters, they merely reported boring and unimportant chit-chat from home, but on next meeting my father, he took out a bundle of letters when we were alone in a hotel room, and asked in an embarrassed tone, which also expressed concern for my well-being, "What do you mean by this, 'I hate my new school?'"

In that situation, I too was overcome with a feeling of awkwardness and shame at this direct confrontation, and so I denied "hating" the school, saying that I now "liked" it. My father at once perceived I was not speaking from the depth of my heart, for he replied, "Things'll get better later on. You're a new bug now, but one day you too will be a prefect – and maybe even a Head boy – and then you too will have authority to tell others what to do." I found this little consolation, but I accepted the distant hope.

Letter writing to our parents was an obligatory occupation on Sunday afternoons, although we could write at other times if we wished. At these Sunday afternoon sessions, we sat at tables in the living hall, whilst the House Master passed round sheets of lined paper on which to write our letters. Our parents' addresses had to be written on the top left hand corner of the sheets, and on completion of the letters, they were collected by the House Master, who put them into envelopes that he was obliged to stamp and address himself. If a system of censorship did not prevail, there was nonetheless the possibility that everything we wrote came to the attention of the House Master.

One evening a boy was caught by a prefect writing a letter home complaining strongly against the tyranny of the school. I first knew of this as I was walking up the hill towards the Junior House when I saw four prefects, followed by a number of other boys, dragging the culprit out of the building. He was yelling, the tears rolling down his cheeks. "What's up?" I asked. – "He's a stinking traitor," someone replied. – "The wretch was caught writing against the school," said another.

The culprit was taken out to a nearby field, and it was debated as to what degree of punishment should be meted out in fitting the crime. The penalty was eventually decided by the Head boy. The culprit was carried to an ants' nest in the field of long grass that was turning to hay with the advance of autumn and the dry weather, his trousers and pants were taken down, a straw inserted into his penis, and ants put into the protruding end of the straw. When he began struggling violently and screaming, his mouth was smothered by one of the prefects, so the torture could be administered with as little fuss as possible. About twenty of us were standing around as witnesses, for it was usual to call out the entire House in witnessing punishments and ritual torture. After some 15 minutes it was all over, and the Head boy turned to us and yelled, "And the same goes to anyone who betrays the school again!" From that day onwards, I never risked compromising myself by writing against the school.

During this term I had another phase of sleep-walking, going into the corridor and entering a strange dormitory, but I always returned to my bed again and continued to sleep normally, and only learned about these episodes on being told the following morning. A boy in another dormitory reported this sleep-walking to the matron, and she arraigned me in front of a group saying that I must be afflicted with some form of "insanity," and this inevitably drew laughter from those standing around. On subsequent nights, the bed of one boy was laid against the door, so that I could not leave the dormitory and come to grief.

There was one particular bully, Tuffield, whom I especially loathed, for violence and fighting seemed the only occupations in which he was engaged. Almost daily, I was the victim of his assaults, and one day I exclaimed in anger under my breath that I was going to fight him. The remark was overheard by another boy who laughingly at once reported it to Tuffield, who approached me exclaiming, "All right, it's fixed! You made the challenge and I accept. We fight tomorrow in the morning break."

The sensational news at once spread round the Junior House, for Tuffield was far larger than me, and besides, I had challenged a senior to a fight and this could not be retracted, and was an event of rare occurrence. When the time came, the entire Junior House was assembled before the building, and even the matron was called out to watch the fun, which promised some excellent sport. All the boys were laughing, for it was regarded as absurd I should fight this much stronger boy, and the matron, who stood in the doorway in her white tunic, was laughing also in anticipation of the outcome of the match.

The bully and I removed our coats and rolled up our sleeves, and the fight began. I was no match for my opposite number, and although I struck out as best I could, I was punched with hard and successive blows in the face and ribs, and the blood ran down my face and shirt front. Tuffield was cheered on to press his victory even harder, and I well remember the mocking laughter of the matron as she stood by the entrance to the building, and the bully hit harder and harder, and the harder he hit the more he was cheered, until eventually, I was knocked down and could not rise again to resume the fight. At this, everyone walked away laughing, and I had learned yet another lesson: never to challenge anyone in authority, in thought, word or deed, howsoever vile or contemptible he might be.

One evening, after supper, a crust of dirty bread was found lying under a table by the Head boy. All who dined at that table were lined up against the wall, whilst the Head boy bawled at us like a regimental sergeant-major: "Who threw this bread under the table?" No one owned up. "All right, we'll soon find out," cried Davey, and he began thrusting the dirty piece of bread between our lips – the ordeal being that he into whose mouth the bread could be forced must be the guilty party.

At this point the House Master's sister came into the room, and began watching the proceedings with smiling approval. When the ordeal failed to identify the culprit, the bread was broken up into separate pieces that we were each obliged to eat. – "Good! I'm glad to see you're ensuring there's no wastage of food," exclaimed the sister with satisfaction to Davey. "If you're hard on them all the time, it'll keep them in order." The attitude of the House Master's sister was that all the boys under her brother's charge were little less than felons and therefore should be treated as such.

There was yet another prefect who was the object of great brutality at the hands of the Head boy. This was a younger brother of the previous terms' Head, of whom it was thought that he had been too protected during the earlier terms by his elder brother who was now in the Senior school. One Sunday evening, Davey began to violently reproach the prefect because of the "protected" circumstances he had enjoyed for so long, and that he had not yet been made to "suffer" sufficiently to justify holding his present position as prefect. The latter at first was astonished and speechless at this unexpected attack, but as soon as Davey ordered his henchmen to seize hold of the offending boy, surprise turned to panic. The victim was dragged into the changing room by four of the thugs, with Davey in charge, and the door was slammed shut. Those of us remaining in the living area were aghast at what would happen next, and we waited in silence. A minute or so passed, and then came a great clattering of thrown objects from the changing room, followed by yells of pain.

This continued for about twenty minutes, after which we had to file out of the building for Sunday Evensong. As we passed through the changing room to the cold air outside, we saw the latest victim of the Head boy's rage, suspended by his wrists tied with boot laces to the coat hooks, his arms outstretched in crucifixion fashion, his face and suit covered in blood and dirt. Up to that time I had never witnessed such a gory mess. He was petrified and whimpering, and at his feet lay dozens of football boots which had been thrown at his suspended body.

All our boots had been removed from the lockers for this purpose, and I amongst others never retrieved my own proper boots again, for name tags soon worked loose from footwear. The ironic epilogue to this story is that the unfortunate boy was caned by the House Master for failing to attend chapel that evening. He could not possibly have cleaned himself up in time for the service, and it was especially a disgrace for a prefect to miss evening prayers, since it set a bad example to the juniors.

During the compulsory rest hour one afternoon, whilst lying on our beds in the dormitory, we were startled by an explosion followed by screaming which came from the direction of the woodwork hut just outside our window. There followed an excited running to and fro of persons in the passageway, as if rushing to an emergency, and then someone cried, "Tuffield's been killed – blown to bits with gunpowder." *Schadenfreude* was my immediate instinct as I concluded that natural justice had been visited on my worst enemy, and I went downstairs with others to see a trail of blood leading from the woodwork hut into the Junior House.

Apparently, Tuffield had been engaged in a scientific experiment of sorts in trying to make an explosive for his personal use. A number of us used often to break into a small woods and rifle range within the school grounds and collect used cartridges, and sometimes, if we were lucky, live bullets. The area was fenced off with barbed wire and danger signs, and anyone caught in this out-of-bounds area was immediately caned, but this was no deterrent to our collecting these treasured possessions of war. Some of us would hide the cartridges in the woodwork hut, scrape the powder or dust from out of the inside with a penknife, and store the collected chemicals in envelopes or tins. Tuffield had succeeded in retrieving several live rounds of ammunition he had stolen from an ammo case, and he carefully broke open the cartridges, pouring the powder into a bottle. It was whilst shaking the bottle, which also contained other chemicals stolen from the school laboratory that the container exploded in his face.

He was put to bed, and for some days he lay motionless, his face bandaged over, and we were asked to be silent whilst passing his dormitory. In regarding my own welfare, I could only pray that his injuries might be permanent, or that blindness would be his punishment, but my secret wishes went unanswered, for in a few weeks he had recovered, apart from superficial flesh wounds from broken glass, which were to be the only reminders of what turned out to be a trivial accident.

One Sunday afternoon, the matron and the House Master's sister took some of us juniors for a country walk, and having passed through the town and reached a ferry by the River Deben, we were rowed across. It was low tide, and on reaching the opposite bank, the oarsman bid us be careful in stepping onto the wooden jetty as it was slippery. The House Master's sister, who rarely heeded advice, was the first to leave the boat, and she slipped and fell straight into the soft mud, sinking up to her knees, and screaming and waving her arms in panic. The oarsman and matron rushed to her rescue, dragging her out of the mud in a life-saving gesture, whilst we boys sat passively on our seats, not deigning to assist in such an unworthy cause. Perhaps we would have gladly watched her slowly sink up to her neck, as she was smothered by the mud.

Amongst one of the ritual tortures I had to undergo alongside others, was to lean over an ancient fallen tree trunk, and be beaten across the back by prefects with heavy logs. When it came to my turn, after the first few blows, I experienced excruciating pain which seemed to paralyse the lower part of my body, so that it could not support the top half of my weight. I collapsed in agony to the ground, and was ordered to get to my feet, only to find that a paralysing pain could not support my weight, and I fell back onto the earth in agony.

It was concluded I was feigning a non-existent injury, and so I was kicked in the ribs and face, and left bleeding on the ground. I remained on the earth for about half an hour in this miserable condition, unable to move my legs or hips because of the pain, and then miraculously, the pain abated, and I could rise to my feet and walk. Over the next few days, I suffered a stiffness and rheumatic pain in the back, but not sufficiently severe, as I then judged, to complain to the matron about my condition, and after several weeks, all seemed well.

On three occasions during the next few years, however, I was suddenly and unexpectedly struck down with excruciating spinal pains, and obliged to immediately lie down for an hour or so. During my medical inspection for National Service, eight years following this episode of ritual torture, the inspecting officers were amazed at discovering the characteristics of a spinal curvature I had incurred. "Come and have a look at this," said the chief to his colleagues, "it's most remarkable," and about five doctors stood around and dug their fingers into my back, telling me to bend forward and backwards. They were even more surprised when I told them it had caused me no "trouble."

Distrusting my word, I was sent to a Harley Street specialist. After the examination, I asked, "What's the cause of the curvature?" – "It's due to a direct injury at some time – there's no doubt about that," answered the doctor with certainty. As a result of the specialist's medical opinion, I was not enlisted into an infantry regiment as requested, but into a corps – but this made little difference, as recruits to this particular corps supposedly underwent a basic training which in rigour was only second to the Guards. Over the next few years I had no more trouble with my back until the first winter of my long residence in Finland in 1961. On encountering another attack of excruciating back pain and examination by a specialist, I was told that this was a chronic life-long condition, although physio-therapy would be helpful in warding off the onset of attacks.

During the first physio consultation, my therapist was appalled I was dressed in English underwear in such a climate, and from that time to the present, I have always worn long thermal underwear during the winter months – despite the ridicule to which I was subsequently exposed on occasion by those English people who discovered the fact. The reality, however, is that the warmth of underwear reaching to wrists and ankles, is not only the best insurance in protecting a weakened back, but also in fending off all other winter ailments as colds and influenza.

Another ritual torture that was to end in unfortunate circumstances, arose from an occasion when we were obliged to kneel down with our arms outstretched, supporting our bodies above the ground in a horizontal position, whilst the senior boys and prefects took a flying leap at us, throwing their full weight onto our shoulders. This resulted in a greenstick fracture of my right arm, and thus within the period of a year, I had encountered two broken limbs.

On returning to the Junior House, in great pain, the arm swollen and paralysed, on being asked by the matron what had happened, I gave the stock answer expected on such occasions, explaining I had "fallen over," and nothing more was looked into the cause of the "unavoidable accident." An ironic epilogue to the story is that on arriving back from the hospital, my arm in plaster, the House Master's sister met me at the door, and glancing at me with disapproval, she exclaimed, "That's God's punishment for not learning to write with your right hand!" As a result of the injury, the elbow has since remained twisted out of shape.

One morning, whilst still in plaster of Paris, a boy was beaten up by several others for some offence I have forgotten, whilst I stood by idly watching. "Why don't you help us?" exclaimed one boy. – "How can I? My arm's in a sling," I replied. – "We'll hold him down and you can kick him in the face," said the boy. The culprit was held down by four or five others, and not wishing to appear "soft" or "effeminate" in refusing to accept the suggestion, I ran at the boy and kicked him hard on the chin. Blood poured from his mouth and one of his front teeth was badly chipped, and a cheer went up from the others because of what was seen as an uncharacteristic act of "heroism." Before the day was out, the news had spread round the school that I, a mere invalid, had helped to beat up So-and-so, and I was congratulated for what was considered exceptional endeavour and bravery in view of my physical incapacity.

It was alleged that the Junior House was built on a Viking burial mound, and every year on 23rd November, it was believed by the junior boys, that the Viking rose from his grave late at night and walked around the school, visiting all the dormitories, and killing any persons by his glance who looked upon his spectre. It was believed through hearsay or myth that several pupils had actually been killed in their beds on this very date. Consequently, the weeks preceding the 23rd November were anticipated with a kind of superstitious dread, although it was not agreed in what form the ghost appeared, and it was debated as to whether he was a monster with fiery eyes and clanking chains, a skeleton bearing a cloak and sword, or merely a white and luminous phantom.

On the night of his expected appearance, and partly in retaliation for injuries received, I decided to play a harmless practical joke on my peers. About twenty of us were lounging outside the Junior House and the woodwork hut, when suddenly pointing to some bushes, and in petrified terror at the top of my voice, I yelled, "Look, the skeleton!" Instantly, every boy made for the entrance of the building as fast as his legs would carry him, and several bruised themselves in the crush at the doorway, and Tuffield sustained a grey mark on his forehead that he wore for a fortnight. No humour was seen in my joke, and I was accused of cowardice. "You might have killed us with shock," exclaimed Tuffield resentfully. It was for this that I was forced to walk round the inside of the sandpit as punishment as described in the previous chapter.

It was usual for the junior boys to play in one part of the school grounds, and for the seniors to play in another, although there were no formal rules concerning this. However, there was one circumstance when the juniors could always "trespass" onto the senior school grounds, and that was during those events when there were battles with the outside world. These were frequent and sometimes large scale, but I usually remained a passive observer during these dangerous skirmishes between hordes of boys. I remember on several occasions standing by a wall, high up in the valley, looking down at the excited yelling and stone throwing mobs from the Public school defending their territory from the slum children or "guttersnipes," as we called them, who invaded our territory.

It was a disturbing scene, with different groups of fighting boys spread over a wide area. On the other side of the valley, just beyond the school grounds, was a small cottage, and an old woman would excitedly wave her arms and vainly shout at the boys to desist. On a number of occasions we were instructed by the school authorities to refrain from these conflicts, but we ignored the behests.

The greatest of these battles occurred shortly after the general election, when a party of youths, somewhat older than the usual trespassers, confronted a group of juniors with provocative taunts of, "pampered kids" and the "privileged rich." One of the juniors ran over to the Senior House to summon reinforcements. Minutes later, dozens of teenage seniors, running to the rescue and shouting at the top of their voices, advanced on the village interlopers. Missiles began to fly, and in response to the shouts of the invaders, came the cry, "Death to the working class – death to the workers!" After the battle and hand-to-hand fighting had continued for some minutes, the old woman emerged from her cottage, pleading an end to the conflict as one of the village boys had been struck in the eye by a stone, and with this appeal, both parties withdrew from further aggression.

This was class war displayed in all its hatred, and the first time I witnessed its practical application. It was also my first experience of political life, although I had already given some thought to political issues. My immediate response was one of horror, and from that day to this, I have repudiated class-based politics as mischievous, destructive, irrational, and inevitably a barrier to appreciating the kind of understanding and knowledge necessary for achieving a free and egalitarian society in benefiting the total population of a nation state. Class war was not an essential component of democracy, but on the contrary, a travesty of everything which democracy has to offer, since it exploits the subjectivity of prejudice, and tramples on the cool thinking which is necessary for constructive intelligence.

One day a labourer's son, a thick-set almost fully grown youth, came into the school grounds, saying he wanted to challenge one of the boys in the school – any boy who might be chosen as the school's champion – as his younger brother had been severely beaten-up in what he described as a "cowardly manner." With solemn formality, a fight was arranged, and one of the toughest boys in the senior school was chosen to champion our cause. Perhaps it would have been more prudent had the labourer's son brought along with him a second or witnesses, but he came alone, and must have trusted in the fair play of the boys from their "soft upper class" homes.

The fight took place at the bottom of the valley beneath the Senior House. At first, each contestant seemed equally matched, but as the fight became more heated and blood ran from their faces, the labourer's son began to overpower his adversary. Naturally, we all cheered on our champion, but when at last he was knocked onto the ground, panting and helpless, and the labourer's son began to drag him to his feet, this was too much for most of us to endure. The thought of a proletarian beating-up a Public schoolboy and in the school grounds, was a galling humiliation to us all, and at once, four others leapt onto the labourer's son, and overpowering and pummelling him soundly, left him a semi-conscious heap to lie on the ground until he was fit enough to drag himself away.

One day towards Christmas some fudge was prepared by the House Master's sister for the juniors, and served out after supper. I had already been given and eaten my piece, but many pieces still remained on the tray, and being hungry, I approached the sister from behind, and hoping not to be caught, I surreptitiously snatched another piece from the tray and slipped it into my mouth. She quickly turned round, exclaiming, "Don't be greedy," and immediately I experienced a deep sense of guilt, but not from the accusation of greediness but from the act of committing a "theft." Nothing more was said or done about the matter, but I have instinctively felt that theft is the most shameful of offences, and consequently, I have always felt incapable of stealing from others.

As at most schools, dares were often made. One day, a boy in one of the senior dormitories of the Junior House dared another to throw a chair out of the window. The dare was accepted, and as misfortune would have it, it landed square on the bald-pated head of the House Master, who happened to be passing beneath. Naturally, the boy got six of the best, whilst the House Master wore a plaster on his pate for the next week or so.

About three weeks later, an ironic incident occurred partly resulting from this, and something which was to rebound and have far-reaching consequences for my own future. Early one morning I had a violent quarrel with another boy in the dormitory, and picked up a chair and threw it at him, at the very moment that the House Master entered the room. "I thought it was you shouting again," he said. "You know perfectly well that fighting before breakfast isn't allowed – and besides, I've never seen anything so brutal or cowardly in my life as throwing a chair at another boy. You're a menace to the school. I shall write to your father about this."

By this time the House Master had doubtless formed a complex about chairs, and after all I had suffered at the school, his upbraiding me for an alleged act of "brutality" and "cowardice" seemed hypocrisy verging on the comic. However, he kept his word about writing to my father for he asked that I be withdrawn from the school at the end of the term. When I learned about this, nothing pleased me more, and I proudly told my fellow pupils that I was leaving the school. When Tuffield, my worst enemy, learned about this, he seemed genuinely sorry. "Why are you leaving?" he enquired in a concerned tone, one afternoon in the woodwork shop as we were carving out boats. – "Because I don't like the school," I said. – "What's wrong with the school?" he asked. – "I don't know exactly," was the only answer I could give at the time, and there the conversation ended.

Late one afternoon towards the end of term, on a gloomy overcast day, I stood alone under a tall tree between the Junior and Senior playing fields, pondering my future. I asked myself: where shall I be in five, ten, or even, twenty years from now? Is my life to be a failure or success? The future looked grim. I was friendless and alone with no expectations of happiness ahead. I reflected on my sufferings, and the injuries I had so unjustly and unnecessarily received, and then for the first time, I began to ponder seriously on questions of philosophy and politics. In reality I was not alone, but one amongst millions, and surely my sufferings must somehow be replicated in reflecting those of the world at large.

It was the practical business of government which was to blame for all the world's ills, and religion was a hypocritical and wicked fraud in promising a future Never-Never land to those who obediently submitted to tyrants on earth. What the world lacked was the rule of law to protect the good and punish the wicked. Those were my thoughts at the time.

Some days before the end of term, we junior boys were invited to the Senior House to watch a Christmas performance of Moliere's play, *The Miser*, and also to attend a chamber concert of music by Bach and

Mozart. This was the only culture I ever encountered during the entire period of my time at the school, apart from two Saturday evenings when the House Master invited volunteers into his study, to sit at his feet as he read to us. On the first occasion, he read the horrifying Sherlock Holmes' story, *The Speckled Band*, and on the second, Charles Lamb's delightfully humorous account of how the Chinaman first discovered roast pork.

CHAPTER 9
A Tutor and his Obsession

"There is nothing makes a man suspect much, more than to know little."

Sir Francis Bacon, *Essay: Of Suspicion*

Woodbridge and its influence: a summary – The tutor's methods – His self-pity – The curriculum – His rages – I am falsely accused – I join the scouts – Communists in Muswell Hill – Why I avoid public conveniences – Unnecessary death of my maternal grandfather – The fear of socialist dispossession – I offer to forego my pocket money – The Labour government ensures the further enrichment rather the impoverishment of our family – Our new residence – How I broke with my brother

The news of my having to leave the school was brought to me personally by my father, who came down to Woodbridge to outline what he had arranged for my future education. At last he had been brought upon to agree that perhaps the school was a little too brutal for my sensibility, and although I had vividly described to my parents during the long Summer break all the horrors of the school, it took the House Master's letter to bring about the final rupture.

My father had come to the conclusion that for the time being I was unsuited to school life, and that my education should be completed by a private tutor. I was overjoyed at the idea! Furthermore, my father had actually found the "ideal" man who would accomplish this mission. His name was Mr. Partridge, who had had thirty years experience as an assistant Junior House Master at a famous Yorkshire Public boarding school. My father gently assured me, in a confidential tone of voice, that I would find him to be a man of great humanity, who understood the problems and "habits of small boys." Just what those "habits" were I was soon to learn in the weeks which followed.

*

In summary, what were the benefits of my life at Woodbridge? On the surface or immediately recognisable level, in identifying specific areas of knowledge gained or experience in skills acquired, they were almost nil. On the deeper or subconscious level, in character forming, there may have been some benefits but they are all of a questionable value. I believe that bullying and ritual torture is wholly harmful with no benefits to commend them. They may be of lesser harm to those of little sensibility and less intelligence, and even if they are justified as "toughening-up" by which is meant the instilment of courage, they are unnecessary, and more likely to instil a streak of cruelty into those involved. The millions who braved the artillery batteries in the First and Second World Wars, in charging forward with bayonets fixed, and sacrificed their lives, did not receive their training through Public school bullying or ritual torture. In the First World War it has been described as a case of lions being led by donkeys.

And neither is violent robbery, or surreptitious theft, or the breaking open of tuck boxes, an ideal preparation for entry into a law-abiding society. And neither would the school have said so - or would they,? see my reference to Sparta in the previous chapter. But what were the ideals of the school? To produce Christian gentlemen? Not only was every influence of the school anti-Christian but also anti-gentleman when that term is interpreted in its most favourable light. The Latin motto of the school, *Pro Deo Rege Patria* is excellent as it stands, but its free translation into, *For God, Monarch and Country*, conveys a different sense – quite apart from the fact that our Roman Republican forebears contemned the idea of monarchy. It is laudable we should support in both theory and practice, God, Monarch and Country, but linking them together in this way sends out a subliminal message of quite another kind.

It is too reminiscent of the motto heading the colourful discharge certificates given out to young conscripts of the Imperial German Army, *Für Gott, Kaiser, König und Vaterland* (For God, Emperor, King, and Fatherland), with its illustration of soldiers flat on their bellies, with bayonets fixed, pointing across the Rhine in the direction of France, their centuries' old enemy. That is, the words, *For God, Monarch and Country*, convey a tunnelled-vision subliminal message which is aggressive, fanatical, provincial, narrow-minded, brain-numbing, and simply stupid. It is a motto which in all respects is anti-educational, whilst remaining pro-Woodbridge Public school in all respects.

What kind of human beings could such a school hope to produce? Unimaginative, certainly, since creativity was disparaged and ridiculed as illustrated in Chapter 7. Self-control, of course, is regarded as a virtue, but when it is linked to an unfeeling attitude it then becomes questionable. Sensitivity is an essentially human quality – even an animal quality, since we would expect to find it in our dogs – but everything at Woodbridge was designed to suppress or erase sensitivity from the personality.

The school boasts it was amongst the first in the country to form a Cadet corps, and we can accept its educational methods are apt in training its boys to be "first over the top" in a battle situation, but the virtues of warfare do not comprise an all-rounded preparation for life – and certainly not for a peace time existence. In view of the duties of the modern British Army, in liaising with the UN or civilian populations, such as in Kosovo or Afghanistan, it is even doubtful that Woodbridge is capable of producing the right kind of soldiers or officers in meeting contemporary requirements.

Perhaps Woodbridge intended to produce the ideal Empire builder, but again, its success in that direction would have been very doubtful. The type of education instilled would tend to undermine rather than strengthen the Empire. The stupidity of a Woodbridge education would tend to encourage those qualities responsible for the Amritsar massacre. The ideal qualities for successful and long-lasting Empire building call for those of a Lord Macaulay rather than those of a Brigadier-General Reginald Dyer – two such men who stand at the opposite poles in building up British India within a hundred-year period.

What was the response of the school to the growth of Fascism in the inter-War period? It is recorded in the book, *When Duty Calls*, that "There was a growing awareness of political extremism and a fascination with events in Germany, the more sinister aspects of which were not yet recognised. The debating society, in a balloon debate, ejected Mae West in order to save Hitler; one teacher's scrapbook, held in our archives, contains enthusiastic cuttings of the Hitler Youth on camp. The general opinion was, 'whether we sympathised with Hitlerism or not, we had much to learn from it.' Indeed the observers at school stated that Nazism 'was largely a youth movement.'" [*] In fairness, it should be noted that the above should not be taken as particular to Woodbridge School. Many schools throughout the length and breadth of the country, and indeed, other institutions and individuals at the time, were sympathetic towards Hitler and Nazism, whilst also choosing to keep a safe distance from Sir Oswald Mosley's British Union of Fascists.

With regard to the influence of the school on my own personality, I was certainly hardened by the experience of the horrors I had witnessed there, and in later life, I was able to respond to scenes, such as public executions by stoning, with greater equanimity than most 20th century Europeans. After attending one such episode in Arabia, and describing it to a German fellow hotel guest, I remember him telling me he had actually been physically sick after seeing one such event, and that he could never endure to see a second. Our ancestors, of course, thought

---

[*] Carol & Michael Weaver, op. cit., pp.34-35.

little of attending public executions in England until they were ended in the middle of the 19th century, and some hundreds of years previously, our forebears were packed in their thousands to watch the horrors of a hanging, drawing, and quartering.

If Woodbridge, therefore, may have left a permanent de-sensitising mark on my character, this was to be amply compensated by the development of a strong rational sense. In facing problems, therefore, irrespective of whether they were personal or those of the world, I have rarely turned to my heart or conscience for an answer, but instead have resorted to reason as the ultimate guide to the truly ethical life. Hence I may need to recognise a debt of gratitude to Woodbridge School for the particular path of intellectual life I was to pursue in confronting the difficulties of existence. Psychologists maintain it is impossible to think and act throughout life without *feeling* as a primary motivation, but it should be remembered that if we do not *attempt* to transcend the limitations of our senses in putting a more objective light on events, then forgiveness is impossible and resentment will remain a corrosive evil in the soul.

I often wondered what became of those boys with whom I came into contact all those years ago. I am loathed to speculate on the possibilities. The most sadistic character of all, the Head boy, Davey, left the school in 1946 but nothing is known of his eventual fate or future whereabouts. It is recorded that he was the son of a William Davey, a NAAFI manager. I do know that Williams joined the RAF, and that Tuffield joined a foreign police force – because that is what was eventually entered into the Admissions book as the last entry alongside their names. Perhaps it is not entirely coincidental that my relative and fellow Woodbridgian, Roger Smith, also entered a foreign police force. Such forces would most probably have been situated in newly independent colonial territories, and almost invariably, routine torture would have been integral to their administrative policy. Police forces beyond the boundaries of civilised Western Europe have none of the law-abiding ideals cherished by the Geneva Convention or other international bodies with a benevolent purpose.

Even today there are a number of Islamic countries with Shariah law which as a matter of course arrest and torture suspects, before placing before them a confession document for signature written in a language they do not understand, without any attempt at an interrogation or even an accusation at any point during the proceedings. Western technology through the invention, manufacture, and sale of sophisticated electrical implements of torture which leave no marks on the body, have aided these procedures, as they have been promoted unscrupulously by those with a Woodbridgian-type background. In this way the worst aspects of our Public schools have contributed to the worst atrocities of the less developed countries of the world.

In researching the forgotten names of certain staff members I was obliged to consult the school's website, but this is disappointing, for it presents a sanitised smokescreen for all its "virtues;" but then through accident, I came upon a far more interesting site, the school's entry in Wikipedia. This included a list of notable ex-Woodbridgians, all of them obscure, apart from Edward du Cann, the Tory grandee who was my elder contemporary, and one other name which stands out as recognisable to the majority in Britain today. And that name is Nick Griffin, leader of the BNP, and a European member of parliament.

Whilst every person should be guaranteed the expression of free opinion – howsoever distasteful – for that is the condition of democracy, I would suggest that no obloquy or responsibility be cast on the shoulders of Nick Griffin for the human being into which he may have developed, bearing in mind that any cause or moral blame should be cast instead entirely upon the school which made him what he eventually became. For anyone who has read the previous two chapters no further explanation need be given in positing such a point of view. Nick Griffin must have joined Woodbridge a quarter of a century after my attendance there. Assuming that every school changes over a period of time, it may be concluded that Woodbridge changed little between 1944 and the 1960s and 70s. This supplies part of the answer to my speculative query as to what may have become of those Woodbridgians who were my peers in the 1940s.

Whilst I endured the ritual torture and other sufferings at Woodbridge School, at about the same time, across the North Sea in various parts of the Third Reich, many thousands were meanwhile being subjected to the dreadful deprivations, physical torments and death in concentration camps. But at least the prisoners in those camps had the consolation of one another's company in sustaining some kind of morale, whilst the "new bugs" and other juniors at Woodbridge school had none. Every boy stood alone and helpless, mocked and insulted by all with whom he came into contact.

Whilst it is unquestionable that the prefects at Woodbridge were no less sadistic than the Kapos who exerted their authority at Auschwitz-Birkenau – and I defy any reader to question this fact – in my view, the House Master, his sister, and the matron of the Junior school, were no less evil in their actions (and probably in their hearts) than the SS officers who managed that notorious concentration camp. And yet, whilst the SS guards and their commanders are still being hunted down for prosecution, until this day no one has sought to punish the teachers, and their ancillary personnel in our English public schools for their comparable criminality, and neither has any attempt been made to execrate their memory.

Before completing the above two chapters, I thought it would be obligatory, in ascertaining certain facts, and in ensuring the fairness of my account, to make one final visit to the school. For this purpose I made contact with Michael Weaver, Secretary of the Old Woodbridgians and the School Archivist, and visited the School in May 2010 after an absence of 65 years. Michael Weaver was not an Old Woodbridgian himself, but a retired history master who had worked for more than 30 years for the School, and I am indebted for his kindness, time, and help in researching through a mass of papers in checking on the information requested. Although in the 1940s much record keeping was lax, and many entries on forms were only partly completed, he was nonetheless able to supply some useful information; whilst his own publication, *Woodbridge School: Memories of the Twentieth Century*, which appeared in 2001, includes contributions from Old Boys which would seem to reflect the general character of the School as portrayed in the previous two chapters.

Physically, the School today is very different from my time in the first half of the last century. Gone is the wild woodland area, and nowhere is the grass left to grow to its natural height, as well-cut lawn areas and cultivated bushes and trees have transformed a wilderness into neatness and order. Many new buildings have been added to the fine Victorian Houses for either boarders or teaching around the original quad. Only the swimming bath remains exactly as it was 65 years ago, to which Mr. Weaver added the comment that pupils no longer have an interest in outdoor swimming, and that the derelict buildings might best be cleared for something better to replace them.

The School now takes in girls, and has many extra-curricular activities outside the School for every kind of cultural and sporting interest. "The School has changed more over the past five years than over the past three hundred," remarked Mr. Weaver, and I do not doubt the veracity of this. Change has been enforced through a mix of legislation and the transformation of society over the past 60 years. I remarked on the huge number of cars parked within the bounds of the school, saying that surely these could not all belong to staff members. "No, they belong to the pupils," replied Mr. Weaver. I was left with the impression that today's boys and girls at the school could not possibly imagine how the School would have been in the 1940s, or envisage what ghosts of the past might haunt the hallways, passages, grassy mounds or valley, bounded by the low grey wall around the estate.

*

After leaving boarding school I had recurring nightmares of my horrific experiences for months ahead. I also suffered abnormal timidity and shyness over the same period, having little desire to engage in social activity or meet new people. I chose the life of a recluse in my bedroom, reading and writing historical novellas. The fact that they were historical may have stemmed from my abhorrence with all aspects of the contemporary world, and hence the need to seek comfort from a mythical golden past. One afternoon I was asked to buy an evening paper from the local newsagent, for my parents were desperate for any excuse to get me out of the house into the fresh air.

On leaving the newsagents, a little urchin, half my age and size, stood on the pavement in ragged clothes, holding a whip made from a piece of string at the end of a stick. Timidity must have betrayed my countenance, for he grinned and cracked the whip on the pavement. In terror, I rushed across the street as fast as I could, and on reaching safety, I turned around and saw him laughing, and he had not budged an inch from where he stood. That must have been my lowest point. I cannot recollect a comparable incident of such timidity or cowardice.

That Christmas we spent with my grandparents at Sampford Place, and I was not to know at the time that that was to be the penultimate occasion I visited their home, and that apart from one or two brief visits within the next few years, it was to be three decades before I visited the Keens farm again. My grandmother was particularly indignant on hearing about the brutality of Woodbridge, for she hated any kind of violence, and one night whilst lying in bed in the Bamboo room, I overheard her remark to others, "It's enough to affect the child for life. Such schools shouldn't be allowed to exist." One night after awakening from a particularly bad nightmare, she climbed into my bed to comfort me.

Several weeks later, early in January 1946, I began my tuition with Mr. Partridge, hoping – and thinking at the time – that I would never need attend another school of any kind. He occupied a house, about 15 minutes walk away, at the other end of Muswell Hill Road, backing onto Highgate Wood. He shared the house with his mother and an elderly aunt, both of whom were disabled and never left the house. He was a short thick set man, slightly lame and so he walked with a stick, almost bald, but a layer of dandruff always lay on his scalp, and I wondered to myself why he never washed this off. He was also a deacon at St. Andrews, the high Anglican church in Alexandra Park Road, where eventually I was to be confirmed.

The pupil who preceded me for tutoring every morning was a precocious cheeky Rhodesian boy, about a year older than me, who had never been to a school in his life, and on arriving early, I sat awkwardly in the over-furnished living room with the two elderly ladies, trying to make intelligent conversation. They were conventional and conservative in temperament, and early on explained that every week they were visited by a pastor from their church who administered the Sacrament, as they were too old to leave the house, and on Sundays they had to content themselves with the religious services on the BBC. The only topics of conversation I felt competent to raise were those of history, and I remember asking them whom they thought was England's worst ruler, to which they both replied, "King John."

After the cheerful young Rhodesian bounded downstairs, after his two-hourly session in the cramped study at the top of the house, I was then ushered up the stairs of the dark staircase. I sat at a desk with my back to a gas fire turned low, which gave out little heat, whilst Mr. Partridge sat at my side or stood at the front of the desk. For the first few weeks he set me to work on a quite easy curriculum, and then gradually stepped up the standard until I was faced by more difficult tasks. It was then that his impatience set in, followed by rages, and false accusations according to his pseudo-psychological ideas as to whether or not I was playing him up.

In the middle of the morning, to keep us warm in a cold room, he would go downstairs to prepare what he humorously referred to as our mug of "asbestos," leaving me to resolve some difficult exercise, and some minutes later he would re-appear with Ovaltine and biscuits, and this was always the best part of the session. During these breaks he would often talk about himself, and the sufferings he had had to endure earlier in life. He explained that his limp was the result of a rugger accident many years ago, and that it had also affected his groin. He remained vague about the latter injury, but I was led to believe at the time that he perhaps had lost his testicles through Rugby – but later I became sceptical about such a conclusion. He kept me in a kind of mysterious suspense, but he always ended by saying, "You don't know how lucky you are to escape what I've had to endure."

On another occasion he told me about a car accident, and how a tobacco tin in his side coat pocket had saved his life, when the handle bars of a motorbike broke through the panel of the back door passengers' seat. "I've been through it, my boy, I've been through it," he exclaimed in trying to win over my admiration for his pluck, but I was left cold by these sordid descriptions of painful injuries – and I was certainly not moved towards admiration or even sympathy. I had already heard and experienced enough of pain and injury at Woodbridge, and I was in no mood to hear more.

His most dramatic picture of past injuries arose from another rugger accident when his head was kicked in. "You can't imagine what I went through at the hospital," he began to explain. He described how they operated on his brain, and had to remove the top of his head without the use of anaesthetics. This succeeded in arousing my curiosity somewhat. "Then you must have screamed," I suggested. He said he was put into a padded sound-proofed room for the operation where patients were allowed to scream as loud as they liked, but not even these horrors aroused my sympathy. There was a moral to these stories, however, which I recognised at once, and that was to refrain from playing rugger or placing oneself in dangerous situations. How could a man be so stupid as to lose his testicles in one game of Rugby, and then have his brains kicked out in another?

The curriculum of subjects taught tended to be narrow and tiresome. Mathematics was naturally the most important as I loathed it the most; then came Latin, in which I had little interest at that time, and then English and History in which I excelled; and finally, Geography in which his knowledge was shaky. French was not on the curriculum, possibly because it was beyond his ken. I was always candid, and not afraid of confronting him with insolence if I knew I was in the right. This occurred on one occasion in regard to geography, when he wrote out a list of the European countries and their capitals, which I had to learn by heart, but I was quick to note he was muddled by Sweden and Norway in transposing the capitals of each. I detected the error as soon as I glanced at the atlas at home, and the following morning I pointed out the mistake he had made. His immediate response was to say I was "insolent," and he continued to insist that Oslo was the Capital of Sweden, and Stockholm the capital of Norway. At this, I pulled the atlas out of my satchel and put the map of Europe in front of him. "Oh, we all make mistakes in *writing* sometimes," he replied, and dismissed the matter at that.

When it came to essay writing, he said, "At least you write sense, which is a far cry from what I get from the others." On one occasion I brought a book along which I was writing at home, and this included my own illustrations. In response to one illustration, he remarked, "What vulgar legs you've drawn," by which he meant shapely or with sex appeal. It had not been my intention to draw in that way, but only to reproduce what was anatomically accurate. When it came to history, he was uninspiring, and we started with the reign of Charles II, and I had to learn about Habeas Corpus, and the fall of Clarendon, and the Cabal, but nothing about Titus Oates and the Popish plot. I asked him why he had started me on this period of English history.

He thought for a moment and then replied it was the most important period, as the monarchy was restored after a dark period, and the Church of England produced the Book of Common Prayer during the reign of the Merry Monarch. When I questioned him on the value of Latin, he replied, "An educated person can get by with Latin in any part of the world with any other educated person," and then he added as an afterthought, "Besides, the prime object of Latin is as a mental discipline." I felt the latter explanation more truly hit the mark as far as Mr. Partridge was concerned, for learning the declensions of verbs by heart was his obsession in teaching the subject. Biology was not included on the curriculum, possibly because he knew little about science, whilst religion was excluded as I already had enough of that at home.

As the months passed by his impatience, rages, and false accusations became ever more frequent. If I slipped up with a Latin declension, or failed to solve a mathematical problem, he would be thrown into one of his tantrums. "Go on, go on – you can do it," he would say excitedly, working himself into neurotic tension, and staring me in the face with his beady eyes. On still failing to come up with the right answer, he would begin to stamp and fume, and bang his fist on the desk, sometimes exclaiming, "Now in a moment, my lad, you're going to make me do something really dangerous – so dangerous you'll regret it. I know you're playing me up – but I can see through you, you know."

The breaking point would come when he subjected me to his own system of ordeal, in determining truth or falsehood. "Stand up!" he would order. "Now come to the front of the desk, and stand before me." I would obey his instructions. "Now put your hands down by your side, and look straight into my eyes. Keep still, and don't shift your eyes from mine," he commanded. He then raised his fore finger and slowly began moving it between the end of his nose and mine, all the time maintaining an intensely hardened expression as he fixed me with his gaze and beaky nose. After half a minute or so of this pantomime, the side of his mouth began to twitch – apparently involuntarily – and it presented such a comical appearance, it was impossible not to burst out into laughter.

This was all he needed to prove my guilt. He would burst into a tantrum, crying, "I knew it – I knew it all along. You're just playing me up. Don't attempt to deny it." As these tests never achieved positive results, it is surprising he persisted in them, or believed in their validity.

One day he asked me, "What do small boys do in their beds at night?" – "Sleep," I answered innocently. "And what else do they do?" – "Sometimes they read a book," I replied bewildered as to what might be the next question. "And what else do they do? What do they do when they get under the bedclothes at night?" He added with a wry smile. "Now don't try to tell me you don't know, because I know you know. I haven't worked with small boys for thirty years without learning something about their nocturnal habits. And let me tell you, that I know you do what other small boys do," he concluded with a significant smile.

"But I don't do it, Sir," I replied, for the truth was that at that period of my life, I was not guilty of self-abuse. It was true I indulged in

it at a much younger age, and I certainly indulged in it several years later
with the advance of puberty, but I was not guilty of the habit during any
period when tutored by Mr. Partridge. "Ah, so now you understand me
quite clearly," he said enlightened. "Now I know you do it. I always
know when small boys do it." – "But I don't do it, Sir, and you can't
prove it," I exclaimed resentfully. "There's a secret method of knowing,"
said the tutor with confidence. "You can always tell. When you've
worked with boys for thirty years, as I have, you learn a lot. – The eyes
betray it," he added under his breath in carelessly revealing the secret
method.

On returning home that morning, I looked into a mirror, but to me,
my eyes appeared no different from any other morning. These
accusations of self-abuse were intermittent, and sometimes he would tell
me, "now you've started it again – I know you have. For the past few
weeks you've been a good boy in your bed, and now you've started to be
bad again." These baseless accusations were usually attended with gentle
warnings to heed the dangers to my physical health. "It's very bad for
you," he would say in a concerned tone. "It impairs the brain and softens
the tissues in all parts of the body. If you refrained from the habit, you'd
find mathematics and Latin grammar much easier to master."

He also subjected me to other false accusations, accusing me one
morning of having cut him dead in the street the previous afternoon.
"You saw me – you know you did – you passed me by inches. But you
chose to ignore me," he persisted resentfully.

He also took on the role of being my moral guardian, accusing me
on one occasion of being with a "girl," a thing that shocked him
profoundly, as he thought that the female influence was wholly
corrupting to a boy's future. When I told him the girl was only my
cousin, he remained suspicious, remarking under his breath that he hoped
I wasn't "falling under bad influences." The girl was Anne Brown and as
all three Brown children were shortly to be tutored by Mr. Partridge, their
parents' having heard good accounts of him from my father, the
accusations of the private tutor were soon made to seem ridiculous when
he realised I had told him the truth. The Brown children liked him no
better than I did, and I remember when Anne followed on from a session
which I had, and as all three of us were in his study, as I was preparing to
leave, she put her tongue out at him behind his back.

After several months I showed Mr. Partridge a romantic novel I
had written, and we went through its pages together, correcting
grammatical and spelling errors. "You seem to know a lot about women
for someone of your age," he remarked afterwards.

One day whilst going to his house, I picked up a popular
psychology magazine from off the pavement, as I was attracted by its

leading article displayed on the front, entitled, *The Battle of Married Life*, but when I showed it to Mr. Partridge, he was taken aback, saying that such periodicals were "dangerous to the mind." He gently persuaded me to surrender it, and after seeking my permission, he tore it into pieces and dropped it into the wastepaper basket. One of the illustrations in my Latin primer was taken from an old Roman painting, and showed a naked boy being laid across the shoulders of another whilst he was birched by a master. On casually opening the book one morning to reveal this picture, Mr. Partridge turned to me with a lurid smile, saying, "Sometimes I'd like to see that done to you."

As I was not attending school my parents said I should nonetheless attempt to mix with people of my age, and I was persuaded to join the local Church Scout group. These took place every week in a church hall in Fortis Green Road, and whilst I was proud to wear the uniform and carry a long staff, I was uninspired by the monotonous activities of learning ever new knots, listening to talks on the ideals and good deeds of the movement, and the chasing after all kinds of badges in raising our personal status. All the activities were inside, and there was no scope for outside adventures or camping of which I had heard so much.

The members of the group came from all backgrounds, and there was one boy from a working class environment with a huge chip on his shoulder about class differences. I tried to ignore him, but he used every opportunity to abuse me verbally, and although he knew nothing about my background, he accused me of coming from a home where all rooms had carpets and where coal fires burned all day. He also made much of the fact that he had had to pay for his own uniform through working on a paper round and saving pennies by the week, whilst I obviously had had mine bought for me by my parents. After a particularly boring evening, as we left the church hall, he struck me from behind with his staff. An angry fight immediately ensued in the street, and we both drew blood from each other with our sticks.

A passing couple, possibly a mother and daughter, told us to stop fighting at once, and we laid down our staffs. The elder woman then asked, what was the matter and that we should both behave ourselves, but when I responded by justifying myself, by saying, "He started it,!" the women laughed and passed on. This was a lesson I learned on the question of justice and power politics. I already had a strong sense of justice, and appreciated the need for morality, but on that day I learned that very few are prepared to stop and weigh issues as to right or wrong, for such considerations are too heavy a burden on their intellect. Most people are ready to use their intuition in decision-making, but that only makes for short-term solutions, but few are prepared for the hard thinking necessary in achieving justice for the longer term. Those two women, I thought, were a metaphor for all the ills of society, and especially in undermining the purpose of democracy in achieving equity and fairness.

At this time I saw several Communist demonstrations and marches in Muswell Hill – albeit small numbers of people – always a poorly dressed crowd with resentment and hatred on their faces. I especially remember a big pregnant woman, with a scarf and two or three children, pushing along a pram, who always attended these demonstrations, and seemed to symbolise a nice combination of ignorance, arrogance, stupidity, and hopelessness. Miss Wall, who had recently moved into a flat in Church Crescent, immediately behind where we lived, confided (as if she had unearthed a secret conspiracy) that the house next door to her was full of Communists. I visited Miss Wall on several occasions to clear her back garden of overgrown weeds and bushes, and it was apparent that the next door Communists were down-at-heel middle class intellectual types.

Although I have never supported the principle of nationalisation except in special circumstances, I must applaud the State-run British Restaurants which flourished in the immediate post-War period. In the parade of shops, adjacent to the Odeon cinema, at the start of Muswell Hill Road, just two minutes walk from our home, was situated a large British Restaurant which I frequently patronised. They always served substantial meals, and I remember with fondness their shepherd's pie, and most of all, their fish pie, served with plenty of parsley sauce. This was the State expressing its power in the most benevolent form in satisfying the stomachs of the British people. I still feel that the closure of the British Restaurants was an unfortunate political decision for it guaranteed that the poorest in the community were always within reach of being fed a healthy diet.

My only outdoor activities in London at this time were to walk in the nearby woods, or visiting Paddington station in collecting the names of locomotives, and enviously watching those lucky travellers destined for the West country. When Mr. Partridge came to know of this, he objected strongly, saying that travelling alone in London was dangerous – especially for a small boy – and he told me the story of how he was robbed in Selfridges. He had been pushed into an alcove, and his wallet was snatched, and when he raised his stick in anger, the thug replied, "If you hit me with that, I'll kill you," and so the tutor was robbed. "But now I have a secret pocket," he concluded, and he opened his jacket and showed me the special lining that the tailor had fitted.

One day I noticed he was wearing a black tie, and when I asked the reason for this, he explained he had just come from the funeral of a former pupil, and "a really good Christian." Some months earlier this pupil had been involved in an industrial accident: whilst swinging a rod backwards and forwards in a furnace room, when the implement had caught him between the legs and he was instantly castrated. The doctor gave him three months to live, foretelling the exact day of his death. The tutor visited him daily before the final hour, and described the high spirits in which he always found his ex-pupil, and the joy in which he anticipated life in the world to come. Mr. Partridge thought this stoicism remarkable in view of the excruciating pain his ex-pupil had endured.

But this story was used as an excuse in turning to my own situation. "Your father tells me you make a great fuss when he canes you," he said. I felt embarrassed and ashamed that my father had ever discussed the matter. "You know, you don't know what suffering is, my lad," and he embarked once again on the operations on his head. He explained he was allergic to gas as it made him retch, and so ice-packs had to be used instead, and after being strapped down into a chair and held into position by five or six muscular male nurses, the surgeon began cutting into his skull with a saw before removing parts of his brain. But one benefit accrued from his sufferings: he could forecast the weather – or at least, rain, snow and thunder. To me this seemed a poor compensation.

Much has been written in this chapter which may be seen as critical of Mr. Partridge, but he was probably a pitiful and lonely old cripple, lacking appropriate social contacts with his own generation, and mitigating circumstances may hence be pleaded on his behalf in view of burdensome responsibilities exceeding his natural capacity. He had to shop, cook, and care for two elderly housebound relatives, maintain and clean a house with awkward and steep staircases, and in addition, earn a living to cover expenses for three persons.

As with many teachers, he spent far too many hours in the day confined to the annoying company of children, with whom he had no alternative but to occasionally vent his varied pent-up emotions as the only course in retaining his sanity. If, therefore, I was afflicted with having to endure horrific accounts of his medical conditions, past and present, together with the fears and complexes he was to transmit to his innocent charges, at least a reason, if not a justifiable excuse, was evident.

It was probably Mr. Partridge and my father together who inadvertently turned me away from any inclination to take up medicine or surgery as a profession. At home I often heard screams from downstairs as younger patients had to be dragged physically by their parents and my father's nurse, yelling and struggling, from the waiting room to the surgery. On one occasion agonised screams pierced the house for almost half a morning, and at lunchtime, my father explained that a little girl had

had several teeth removed, but that the parents had refused consent to the use of gas as it was "against their religious principles."

This was during the days before local anaesthetics were commonly used, and my father was the only surgeon in the neighbourhood prepared to undertake operations in such circumstances in satisfying the needs of religious bigots. He upbraided the "cruelty" of conservative-minded parents who had no faith or belief in modern science. On other occasions he attended to patients from the nearby Colney Hatch lunatic asylum, whom no other dentist was prepared to treat, and he described how they lashed out with their fists, and could only be treated for any kind of dental ailments after being rendered unconscious.

It was about this period that an incident occurred which left me with a lifelong anxiety until the present day. One afternoon I was with my cousin, Michael, both of us in our school uniforms, wandering around Muswell Hill, when we wanted to relieve ourselves. We therefore went to the Gents on the bus roundabout in Muswell Hill Broadway. On ascending the steps to leave the toilets, we were confronted by an old man with a white goatee beard, boater, white jacket, and carrying a walking stick.

"What are you two boys doing here,?" he demanded gruffly. Like two well brought-up Public schoolboys, we politely and promptly replied, "Being excused, Sir," – this being a synonym for visiting the toilet. – "Haven't I seen you boys here before this afternoon?" exclaimed the old man irately. – "No, Sir," we replied. – "Oh yes I have," said the old man, his cheeks reddening with anger, as he tapped his stick on the ground. – "We've just come from Barnet," explained my cousin. – "You've been hanging around this place. I saw you half an hour ago. If I catch either of you two boys around these toilets again, I'll call the police. They're on the look-out for boys of your kind," and he descended into the Gents, whilst Michael and I shame-facedly made our retreat, although we had done nothing wrong.

This story illustrates the instilment of guilt, not only when no wrong-doing has been committed, but even when the accused retain a clean conscience of not having committed any wrong-doing. It also illustrates the nonsense of appealing to conscience as a criterion in assessing right or wrong, and the gross injustice inflicted by schoolmasters and others in punishing the compliant, the timid and shame-faced, as soon as they are upbraided for alleged misdemeanours, when the expression of fear alone is taken as the proof of guilt.

Consequently, I have always avoided the use of Public Conveniences – or at least urinals – through the irrational fear of being confronted falsely for some kind of inexplicable wrong-doing. Nowadays public toilets are few and far between, but if I am caught short whilst away from home, I always make for the nearest pub, restaurant, or hotel, without any compunction or sense of guilt. I must add, however, that this irrational fear only exists within the boundaries of the United Kingdom. As soon as I reach the Continent I am free of any such complexes.

On 7th February 1946 my maternal grandfather died at the age of 78 due to an incompetently performed operation for a critical although routine illness. Early in the morning he was taken ill with prostate trouble, and because of an emergency situation, he was taken away in an ambulance. On passing the newsagents, he insisted on stopping the vehicle, so that *The Times* could be fetched for him, as reading the paper was his priority at the beginning of the day. My parents went to the funeral, whilst we children remained in London, but whilst in Melksham, my father took the opportunity of investigating as to why such a simple operation had gone awry, for my grandfather was otherwise a fit and strong man, of whom it was said he should have lived to be a hundred.

It happened that the operation was carried out without draining his bladder and this led to inevitable complications. It was decided by my parents that the cause of my grandfather's unnecessary death should be kept secret from his widow. I have since wondered as to whether he might have made a fuss about the need to drain his bladder, which is an unpleasant and not an un-painful procedure carried out without an anaesthetic, and in view of the natural authority he seemed to wield, as to whether he persuaded the medical staff to waive the normal precautions. If this was the case, then the medical staff were entirely to blame for his death, both on the grounds of weakness in failing to stand up to my grandfather as well as incompetence in performing the operation.

The local paper produced a glowing obituary, saying he "had been a pioneer for the cause of the British Legion," and, "his death on Thursday will mean a great loss to the Legion, both in the Melksham branch and the whole county. He was one of the outstanding personalities of Melksham, and had always devoted part of his time to the social interests of the town, where he had lived for 20 years. He was Vice-Chairman of the Melksham branch of the British Legion and treasurer for the county. During the First World War he had served on HMS Glory, and retired in 1919 with the rank of Engineer Captain. Until recently he had been for some time Secretary to the Soldiers', Sailors' and Airmen's Families Association."

As the year progressed my father and grandparents became increasingly pessimistic about the future of the country in view of what the Labour government intended to do in the years ahead. My grandfather said the consequences would be Soviet-style government with the abolition of property and all the rights to freedom which 300 years of struggle for democracy had succeeded in achieving. My father became increasingly depressed by his parent's predictions, for although both were Conservative in a reactionary sort of way it was my grandfather who was more coherent in expressing his political although fallacious ideas, whilst the younger man followed in the footsteps of the elder. I remember exclaiming during a particularly alarming discussion in Ashmount, "Well, if we're all going to lose our property and live in poverty, why doesn't someone shoot the Prime Minister?" – "We can't do that because this is a democracy," replied my grandfather with resignation.

One day whilst my father was pottering around the garden, moping about all the financial constraints which would affect us all, he indicated we might have to sell the house. This was an appalling piece of news! My father explained that the socialists wanted to get rid of the medical profession by turning doctors and dentists into civil servants who would be paid by the State. That's how things were in Russia. It would be difficult to carry on as a dental surgeon whilst meeting all the heavy expenses. At this, I immediately offered to give up my pocket money of ninepence a week. My father responded generously by saying I could continue receiving my pocket money, as the crisis would only occur a year or two ahead. I was left worried by these thoughts and the prospects of financial insecurity.

Poverty was not to be our fate in the years which followed, for quite the contrary occurred, but despite our changing circumstances for the better, there were constant efforts to hold back expenditure. The turns of the stock market overrode all other considerations when it came to financial matters, and so when stocks tumbled, everything was interpreted in a bad light, and there was insufficient wherewithal for all kinds of extras. The anxieties of these times was to ensure I would always be careful in money matters – but care is not necessarily the same as financial wisdom, for the latter is something more than mere financial prudence. Care means retention or saving, but the creation or clever use of money calls for a more pro-active approach. As a pre-pubescent boy I still had sufficient naivety to ask my father point blank how much money he had. Of course he never gave a straight answer, but when I suggested specific sums and asked for "yes" or "no" answers, he indicated he had a sum exceeding a million. Several years later, a member of the Brown family (an aunt of my cousins) mentioned to me that my father was a man of "considerable wealth," and since she was probably in-the-know, it may have been true he was a millionaire by that time.

He certainly had a successful practice, and always had patients who were well-known in the public sphere, although he did not always appreciate their patronage. There was the American, Mary Martin, who starred in *South Pacific* in Drury Lane, but he was disappointed when she failed to deliver promised tickets for the show. And then there was, Sir

Leonard Gammons, the local MP from 1941 until his death in 1957, of whom he complained was always hogging the phone with "urgent" telephone calls whenever he visited the surgery for dental treatment. Ronald Shiner, the comedian and film star was another patient, as was the family of the radio comedian Ted Ray.

In the middle of 1946 my father bought another house for use as our main residence. This was 105 Muswell Hill Road, almost opposite the dental practice, and occupying a site adjacent to the car park at the back of the Odeon cinema. This property had belonged to an elderly Dr. Mannington, who died earlier in the year. It was a magnificent late Victorian house, with large rooms and high ceilings. There was a portico leading into a hallway, and on the left a door led into what became the playroom. On big family occasions it also became a dining room. To the right of the hallway was a smaller room, which was a breakfast room, and many years later, after the house was divided into three self-contained flats, it became my bedroom.

Straight ahead to the left was the lounge, with French windows leading onto a flight of steps down into the back garden. In this room we had coal fires. To the right of the lounge was a very large kitchen which also served as our dining room, and beyond that were some steps leading down into a scullery. To the left at the far end of the kitchen was a door leading into a pantry and another door into the lounge. From the scullery were a flight of outside steps leading down into a passageway, which on the left led into the garden, and on the right to the back of the garage and a door leading out at the side of the house. The garden was at least a third larger than that at 196. There was a substantial cellar with coke and coal bunkers, and a tool room; and a broad staircase led from the hall to the first floor. Here there were four spacious bedrooms, one with an en suite, plus a bathroom and an airing cupboard. Another two flights of stairs led to the top floor where there were another four bedrooms and a kitchenette.

My first bedroom was on the first floor at the back, then after some years I occupied a room at the top of the house at the front, and finally, after the conversion of the house, to the ground floor room referred to above. These moves were decided by periods when we chose to have lodgers or not on the top floor. The nursery, occupied by my youngest brother, Oliver, was on the first floor, where the ceiling promptly collapsed, and so his cot was afterwards covered with a sheet of plywood. The house was cold, for of course there was no central heating, and we relied on gas fires in the upstairs rooms. It was good to have a room of my own which I was free to decorate in my own way, and this I did with my own artwork, comprising portraits copied or traced from the *Illustrated War News,* of leading First World War generals and admirals, or else portraits of great English writers copied from Arthur Mee's *Encyclopaedia*. These portraits were stuck onto large black rolls of paper (intended as blackout paper during the War years) before being fixed onto the wall.

*

Not long after moving into 105 Muswell Hill Road, when I was 10 years of age and my brother was 7, there occurred a serious break in our relationship which lasted until well into my teenage years. When we played together, I was always the dominant party, i.e., I laid down the rules or gave orders, and I expected him to obey, and so I suppose this amounted to the verge of bullying. One day as we were assembling Uncle Harold's magnificent clockwork Hornby train set, which by now had been equally divided between our family and the Browns, he suddenly protested against my instructions, shouting defiantly, and stamping his foot on the floor, in insisting he was no longer going to be ordered around.

At that moment, as we stood glaring opposite one another in the playroom, I realised that my authority had been broken, and that therefore he was no longer a fit play fellow with whom I could associate. From that time forward, I made every endeavour to play alone and avoid his company, for I realised that the disparity between our ages meant there was little opportunity for cooperation between us. I sensed that the degree and strength of his protest was final and came from the depth of his heart. There could be no return by either of us to an earlier stage in our relationship.

Whilst this historic event may have initiated that rebellious streak in his character against the imposed conditions of life; for me it may have marked the beginning of a new inner loneliness and introspection. In any event, from that day forward, we developed our own separate interests and ways of thinking, and mutual avoidance was the best course in maintaining peace and avoiding a quarrel. For the second time in my life, I decided that this was a person whom I should dislike – although not to the same degree as I disliked my father, for the latter was the greater cause of pain and a far greater threat. However, this second dislike only represented a temporary break of several years, as other factors were soon to play which brought us towards a common alliance.

When we visited relatives, such as my grandparents or the Browns, my father had a comical way of announcing our arrival by sticking his pipe through the letter box, and making a squeaking noise. On one occasion when arriving at the Browns, we found that my cousins, together with several other friends, were playing with air pistols. This was too much for my father, who was averse to dangers of this kind, and to the disappointment of us children, he insisted on immediately driving home again.

It was at this time that my paternal grandmother complained about my ears sticking out, and that as this was taken as a sign of a child who had been bullied, something should be done about it. It was debated as to whether I should undergo an operation, or merely have my ears stuck back with sticking plaster until they remained naturally in that position. It was finally decided that my ears should be left as they were as being part of my normal anatomy.

At different times a varied assortment of lodgers occupied the top floor at 105. At first we had an academic and his wife who had just returned from India, and my mother suspected he was possibly of mixed race because of his well-tanned skin. Then we had an American married couple who were very friendly, and the woman was a strange curiosity because of the unusual facial expressions and turns of phrase of the American race. During the Coronation year we decided to take in lodgers from South Africa, charging them the exorbitant rent of £5 a week and a correspondence followed with regard to prospective visitors from that country. We anticipated the possibility of accommodating black people, and this excited our expectations, for we had never met or even seen any natives from the African continent, but in the end, no one decided to take up the offer, as the house was situated too far from the centre of London.

We then had a young married couple from the Orkneys, who quarrelled violently amongst themselves, and had aspirations towards a better status in life. Early one evening, the young man came into the lounge and alerted us to the fact that he was expecting the "delivery of some encyclopaedias," and would we be so kind as to take them in. Of course we agreed but my mother ridiculed the couple because of their pretentiousness, saying she did not believe that any such encyclopaedias would arrive at the house, and indeed she was correct in her prediction. She held them in disdain as working class people who were making every effort – but failing in the attempt – to project themselves as middle class, to which they had no proper qualities or right of entry.

CHAPTER 10
Back to Public School

"The whining schoolboy, with his satchel
And shining morning face, creeping like snail
Unwillingly to school!"

Shakespeare, *As You Like It*, Act II, Sc. 7, 147.

My examination for Highgate – Jew-baiting at school – Causes of this – My affinity with the Jews – Inspirational teaching of History, English and Latin – An art work is condemned

After a term with Mr. Partridge it was decided I should be sent back to school again, so I could mix with boys of my own age. I did not much fancy the idea, in view of past experiences at school, but it transpired I was never to be bullied again. In the future I was to inflict bullying rather than receive it, for I had gained a greater self-confidence in the intervening months since leaving Woodbridge. I was put forward as a candidate for entry to the Junior School of Highgate. I sat an entrance examination consisting of mathematics, English, and a general intelligence test, and an oral interview, and I was 10 years old at the time.

Having completed all the papers on the day of the examination, I was taken to one of the masters in a small room for a personal interview. This was with Mr. E.A.D. Hamilton, a short bespectacled little man with a thick red moustache and a rather strong smelling breath. "Corfe! I've heard that name before," he said reflectively. "Have any of your relatives been to this school?" – "Yes, Sir," I replied, and gave the names of my father and his two brothers. "Ah, Harold Corfe, a marvellous boy. I remember him well," exclaimed Mr. Hamilton, his eyes lighting up behind his spectacles. "One of the finest pupils I ever taught! How is he nowadays?" I explained he had been in the Tank Corps, and was now in the City, training as a stockbroker. "He was a born success! A wonderful boy. He'll go a long way in life," said the master with enthusiasm. "How fine it will be to have another Corfe in the school," he added piercing me with his eyes. "Now let's get down to the test. Can you give me the names of six different cars?"

I gave the name of my father's car, which was an Austin 16, and I thought strenuously, but could not think of a single other make. I had no interest in cars. "Oh well, it doesn't really matter," said Mr. Hamilton reassuringly. "Now, can you give me the names of six different industrial cities in the Midlands and the North?" I thought with effort but was unable to identify a single city. I had no interest in the North, and at that time, even less interest in industry. Had he asked me to name six different towns and cities in the West country, I should have had no difficulty in answering. "Don't worry," he reassured. "Now here's an easy question: give me the names of six leading football teams," he said with confidence in receiving a satisfactory reply. I had no interest in football and neither was I ever to develop an interest in the sport.

Sometime later, when I was to hear the name of Arsenal, I decided to describe myself as an Arsenal supporter (as it was a North London team), and from that day to this, I have always boasted about the successes of Arsenal without knowing anything whatsoever about their listing in the league. I also came to know the name of Stanley Matthews – but of no other footballer until the arrival of David Beckham many decades later – and whenever I found myself amongst a group of soccer bores, I would always exclaim, "You can say what you like, but there's no one today who's a patch on Stanley Matthews. You should have seen him at the height of his career!" This clever piece of hoodwinking was sure to arouse a lively discussion which was of interest to everyone except to the person who had initiated it.

When I drew a blank on the third occasion, Mr. Hamilton excused my ignorance with, "Well, it's not very important, what really matters is that you enjoy *playing* sports. I trust you do?" he asked. "Yes, Sir," I lied, for at that time I loathed engaging in any sport. "Very good! I'm sure you'll make out very well at our school once you're settled in. That's all for the present – and give my regards to your uncle." – "Yes, Sir. Thank you, Sir," I replied, and hurriedly left the stuffy room, relieved to be free from having to answer stupid questions.

Some weeks later, over the breakfast table at home, my father awkwardly and rather disagreeably explained he had just received a letter from the school. "You've failed all the exams," he began slowly, "but, however, as two of your uncles and I attended the school, they've decided to allow you in. It means you'll have to work hard in the future if you're going to complete your education at the school." It seems, therefore, that I was accepted into the school on the strength of my Uncle Harold, whom my mother had first known as "a selfish, moody, and rather charmless teenager."

On joining my second Public school as a day boy, I was placed in the highest class of Ingleholme, these comprising the Reception classes of the Junior school. This was a school where the teachers often took a like or dislike to boys for no particular reason – or none that I could conjecture – and at different times I was liked and disliked by different masters for reasons that had nothing to do with my behaviour, efforts, or academic progress. I found myself in a class of 18 under the watchful and benevolent eye of Mr. Hamilton, who was going to mould me into the perfect Public schoolboy, with the name of my Uncle Harold never far from his lips.

On the first day at school, and before the lessons had begun, Mr. Hamilton called out two boys to the front of the class, and as they stood side by side, he reprimanded them in the strongest terms not to fight together or make a nuisance of themselves. One of them was a pallid blond boy, R.G.C. Osbourn, whom Mr. Hamilton especially loathed, and who soon became my friend, and the other was a dark haired boy with a foreign sounding name. Although I was not to know it on the day, this reprimand was concerned with Jew-baiting, and I was soon to find that Jew-baiting and bullying was an obsessive occupation throughout all year groups at the Junior school. The school staff were fully aware of this, but whilst on the one hand the terms "anti-Semitism" or "Jew" were never used by teachers (perhaps wisely), on the other hand, the Jews themselves sought to adopt a low profile, never calling attention to the fact of their victimisation.

"Now, I want no trouble from either of you this term," concluded Mr. Hamilton. "If either of you begins a fight or hits the other, the offender will be caned. Is that clear? And that goes for the rest of the class. If anyone begins fighting So-and-so," naming the boy with the foreign sounding name, " – I don't care who it is, he'll get a caning." All this was incomprehensible to me, since it was my first day at school, and I did not know what had occurred the previous term. What was the cause of this anti-Semitism? In retrospect, my own view is that it stemmed from the political situation in Palestine, i.e., the clash between Jews and Arabs, and the efforts of the British authorities to keep the peace, and the blame and hatred which rebounded on Britain from both sides because of this. But the political situation was never mentioned by the 7 to 12 year olds who belonged to the Junior school, and so their anti-Semitism must have been generated through misunderstood comments of their newspaper reading parents across the breakfast table.

I, and doubtless others amongst my peers, had romantic notions about the Arabs. I possessed a set of German manufactured lead Arab horsemen with movable arms carrying scimitars, in addition to a magnificent lead set of German made Crusaders, some with black crosses on their shields, and others with red crosses, as well as 15th century foot soldiers – all beautifully crafted before the First World War. Furthermore, the gallant exploits of Lawrence of Arabia were still fresh in the memory of the younger generation, whilst the Hollywood films of Rudolph Valentino were to give the impression that the Arabs were the most romantic, outgoing, and adventurous race on earth, and that Arabia was awash with wine, freedom, and laughter. Such a deceptive impression, of course, was most strongly conveyed through the colourful

Tales of The Arabian Nights, which in origin were not Arabian but Persian. The fact that the Arabs and Arabia were in reality endowed with characteristics completely opposite to those cited above were unknown to ignorant schoolboys at the time. We lived in a world of delusion.

When, therefore, Osbourn approached me, as he did others in our year group, with the accusation against the Jews that they didn't "believe in Jesus," I was truly shocked. This was followed up with the contention that God wanted us to "beat up the Jews." The Jews could easily be identified as those boys who were excluded from morning assembly – even though there were Jews who sought to hide the fact, by creeping into assembly all the same. Boys who failed to attend assembly were therefore immediately marked as suspect, and during breaks were confronted by a group to explain themselves.

It seemed to me at the time – as it still seems today – that Mr. Hamilton was especially brutal to Osbourn, picking on him arbitrarily without justification – or none which was specified. On one occasion he called Osbourn out to the front of the class, gently laid his hand on top of his head, and then with a sudden tug, pulled out a handful of his hair. "This is yours, I believe," said Mr. Hamilton handing the lock of blond hair back to the pupil. "Now go back to your seat and be quiet." Some days later Osbourn's father, a naval lieutenant, visited the school and walked into the classroom in his uniform, to enquire about the problems of his "erring" son. One might have anticipated a row between the parent and schoolmaster, but the older man had control over the situation and there was a calm exchange of words before the lieutenant departed from the building.

Because of my legendary uncle, I immediately became the teacher's favourite in our class, and never experienced a harsh or impatient word whilst under Mr. Hamilton's wing. He was full of advice and gentle instruction in best attending to my education and future. I remember on one occasion when called upon to speak, he exhorted me never to gesticulate or move my hands as I spoke, as that was "not English." When walking to school in the morning, we often met on the footpath, and sometimes he lay his arm across my shoulder (which gave me an unpleasant shiver down the spine) as he lauded the virtues of Public school life.

"You know, Corfe, in later life you'll come to realise your Public school days were the happiest in your life," he once exclaimed – but the realisation was never experienced. "They're the years of our greatest fulfilment and success. Every man comes to look back on his Public school days with a longing for their return – so make the most of them." – "Yes, Sir," I only replied. – "Those great days on the playing fields in the first eleven; the fair play and sportsmanship of the school, and the opportunity for moral leadership as a prefect," he continued in a sentimental tone." – "Yes, Sir," I repeated coldly. – "Have you read, *Tom Brown's Schooldays?*" – "No, Sir." – "Then get it. It's one of the great classics of the world," he said with conviction.

He would often keep me at school for up to an hour after hours, not as a punishment or formal detention, but to give me an opportunity to improve my mathematics. This pleasure at having another "Corfe" in the school seemed to go unnoticed by my classmates, probably because he gave equal individual attention to other boys under his direction, even if it tended to reflect a harsher attitude. At this time, during breaks and after school hours, the boys of Ingleholme participated in helping to lay a concrete path and playground, breaking up bricks for the foundations, mixing cement, and pushing wheelbarrows loaded with concrete and laying it on the ground. When the work was finally completed, Mr. Hamilton publicly congratulated me, saying that I had been the most enthusiastic and hardworking boy engaged on the task. If this was so, it was probably due to the experience and habit of work I had picked up over the previous years at the Keen's farm.

During a history lesson on life in Saxon England, we were told that the human race was becoming weaker and smaller with every generation, due to the increasingly soft life that people experienced in civilised communities. The Saxons were tougher than the Normans, the Romans were tougher than the Saxons, and the Greeks were tougher than the Romans. He cited how Socrates had marched bare-footed in the snow during his military service, and had slept on a wooden board without any ill effects. "Your generation is particularly short in stature," he continued, "but in the days when Corfe's uncle attended the school, boys were taller as they led tougher lives."

He then unbuttoned his shirt, and baring his chest (and this was during the cold season), he showed us that he wore no vest beneath, explaining that if everyone kept to his summer wear, rather than changing into a lot of woollens, it would help regenerate the human race. This was inspiring talk for 10-years olds, but of course it was utter nonsense, and proffered bad advice, but cold baths, open windows, and light clothing in all weathers, was genuinely accepted at the time in contributing to a healthier life-style.

Sometimes, if my father had consultations at the Middlesex Hospital in Holloway, he would drive me to the junction of Archway Road, from where I would walk the rest of the way to school, but there were two parting exclamations which he always made, either, "Work hard and play hard," or else, "Keep your mouth shut and your bowels open." The first was comprehensible, although "playing" in this sense did not refer to sport but rather to leisure break-time activity, and I do not think it was the right kind of advice, since leisure should put its emphasis on relaxation if good social mixing is its purpose, as otherwise, "hardness" contributes to tension or conflict – or at least, to an abrasive cast of mind. With regard to the second piece of advice, it reflected my father's obsession with the need to defecate, but the first half of the sentence was meaningless. This is because a closed mouth ensured silence and refraining to participate in either class or social activities. What other meaning could the words have meant unless it was an exhortation against illicit eating?

The bullying of Jews throughout all year levels was random rather than systematic. It was an activity which was puerile, and childishly irrational in the sense it could not be supported by the reasoning of an adult mind. It was superficial in the sense of its immaturity, as a temporary phase of pre-pubescent boys – but was nonetheless reprehensible for that – in fulfilling the instinctive need for gang warfare of the particular age groups at the time. If, therefore, we were guilty of anti-Semitic *acts* – and we were – the usual excuse was always the non-belief in "Jesus," but such a justification was made by those without an iota of religious feeling, and so this made nonsense of the reason given for our aggression. It was an excuse for playground gang formation, as cowboys against Indians, except for two factors: firstly, in that Jews were a ready made group in not attending morning assembly; and secondly, in that they never formed a gang of their own. They were always attacked as separate individuals, and so this was pure baiting and bullying by a gentile majority.

Such racially discriminatory activity could hardly take place in the 21st century – even if laws against racial discrimination had never been enacted. Why, then, did it take place in the immediate aftermath of the Second World War? My explanation is that the War time churchgoing of my particular age-group, i.e. those between 7-12 in 1946, was particularly damaging to their moral upbringing. I was clearly not the only boy at Highgate exposed to the kind of sermonising I listened to at St. James's church over a number of years.

That was a time when churchgoing was much more common than it is today, and it must be assumed that sermons, and moreover, Bible readings, in the typical church throughout Britain between September 1939 and May 1945, was hardly less hostile and bloodcurdling in confronting an enemy than that of St. James's in Muswell Hill. It is true that in a sermon shortly after the War, the Rev. E.A. Dunn said that we "should never hate anyone – not even Hitler," but the damage had already been done. I am not suggesting that the War time contribution of the churches was harmful to the adult population at the time, but only to pre-pubescent children who had never formed a consciousness of what a peace time or normal world was like.

As I noted in an earlier chapter, when church services were concluded, the adults resumed the normality of cheerfulness, despite having heard of God's commandment, "to massacre the Hittites, the Girgashites, the Amorites, and Canaanites, Perizzites, the Hivites and the Jebusites , and to show no mercy unto them," but the children who had listened to such bloodthirsty exhortations remained silent and solemn. Inevitably, exposure over a long period to such calls for vengeance and mercilessness was bound to have some kind of detrimental effect on the younger generation. It was bound sometime to encourage a level of intolerance, cruelty, and ganging-up in the playground, above what was usual amongst pre-pubescent boys who had never known an age of peace.

I remain convinced to this day, that on balance, the Bible is a bad moral and psychological influence on human character – irrespective of where it is propagated. It cannot be denied that the King James version is a great work of literature in influencing the better development of the English language. But as a work of literature its value is not to be found as a book of ethics, but as a profoundly remarkable study of psychological resentment during the emergence of nationhood, as has been observed by such leading thinkers as Renan and Nietzsche. In that lies its greatness. But as a book of morality it is grossly wanting on account of its multitude of contradictions and absurdities, and these have been compounded by theologians over the past two millennia through every kind of fanciful intellectual acrobatics.

If a person is really seeking morality or goodness, his or her time would be better spent in reading the tranquil and well-composed thoughts of Cicero, Seneca, Epictetus, Plutarch, or Marcus Aurelius – not to mention the towering giants of 4th century BC Greece – than the hysterical ravings of self-declared prophets who only promised death and destruction. In turning to the contemporary world and contemplating the outrageous dispossession of the Palestinian people, and witnessing the endemic and arbitrary murder of unarmed men, women and children, there is only one source which has given *moral* credence to these atrocities, and that is the Holy Bible. Without that book, such policies could never have been initiated in the Near East of the 20th and 21st centuries. And it is the same book which was responsible for Jew-baiting by crowds of pre-pubescent boys at Highgate Junior school in the 1940s.

Although I can never recollect having actually struck a Jew, or used abusive language against such an individual – for verbal abuse was never "my style" – I can recollect chasing a Jew amongst a crowd of others on a playing field during break, whilst shouting in unison, "Get the Jew,!" or words to that effect. In any event, I could hardly have won for myself a reputation for anti-Semitism at the school, for on several occasions, I invited Jews home for tea, when they were always made welcome, and I remember my mother remarking reassuringly on several occasions that "he was a nice Jew" who could be invited back again. My parents' attitude to the Jews was probably typical of middle class people at the time, i.e., they were respected if not exactly liked. The reservations with regard to the race was, on one level, their pushiness, and quickness and versatility in business above what was considered proper; and on another level, their foreign (or East European) mannerisms and accents.

Whilst my parents – alongside most people – were not averse to jokes at the expense of Jews, they would certainly have been horrified by any kind of anti-Semitism which was political in intent. My father associated with a number of Jews with whom he was friendly, both professionally, and in such organisations as Rotary and his Masonic Lodge, and as a golfer, he was never a member of a club which excluded Jews. When he heard about the bullying of Jews at Highgate, he took a disapproving stance, exclaiming, "How would you like it if you were bullied for what you are?" – "But they don't believe in Jesus," I exclaimed with moral conviction. My father had no answer to that.

One of my best friends at Highgate was Robin Olden (1934-98), the son of Ted Ray (1905-77), the successor of Tommy Handley (1892-1949), and the leading radio comedian in the immediate post-War period with his weekly show *Ray's A Laugh*. Robin was a year older than me and in a higher class, but we struck up a firm friendship, and on Friday after school, he treated a small group of us to Coca-Cola at the newsagents at the corner of North Hill and Broadlands Road, on our way home. The newsagents still exists. He purchased a large bottle of the cordial and the proprietor gave us each a beaker into which it was poured. This was the first time I had tasted Coco-Cola, and we all regarded it as a great luxury.

On one occasion there was a discussion about the bullying of his race by his year group, and I remember him recounting how he always used a trick, which he advised others to follow, which was to go limp and feign unconsciousness. "If you do that, they'll get frightened, and always go away," he said. "It always works." He was often a guest in my home, and my mother described him as the "most polite and charming boy" for his age, she had ever met in her life. She said he had a "sensitivity" and ability to "please" she had never found in any other boy. On several occasions I went to parties at his home at the bottom of Muswell Hill in the direction of Crouch End.

He lived in one of the elegant two-storey early 19th century houses which had been constructed before Muswell Hill became an urban centre at the start of the 20th century. It was surrounded by a fine garden. At a children's party the great comedian was there with several men friends, but he took little notice of us kids. He had a serious expression, and remained deeply engaged in conversation – quite unlike my impression of a comedian. At another party there was a beautiful blonde girl whom I found most attractive, but I lacked the courage to ask my friend to put us into contact. On going to tea there on other occasions, I saw his younger brother, Andrew Ray (1939-2003), who later became a famous child star in well-known films, whilst Robin himself, under the name of Robin Ray, eventually became a well-known radio quiz master as the initiator of *Call My Bluff*, and a popular TV panel member of *Face The Music*. On birthdays we exchanged presents and I remember he gave me a volume of Wild West stories.

For me, I was to find that friendship with those belonging to the Jewish race was not so much a question of choice, as the result of inevitable circumstances. This was because of my questioning attitude to the world, and because I never accepted anything at its face value. I developed into a thinking and enquiring person to a greater degree than most of my age – and I was never to lose these characteristics. I saw the world from a different perspective from the humdrum middling gentile majority, and wherever there were Jewish people around, there was a mutual attraction. My deepening interest in literature, the arts, music, and the social sciences, over the following years, which transformed me into the most despised species in the English speaking world, viz., an *intellectual*, was to strengthen this mutual attraction.

A thinking person always feels in some way alienated from the rest of society, in the same way that a Jew never feels entirely integrated because of his natural integrity to his own culture. But a Jew is nonetheless a national of the territory in which he finds himself, and hence is keen to understand and absorb the national culture from his own perspective. In fact he often tends to have a deeper understanding and a broader knowledge of territorial cultural traditions than the so-called gentile inhabitants. For all these reasons, therefore, I often found there was more common ground between myself and members of the Jewish community than with others in the population. Thus, in the last school I attended, as also in the Army, my best friends were often Jewish.

The Headmaster of the Junior School, Mr. H.F.R. Miller, clearly disapproved of the bullying of Jews, and during breaks when wandering around, on several occasions I saw him approach groups of boys with the words, "If I see any of you chasing *that* boy again, he'll be caned."

One afternoon, classes were interrupted, and the entire Junior School was called into the assembly hall for a special meeting, and we waited apprehensively to know the purpose of this roll call – and all the teachers were also present. The Headmaster came into the hall, and speaking in a slow deeply serious tone from the platform, be explained that shortly after lunch break, the master on orderly duty had found a certain boy in a senior class who was named, and whom we knew to be Jewish, had had his trousers taken down, and was held to the ground by his testicles. The guilty boy, who was also named, had just been caned, and we were warned that any similar incidents would be followed immediately by expulsion from the school, and without direct reference to the race of the victim, we were told that attacks of any kind in future against "these people" would be seriously punished. Thereafter the baiting or bullying of the Jewish community diminished.

On my second term at Highgate, being the Third Term of 1946, I was moved with the rest of my class from Form IV B to III B, where Miss E.A. Hay, an attractive fair-haired lady became our class teacher. She was also the leader of the Boy Cub group, which I joined, and this was demotion for me, in view of the fact I had already been a Scout within the past year and had successfully taken my Tenderfoot examination. I remember that when our Cub group was in Kenwood one hot summer afternoon, she taught us that when cutting our nails, our fingernails should be cut rounded whilst our toenails should always be cut straight. I cannot remember anything else I learned in the Cubs, as we seemed to spend most of our time playing enjoyable games. As a class teacher, I do remember she told us it was our duty to marry and produce children on reaching manhood as there was a shortage of Englishmen in the world, especially in Africa.

After two terms with Miss Hay, we were moved out of Ingleholme up to the Junior school proper into Mr. Q.T. Robinson's class, this being the second term of 1947, where we remained for two terms until the first term of 1948. From this stage in our education we had different masters for different subjects, Miss Hay being one of the few female teachers in the school, and my rapid absorption of factual or academic knowledge both within the curriculum of the school and outside it, may be dated from this period when I was 11 ½.

It was at this exceptionally early age that I entered puberty and grew pubic hair, an embarrassing and painful experience in view of the fact that none of my peers underwent the same transformation. When, therefore, we had to undress and shower after football or PT, or during the twice yearly medical inspections which took place in the premises of the Senior school, I was made to feel not merely abnormal but a horrific freak of nature. None of my class mates confronted or teased or bullied me, or even remarked on this visually dramatic bodily change, I think because they sensed my embarrassment and felt pity rather than amusement.

Once in the dressing room, when a boy looked at me in surprise, another in an undertone remarked to the first, "It's only normal." There was a French boy in our midst who always had an erection as soon as he removed his clothes, which should have been more embarrassing as he was unique in this respect, but later in life in communal washing areas in Continental youth hostels, I noted that Frenchmen (and only Frenchmen) often had erections in such places without any sense of shame. One boy in the changing room remarked that I smelt like his father but he intended this as a compliment.

Our lessons in English history comprised learning about the reigns of the English monarchs since the Norman Conquest, which whilst ridiculed today, I still maintain is the best approach to teaching English history, since the dates presented form a skeletal framework, as well as an intelligent narrative, for building every aspect of historical knowledge. In our classroom were portraits of all the kings and queens of England, and very soon I learned to recognise from any portrait the face of every monarch from Edward III (1327-77) to the present day. The teaching of history was very much better in the 1940s and 50s than it is at the present day.

At that time there was a progressive narrative which had meaning in instilling both individual and national pride; but today, through a variety of influences, e.g., Marxist educational theory; deferring to the cultural backgrounds of immigrants; the need to highlight the negative rather than the positive aspects of British influence throughout the world, etc., have culminated in confusing the purpose of history and trashing it as a subject for teaching in schools. The teaching of history to schoolchildren in the lower grades cannot be undertaken as a scientific or totally objective study, as with a university course, but only as an intelligent narrative with *moral* purpose, as otherwise factual information will not be sufficiently retained.

The teaching of reading also sought to inform our knowledge of history. I remember one book about the Peasants' Revolt, and how a boy serf had thrown a clod of earth at a nobleman, for which he had to be flogged with a rope, and how the story ended gloriously with the heroic 14-year old Richard II suppressing the unruly peasants. Another book dealt with the daily lives of London apprentices during the reign of Henry VIII, and how the king jousted with a ridiculous schoolmaster, and jumped into the Thames and swam in his armour.

Another book was a simplified version of Charles Kingsley's, *Hereward The Wake*, and I well remember the Saxon comrades in arms, cutting their flesh and letting the blood flow into a drinking horn, before swearing blood brotherhood in their struggle against the invading Normans. It was in this book that I first learned about Lady Godiva and how she rode naked through the streets of Coventry, so that her husband, the Earl of Mercia, would agree to the remission of an unpopular tax.

In moving into Mr. Robinson's class, I was also happy to begin my study of Latin under his tutelage. We were fortunate in having an exceptionally good text book, *Latin For Today* (the first in a series of six), which some boys scribbled on the front cover to read, *Eating For Today*. The value of the book consisted in inspiring narrative pieces followed by grammatical examples, and the declension of verbs, etc. The books were richly illustrated and sought to give a vivid picture of Roman life and history, with many heroic stories taken from the pages of the great Augustan historian Livy.

It was only through re-reading simple and interesting narratives that a large foreign vocabulary can be learned, for the exercise in attempting to memorise lists of words out of any meaningful context is futile, since they are soon forgotten. We were inspired by the stories of the great Republican Romans as Appius Claudius, the blind Censor; Mucius Scaevola, the upright governor of Asia; the virtuous Cato; and the heroic Scipio Africanus, who brought Carthage to her knees. Some years ago when wanting to brush up my Latin, I was dismayed to learn that these text books were not only out of print, but had been discontinued by Longmans, and in searching for a comparable replacement I could find nothing which approached the high standards of *Latin For Today*.

Occasionally, Mr. L.G. Markham, an elderly but nonetheless virile schoolmaster, took us for Latin. He was a large red-faced man with a bad temper, and he would enter the classroom with a walking stick in one hand, to aid his limp, and a splintered officer's bamboo baton, in the other, with which he had beaten innumerable pupils across the shoulders over the past decades. When he fell into one of his uncontrollable rages, his face would twitch in a comical fashion, as if he had been seized with a kind of paralytic attack, and this would throw the entire class into fits of laughter. This, of course, only increased his anger, and he would hit about wildly with his battered cane.

It was said that his leg, which had been injured whilst on active service in the First World War, was a cause of constant pain, and that this was the real cause of his rages rather than the irritation of his pupils. Whilst reciting the conjugation of Latin verbs, he had a habit of walking up and down between the desks, and beating us across the shoulders in unison to our chanted recitation. He also had a habit of resorting to more subtle punishments, such as pressing the point of a compass into the palm of the hand. My Uncle Maurice was punished by him in this way, and joked about the number of canes he must have broken across the backs of innumerable pupils.

Mr. Miller, the Headmaster took us for science, which was superficially taught, whilst our class teacher, Mr. Robinson, took us for art, a subject in which he had little interest. He once supplied us with drawing paper, and asked us to draw whatever was of most interest to us. I thought about the matter, and in view of the psychological influences over the past two years, I was driven to draw a picture and ground plan for an ideally defensive fortress, with heavy guns pointing out in all four directions, ammunition rooms, dormitories for large numbers of troops, dungeons with numerous torture chambers, and in the safety at the centre of the building, a fine residential suite for the Commander and his family. When Mr. Robinson passed by to inspect my work, he made the comment that, "only a warped mind" could produce such an illustration.

CHAPTER 11
My Escape into Literature

"Literature, taken in all its bearings, forms the grand line
of demarcation between the human and animal kingdoms."

William Godwin, *The Enquirer: Early Taste For Reading*

My psychological attachment to *The Three Musketeers* and the 17th century – Broadening interest in the classics – Illness and absence from school – The dreaded art lessons – The influence of the PT master – Visits to antiquarian bookshops – Holidays and other relatives in Swanage – Two new loves

During the earlier part of my time at Highgate I subscribed to the comic *Knockout*, which I chose in preference to *Beano* and other similar weeklies which were then available. In addition to the usual comic strips with Desperate Dan, Billy Bunter, and Lord Snooty, etc., they also carried the comic strip of a well known classic, and at the time of subscribing, it happened to be, *The Three Musketeers*. I was immediately captured by the wonderful adventure story, and the enchanted freedom which seemed to be enjoyed by D'Artagnan, Athos, Aramis, and Porthos. Here were four men who were not prepared to take any insults or rebuffs from any man without drawing their swords to avenge an injury. What manliness and swashbuckling lives were pursued at that time by comparison with the squalid rule-driven lives of people in the boring 20th century! That was my romantic impression. As I followed their adventures from week to week, I was enchanted by everything which the 17th century presented.

All this, of course, fulfilled the vacuum of a deep psychological need in answering an inner discontent with life at home and elsewhere. If it had not been *The Three Musketeers* and the 17th century, some other convenient obsession would have seized my imagination. I was filled with a greater self-confidence and also with a greater degree of self-justified aggression, and general feeling of enhanced well-being. My interest in the historical period took me back to peruse the pages of Arthur Mee's *Encyclopaedia* with greater care. And there I found what I wanted: informative articles with well chosen accompanying illustrations on the English Civil War with portraits of all the main participants.

Now I was emotionally (but not yet deeply) absorbed in the issues of history for the very first time. My sympathies were wholly with Charles I and the Royalists. I was moved by the sadness of his expression, his kindness and humanity as a father and lover of dogs, and I sympathised with the political difficulties with which he was confronted. How dare the insolent upstarts in Parliament question his authority, or Divine Right as conferred by God! Surely anarchy was the only alternative to Kingly rule. I saw Cromwell and the Parliamentary cause as law-breaking, and felt the vacillation of the prevaricating king as justified in maintaining public order.

A year or so previously I had heard my father and grandparents rail in futility against the overthrow of the great war leader and champion of Britain, and the injustice of "dispossession" by a rebellious incoming Labour government, but they did nothing in attempting to correct the situation, except sit back and complain. And now I had found a hero who had the courage to stand up against the resentful mediocrities of the world, even though he ended up as a tragic figure in losing his head on the block. I was to hold onto these reactionary if romantic ideas for another five years or so until about the age of 16, when I fell under the influence of the radical ideas of the Enlightenment, towards the conclusion of my schooling, when I was obsessed by the very different virtues of another century.

When *Knockout* concluded its pictorial serialisation of *The Three Musketeers*, it then began to serialise Charles Kingsley's great Elizabethan novel of the Spanish main, *Westward Ho!* and I was equally entranced by the youthful rebelliousness of its hero, Amyas Leigh. Here was a drama of independent-minded Englishmen fighting against the might of over-rich, decadent and Catholic Spain, with its determination to destroy the freedom of the world. The editors of *Knockout* certainly knew how to appeal to the imagination and sensibilities of the schoolboys of the immediate post-War period!

It was at this time that I struck up a friendship with a boy called Newman, from a higher class, who also had an interest in literature and the arts. He had led an interesting life and had lived in China, and he described how he had seen criminals hanged or wandering around the streets with kangs round their necks, before returning to Britain. Together we explored the Southwood Bookstore, a second hand shop which still exists, albeit under a different name, in Archway Road at the bottom of Southwood Lane. I visited and browsed through the store every week, in this way quickly accumulating a broad knowledge of literature and books and the many editions in which they appeared.

Quite early on I saw a cheap edition, with smelly yellowing pages, of *The Three Musketeers* and its five sequels, *Twenty Years After, Louise de la Valliere, Vicomte de Braglonne, The Man in The Iron Mask,* and, *The Son of Porthos*, in a bookcase placed out on the street for 6d each. I bought the lot and read them avariciously over the next few months. At home my mother had inherited some 8-10 volumes of Sir Walter Scott's novels and Thackeray's *Pendennis*, bound in pigskin and printed on Japanese rice paper. They were kept on a chest of drawers in my parents' bedroom, and these books, too, I began to read – although I found Scott's long introductions rather heavy going. Amongst the first of Scott's novels I read were, *The Talisman, Ivanhoe, Kenilworth, Woodstock,* and, *The Bride of Lammermmoor* – the last two set in my favourite 17th century. Thackeray's *Pendennis* seemed to present the ideal life of the leisurely but young professional man entering the world after completing his education.

History remained my first interest and I flourished at this at school, succeeding to outshine my other classmates, although I remained almost at the bottom of the class in most other subjects. One day I saw in the window of the Southwood Bookstore, Fletcher's 4-volume History of England, but it was priced at 15 shillings – far beyond any sum which I could afford. I asked my mother to intercede on my behalf with my father in buying the set, but the answer was "No," on the grounds that he was not a well-known historian – not that my father was an authority on the matter. It should not be suggested, however, that my father was mean towards me when it came to the purchase of books on gift-bearing occasions. In the late 1940s I proposed a choice of two sets of books I had seen in the Southwood store: a fine 18-volume set of Dickens' Works published by the Educational Book Company priced at £4 10s 6d., or a nicely printed 28-volume set of Kingsley's Works at £3 10s. 6d. My father wisely chose the more expensive set as being more suitable reading material.

Some weeks after I had seen the Fletcher set, I bought a cheap small print 3-volume edition of Hume's History of England. The books which I read at this period were far above the reading level of my peers, and this made me seem a snob – if not actually a snob. I remember sneering at a classmate who was hooked on Enid Blyton, saying that such books were "soft" and only "written for girls," upon which he responded that I was just trying to be a "clever-clever." On the other hand, I was fond of popular radio programmes, and never missed the daily 15-minute slot of *Dick Barton Special Agent*, and later the successor programme, *The Daring Dexters*, which lasted until the inception of *The Archers*, which remains until the present day. I also regularly enjoyed the weekly programme, *Ray's A Laugh,* which I found immensely funny.

During these years I was often ill with colds and influenza, and after moving up to Mr. C.D. Chottin's class in the first term of 1948, I fell ill with mumps and then complications with orchitis, and was confined to bed for three weeks. The family doctor (Blackburn) called daily and examined me, and I was obliged to drink endless liquids throughout the day and sweat profusely, for in those days there were limited drugs to treat the illness. My father showed great anxiety, for there was the danger I should become infertile, but fortunately only one testicle became infected. Shortly afterwards, my cousin, Mervyn, was struck down by the same ailment whilst working in London, and his mother, Joan, made desperate phone calls from Australia to ascertain the condition of her son. He did not have such good medical attention, and became infertile as a result, but that did not prevent him from becoming a successful womaniser for the rest of his life.

Shortly after rising from my sickbed I convalesced for three weeks at a holiday home my paternal grandparents rented at Westcliffe-on-Sea, and it was relaxing and pleasant to stay with them and enjoy the sea air of the Thames estuary. I remember reading Dicken's *Child's History of England* in Westcliffe, and being taken on brisk walks along the promenade. When I returned to school later in the term I was met by a torrent of abuse from Mr. Chottin, who upbraided me in front of the class as a "worthless weakling" who had been idling away on holiday and avoiding work. I was astonished by this outburst – as indeed, were the rest of the class - and could not respond to it in any way. Although Mr. Chottin was our English master as well as our class teacher, and I was good at English, it seemed he had taken an irrational dislike to me.

Strangely, the most dreaded subject of all was art, which was treated "seriously" once we reached the higher grades of the Junior School. Previously, we had been encouraged to draw whatever we liked, but the new teacher was a physics master, sent down from the Senior School. He was bald and pompous, with a contempt for paints or colour, explaining that colour was merely an illusory thing, dependent on the light spectrum, and that we should be more concerned with "realities," which he defined as line drawing.

"The first and most important principle in art is the drawing of a straight line," he declared at the start of the first lesson, and drawing a white line on the blackboard to set an example. "A straight line means the closest distance between two given points. It calls for a firm hand and a steady nerve." We then spent the entire lesson attempting to draw a straight line, and as the master walked up and down between the rows of desks, he bawled at each in turn, "That's not a straight line. Rub it out and start again. What's that supposed to be? It's full of curves. What's wrong with you boy?" By the end of the lesson our sheets of drawing paper were almost rubbed through with holes.

During the second lesson, we learned to draw circles and arches, and from the third lesson onwards, we were actually allowed to draw from a model – a milk bottle being placed on a table at the front of the class, and it remained there during the art lessons for the next six weeks. These were weeks of frustration and failure, for nothing was ever perfect: the left side of the bottle never exactly corresponded with the right side, the proportions were always wrong, and no one was allowed to use instruments of any kind. During the second half of the term, by which time we had supposedly grasped the principles of drawing a milk bottle, we were given a more exciting object, viz., a pot with a handle sticking out at the side. This remained our model until the end of the term, when the classroom was then decorated with several dozen line drawings of milk bottles and pots, all of which were intended to be indistinguishable from one another.

Music lessons were valuable, I found, because they concentrated on an appreciation of the classics. The music master carried a cane, which he was entitled to do in conducting our singing, but he frequently beat the hands of recalcitrant pupils who usually deserved it, for he was constantly subjected to ragging. He sometimes attempted to teach us things above our heads, such as a twenty minute lecture on how to write music, followed by a request that we should then write out the National Anthem – something which foxed us all.

It was during the singing lessons that he was most often subjected to ragging, and after waving his cane backwards and forwards in conducting us, he would suddenly lay it down, exclaiming that someone was making a strange unnatural sound. He would commence again, and a second time would interrupt the performance, saying that someone was trying to spoil the choir. "Who is it?" he exclaimed irately. "It's a strange stuttering sound." – "Then it must be Corfe," said one boy. "He stutters." – "No, this is an affected sound," replied the music master, and he began conducting us again. When the disturbing noise occurred again, he threatened in exasperation to send the culprit to the Headmaster for a caning, and he walked up and down the lines with cocked ear, but as soon as he approached the guilty party the strange noise ceased, and so no one was ever caught. Our introduction to classical music, when we listened to Beethoven's *Pastoral*, and were taught about the structure of music, proved very helpful in opening up an entirely new world of entertainment.

The physical training teacher was the man who most commonly sent boys to the Headmaster for caning. During PT sessions there was always a 5-minute period when we had to sit on the floor cross-legged with arms folded, quite motionless and silent, he sitting in front with his back to us in a similar position. He was an ex-naval man with a strong provincial accent, and every few moments, as we sat in this position, he would call out the name of a particularly mischievous Irish boy, exclaiming, "I'm watching you, Doyle. I see your every move. If you don't keep still, I'll send you for a caning." It so happened that the PT master was always correct in his assumptions, although whilst none of us could quite understand his uncanny powers, the explanation was soon bawled out, "I've got eyes at the back of my head, you know!" If he wore glasses, such an explanation could have been easily accepted, as with a maths master who was ragged whilst he wrote on the blackboard. In those instances he was candid enough to explain, "I can see everything that happens in class through the reflection in my spectacles."

During my early terms at the school, the PT master did not take a liking to me, often subjecting me to mild ridicule as a "weakling" and "poor runner," etc. It is true that I was not brilliant on the football pitch, primarily because I was a poor runner, due to the back injury I had sustained at Woodbridge. On sports days, I invariably came last in all races. As a walker, however, no one could outpace me, and even now in my mid-70s, I can usually outpace those who are half my age, since I maintain a fast walking pace whenever I am in the open air.

One day whilst at lunch, when our PT master headed the table, there was a discussion on life expectancy, and I chipped-in with the remark that I hoped to live till ninety. He laughed at this suggestion, saying, "You're such a weakling, Corfe, you'll be lucky to reach fifty. If you want a long life you must be tall and muscular with hairs on your chest." I was hurt by these remarks, and soon fell under the firm conviction that I should live to be 54 and then drop dead from a heart attack. On reaching 55, I realised I had been deluded, and when about a decade later a friend asked me how long I expected to live in reference to an insurance matter, I replied confidently, "Ninety-three or ninety-four, bearing in mind my forebears, and barring an accident and unforeseen disease which might kill at any time."

During those periods when we were scheduled to play games outside, but the weather was too inclement to make that possible, the PT master would take us to a vacant classroom and tell us about his experiences in the Navy, inviting questions and discussion afterwards. We greatly enjoyed these sessions as he drew plans of battleships on the blackboard, explaining the uses of the different decks, how the guns were operated, and their range of fire and the damage that the different shells could inflict on other naval vessels. We gasped in awe as he described the huge size of these vessels and deck was added to deck. We also learned more about the purposes of submarines and torpedoes in naval warfare.

Most vivid were his descriptions of naval life and discipline. "We ratings were stood to attention on the deck alongside the guns whilst 16-pound shells whistled passed our ears, and if we flinched or batted an eyelid, we were flogged," he once told us. "Always there were officers watching us. I've known storms at sea, when the waves were so great, that they tore open the steel deck and rolled it up like tinfoil. I've seen men washed off the deck of a ship into the ocean, and then the next wave washed them back again. They were saved by a miracle!"

His descriptions of floggings were especially horrific. "You boys don't know what flogging is," he told us. "When the Headmaster takes you into his study for a caning, it's nothing compared with what we went through. I've been flogged many times," he exclaimed proudly in further winning our respect. "The entire crew would be assembled on deck, and we'd be brought up stark naked from the punishment cells and tied to the hand rails. We'd be flogged with a rope soaked in sea-water, and after every stroke the cook would rub salt into our wounds to prevent them festering. The blood would run to our feet, and if we let out a squeal, the officer would order the flogging to be doubled."

Boxing was a new sport to which we were introduced by our PT master. In introducing the sport, he explained the necessity of learning to box as one of the essentials in life. "When you go out into the world," he began, "you'll find there are periods in your life when you have to put up a fight. It may be when a man has deceived you, or told a lie behind your back, when you have to defend your honour with a round of fisticuffs. But more often, it happens when a man has to prove his liking for a girl, and he has to fight a rival to maintain his rights. For all these reasons, you have to learn the rules of boxing so that the fight is clean and fair." Consequently, I gained the impression at the time that it was quite normal for the majority of men to go through life and engage in fisticuffs from time to time.

This impression was not only gained from a reading of, *The Three Musketeers*, but from the frequent exclamations of my father, who was always threatening to knock someone down or punch them on the nose. This usually occurred in such petty situations as when someone beat him to a parking space at the side of the road, or when his stockbroker failed to sell or buy when the market was right. However, I never knew my father to become actually involved in a fight but the threat was never far from his lips. We 11-year old boys knew nothing about laws against causing an affray, or maintaining the peace, and so there was no reason why we should not believe that adult males spent much of their time fighting one another.

One Christmas my wish was fulfilled in receiving a pair of boxing gloves, and I took up the sport with enthusiasm at school. Towards the end of one term I was entered as a candidate for the finals for the Junior school championships. I successfully defeated three boys and had only one more fight to go before entering the finals. Although the PT master oversaw the matches, it was Mr. Chottin, my form master who actually decided as to who should fight whom. As I said, he disliked me intensely, and for this crucial match he set me against a boy who was very much larger. My classmates at once thought that this was unfair, and warned me against accepting such an unequal challenge, whilst the PT master, who had come to appreciate me as a boy with pluck, quietly confided, "You needn't take on the fight if you don't want to."

But I was determined to go ahead with the challenge. I had come so far, and I was not going to back down now. On the day of the match, after the first few rounds, the blood began to run freely from my nose, and during the intervals, my face was washed and ice applied to my forehead, and the PT master repeated his warning, "You needn't continue the fight if you don't want to," but I was determined to carry on. It was a futile hope, for I simply did not have the stretch to return the blows, but when I did successfully drive home a blow, the school cheered me on, and I saw that I had won over the sympathy of the majority. The fight was concluded after the twelfth round and was won on points. After that eventful match I rarely engaged in boxing again, as Mr. Chottin had succeeded in his efforts to exclude me from any serious competition.

*

Not long after discovering the Southwood Bookstore, I found an even more interesting bookshop in Highgate Village, viz., Fisher and Sperr, being the largest second hand and antiquarian bookshop in North London. During the weekends I regularly walked from home through Highgate Wood, visited Southwood Bookstore, climbed the steep hill to Highgate Village and spent at least an hour or so browsing through the three or four floors of Fisher and Sperr. This was a paradise for any bibliophile, for not only was it stocked with all the established classics of literature and history, but also with the ancient folio tomes of Camden, Holinshed, Stow, State Trials, etc., of the 16th and 17th centuries. My knowledge of books, history, and literature was again increased tenfold, for of course, I engaged in further research as soon as I reached home on those works which struck me of most interest. From Highgate Village I walked through Hampstead Heath and Kenwood to several smaller, but nonetheless excellent second hand bookshops in Flask Walk, Hampstead.

I developed the habit of fast walking so I could be home again in time for the early evening meal.

One day I discovered a set of Scott's complete works in 19 huge half-calf bound volumes, printed in the 1840s, the novels richly illustrated and two to three to a volume, and the miscellaneous works, i.e., Life of Napoleon, poetry, and Lockhart's Life of Scott compacted into 5 volumes with small print and double columns, the lot priced at £4 15s 0d. Somehow I had to raise the money to make this purchase. For almost two years I had kept a pair of Dutch rabbits, appropriately named King Charles I and Queen Henriette Marie, which I had kept for breeding, and I sold these profitably to raise the required sum. My father had looked favourably on my keeping rabbits as educationally beneficial in learning about the "facts of life," and my mother was not adverse to their sale, as the male rabbit intimidated the dog when they were both let loose in the garden. This originated one day when the dog apprehensively approached the rabbit's food bowl whilst the latter was eating, and was attacked for its intrusive curiosity.

My father agreed to drive the car to Highgate Village, and the books were paid for and loaded into the boot of the car. That was in 1948. Some time later Mr. Sperr sold out his partnership to Mr. Fisher, and the latter is still managing the shop 62 years later in 2010. When I occasionally visit, perhaps once every two years, I find Mr. Fisher at the back of the shop, hunched over a computer nowadays rather than a typewriter, somewhat aged – as he must now be in his *late* 80s – but still recognisable as the man he once was all those years ago. Today the shop is only open several days a week, but exploring its rooms is still as exciting as it ever was. "I see no sense in retiring," said Mr. Fisher, the last time I called in. "Work keeps you fit and active, and so why should I sell up?" He once asked me after I had made a rare purchase there, "Are you in the oil industry?" – "No," I replied.

Another shop I often visited, amongst a dozen or so others in the same street, was Foyles in Charing Cross road. At that time Foyles was double its present size, for it owned properties on both sides of Manette Street, and most its stock was then second hand or antiquarian. It was a veritable paradise for bargain hunters, for most antiquarian books had a negligible value in the immediate post-War period, whilst I found new books too expensive to buy. I spent my pocket money in the late 40s on such multi-volume sets as Dr. Robertson's Works, Nathaniel Hooke's *History of the Roman Republic*, Gibbon's *Decline and Fall*, Pope's Homer in 11 volumes printed in 1757, and Nicholas Rowe's translation of Lucan's *Pharsalia*, glorifying Caesar's role in the Civil War, and L'Estrange's translation of Seneca's *Morals* printed in 1699 – all highly enjoyable books. I even succeeded in arousing the interest of my cousins,

Michael and Howard to accompany me, on one of these expeditions to the West End, but I could not capture their serious interest in these antiquarian works.

But my interests soon extended beyond literature and history, for the latter has to have a purpose if it is studied with intelligence. I therefore graduated towards the social sciences, politics, and philosophy, and I remember bringing home a volume of Macaulay's Essays, which seemed so deeply concerned with interpreting events, and pressing my father in an almost desperate fashion to explain the purpose of the Essay as a literary medium, which he attempted to do to the best of his ability in recognising the urgency of my question. One afternoon whilst reading Plato's *Republic* in Oliver's nursery, I was disturbed by a mouse by the gas fire, and I took up a walking stick with a cudgel at its head and killed the intruder.

*

For the summer holidays we were taken on several consecutive years to the Ocean Bay Hotel in Swanage, which overlooked the beach, and we were fortunate with the weather. On one occasion, the comedy actress, Margaret Rutherford and her husband, the character actor, Stringer Davis, were also staying at the hotel, and my father was amused that they had flowers on their dining room table whilst none of the other guests enjoyed this privilege, and he made a pretence of being offended by this. The owners of the hotel were great Thespians, and when we visited the local theatre to see a variety show, we were amused to see our hostess stick her head through the curtains at the end of the performance in talking to the artistes.

In the evenings I sat in the lounge reading a Scott novel, whilst Margaret Rutherford perused the papers, and her husband played the piano. The couple refrained from mixing with the other guests, and the latter respected the privacy of the famous stars who only sought peace and quiet. On Saturday afternoons as I walked from Fisher and Sperr to Hampstead, I occasionally saw Margaret Rutherford through the wrought iron gates in the garden of her magnificent Queen Anne property situated in South Grove in Highgate Village. It was the kind of house I yearned to live in myself.

My paternal grandparents and Harold also came to stay at the Ocean Bay Hotel, and I remember when my grandmother became angry when an attractive red-headed waitress made eyes at my young uncle as we were purchasing our sandwiches and afternoon tea to take on the beach. She thought it most improper that a woman should behave in that way and she kept her eye on her son to ensure he would not wander too far. My mother's elder sister, Joan, and her boy friend (of the time), also came to stay at Swanage. Joan had been divorced several years earlier following the adultery of her husband (my Uncle Reg), and although she never re-married, she had a string of muscular-type lovers. She also had an interesting career: immediately after the War she was in Germany in the WVS, bringing over groups of refugees to Britain, and later in Italy, and I remember her vivid description of having seen *Tosca* at La Scala in Milan, and this first stirred my interest in opera.

As a birthday present she gave me an early Chapman & Hall edition of *Oliver Twist* which she had found in a shop on the Christmas Steps in Bristol. Later she was self-employed in selling encyclopaedias, and at that point in her career, I showed genuine interest in the product she was selling, but she adopted a snooty attitude, saying that the encyclopaedias were "not for children," but only for those involved in further education. She tried to sell these books to my parents, but got nowhere. She then went off to South Africa in pursuing her sales career, but she returned after a year or two, quite disillusioned with the country. "Those poor little piccaninnies," she exclaimed, "you really want to pick them up and kiss them – they're so sweet. You can't imagine how badly the government treats those black people," she told my parents. "It's so unfair it makes you want to weep."

She then went off to Australia, in the wake of her daughter, Carol, who had already been working as a nurse there for a year, and somewhat later she was joined by her son, Mervyn, who rose to a senior managerial position in Qantas. The family remained there for the rest of their lives but returned frequently to Britain in visiting friends and relatives, always insisting they preferred Britain to Australia. Aunt Joan became intolerably snobbish with regard to Australia, saying that she knew everyone who was "worth knowing" in the country – and this included Dame Elizabeth Murdoch, the mother of Rupert. Both my aunt and my cousin, Carol, were closely involved with her charitable activities. When Joan was eventually put into an old peoples' home many decades later, she only deigned to socialise with those who were born and bred in Britain.

One day whilst in a newsagents shop in Swanage I saw a beautiful leather bound edition of Hume's and Smollett's *History of England* in 13 volumes, with gilt edging and illustrated by Houbraken, and printed in 1820. When I asked the price of the books, which were lying on the dusty floor, the middle-aged assistant looked at them contemptuously, and said, "You can have that lot for thirteen bob." I bought them at once. I still possess these books, and today their value could be in excess of £1,000. A few days later I visited the shop again and bought for a few pence Adophe Thiers' famous, *History of the French Revolution*, compacted into one leather bound volume, with double columns and small print but profusely illustrated with blood-curdling pictures.

It was during my first trip to Swanage at the age of 12 that I fell in love with a girl with whom I was eventually to develop a friendship. Her name was Angela Nickels and she came from Maidstone, the ancestral home of my grandfather. During the days at Swanage, we had no physical contact, but our exchange of glances indicated there was a mutual affection between us, and a day before she left with her family, she quickly passed me by, exclaiming under her breath, "It seems I've found my husband at last." After her departure I felt devastated, but there was little I could do, and I did not even confide my feelings to my mother who I knew might be sympathetic.

Some months later, however, I told my mother I wished to form a friendship with the girl. "Then it's for you to write to the hotel asking for her address," replied my mother. I did just that in January 1949, and some days later received a friendly letter from the hotel proprietor with the information requested. A correspondence then ensued between us, and I prayed every night that God would bless our friendship, and that it would lead to an early marriage, and eternal love. I could not have anticipated at the time that God, in his sense of humour, was to place me in a paradoxical situation. After several months of pen friendship she was invited to visit for the weekend but I was disappointed in the transformation of her appearance.

Her slim lithe figure had been sacrificed in the cause of puberty. God had half-answered my prayer but I no longer found her physically attractive. In my disappointment I therefore felt I had been short-changed by the Deity, and that ironically he had chosen to misinterpret rather than misunderstand my true wishes. And because of this circumvention I have never prayed from that day to this. I had embarked upon prayer in testing it as a strictly practical proposition. I had fulfilled my part of the bargain but He had not fulfilled His. I therefore concluded that prayer was a waste of time, although I would have been fully prepared to continue the superstitious practice if it brought a measurable return.

Nonetheless, I was determined to maintain the friendship as a point of honour, hoping that her sexual attraction might somehow reappear. We went for walks together along Woodside Avenue to Cherry Tree Wood, my brother, Gavin, traipsing behind, smiling in amusement and generally being in the way. He followed us everywhere until my father told him at last not to be a nuisance. I was excused churchgoing that Sunday so that I could entertain my guest. When I put my arm romantically around Angela's waist, she said, "Don't do that," so clearly she was defensive. That Sunday my grandparents visited after church for a glass of Sherry, whilst Angela and I were out at the park, and later in the week I overheard my father telling my mother that my grandfather had "spoken a lot of nonsense" about the "dangers" of "having a girl in the house," and that a boy of my age should not be associating with girls.

Some months later I returned the visit by spending a weekend at Angela's home, but I found her no more attractive than before, and so my libido was not uplifted. I felt awkward in their home. Her parents were pleasant but modest people who supported the Liberal party, and I felt that our friendship was becoming formal and dull, and certainly it had lost the spark and excitement enjoyed at Swanage. On returning home the pen friendship was maintained as a kind of moral obligation to the memory of the love I had once experienced, but I soon tired of this half sentimental and half altruistic attitude, and sought a way to break off the friendship. At last I found a convenient excuse. She went on a school trip to France, and promised to bring me back a box of chocolates, and when these did not arrive, I confronted her with the broken promise, stating that I wished to discontinue the friendship. I never heard from her again.

Our friendship and correspondence ended in August 1950 or shortly thereafter. Although none of my letters to her survive, her letters remain. On re-reading them, she seems to have held some affection for me. Whilst I wrote to her about my novel I was then writing, *Anthony Anvil*, and my interest in literature and historical subjects; she wrote to me about her horse riding and her pony, her pen friendship with a French girl, and her success at school. She attended the Maidstone Grammar School for Girls, and recorded her high examination marks for most subjects. She had her own pet spaniel, called Benny, and was clearly a happy girl with a well adjusted personality. She told me her father knew a great uncle of mine who served on the County Council, as her father was also involved in public life.

The following summer whilst on holiday in Swanage, at the age of 12, I fell deeply in love with Cynthia, but she was six years my senior, and I dared not declare my love. She was a great beauty, tall and slim with long brunette hair, and worked as a post office clerk in Southampton. She was on holiday at the Ocean Bay Hotel with her parents and 16-year old sister who was not nearly as attractive. She was full of life and initiative, and together with her sister, organised a fireworks display, and collected money from other residents for this purpose. There was a lively party on the eve of her departure, with Catherine wheels and rockets shooting into the sky, and I felt deeply depressed after she had gone, whilst also appreciating that a love affair would have been impossible between us because of the disparity between our ages.

*

It was about this time that my father proudly obtained his own dog, a golden retriever puppy name Judy. I think he had come to realise he was entitled to the joys of dog ownership in the same way as my mother. Judy developed into a good-natured but undisciplined and totally mischievous dog – often responsible for inexplicable damage. It was probable she was not given sufficient exercise for her size, or that my father was over-indulgent and not sufficiently severe. Although young humans might be flogged because they were guilty of original sin, such blame was inapplicable to dogs which called for gentler treatment.

One day when I came down into the kitchen to prepare breakfast before school, I found that Judy had pulled the table cloth and all its laid contents onto the floor, and was standing triumphantly on the table happily wagging her tail. A situation soon arose when my mother frequently confronted my father with "Your dog" has done this or that damage. Eventually these incriminations took the form of a joke, and my father with humour, occasionally retaliated by confronting my mother with some misdemeanour for which "her dog" was possibly responsible.

The point was reached when it was decided that Judy was unmanageable and hence would have to go, and other owners were found for her. This was therefore the second occasion when a dog had failed to integrate successfully into our family life. After her departure, and for decades following, my father would jokingly on occasion turn to my mother, referring to "Your dog has done" this or that, if some inexplicable upset could possibly be blamed on the particular dog we happened to have at the time.

CHAPTER 12
The Conflicts of Home Life

"He that loves not his wife and children, feeds a lioness at home, and broods a nest of sorrows."

Jeremy Taylor, *Sermons*, Vol. I, Bk. 1, Ch. 9

Mabs, my father's friend – A suicide gesture – Jane, the maid – Pleasures of the pantomime – My father's contradictory attitudes on class and status

Home life was inexplicably depressing, for there was a soulless, purposeless, even deathlike environment. My parents never quarrelled – or at least, we children never witnessed any such quarrel, but clearly their relationship was far from happy. At school, boys occasionally referred to angry arguments between their parents, and I remember one morning my friend, Ray Olden, referring to a quarrel which had taken place during breakfast that very day. "Do your parents quarrel sometimes?" he asked as we boarded a bus to take us to the top of Muswell Hill road. "Never!" I replied with confidence.

At this time my father became friendly with an attractive young blonde called Mabs, who worked as a radiologist at the Middlesex Hospital in Holloway. She was engaged to a young aeronautical engineer with strong left wing, even Communist sympathies. He was fairly well read and far more politically literate than my parents, and highly skilled in marquetry in making small wooden objects which we sometimes received as gifts, such as cigarette boxes or jewellery cases. My father was greatly impressed by his workmanship and welcomed him into the family circle, although, Bill Symonds (which was his name) did not feel entirely comfortable sitting amongst these people with their high Tory principles. My mother said he seemed to take a particular dislike to my stockbroker Uncle Harold, who since his demobilisation preferred to be known as "Martin."

My father's friendship with Mabs naturally necessitated that her fiancé should be included in this *famille à trois*, quite apart from the demands of appearances and decency in satisfying the sensitivity of my mother and other relations. Soon Mabs was employed part time as my father's dental nurse, and after the retirement of my grandfather another partner was taken on, a Mr. Vine, who later made a distinguished name for himself in the profession when he established a practice in Westminster. One day when I went into the nurse's office, I saw that Mabs had a high class American magazine illustrated with pornographic but not erotic cartoons, which I found fascinating as I had never seen such art before.

Mabs and Bill were not financially well off, and they had no home of their own, because of the acute post-War housing shortage in London. As we had now moved to 105 Muswell Hill Road, my father kindly offered the couple the top floor of 196 as a flat for a nominal rent, and this they gratefully accepted. The floor below was now occupied by the new dental mechanic and his wife, following the retirement of Mr. Kemp the previous mechanic. Mabs and Bill, therefore, had no objection to sharing the bathroom and kitchen with the other tenants.

One day my father took Mabs, Gavin and me for a long weekend holiday to the East coast, where we enjoyed the bracing air from off the North Sea. I do not know whether Mabs and Bill were already married by this time or not, but in any event, he had to accept the seigniorial rights of my father irrespective of his marital status. Gavin and I sensed nothing improper in this arrangement at the time, or that we had been taken away for such an unusual holiday. Perhaps we were seen to fulfil the function of some kind of chaperone, or otherwise act as a cover for respectability, or to salve the conscience of the erring pair. My father and Mabs were happily enjoying themselves, and I was pleased to see that my father was in a much better frame of mind than usual. Mabs was joyful and full of conversation, saying she had read several of Scott's novels and loved his style. A common bond was therefore immediately forged between us, and the holiday was a successful foursome enjoyed by all.

Two double-bedded rooms had been taken in the three star hotel, and whilst supposedly Mabs had her own room, my father, Gavin and I were crushed into a rather narrow double bed in the other. In fact, however, my father spent the greater part of the night with Mabs, and when he retired to our room (at some unknown hour) my brother and I were awoken, and from then onwards we had a sleepless night, as my father complained bitterly every time we wanted to turn over in the bed. "Can't you keep still,?" he kept pleading. That was the only grating aspect of the holiday.

Years later, my brother always used to say that Mabs was "great fun." Bill, meanwhile, was very passive – and seemed increasingly so as the years passed – as indeed he was obliged to be in helping maintain a complex pattern of relationships. Several years later my father took my mother, together with Mabs and Bill, on a tour of the Scottish Highlands. When a decade or so after that event I remarked to my mother, that "that must have been a wonderful holiday seeing so much of Scotland," she replied, "No, it wasn't. It was a horrible holiday!"

When my parents saw the film, *Cry, The Beloved Country*, being an adaptation of Alan Paton's bestselling novel on the early Apartheid years, my mother was deeply moved, and felt that something should be done to relieve the suffering of the blacks in South Africa. She broached the subject with my father, asking what could be done – or what could they do? My father then discussed the matter with Bill, and then came back with what he thought was a self-satisfied answer, saying, "Bill says there's nothing that can be done about it. Bill says they're so uneducated that there's no hope for improving their lot." This, perhaps, was the classic Marxist answer one might have anticipated from Bill, viz., that the Blacks had to endure their suffering until they were sufficiently industrialised and then overthrow the capitalist order. In any case, my father had salved his conscience by consulting the superior political nous of Bill, although he may not have come up with an answer to satisfy my mother.

*

One day I was given for history homework at school the task of writing an essay on the "Papal Bull." At home I could make no sense of this, only realising it was in connection with Henry VIII arising from his application for divorce from Catherine of Aragon. I searched in the Index of my Hume's History of England to no avail, and became very despondent. No question of history had ever stumped me before, and I felt particularly humiliated that I had not found the answer in Hume, whom I foolishly assumed could be relied upon to answer anything. On having read the first of the eight volumes of Hume, I asked my mother to test me on my knowledge of the volume, for I was confident of the retentiveness of my memory. She agreed to my request but was unable to uncover anything I failed to know. At last she threw aside the book, exclaiming in despair with a suggestion of disapproval, "You know everything!" This doubtless added to my arrogance. At that time I was too naïve to realise the infinity of knowledge, and that no book is comprehensive on anything in all its conceivable aspects.

At that moment I became so depressed and filled with a sense of worthlessness that I decided to end my life. I took a rope from my cupboard, tied one end around the bookcase and the other with a suitable noose around my neck (one of the few beneficial things I learned during my scouting days), opened the window, and was just about to climb out, when Miss Wall suddenly entered. She burst into tears and pleaded that I refrain from hanging myself, and in this way I was reluctantly persuaded to desist, and I never made such a serious gesture of suicide again. That evening, my father expressed his shocked surprise that I had attempted such a thing, explaining it would have left an indelible mark on the mind of my youngest brother who was then only four years old.

My mother frequently complained to Jane, the maid, that she never washed herself properly, and that often there was a piece of food left on the side of her mouth, and she was suspected of pilfering from the rations of others. There was one occasion when my mother fell into an especially violent rage, when the maid returned from the shops without a proper receipt for all the goods purchased, and after an angry verbal exchange, Jane was knocked to the floor. The maid began yelling, and grovelling about the floor in searching for her spectacles which had fallen from her head, upon which my mother beat her upon the back with clenched fists.

This scene took place in the doorway leading into the kitchen, whilst Gavin and I stood halfway up the staircase witnessing the row, and as we had never before seen an adult crying (apart from episodes in Laurel and Hardy films), the incident struck us as highly comical and we could not resist laughing. – "Why do you let them laugh at me? Why do you treat me like a fourteen year old?" cried the maid as tears rolled down her cheeks. – "If you behave like a fourteen year old, you'll be treated like one," my mother yelled back. – "I'm over sixty years old – I'm due respect," moaned the maid. – "In that case you should be drawing a pension, you old fool," replied my mother.

The upshot was that the maid visited the Post Office and then the Ministry of Pensions, and on receiving two years back payments and finding herself so flush, she bought a present for every family member. Some years later, following her final dismissal, my mother acknowledged that Jane was the finest cook ever employed in the household, adding, "I never knew anyone who had the art of baking finer pastries than her."

During this period the National Health Service was established, and put into full working order, but it did not lead to the impoverishment of the medical profession as predicted by my father, although he decided to maintain a purely private practice, which seemed to flourish. Over the years ever-larger cars were purchased, and driven down by a manufacturer's representative direct from Birmingham. The ultimate car was a luxurious Austin Sheerline, which were often purchased by local authorities for ferrying around their mayors or chief executives. My father also purchased a wooden seafront single storey property at Elmer Sands, adjacent to Bognor Regis. This was known as "Woodhouse," but after several years it was torn down and a fine two storey brick house, rendered in white, was built in its place. This was known as "White House."

As our parents were often away at the seaside, or elsewhere, during the weekends, we three children were looked after by Miss Wall, who cooked for us as well. She always insisted on working alone in the kitchen, and called us as soon as our plates of food were served up on the table. She always presented us with piled-up dishes of food, to fully satisfy our hunger, and as we sat down to eat, she always used to say, "Now you won't hurt!" This eventually became a family joke, and whenever we three brothers served up a family meal to one another, we customarily exclaimed, "Now you won't hurt!" and laughed at the joke which we always understood from the generous portions served up in the 1940s and early 50s.

As Miss Wall had travelled as the employee of a diplomatic family in Malaya, the South Pacific territories, and Canada, she told us remarkable tales about these lands: of how chimpanzees were trained and used as navvies in Malaya; and how a great wailing would be set-up throughout the jungle when a coolie had been mauled and half-eaten by a tiger; of the Malayan woman with an enormous worm in her stomach and how it occasionally climbed up her gullet, the head appearing in her mouth; of the kangaroos who could knock over a cart with their tails; of the mud geysers in New Zealand, commenting that, "one day the whole of New Zealand will be blown up into the sky;" and, of the wolves which howled outside the log cabins in Canada, and of how wooden shutters had to be fitted over the windows to prevent the animals from jumping into houses and eating their inhabitants.

During Christmas, Gavin and I were always taken on several occasions to pantomimes in the West End, or at the Golders Green Hippodrome, and we were often accompanied by our three cousins from the Brown family. We were either taken by our parents or by Uncle Dick and Aunty Joan. Occasionally our grandparents took us to another kind of show, such as a conjuring performance or to see *Peter Pan*. When we went to the pantomime in the West End we often sat in a box. When the Browns took us, I always remember that Aunty Joan went into raptures over the dancers, almost expressing envy over their skill and the "perfection" of their legs, even though she had a slim figure and shapely legs, and hence no reason for envy.

The pantomime was always a pleasure, and as soon as the baton was taken up and the first few bars of the orchestra were played, a thrill went down my spine. When the curtain rose on the brightly lit stage, I entered a world of enchantment, for this was how the world should *really* be. Everything seemed clean, happy, and predictable. Barons, Kings, Princes, and Princesses, were good-natured people, who easily rubbed shoulder with footmen, butlers, and idiotic nincompoops and ridiculous old dames, without offence being caused on either side – despite a fair amount of cheekiness and outrageous behaviour. This was a world in which all classes were presented in a totally *classless* environment.

If there was injustice or nastiness, it was a foregone conclusion that the baddies would lose out, and the oppressed would be awarded their prince or princess and live happily ever after. There were no psychological complications, for psychology simply did not exist in the world of the pantomime. Evil-doing or nastiness had to be invented as a kind of comical fantasy, which defied the boundaries of the orderly pantomime world, so that the power of magic could be relied upon to bring happiness at the conclusion. Thus mice had to be transformed into horses, and pumpkins into coaches, and the good fairy with her wand was guaranteed to overpower the wicked witch.

Surely the pantomime world was the world we should seek to create on earth! It was a world where all problems were hidden in a joke or a song, and where idiocy was a cause for laughter rather than a cause for concern. Any behaviour seemed acceptable because no behaviour caused real offence. If everyone could be as good-natured as pantomime people, the world would be a better place. And that was perhaps the only *real* lesson one could learn from such a fantasy world. The pantomime was the one time in the year for escaping into a paradisiacal universe.

*

During one of the rare occasions when my cousin, Carol, and my godmother, Joan, both stayed with us together, I was one night left alone in the house when my parents had gone out. It was late in a summer evening and I was already in bed reading a book, when Carol and her mother entered the room. Carol began to act in a flirtatious sort of way, and she sat on my bed and began passing her hands over my legs above the bedclothes, encouraged by her mother.

At first they asked about the book I was reading, but then my aunt said laughingly that she wanted to know "what kind of a man" I was. I began to struggle coyly and resist their advances, for I was both afraid and found their behaviour unpleasant, but they laughed all the more. At last my aunt exclaimed, "Let's leave him to his own manhood," and they left the room together. I always wondered afterwards as to what were their real intentions, or as to what degree they would have pushed their advances had I been more compliant. In any event, Aunt Joan either took offence at my response, or decided in her own mind that I must have homosexual leanings, judging by the veiled insinuations she made about me in the years which followed.

During these years at 105, we often had workers in the house: carpenters, roofers, tilers, and electricians, either to carry out repairs to a building which had been long neglected, or else to update plumbing or electrical wiring and points. The electrician was a Mr. Rogers, who allegedly was very slow in his work, and was therefore labelled as "lazy," and possibly a "Labour party supporter", and eventually he emigrated to New Zealand. There were two men, however, with whom my father struck up a firm friendship, Mr. Lister, a carpenter, and Tom, a handyman, both of them hard workers and supposedly Tory supporters. Mr. Lister became a regular tennis partner of my father, for although the latter was both status and class conscious, he was always happy in mixing socially with those who looked up to him. He had few friends in his own age group, with whom he might be described as a social equal, apart from friendly acquaintances at Rotary, the Old Cholmeleions (his old school) or freemasons, for he disliked anyone who might put him in the shade intellectually or knowledge-wise.

He had a particular dislike for women who showed off their knowledge in any way, and that is why he tended (alongside my mother) to ridicule Aunt Anita, who was also Gavin's godmother. I remember on one occasion at a hotel, when my father took a particular dislike to a well-dressed lady who was lecturing her two boys about some literary topic at the dinner table, which he dismissed as "affectation and pretentiousness." I would rather have described such behaviour as "educational," but my parents felt that such talk should be left to school teachers, and it was certainly rare that my mother sought to impart information of an intellectual nature unless it was something impinging on personal status.

Once my father took me for a walk in the West End, and as we passed down Pall Mall, he said that if I did well in life, I might one day join one of the imposing clubs situated in that street. On another occasion, however, when I must have bemoaned my situation in life, he responded with the democratic notion that we were "now living in the post-1914 world," and that today all of us were equal. His opinions, therefore, had advanced somewhat beyond those of his parents' generation. Contrariwise, as soon as television began to interview or otherwise present people who spoke non-southern standard English, he was outraged, and complained about the undermining of culture. As with most people, he was therefore inevitably full of contradictions in a complex and fast-changing society.

On one occasion, Tom, the handyman, approached my parents as to whether he might take Gavin and me to a football match. My mother then approached us for our own answer. My response was a firm "No," and so that applied to my brother also. Decades later I regretted having taken such a decision as a gesture of rudeness in response to a kind invitation. On the other hand, Tom's attitude was that every young boy should have the opportunity of attending football matches, and if my brother and I had accepted the offer, we might have bound ourselves to a regular time-wasting habit which became a nuisance because of that.

During a Christmas which we celebrated at 105 at this time, whilst the Browns, and Uncle Quentin, Aunt Sybel, and Aunt Ruth, were seated around the dinner table, towards the end of the feast, Quentin began to rag and ridicule his rather eccentric sister. Ruth was a little old lady and spinster, deeply religious, and little seen by her other relatives (apart from her brother Sidney) since she lived in an ancient thatched cottage, hidden away in the remote wilds of East Suffolk. We all laughed dutifully, after a substantial meal of turkey and a glass or two of wine, as great Uncle Quentin described how "electricity" and "gas" were commodities of which Ruth had never even heard the existence of.

She lived in her cottage and little patch of land with only oil for lighting and faggots for cooking, and to remain in good health, every day of the year she walked the four miles from Westleton to Dunwich to bathe in the cold North Sea. Earlier that Christmas day she had brought ridicule upon herself by discovering in the Bible (which was the only book she read) that a man was allowed more than one wife, and this greatly disturbed her. Quentin reminded her that this was a question which should hardly worry her, as she was unlikely to find a husband at her time of life – and even less likely a bigamist.

My cousins, Michael and Howard, however, used to stay with her every year for a week or so, and always had happy memories of holidays with their great aunt in an environment which could hardly have been a greater contrast from their own home. I was taken to tea there on one or two occasions, and remember that the upper floor was so uneven that it was almost like walking across the waves of the sea. There was also a large oil painting of an attractive looking ancestor from the Victorian period, who contracted a disease requiring the amputation of a leg, and as

Author's paternal Grandfather
Ernest William Corfe
(1878 - 1963)

Author's paternal Grandmother
Ethel Corfe, nee Smith
(1885 - 1951)

Maternal Grandfather
Capt. John Figgins, RN, OBE
(1868 - 1946)

Maternal Grandmother
Grace Figgins, nee Bedbrook
(1876 - 1965)

Great-Grandfather
Rr Admiral
James Albert Bedbrook
(1845 - 1902)

Author's early
childhood & later
teenage home:
196 Muswell Hill Road

Author's Father,
Felix Norman Corfe
(1906 - 1990)

Author's Mother
Joyce D.P.Corfe, nee Figgins
(1906 - 2000)

With paternal Grandparents
at Ashmount, with l. to r.
Uncle Harold & Father, 1936

Author age 2 in
London home, 1937

With Old Nanny
in garden, 1937

With maternal
Grandmother in
Melksham, 1937

Easter weekend picnic 1937, with seated l. to r.
Aunts Anita, Betty, Great-Aunt Lou, cousin Maris,
Great-Aunt Blanche, maternal Grandmother, Aunt Pam
and Mother; standing: Uncles Denys and Vaughan,
Great-Aunt Gwladys and Great-Uncle Percy

Whitsun picnic 1937, l. to r.
Uncle Dick, Author, Mother, cousin Anne,
Aunt Joan (Brown), cousin Michael and Uncle Harold

In London age 3

Sampford Place, Melksham

With Ealing Nanny, 1938

Author age 4 at Kingsdown
September 1939

On "My land" at the
back of Sampford Place
1942

Author in background with
cousin Maris, & brother Gavin
in foreground, 3rd September 1939
at Sampford Place

At Weddon Cross, Somerset, 1943

Author with his two
younger brothers & Miss Wall
at Sampford Place, 1944

Hampton Hall, Bath

With paternal Grandparents, Mother
and youngest brother, Oliver, 1945

G.B.Riddell, Housemaster
Woodbridge Junior School

With Mother & Gavin:
Half Term at Woodbridge,
1945

With parents,
Great-Aunt Ruth,
& Gavin in Westleton,
Suffolk, 1945

The Revd. E.A.Dunn

Author's later childhood
& early teenage home,
105 Muswell Hill Road

The brothers with dogs, Judy &
Woofa in Highgate Wood, 1946

Highgate School, July 1947

The Author

R.D.Newman

R.Olden (Robin Ray)

R.G.C.Osbourn

Highgate Schoolmasters: l. to r.
L.G.Markham (Latin Master),
H.F.R.Miller (Junior School Head),
G.F.Bell (Senior School Head)

Author's Father in sailing dinghy
1950

Woodhouse, Elmer Sands

Author's parents with
Mabs on left

Back row: paternal Grandparents,
front row: Uncle Quentin,
Mother & Aunt Sybel

Author's parents with Aunt Joan
(Brown) on left

Mother with Mabs & Bill Symonds
in Scotland

King Alfred School, June 1951

The Author

Raphael Samuel

Jonathan Davis

Sarah Miller

King Alfred School Staff

The Heads: Mr.B.H.Montgomery
& Mrs.H.M.E.Barber

Mr.F.C.Johnson (History)
& Mr.R.Fuller (English)

16 Conduit Street as
it appears today

Patricia Dainton
November, 1950

White House, with l. to r.
Father, Uncle Quentin, Mother,
Aunt Sybel & Aunt Joan

10 Sion Hill, Bath

Aunt Inez in
WREN uniform

The Author in
December, 1953

Uncle Bill at
Sampford Place

2 Old Burlington Street as
it appears today

this was before the age of anaesthetics, she chose to die rather than undergo the pain of the operation.

On approaching the age of 13 I faced the examination and selection process for entry into the Senior School at Highgate. The selection of pupils according to "character" was openly treated as more significant than the examination itself, and indeed, several of the most brilliant scholars were refused entry, including my friend, Newman, who was bright in mathematics, and with whom I had enjoyed many an hour in browsing through the Southwood Bookstore. The selection system was explained to us one day in class by Mr. Chottin, when he pointed to one of the dimmest boys in the form, saying that although he was academically backward, his "determination on the playing field" would assure him a place.

When my father came into my bedroom one evening, in interrupting my reading, to solemnly announce I had failed my entrance examination, he explained that I was not suitable to continue as an "academic student." He had been informed by the school that the occupation which would best suit me would be as a "market gardener running my own business in growing and selling plants." I said nothing but suddenly realised that my teachers at Highgate remained ignorant of both my abilities and inclinations, and that I was hated by my form master, Mr. Chottin. His judgement was not based on any kind of reasonable assessment, but rather on pure malice. The very idea of market gardening filled me with contempt and disgust.

On being rejected for entry, I was not over-worried as I had little interest in my formal education, feeling that what I taught myself was of greater significance to my future. It was, however, of great concern to my parents, and I was sent for psychological testing by the local government education authority to ascertain the best way ahead. It was recommended, in view of my personality, interests, and abilities that I be sent to King Alfred School in Manor Wood, North End road in Hampstead, just to the south of Golders Green. This was a progressive co-educational institution established in 1897 and incorporated as the King Alfred School Society (KAS) the following year. I entered the school in spring 1949, several months before my 14th birthday and remained there for three years, completing my school education at the age of 17.

I felt a little apprehensive – almost shameful, at the idea of being educated alongside girls, but these feelings were soon countered by high hopes of becoming a successful Casanova in winning over the heart or hearts of the most beautiful girls in the school. It was many years since I had last been in the company of many girls assembled in the same place – not since I was a 6-year old at Convent school, or possibly, at St. Michael's, at Melksham, although I could not remember speaking or associating with any girl at the latter school. In any event, being sent to a co-educational school would offer me the opportunity of a lifetime, and I could only imagine myself as a dashing future Don Juan.

CHAPTER 13
A New School and New Values

"Education has for its object the formation of character."

Herbert Spencer, *Social Statics*, Pt. ii, Ch. 17, Sec. 4.

King Alfred School: its values and success – Its system of discipline – The psychological problems of social integration – The teaching of history – Ronald Fuller and English literature – Political interests and the debating society – Raphael Samuel and our differences

The education I received at King Alfred's in literature, history, the arts, and social sciences, could hardly have better prepared me to succeed in my ultimate aspirations in later life, if not in the immediate occupations I was to take up towards the close of my teenage years and early 20s, then certainly by my early 30s and onwards. This was due to the high quality of the inspirational teaching, and also to the intellectual stimulus of many of the pupils who were my peers.

The school prided itself on teaching those from many nationalities and cultural backgrounds. There was a high percentage of Jews who dominated the cultural and political thought of the school, and many belonged to the left or even the far left. Most must have come from a fairly affluent background, since this was a fee-paying school, and there was an intellectual liveliness and quality of debate exceeding the level to be found in most well-known schools of the country.

Many were the children of diplomats or those who were prominent in many walks of life. There were David and Peter Wasserman (who many years later changed their names to Waterman) the sons of the founder and proprietor of the left wing chain of Collets bookshops; Sarah Miller, daughter of the novelist and biographer, Betty Miller (née Spiro 1910-65) and the psychiatrist, Emanuel Miller (1892-1970), the first person anywhere to establish a series of child psychiatric clinics, first on the Continent and then in Britain, and brother of the theatre and opera director, Sir Jonathan Miller; and then two daughters of Hugh Gaitskell, the former moderate Labour party leader, who tragically met an early death in 1963, also attended the school. I remember selling a programme to Hugh Gaitskell at one of the school's dramatic productions. He was somewhat more podgy than he appeared in press photographs, and he wore a pair of heavy horn-rimmed spectacles.

There was also the beautiful flaxen-haired, Sofia Johannsdottir, about a year younger than me, who became a talented pianist and then the wife of the world-renowned conductor and pianist Vladimir Ashkenazy. She was the daughter of our music teacher, and later in the 1960s the young couple took up Icelandic nationality although choosing to reside in Switzerland.

The above were my contemporaries, but over the years many others, especially prominent in journalism or the arts attended the school, such as the actress, Zoë Wanamaker, the documentary photographer, Janette Beckman, and the journalists, Richard Clements (1928-2006) and Ian Aitken.

The school had a uniform but only a minority (in which I was included) chose to wear it, whilst most wore whatever they wished, providing it met certain standards which changed from time to time. I remember several occasions when pupils were sent home for wearing dress considered unsuitable by the Headmaster. Older boys were not allowed to wear shorts during summer, and they had to have proper long-sleeved garments, and on at least two occasions, boys known to be Communists were sent home for wearing red shirts, for this was considered tantamount to displaying a political uniform, which of course had been made illegal in 1936. If a pupil appeared at school in a dirty or ill-dressed state, he would be publicly warned against a recurrence of this at the morning assembly.

The school was headed by two joint heads: Mr. B.H. Montgomery and Mrs. H.M.E. Barber, whose son, Chris, became an internationally famous jazz band leader, some years after he left the school. He also had a younger sister, Audrey, several years older than me, whom I came to know quite well during debating sessions. Mr. Montgomery taught geography, and could be quite severe at times, whilst Mrs. Barber was the chemistry teacher.

It was the policy of the school not to inflict punishment, but to depend on self-discipline, and so the teachers neither carried canes nor wore mortar-boards, and could be addressed by their first names, whilst the pupils in turn were invariably addressed in this way. I and others chose to address the teachers in a more formal way, as Mr. or Mrs. So-and-so, but the use of the title "Sir" was unknown. On joining the school I was placed in Miss Marsh's class (who was the biology teacher), and she explained to the new intake the basis of authority, and that the pupils were ultimately responsible to themselves and to the school. Self-discipline seemed a workable form of authority, and during my three years at the school, I never saw an incident of rudeness to teachers, or any serious insubordination against the rules of the school, although some democratic procedures, as described below, did lead to tension from time to time. Naturally there were occasions when children were rowdy or disorderly, but this was successfully corrected by the immediate and sharp reprobation of the teachers.

The head boy of my class was Richard Thomas, with whom I soon became friendly. He was the son of a film director, and later joined the Royal Shakespeare Company, where I visited him behind the stage at the Princes Theatre, after a performance of *Anthony and Cleopatra*, and later he became a well-known producer, the apex of his career coinciding with his production of the renowned television drama, *The Jewel in The Crown* in 1984. Towards the end of the term, he was discovered to have tuberculosis, and was away from school for almost a year. When he returned, following the loss of a lung, he returned with a hero's welcome, and resumed all the activities in which he had participated before – particularly drama, where he was given key roles. I, meanwhile, distinguished myself as a critic with essays on school dramatic presentations, and this led Richard and me to some lively albeit friendly discussions as to how Shakespeare should be produced.

The head girl of the class was Penelope Ionides, who later became a physicist and then an economist, and whom I was to meet for the first time after leaving the school 45 years later, at a function at the Reform Club, when we both happened to be members of the Labour Finance and Industry Group, in those heady days when the Labour party seemed destined to change the country for the better. Both of us became disillusioned with the LFIG, alongside many others, shortly after the Labour government was elected into power in 1997, and we left the association.

The school comprised a ramshackle yellow brick building constructed around a covered courtyard, with the library, chemistry block, offices, cloakrooms and other classrooms; a hall and theatre with kitchen, nearby the entrance to the school and the caretaker's lodge; several other classrooms comprising separate buildings spread around; Squirrel Hall, an open-walled roof structure built around a huge tree stump, used for daily assemblies; and a generous playing field fringed with open land and bushes. At the assembly every morning we sat on logs approaching a metre in diameter.

It was even contended that the school was part-run by the pupils, for there was a parliament to which each class sent several representatives, and it met for an hour on the first Friday of every month. Its discretion, of course, was limited, for it was overseen by the Headmaster or Headmistress and other teachers, and confined itself to discussing and passing decisions on catering matters; looking into complaints against such facilities as the cycle sheds, or the cleanliness of the cloakrooms, etc., or requests for special sporting equipment. The inculcation of these democratic ideals naturally ran counter to everything which had been implied through a Public school education, where the very word "democracy" was almost taboo, whilst its reality was either ridiculed or abhorred.

Soon after settling into the school I was to realise that my romantic inclinations were not to materialise. Firstly, I did not see any girls whom I found sufficiently attractive, and secondly, although boys and girls were seated together in the same classroom, there seemed a natural division between the sexes. Although there was full and equal cooperation between both in a classroom environment, during breaks each divided into their separate groups for conversation or play. Of course there was communication between boys and girls outside the classroom, and even friendships of a Platonic nature, but none of the craze for "dating" or romantic links, found throughout the American educational system. If romantic relationships were formed in the higher classes, they were maintained with quiet discretion.

During my time, I never knew of any sexual misconduct at the school, although there were authenticated rumours concerning a girl who had attended a year before I joined. She and a small group of boys from the lower forms had consorted in an improper manner in a kind of low-ceilinged cupboard by the cloakrooms. When discovered, she was obliged to leave the school, and later became an actress. There was another girl who was said to be prepared to lower her knickers and show her pudenda for the sum of ten shillings, but I never knew of anyone who took up the offer, probably because at that time one could have full sexual intercourse with a Soho prostitute for a sum which was only marginally more than that.

This is not to suggest, however, that feelings of affection between the sexes were not experienced, even if they may have been suppressed. On several occasions it was conveyed to me that different girls had formed an affection for me: on two of these occasions, friends of the girls laughingly informed me of the fact, and then ran away shyly; whilst on the third, a girl who was standing behind me, drew a deep sigh, and exclaiming my name, said, "Oh, how I like you!" I found these occurrences embarrassing as I was not prepared to reciprocate their feelings, and I usually avoided the social company of girls, although I was at ease with them in the classroom, or in debates, or in discussing literature or the arts. All this marked the collapse of my romantic aspirations within a school environment.

The most difficult problem I encountered at the school, which I never entirely overcame, was the need to adapt psychologically to a cultural milieu which was strange and entirely new. There were attitudes and customs which continued to grate, for they seemed to conflict with all the values and beliefs in which I had been ingrained. Until I joined King Alfred School, I had been subjected to cruelty and the brute force of authority, and this of course, continued at home. Few of my sensitivities had been respected, and if I expressed an opinion which clashed with that of my parents, my father would even go so far as to threaten to "cut me off with a shilling," in the same way that his friend, Dr. Greenway, in Bognor Regis, had "cut off his son with a shilling," and sent him out into the wilderness.

I felt awkward and embarrassed by the informality of the school, and especially by the use of first name terms, for at the Public schools I attended, we only addressed one another by our surnames, and only came to know the existence of first names if a personal relationship developed, and friends were invited home for tea. At King Alfred's we knew the surnames of all pupils, as they were read out at the daily register, and were marked on our exercise books, but in personal address only first names were referred to. Eventually, the sound of my middle name became so odious to me, that on leaving the school, I chose only to be known by my first name from then onwards.

A strange example of my refusal to be even acknowledged by the name of "Nigel" may be cited by an incident which occurred some five years after leaving the school towards the close of the 1950s. One day whilst passing by the London School of Economics in Houghton Street, I encountered Raphael Samuels, who was studying there at the time, and as will be clarified below, I came to know him well at King Alfred's, and had even attended a function at his parents' home. When I introduced myself as "Robert," he feigned not to recognise me, although the failure of mutual recognition between us in view of our abrasive relationship would have been hardly credible after so short a period. As he stood there nonplussed, as if searching his memory, I stubbornly refused to jog his memory with the name of "Nigel," and so we parted as if we had never met in the first place.

There are two possible explanations for this episode. The first is that I was dressed in a smart business suit in fitting the occupation in which I was then engaged, whilst he was dressed informally as a student. The second explanation, however, may be more significant, for following the Hungarian Uprising in 1956, he underwent a moral and spiritual crisis which led him to repudiate his Stalinist views and leave the Communist party, in favour of a more liberal although strong leftist stance. As a consequence of this, he openly apologised to the teaching staff at King Alfred's, as well as to other acquaintances and friends, for his past actions and thinking in supporting the ruthless politics of Stalin. It was thought at the time, by teaching staff and others, that he carried this gesture to an unnecessary length.

The lack of rules and regulations and their enforcement through threats and punishment, placed me in a strange psychological void with which I never entirely came to terms during my three years at the school. During my first weeks at the school, I was laughed at by several pupils for my constant fear of punishment for contravening what in a Public school might constitute minor breaches of rules or customs. I had never been caned or severely punished at any school I attended, for I had always adopted a manner of humility, and never questioned an order given by those in authority. Nonetheless, I always remained fearful of punishment, for I had often experienced the arbitrary punishment and extreme pain inflicted through flogging in a home environment.

During my first weeks I tried to form various gangs with several others, who understood my point of view, in fighting various silly causes, but we received little support, and were laughed at for our childish behaviour. Other pupils had more adult and constructive playtime interests, and later I joined Richard Thomas and his group, who were digging out an underground cellar with a roof of branches and timber. Nonetheless, on several occasions I became involved in several serious fights, and was afterwards severely reprimanded by the Headmaster for my "violent quarrelsomeness."

As a pupil with psychological problems in integrating with the cultural milieu of the school I was not alone. Two other ex-class mates from Highgate School joined me at King Alfred's at the same time, and if their psychological problems were different from mine, they were no less severe and their outcome worse. Both were noisy and undisciplined to an intolerable degree, and were not amenable to the idea of "self-discipline." Whilst one had been in receipt of regular canings from the Headmaster, the other now jumped on the girls in abusing them sexually – i.e. thrusting his hands into their breasts and lifting their skirts in a mischievously humorous manner. Both were withdrawn from the school after the first term, and after the event, I remember Mrs. Barber remarking that "So-and-so was not suited to the school because of his unruly temperament."

I remained at the school, firstly, because I became quickly absorbed in the serious study of English and History; and secondly, because my psychological conflict between the demands of freedom and those of a humiliating obedience to authority was not overt but repressed or hidden. The dichotomy between freedom and oppression arose through the failure to generate a sufficient level of team spirit, or group pride, or feeling of unique superiority, to be found in any Public school – all values of which are false values if viewed in a certain political context. At King Alfred's, such values were reserved exclusively for the sports field, for in the academic sphere, each individual was expected to maximise his abilities as best he or she could, without the need to *seemingly* outshine his peers.

All sports and physical training I loathed – and the latter included ball games which I found physically threatening. This was because I lived in fear of being castrated on the sports field – bearing in mind the stories of Mr. Partridge, and the numbers of eunuchs I believed had owed their condition to football, cricket, and even such gentler games as volley ball. I remember on one occasion during PT at King Alfred's, actually assaulting a boy during a game of volley ball, because the sphere he was throwing landed in my crutch, and for this I was severely reprimanded.

The individualism encouraged at King Alfred's I experienced as alienating rather than self-assuring, for at that time I valued the kind of friendship which comes from solidarity or unity of thinking, and such tendencies were not encouraged at the school. Each pupil was expected to find strength within his own balanced personality, and of course this was implied through the spirit of self-discipline. There was little time for hero-worship in the school in the same way that teaching staff were loathed to impose a system of punishment, or mould pupils to fit a fixed standard of character or personality. All were expected to be civil in their relationships, and respect the different individuality of their peers. This, of course, was a grown-up or mature attitude to the world.

I interpreted the two-way system of informality in communicating authority as disrespect or impoliteness towards those responsible for our nurture and education, but of course in reality, it was nothing of the sort. The style in which authority is communicated has nothing whatsoever to do with its intended ends, for the ends alone have significance, whilst style merely reflects the superficial appearance of the means. Brutality and humiliation do not necessarily ensure discipline or self-discipline, and indeed, more often arouse the kind of resentment leading to rebelliousness of one kind or another. It is far more effective in truly influencing the behaviour, and more significantly, the thinking of people, to use subtle and gentle means in achieving success.

But unfortunately, the external appearances of form and fashion exert a greater influence on the mind than the deeper realities of life. Style is everything to the young and unformed mind, but has little to do with right or wrong action, and too often leads to a deceptive line of thinking. This deceptive mindset and psychological confusion originating from style and the experience of brutality at both Woodbridge and home was to remain with me for several years yet. It was a problem I carried into the Army when the boot was on the other foot. My father wrongly anticipated I would "suffer" under Army life, and took some steps through medical specialists towards my exemption from National Service, but I was nonetheless admitted as fit. During my two years service in the ranks I encountered no problems with either basic training or afterwards.

Our basic training in terms of "toughness" was supposedly only second to the Guards – or so we were told by our Company Sergeant-Major – but I found physical exhaustion and mud, and shouting and swearing no problem to contend with. The Sergeant's bark was always worse than his bite, and we were always fairly treated and well-fed, and there was no bullying or victimisation – or none which could give rise to justifiable complaint – and of course ritual torture was unknown. When I became a junior NCO (whilst still a teenager) I attempted to turn the strict style of discipline into the harder reality it had been in an earlier era. In theory regimental baths and public flogging still existed in the Army of 1954-56 – or at least, it existed in the mythology of the rank and file, and when my unit failed a GOC (General of the Command) inspection, I attempted to introduce a far more ruthless discipline which was within my remit as being a Regimental policeman in charge of the Guardroom.

I did not realise at the time that such disciplinary measures would be intolerable in the British Army, and neither did I realise that so-called "brutality" was no more than pretence in maintaining discipline which rarely if ever mutated into the reality. My error was not to distinguish between the two. Eventually, as a consequence of my actions, I was called before the Commanding Officer, Lt. Col. Purcell, to be lectured and reprimanded, for not even the failure of a GOC inspection could be seen in justifying the course I had taken. The Colonel spoke about leading horses with kindness rather cruelty and the benefits of awards over punishment, and I was relieved of my post as a policeman, although I retained my rank and the armchair comforts of the Corporal's NAAFI.

With such a mindset as I had at the time, I would probably have been more attuned to serving in the ranks of the Imperial Japanese Army of the 1930s, or even that of Frederick the Great of the 1750s – or the British Army of the same period, these two being the most exacting European armed forces of the 18th century, until the reforms of the Comte de Guibert in 1788 which transformed the French Army into a highly disciplined force in readiness for the Napoleonic era. It was not until I settled in Scandinavia, where I resided for almost a decade that I fully recovered from the brutality of the Woodbridge syndrome, with its morality of the devil hypocritically clothed in the cloak of Christianity.

A mind which experiences a sense of guilt through the lack of oppression, fear, suffering, and constant punishment, must indeed be truly sick, but in Scandinavia I found myself living amongst peoples with the highest social morality in the world, where fairness, egalitarianism, and freedom existed in a perfect mix to create a truly sane society. In such an intellectual and amicable environment, I was to psychologically regain the balance of my personality and achieve sufficient objectivity in assessing values and behaviour. It is unlikely that this psychological problem at my last school was ever discerned by the teaching staff or anyone else, since it was a matter I discussed with no one.

The academic standards at King Alfred's were the highest I encountered anywhere: the teachers being not only specialists in their respective subjects, but endowed with a genuine interest in imparting knowledge and stimulating an attitude of enquiry, and it was for these reasons, and others clarified below, that I subsequently considered myself infinitely fortunate in being refused admittance to Highgate Senior School.

Within a year or so of my joining KAS, Gavin's name was entered as a prospective pupil on his finally leaving Norfolk House preparatory school, but my parents' first preference was that he should enter Highgate Senior School, although they were doubtful about his passing the entrance examination. As it happened, he did pass and he went to Highgate. This caused me some embarrassment as I was approached by several teachers and asked why Gavin had not joined me at King Alfred's. I was unable to give an answer. Some years later, by the time my brother had become rebellious and unruly, my mother exclaimed, "Thank God we never sent him to King Alfred's as otherwise we would have blamed the school for everything which went wrong with him!"

The school in which I was now privileged to be taught had an excellent library which was constantly enlarged, including works in Latin, French and German, as well as the major British classics and rare and interesting antiquarian works, such as Neale's *History of the Puritans*, and the *Letters of Junius*. In addition, each classroom had a specialised subject library of its own. During a book sale of titles which had been removed from the library as no longer required for one reason or another, I purchased a 33-volume set of the *Penny Cyclopaedia* published by the Society for the Diffusion of Useful Knowledge in the 1830s, which I found highly educational at the time, amongst other books which I also purchased at the sale.

The lessons at the school were excellently prepared, and usually took the form of lectures followed by a time for questions and answers, in contrast to the Public school system, where teachers merely sat lazily behind their desks and called on different pupils to get up and read a paragraph from a text book, to which additional information was rarely supplied, irrespective of the subject. There were two-hourly examinations every fortnight, and the marks for these were kept separate from our other work. Although most the teaching staff tended to be left of centre, these leanings were not significantly brought into the curriculum. On only one occasion do I remember failing to stand by my own independent judgement, and that was when I wrote an essay critical of Cecil Rhodes, which I subsequently regretted. The master who expressed these anti-imperialist sympathies, Mr. R.J. Handford, nonetheless had a high reputation as a history teacher, and when he left the school, it was to take up a post with University College London.

For the first two years my history teacher was Mr. F.C. Johnson, and we were given a course entitled the Benevolent Despots, covering the careers of Louis XIV, Peter the Great, and Frederick II, and I still vividly remember a large coloured print of this great Prussian monarch looking down onto the classroom. At previous schools I had never been taught anything about Continental Europe, and now I was learning about the great princes who helped to modernise the world as we know it today. I especially admired Peter the Great and his civilising mission in Westernising barbaric Russia. I was awed by his tax on beards, and ruthless crackdown on corruption, when even those who had held the highest offices of State were slowly torn to pieces when their hands were caught pilfering from the Treasury. His principles in maintaining the interests of the modern State were such that he was even prepared to execute his own son when the latter became involved with reactionary interests and he then attempted to flee the country. Such a man stood constantly by the highest standards of political morality since he was financially incorruptible, and no higher purpose could be expected of a ruler.

A girl in a higher class, Anthea Ionides, the elder sister of our girl class leader, approached me on one occasion saying I would be enthralled next term when our form was due to learn about Napoleon – "the greatest man in history," as she described him. Sure enough, the next term we learned about the Enlightenment and the French Revolution, followed by the story of Napoleon. On the wall was fixed a diagram of all the battles he had fought, marking his victories and defeats. It may seem surprising, in view of my admiration for Napoleon in bringing the ideas of the Enlightenment to most of Continental Europe, that I also admired Metternich and the Metternich system which arose from the Congress of Vienna in 1815.

My respect for Metternich arose through the void left by the final defeat of the French Emperor, and the need to impose a secure peace throughout the Continent, and if Austria sought to crush liberalism and the interests of the rising middle class, internal peace was secured until 1848 (apart from the July Revolution in Paris which saw the overthrow of Charles X) – and it certainly suited the commercial interests of Britain. If the policies of Metternich in deferring to the principles of legitimacy and the recognition of cultural and religious differences between nations have been looked upon with askance in the past, they have certainly been revived in the second half of the 20th century through the thinking and advocacy of America's Secretary for State, Henry Kissinger, amongst others.

My enthusiasm for history not only generated a love for the past, but gained for me a reputation for preferring to have lived in an earlier epoch. One day in the library I fell into a discussion with Peter Seglow, who was a year older than me and later became an academic of some distinction, as to what really aroused an interest in history. He had been born in Austria and could not explain as to why he was interested in historical studies. At last he turned to me, and asked incredulously, "Would you *really* rather have been born in another age?" After a momentary pause, I answered definitively, "No, I would not like to have been born in an earlier era." My explanation for an interest in history is that it arises from intense dissatisfaction with life and bad experiences. As a child Peter Seglow had been a refugee from Nazi persecution, whilst I had endured a brutal and oppressive home life. My interest in history had begun through a romantic view of the past, as reflected in the kind of popularity aroused through costume dramas, and only later did it mutate into a more scientific examination of the past linked inevitably to social and political studies.

The best teacher of all, from my perspective, was our English teacher, Ronald Fuller, a man with an encyclopaedic knowledge of literature and history, with a fluency in several modern languages, besides Latin and Greek, and with other cultural interests touching many aspects of life. He was a chain smoker, and a minor piece of information he once imparted to the class was that it was "bad form to light up a cigarette in a holder." One should light up a cigarette and having smoked one tenth of its length, it could then be inserted into a holder. When I took up smoking at the age of 17, it was a piece of advice I followed religiously during the short period of time I could be bothered to use a holder. I eventually gave up smoking cigarettes in May 1963 at the age of 28 on boarding a ship in Helsinki bound for Lübeck, and have never tasted a cigarette since. I continued to smoke cigars for another 20 years, but only during Christmas or Easter, and I gave up this luxury when they made me feel sick after a heavy meal.

Ronald Fuller was the author of several books on literary topics, and a direct descendent of the famous 17th century antiquarian and divine, Thomas Fuller (1608-61), whose most famous book was a *History of the Worthies of Britain*, and on the Restoration he was appointed Chaplain-Extraordinary to Charles II. The lectures of Ronald Fuller were always gripping, and time was allowed for questions and discussion, and during the three years I attended the school he opened up entirely new vistas for learning, and he helped direct my omnivorous but discriminate choice of reading. He once alerted us to the fact that the time for reading the most important books was during our schooldays, as after that period, when we were engaged in an occupation, we would have little time left for personal study or free choice of reading. I was subsequently fortunate in not being placed in such a situation, and I have succeeded in continuing my literary and social sciences studies on a lifelong basis.

One afternoon whilst engaged in the quiet of an essay writing session, he called me up to the front of the classroom having just corrected a recent piece of my homework. He brought my attention to the piece, which was a description of life surrounding the Elizabethan theatre, saying it conveyed an imagination and understanding of the epoch "quite beyond my years," and that I should strive to develop my latent literary abilities. This was good encouragement indeed, and I strove to follow his advice, and in addition to school work, I produced several historical novels over the next couple of years, viz., *Five English Comrades*, inspired by Dumas, about Cavaliers confronting Roundheads; *Anthony Anvil*, a love story taking place during the Glorious Revolution; and, *James Thornton*, an unfinished early 19th century tale with overtones of Thackeray.

Several years later, in the Spring of 1954, after being posted by the Army from my training camp in Devizes to Ranikhet Camp, Tilehurst, Reading, I wrote to Ronald Fuller, proposing to visit him in nearby Maidenhead. He wrote back a kind letter but explaining it would not be convenient for me to visit him at the present time as he was nursing a sick sister. It may have been that I disappointed him in expressing my pride in serving as a soldier, bearing in mind his pacifism, and that he had served in the last War as an ambulance man. He ended his letter with a cryptic sentence explaining that there are many vicissitudes during the course of life, but that what really mattered were those achievements made by the end of life itself.

Many decades later, after the start of the 21st century, I contributed an article about the inspirational teaching of Ronald Fuller to the *Old Alfredian*, and several weeks later I received a letter from Sarah Miller, thanking me for my article and offering to send me a CD of Mr. Fuller's Jonathan Davis Memorial Lecture, delivered at the end of the 1950s. Sarah was a year younger than me, but remembered my pontificating on literary matters in the library at King Alfred's, and on resuming our friendship we met for tea at the Wigmore Hall when she told me she had kept up her friendship with Ronald Fuller until his last illness and death in 1974. She had a "crush" on the English teacher, and had recently taken early retirement after a lifetime with the BBC. She was involved in several good causes of a semi-political and mystical nature, and invited me to attend musical soirées she had arranged at her home, but I found it difficult to travel so far for an evening out.

In 2006 I came across an announcement of her death in the *Old Alfredian*, and sent a note of condolence to her relatives which needed to be forwarded through her legal executives. Many months later I received an acknowledgement from her brother, Sir Jonathan Miller, who wrote in his letter of 15th October 2007, "Although she had a somewhat sad single life" (which I felt were uncalled for sentiments in response to a letter of condolence) "she enjoyed the company of many friends and right to the end was a great enthusiast for music and literature and the theatre and for the various Jewish societies with which she maintained a close contact to the very end of her life." She had never told me that the great theatre producer was her brother, and only afterwards did I discover that they had not been on good terms, primarily because of her religiosity versus her brother's intensive atheism. She had a certain idealism which was missing in the character of her elder brother, and this may explain the unnecessary recollections in the letter referred to above.

One of my best friends at this time was Jonathan Davis, who was already widely read in the English classics, and had achieved a quite remarkable knowledge of English poetry. He was also the youngest member of the Gilbert and Sullivan Society. We spent much time together discussing literature, and also our literary ambitions in later life. Whilst I aspired to becoming a novelist, he aspired to becoming a literary critic and university teacher, but neither of us was to achieve our ambitions in these spheres of activity. I decided by my early 20s that novel writing would be a waste of time on the grounds, firstly, of competition, secondly, because I felt there was no assured market for the kind of novels I might choose to write; and thirdly, because I could not perceive a sufficiently innovative way forward in advancing the novel as a unique literary genre. Jonathan's life, on the other hand, was to end in tragedy, when he was drowned at the age of 18 whilst swimming in Lake Como.

When I did eventually come to write a novel, *The Girl From East Berlin*, in 1961, the motivation arose from unique personal circumstances, and the question of literary form was pushed aside. On 14th August that year I was working as a teacher in a Summer camp in a remote area of Finland, and when I learned about the events which had occurred during the early hours of that day in constructing an impenetrable barrier in dividing a great European city, I immediately perceived I was obliged to write an epic autobiographical novel surrounding the events. This was no occasion for vexing over the niceties of literary style, for the narrative and truth of the story would take on its own style. The task was undertaken in Helsinki and completed after an

18-month period, although the novel was not published until 2006 after two widely separated periods of ruthless self-editing.

Another close friendship I developed at this period was with Geoffrey Dunston who lived in Woodford Green, Essex. The superficial similarities in that we happened to be gentiles and Christians may subconsciously have drawn us together in sharing certain common interests, but our conversation concentrated on books and literature, and we often met in the West End to explore the second hand departments of Foyles and other bookshops in Charing Cross Road. I was the dominating partner in the friendship in imposing my ideas on his, and I still retain many of his letters and cards, either from holiday resorts or in arranging to meet in Foyles, although none of my letters to him survive. He also became my confidant in regard to my love for the stage and film actress, Patricia Dainton, as described in the next and following chapters.

In return, he confided to me that he was the only pupil in the school who had been chosen to have a free place, and as a consequence of this, a close friendship and tennis partnership developed between his father and the Headmaster, Mr. Montgomery. He also had a younger sister, who was tall for her age but attractive, and an older male pupil had fallen for her and bombarded her with love letters which allegedly contained indecencies. As Geoffrey's sister was only 15, and as the letters were considered unacceptable, the boy concerned had to be withdrawn from the school. This, too, was a piece of confidential information, and I was surprised by the episode, as the offending boy had always conveyed the impression of being shy and retiring.

After leaving the school and returning several years later, in the mid 1950s, for an open day, I greeted Geoffrey Dunstan as he sat amongst a small group waiting to bat in a cricket match between the Old Boys and the First Eleven. He responded superciliously, seemed embarrassed, and began addressing another boy in order to avoid my presence. I knew from his rudeness at that moment that our friendship was over. He was then undergoing his National Service in the RAF, and surprisingly, he claimed to be an "Adjutant," a position in the Army which could not be held by anyone beneath the rank of Captain. As I had recently been serving in the ranks, he did not consider it worthwhile continuing our acquaintanceship. It also transpired that his interest in books and literature was superficial, and something he had "outgrown." From that day onwards I never saw or heard from him again.

During this period I developed a deeper interest in politics alongside my interests in literature, history, and the arts, but I was not to be persuaded to support any of the divisive parties of the left or right, in the conviction they failed to promote the better interests of the majority which could only be discovered through a disinterested approach to socio-economic issues. I joined the school's debating society and soon made my presence felt with my ideas which were a nice combination of realism and idealism. I was an avaricious reader of political philosophy, having embarked on Plato's *Republic*, which influenced me profoundly, before reading several histories of political philosophy, e.g., Catlin and Sabine, followed by many of the publications sponsored by Karl Mannheim under the heading of the International Library of Sociology and Social Reconstruction, as published by Routledge & Kegan Paul, over the following years.

With the backing of this objective approach to political life, I forcefully promoted my ideas, but soon came up against the hard Communist left under the leadership of Raphael Samuel, who was later to become such a distinguished academic and historian, and his followers, David and Peter Wasserman, and others. Raphael usually resorted to the instrument of ridicule in attempting to achieve his ends, but he was not always successful in this, and when I was eventually elected to lead the debating society as a representative in assessing subjects for discussion, he protested loudly on the grounds that I was "a history man rather than a politics man," and hence unsuited for such a post, but nonetheless, I continued to retain majority support. In fairness to Raphael, he did support me on other occasions, and when one day he happened to pick up my English exercise book lying on a desk in the library, and came across an essay I had written in the style of Sir Francis Bacon, "On Big Fishes and Little Fishes," he praised me for the excellence of my Marxist interpretation of political power.

Several classmates intimated I must be an "anarchist" in refusing to support or sympathise with any of the mainstream political parties, but I repudiated their accusations as nonsense, saying they had a narrow perspective of political life if their ideas extended no further than the stale old notions of established prejudice. Nothing could persuade me to lean one way or the other, and I regarded it as far sounder to hold all their parties in disdain as being counterproductive to the public good. I was to hold this stance for the greater part of my life, and certainly for the next 30 years when exceptional circumstances persuaded me to join the SDP as a founding member and activist in 1980, and later, on Tony Blair's assurance that class-based politics was out-dated and discredited, I joined the Labour party in 1994, and remained an activist until June 2008, when I resigned and re-adopted the political stance I had had as a teenager at King Alfred's. Thus, within a 50-year period I had turned full circle. I believe as I have always believed that knockabout ding-dong politics is not only demeaning to humankind, but ensures that political discussion is never allowed to rise above the most superficial level.

It was one of my classmates, Simon Ryder-Smith, the son of our French teacher, Mrs. Johnson, and the step-son of our history master, Mr. Johnson, who first introduced me through an act little short of physical force to the writings of Karl Marx. One day whilst in the library, this huge boy dragged me to a seat nearby the shelves of political books, grabbed the first of a 2-volume work of the selected writings of Marx and Engels, opened it at the start of the *Communist Manifesto*, slapped the book down onto a table in front of me, and ordered me to read. I read the pamphlet, which I found factually illuminating, but I was repulsed by the agitated revolutionary style which aroused my scepticism as to the underlying truths which the writers were trying to convey.

My suspicions were justified, for although I could not exactly identify them at the time, the purpose of Marx was not to construct a *positive* political philosophy (a concept he dismissed as naïve), but rather a dialectic for overthrowing the existing order in the belief that the consequences would be the emergence of a stateless socialist paradise. Marx was unconscious of the fact that his scientific critique of the capitalist process only laid the foundations for a utopian dream – and yet utopianism was the element in politics which evoked his greatest derision. This ironic dichotomy was not only to lead to endless quarrels and splits within the socialist movement, but at a much later date, from the 1930s onwards and throughout the second half of the 20th century, to the persecution and slaughter of millions in the name of a false and unworkable ideology. Nonetheless, I came to realise the importance of studying Marxist philosophy, and I carefully read many of his works.

We lunched in the school hall, and each of the tables was headed by a teacher, and there was a table roster to which we signed up on a weekly basis, and there was always a heavy demand to sit at Mr. Fuller's table and enjoy his conversation. No pupil, however, was allowed to sit at one table for more than two consecutive weeks, but I usually succeeded, with other literary enthusiasts, in signing up for his table every other week, and there were always lively discussions during lunch. When the meal was finished, the dishes and cutlery were cleared away, and we had to leave the tables which were folded and stacked, whilst the forms on which we sat were piled against the walls.

It was at one such lunch in the school hall when we were told that the King had died. At the same table sat Stuart West, a Jewish pupil, who surprisingly for a member of his race, was of a dull and unimaginative temperament, with aspirations to become an accountant, and I was astonished in view of his known insensitivity – at least towards the arts – when he burst into tears. Raphael Samuel, who sat at the same table with us, immediately ridiculed his outburst of sorrow, reminding him that "monarchy" was not the road for the future. The following day at the assembly, there was a two minute's silence held in memory of the King, and as we made our way to our classrooms some minutes later, I remember Peter Wasserman, my classmate, exclaiming, "Queen Elizabeth I saw the beginning of British imperialism, and now Queen Elizabeth II will see its end." This was not merely stated as a question of fact (which of course it eventually became) but with malicious intent as if he was to promote the end of British power through his faith in worldwide Communism.

A more significant intellectual influence at the school than Marxism or left wing politics was Freudian psychology. This was not something taught at the school – at least not intentionally – but seemed to be grounded in the cultural mindset of the majority of families from whence my fellow pupils sprung – my family, of course being excepted from such tendencies. Until ten years earlier Sigmund Freud had lived the last year of his life in a house hardly a mile distant from the school. We pupils, irrespective of our political leanings, but probably those inclined towards a more secular outlook on life, constantly prompted or criticised one another according to assumed psychological characteristics, and then followed this up with Freudian arguments. I later came to discover that such a mindset was a generational thing, and certainly not confined to King Alfred School, and in the Army and in the world of work, most young people with a thoughtful attitude to life interpreted humanity in psychological terms, but it was only at KAS that I first encountered this, and psychology has since remained my primary approach in making sense of existence.

Amongst the extra-curricular afternoon subjects, there were besides the sports of cricket, hockey, soccer, tennis and fives, art, drama, wood and metal working classes, printing, and cooking and household management for the girls – and of course debating, where I learned the basic principles of public speaking. The subjects for debate were usually arranged a week in advance, so allowing for preparation, and most centred around political, religious, or other topical subjects. Raphael Samuels usually dominated the debating society, to the exasperation of some, and he would arrive with a great bundle of notes, and would have controlled the proceedings if not held in check by the teacher in charge, who was usually Mrs. Barber, the Headmistress.

Raphael was unquestionably a brilliant speaker, and used the art of ridicule or even open insults in confronting opposition. I remember on one occasion his referring to the father of a senior boy as a "Trotskyist," and this led to a furious quarrel and almost led to blows, and eventually he was obliged to write a letter of apology. His activities on behalf of the Communist party were considered a "problem" by the teaching staff, particularly his subversive leafleting (which was not strictly allowed), and he had a habit of concealing the *Daily Worker* behind the display rack of *The Times* in the school library. *The Times* was the only paper displayed at the school, and when Raphael proposed at the parliament that the *Daily Worker* should also be displayed in balancing political opinion, his view of the situation was almost unanimously rejected. When the Headmaster discovered the *Daily Worker* cleverly concealed behind *The Times*, he removed the offending paper before ceremoniously tearing it into pieces before binning it.

No one could prevent those from the far left collecting signatures for banning nuclear weapons, or supporting suppressed minorities in colonial territories, etc., and I signed such petitions, after we had been assured (usually falsely) that they were "free from Communist influence." Political meetings in central or other parts of London were also announced, although such notices were often posted on boards without proper authority. One day it was announced that a talk on the Soviet Union was to be held at Raphael Samuel's home, and when I joined the small group after school hours to attend this event, Raphael threw up his arms in exasperated amusement when he realised that I would be amongst their company. The talk was given by an elderly man who had just returned from Moscow. He was a grim-visaged Englishman who never smiled once, but he praised every aspect of Soviet life and the heroism and genius of Joseph Stalin. During the question and answer session, he was taken to task by a young White Russian, who had fled to the West in 1942.

During one summer open day at the school, Raphael sported a red shirt, and carrying a thick volume of Lenin, he smoked a Stalinist style pipe. Smoking was naturally forbidden for pupils in the school, but during an open day he could easily mix in with the crowd or even pose as an old boy, for it was a day when discipline could not easily be enforced. Eventually he was taken under the tutelage of Mr. R.J. Handford, the senior history master, who groomed him for an academic rather than a political career, and this was to change the direction of his life.

My paternal grandparents were naturally suspicious of King Alfred's from the start, especially on learning that Communists attended the institution, and one Sunday morning over a glass of Sherry after church, my grandfather exclaimed, "When you meet a socialist I hope you punch him on the nose." I said nothing, but my mother put in rather primly, "At that school they don't fight." – "That sounds a funny kind of school where the boys don't fight," commented my grandfather.

CHAPTER 14

Love for an Actress

"Love has no thought of self!
  Love buys not with the ruthless usurer's gold
  The loathsome prostitution of a hand
  Without a heart! Love sacrifices all things
  To bless the thing it loves!"

Bulwer-Lytton, *The Lady of Lyons*, Act V, Sc. 2, 1, 23.

The beautiful Patricia Dainton – Psychological background for such an obsession – I seek personal advice for courtship – The first love letters – My mental condition – Revelations of the Journal

In Spring 1951 I fell helplessly in love with a film star whose photo I had first seen in the *Daily Mail* in November 1950. The short and medium consequences for my life, of this all-absorbing passion, were self-destructive, and were to destroy any aspirations I may have had for a planned or constructive academic future. The long-term, or psychological consequences of this love, were to direct the future course of my life for both good and ill.

On Saturday 18th November 1950 I read a feature on a film premiere of, *The Men*, attended by three film stars whose pictures accompanied the report, viz., Valerie Hobson (1917-98), who later married John Profumo in 1954, the Tory Minister who was subsequently disgraced following his involvement in a sex and espionage scandal; South African born Glynis Johns, famed for her husky voice and comedy roles; and lastly, Patricia Dainton. I was immediately struck by the beauty of the last-named, who wore an elegant white dress, and her long flaxen hair was neatly tied back in a bun before falling as lovelocks over her shoulders. In the report, "orchids ascended with ferns from the ruched sequin-studded bodice" of her "silver gown to a net scarf worn back to front. Above the orchids were diamond earrings, and below them, near-elbow-length gloves."

I was enchanted by the almost childish innocence and sweetness of her smile, her eyes flashing beneath a high forehead, and the benevolence which seemed to exude from her demeanour as she glanced towards the camera. I cut out the article and retained the picture as a thing of beauty to gaze upon whenever I felt the need for human company, without any idea of developing a friendship with the human being behind this glamour. Over the following weeks and months I became obsessed with the portrait, until eventually I was overcome with a desire to possess the beloved object. I was convinced that spiritually our personalities and desires coincided as a perfect match. There was nothing which could divide our interests except for the falsity and delusions of the external and unreal world.

My first course was to trace her whereabouts, and gain some information about her personal life. The Public Library was the first port of call, and in a directory of British film stars I read and copied out the following text:- "Born in Hamilton in Scotland on 12th April 1930. Daughter of Vivienne Black, film and stage agent. Studied for the stage at Toynbee Hall, and after experience in pantomime and ENSA, made her first film debut in 1942 in *The Bells Go Down* (Ealing). Recently, *Uncle Silas* (Two Cities), *Dancing With Crime* (Coronet-Paramount). 1946-49: on the stage in, *Love in Waiting* (Highbury). Under contract to J. Arthur Rank." Her address was given as c/o Vivienne Black, 16 Conduit St., London, W.1. With this information at my fingertips, I was ready to embark on a passionate courtship and win the love of my life.

Her career was to cover a series of films, television, and theatrical roles between 1947-66, when she suddenly and inexplicably disappeared from public view. Then in 2011, on the Britmovie website, I discovered the following curious entry by a certain Peter Rand, who wrote: "in the late 1970s I was working as a trainee manager at W.H. Smiths, Walton-on-Thames. For a period I worked in the Book department which was managed by a very attractive woman called Pat Dainton. It was a few months later that I discovered she had been a successful actress in the 50s and 60s. She was married to a film director and from memory she had two beautiful daughters. Pat loved books, and was a very passionate person in her role as a manager. She was a joy to work with." What could possibly have persuaded such a glamorous film star to make such a startling career change which must have so totally altered her lifestyle?

Having been struck by Cupid's arrow for an unobtainable being, how could such a crazy scheme have captured my imagination and worse still, been pursued in practice? I had first encountered her image as I said, in November 1950, and in August that year I had contrived to end my friendship with Angela Nickels, as I no longer found her physically attractive. A void (of my own making) had therefore been created in my life. The overwhelming desire for a permanent romantic relationship with someone of the opposite sex, bearing in mind my young age of 15, can only be explained through a deep-seated psychological need. Otherwise such a desire could only be dismissed as perverse in one of such an early age.

It may be that I felt alienated from most of my relatives, in that my interests were different from theirs, and that there was no common bond or basis for understanding to give rise for affection. I was regarded with contempt by my parents, who in the years ahead, not only attempted to create a barrier between me and my cousins and other relatives, but also a barrier between me and their friends, and so I was excluded from anything which could be described as a social gathering except at very special events such as Christmas. Whilst my father treated me with extreme insensitivity, my mother could never be trusted with any piece of information without the fear of its being used against me at some future date.

It should also be noted that my brothers were treated likewise, but we all responded in different ways to this cruelty and repression. Whilst externally I always presented a conventional impression, internally I was boiling with a spirit of rebellion. My younger brother, Gavin, was externally rebellious in his appearance and interests – especially through his enthusiastic playing of jazz on the trumpet, which consequently resulted in his expulsion from home at the age of 15, but otherwise he had a relaxed and careless attitude to life. My youngest brother, Oliver, who was never thrashed, since it seemed at last to dawn on my parents that caning was somehow counterproductive, nonetheless developed into a nervous child and suffered from a bad stammer from which he never recovered.

The contempt of my father for all his sons – and my brothers were undoubtedly held in even greater contempt than their first born – stemmed from the fact that none of us fulfilled the demands of the stereotypical Englishman. In behaviour and interests we were *individualistic*, and this was an unforgivable characteristic. In fairness it should be noted that my father had contempt for the younger generation in its entirety, in that it lacked the polish and good manners of his own generation. Despite my father's opinion, I was nonetheless noted for "good manners" by great aunts and uncles, and sometimes ragged for this characteristic by school acquaintances. "Why do you have to be so polite?" was an accusation sometimes thrown at me by my peers.

My father had little understanding of human nature and little tolerance for the quirks of personality. What he really desired were daughters rather than sons, but if the latter, he craved for *Stepford* sons rather than *human* sons. He wanted pre-programmed robots who would fulfil all the ideal characteristics of the perfect human being: i.e., good at cricket and sports, achieving top marks in all subjects, never behaving in a manner which would displease, and never seeming to be a burden on their parents. Real life was problem-free – or it always had been until the birth of his children – whilst psychology was non-existent, and a deviation of any kind was only explicable through a theological interpretation of good and evil.

This was the household in which I had been nurtured, which was not so much stuffy or constricted, as suffocating, soul-destroying, and deathlike in every aspect. My father's answer to the gloom and depression which overhung the household at particular periods was always the church, but the latter I found even more depressing than home life. After church, my father would often bang away at the piano singing hymns, to the exasperation of my mother, and to the dismay of us all, and when he realised this, he would bang away and sing all the louder. It was in this environment that I yearned for the love of a beautiful woman and for escape from a loveless household where all was at enmity with my feelings and aspirations.

By this time I had outgrown the need for friendship with a girl of my own age. Of course I had briefly enjoyed my love for Cynthia at Swanage. She had been six years my senior, but now she was lost in the mists of time, and I had never accepted the practicability of a friendship between us. The idea of befriending a girl at King Alfred's was dismissed as puerile. I needed to confide my love for Patricia Dainton with someone, and Geoffrey Dunston was to be my confidant in this regard. As he was alternately sympathetic and critical, this led to a dialogue between us, the result of which strengthened my reasoning and conviction in somehow carrying the affair to a successful outcome. Such discussions and occasional arguments could have led in no other direction. Every thought and even every contradiction drove me forward towards the object of my passion.

My love for Patricia Dainton was pure and unblemished by corrupting or carnal thoughts. I longed to embrace and kiss the beautiful features of her face, but would have been horrified to make sexual advances as to endanger her honour or virginity. My attitude was that of the medieval troubadour. She was to be idolised or worshipped from a distance as a being who occupied a higher sphere of existence than ordinary women, and if she was to be approached or touched with impure thoughts, then such a suitor would be condemned to damnation.

This is not to suggest I was averse to the raw pleasures of sex. In the Hippodrome in Charing Cross Road at that time was the Follies Bergère, and outside the theatre was displayed the 30-foot naked image of its lead dancer. Second only to Diana Dors (1931-84), whom I regarded as the most sexually attractive woman on the planet, this was the person with whom I most wished to enjoy the lust of a sexual relationship, and not with Patricia Dainton. At that time I recognised a clear distinction between the unsullied purity of true love which was not to be contaminated with lust, and sexual desire which was purely a physical enjoyment. The two were not to be confused. In this sense I was a true troubadour.

It was not my intention to throw myself blindly at the foot of the one I loved. Before composing any letters, I felt the need for authoritative advice. But to whom could I turn? School friends or family members were not to be trusted, and neither did they have the appropriate experience in such matters of the heart. The obvious choice was to turn to those professionals in the media who devoted their lives to resolving the love entanglements of others. I therefore wrote to two journals: to Jane Blythe at, *Reveille For the Weekend*, at 54 Fetter Lane, and to the world-famed Mary Grant at, *Woman's Own*, Southampton Street, The Strand.

The text of my letters to these advisers of the heart are no longer extant. The first reply was from Jane Blythe at *Reveille*, dated 25th April 1951, and it was not encouraging. It read as follows:- "Dear Mr. Corfe – Thank you very much for your letter. I think it is most unlikely that you could ever become friendly with this young woman, as she must have hundreds of fans, all of whom would like to contact her. I suggest you content yourself with the girls that you meet and stop falling in love with photographs. – Yours sincerely," &c. The second letter from the renowned Mary Grant and her Problem Page, was far more encouraging – or at least, that is how I saw it. It is undated but post marked 7th May. It read as follows:- "Dear Mr. Corfe – Thank you for your letter. Lots of young men fall in love with the photographs of actresses, and the actresses are flattered and delighted, so I assure you that Patricia Dainton will not think you stupid or impertinent if you write to her. As for her address, that is something I cannot supply. But write to the Editor of one of the film papers – or to the *Daily Mail*, where you first saw her picture. – Yours sincerely" &c. When the letter arrived, it was handed to me by my father, who immediately asked from whom it was. He was curious since it arrived in a self-addressed envelope. I felt I had no alternative but to tell the truth, upon which he started blustering about my parents being the proper people to consult on such matters.

With the arrival of the month of May, I resolved on commencing the courtship. The first letter was written on 5th. This and those that followed were long rambling epistles which showed that I had no practical experience in winning the affections of the opposite sex, and their effect would have been to repel rather than attract. There was no "beating about the bush," and in the first letter I was sufficiently candid to declare that, "I have fallen passionately in love with your picture and all attempts of my trying to drive you from my mind have failed." I then apologise for what might be interpreted as "impertinence," but excuse this on the grounds that we are all at the mercy of nature and so cannot be held responsible for our feelings. I then attempt to project my sense of honour by saying that, "I am not the type of person who falls in love with anybody" and then discards them the next moment, and "neither do I collect photographs of actresses for a vain or casual admiration. … I treat few things lightly, especially love, which I greatly respect, and it was this which induced me to write to you."

As if this was not sufficient to arouse aversion for the author, I then indulge in the self-pity of admitting, "so much do I love you, that every time I am alone, a gloomy melancholy breaks over me, which can only be checked by the vanity of beautiful visions, without which I would be ready for the grave." After declaring my love in more forceful terms, accompanied twice by apologies for any seeming "impertinence," I ask her to "please think of the agony and humility in which I stand before you." After several more paragraphs, I draw towards a conclusion with the words, "I have enclosed a stamped addressed envelope together with a sheet of notepaper for your reply. Most likely before we meet, you would rather have further information about me. This I will gladly supply together with a photograph in my next letter." In the only sentence which suggests a glimmer of humour, I add, "I only wish I could enclose the pen and ink also in my envelope!"

Having not received an expected reply after an impatient wait of five days, on 10th I sent a second letter. I began the letter, "May I apologise if my last letter appeared too impertinent" or aroused your suspicion. I then speculate as to why she may not have replied, e.g., perhaps I am seen as a "dark" character; or perhaps she receives much correspondence from other suitors. I then continue, "Last Monday I saw a second photograph of you in the *Daily Mail*, which said you were acting in, *Count Your Blessings*, at the Westminster theatre, and which at least proves you must be staying somewhere in London. ... I have just prepared a present for you, but which is too large and brittle to be sent by post. I would therefore like to suggest that I make an appointment to give it to you in person, on any weekday after 5.0 pm, or any time which is most suitable to you during the weekend, at your present lodging which I assume is 16 Conduit Street. I am afraid I cannot see you during Whitsun, as I shall then be away."

The said gift was an unbaked but varnished clay bust of the Greek poet, Homer, which I had made at school. I then speculate once again as to why she had not answered my first letter, and that perhaps this was due to my poor handwriting, and that she suspected I might be an "uneducated person." I then tell her my age and the date of my birthday: 23rd August – just three months ahead. "If I appear young in years I am mature for my age as you may well observe." After further declarations of love, I suggest that she might prefer to phone me rather than send a letter, and I give my number as Tudor 2106, and conclude, "Remember how so much you mean to me," &c.

Having waited in vain for over a week, a further letter was sent on 19th May expressing a rising sense of exasperation. "Dear Miss Dainton. – This is the third time I am writing to you, and you have not yet answered my first letter. Why do you thus so cruelly despise me? I am sorry that my letters do not impress you, but surely you have some spare moments in which you could write to me, busy as you are. I hope that no prejudicial ideas are the cause of your ignoring me for that would be the greatest injustice. I am not a hunch-back or a one-eyed ogre," &c. I then go on to describe my physique as 5' 7" and weighing 9 stone, and I remind her that it is not my custom to hunt down strange women, although I appreciate that she "must be cautious" with whom she associates. "I hope you do not disdain me for not being an actor. I am a great admirer of good acting when I have time to visit the pictures or theatre. ... Surely you could assign some time in which I could be received into your company, however short that may be. I could not possibly post my present to you without the risk of its becoming broken, and because of its weight, the cost of postage would be prohibitive. Therefore, with kindness, I beg you to answer my letter, and relieve me of this horrible suspense in waiting. Every day I go anxiously to the letter box to sort out the post and am tortured when your letter is not amongst the mail. I would be more grateful to receive a kind letter from you than for all the wealth under the sun. – Yours most sincerely," &c.

The descriptions of my tortured melancholy and suffering may appear naively absurd – and they were – for such expressions were clearly hopeless in evoking a desirable response. Whilst my letters were the product of life's inexperience they were nonetheless influenced by my bookish knowledge. I imagined myself as the love-lorn swain, and was influenced in my approach by the languishing lovesick musings of the Elizabethan poets. But did these poets achieve any *practical* success through their odes and sonnets which have been passed down and re-printed again and again as one generation succeeds another? Probably not!

Their wasted energy and useless words may have been formed into beautiful expressions of unfulfilled desire, and may have expressed psychological sentiments which struck a chord amongst their own sex, but where is the evidence that such poetry in itself won hearts and captured maidens in life's embrace? Such poetry, I would contend, has never served as anything more than a door-opener, which admittedly is a sufficient love-tool in inveigling those who were beyond one's immediate social circle into a compromising situation.

Seven days later on 26th May, a fourth letter was despatched. It begins with the assertion that no poet could express the strength of my feelings of love, and then repeats much that appeared in previous letters. It then continues self-deprecatingly, "Perhaps you think me too young to have the impertinence to fall in love with you," and then elaborates on the idea that love has no "age limits," and whilst some men are not mature enough to marry at thirty, as "their minds are so unsettled" and they are compulsive Casanovas who "jilt" their loved ones, others of a much younger age with firmer convictions are already fit for marriage. I support these ideas with Shakespeare's reference to us as, "This world of fools." I then continue, "On the other hand, you may doubt my love for you," and I use the specious argument that if my love was not genuine I would not be intent on giving her a present.

"When I saw your photograph in the *Daily Mail*, I was so overwhelmed that my breath was taken away; my pulse almost ceased to beat; and my heart felt heavy. A great melancholy came over me, and I almost choked as my throat contracted. Your beauty was so brilliant that I never knew that such a being could exist on earth. Your smile seemed so sweet – so sublime, and your hair was so smooth and lovely, and you seemed to be standing with such a gentle dignity," &c. "I have just written an ode to you, and it is enclosed with this letter. I hope you like it. Perhaps one day I would think of publishing it, but that of course would be impossible without your consent. Please remember me, forever yours," &c. The ode no longer survives.

On receiving no reply to the fourth letter, I realised that a new strategy was called for. I would need to deliver the present to her home in person. There was no other alternative. By now I realised that a significant historical point had been reached in my life, and that the following days would need to be recorded for posterity. On the 1st of June 1951, I therefore embarked on a detailed daily Journal, but it was so extensive and time-consuming, it could only be maintained for eleven days.

The document is not only revealing in portraying my daily routine as a 15-year old schoolboy, but more significantly, in describing the extreme effects of teenage *Angst* and the turmoil of my mind. In reading through the document, and the more concise Journal which followed, covering the period from 29th July 1952 until 20th January 1954, for the first time after a lapse of 60 years, I am appalled by the violence of my feelings and the apparent insanity of my actions. But I was not insane, and my actions did not lead into the tipping point of outrages calling for the intervention of the law – although my projected decisions would certainly have done so. I may have possessed an excess of testosterone, and I may indeed have been unbalanced due to a variety of causes arising from the chaotic influences of home life, and all these factors combined led to a crazy obsession to possess an unobtainable woman and the doomed and fruitless struggle to win her heart.

If I was "mad" it was more the madness of the March Hare, which is not mad at all, but merely following its natural instinct. Nonetheless, for a variety of reasons, it is difficult to imagine that such a set of events as described below could possibly take place in the 21st century without at some point the intervention of the law or the medical authorities stepping in and putting a stop to the nonsense. What seems remarkable today in our supposedly enlightened 21st century, is that I proceeded so far, and was met with tact, kindness, and understanding – although little of this was appreciated by me at the time. In some ways the 1950s was a more free society in that it was unhampered by all kinds of rules, regulations, or laws controlling human behaviour – what collectively we now refer to as the "Nanny State."

For a start, by comparison there is little room for eccentricity today, and although contemporary London is far more racially and culturally diverse than in 1950, there was far greater diversity on the London streets in terms of wealth and poverty, street entertainment, the ragged ex-military and often severely disabled bandsmen who traipsed along the gutters of our main streets in the hope of picking up a pittance; other modes of begging; dress, behaviour, or attitudes, etc., etc. 21st century London is far more conformist because of underlying cultural differences, and the need for a particular kind of toleration; but more significantly, 60 years of the Welfare State, and increasing government intervention into so many aspects of personal life, have led to many controls and forms of observation – quite apart from CCTV.

For example, shadowing or pestering someone of the opposite sex – irrespective of the motives – is now recognised as a criminal offence; private business premises of any kind are no longer open to casual visitors, but are locked and barred, and only accessible through internal communication systems; and professional organisations, such as publishers or theatrical agencies, are far too focused in their marketing approach to tolerate the proposals of interlopers who have not been introduced through formally recognised channels. These are all barriers which I broke through with success in the early 1950s.

If, as a teenager I behaved in the 21st century as I did in the 1950s, I would soon have had the police on my trail, and if I escaped prosecution, I would have been handed over to Social Services, and after trouble with my parents, I would have been despatched to a psychiatrist for examination and treatment. But as someone who was born two generations earlier, I was fortunate to escape the clutches of the law, and what may have been more harmful in the longer term, the panaceas of the shrinks together with the stigma and consequent life-long conviction that one is somehow maladjusted or abnormal, following a medically recognised condition which has been professionally diagnosed.

If I had been suffering from a mental disorder, therefore, it was never uncovered, and I subsequently cured myself through living and experiencing life to the full. As I never surrendered myself to the head-shrinker's couch, I never needed to contemplate my navel or reflect with life-long pathological doubts on my mental condition. The following is an edited version of the aborted Journal which I began at the beginning of the Summer in 1951:-

1st **June** – On Friday evening whilst casually perusing over the day's papers, I chanced to pick up *The Evening News*, and on turning to the second page, I saw the photograph of Miss Patricia Dainton, the one I loved. I bitterly disliked her publicity in the press, although actress as she was. By this time I was becoming used to seeing her photograph, for by now I had seen four pictures of her in newspapers and other periodicals, since the first occasion in November last year. I therefore responded to this one with less surprise and shock, for it was more useful than the others in revealing some interesting information.

I had by this time realised that the advertisement for the play, *Count Your Blessings*, in which she acted at the Westminster theatre, had not appeared since Saturday 26th May – nearly a week past. I was further shocked on Monday 28th that the advertisement was missing from the appropriate column of, *The Daily Telegraph*, and, *The Evening Standard*. This worried me for it indicated that the play had ended its season, and that Miss Dainton might by this time have easily flown to the other side of the globe to perform elsewhere.

Fortunately, my constitution was built to withstand such mental stress, and I thought little more of the matter. I continued to eat much which maintained my spirits, allowing me to pursue my hard-working studies. Being at school all day and mixing with a lively crowd of young people is also a good recipe for quenching melancholy, but it was when I returned and confined myself in my quiet and lonely closet to read or meditate that the disease recurred. Melancholy oppressed me more this week than it had ever done before, sometimes preventing me from reading. I would throw down my book in agitation, go downstairs, and switch on the wireless for the Third Programme, when classical music brought tranquillity to my soul. If the music was dreary I would turn on to some lighter music, although no music worsened my spirits. Most music raised my spirits, and the more thrilling it was, the faster I would pace the room as was my wont, for music took me from the world of troubles into the realm of fantasy, where I built the most glorious castles in the air.

In such a state, I imagined receiving a reply from Miss Dainton asking me to visit her at 16 Conduit Street, on some Sunday afternoon. There I would give her my present and woo her, and she would love me, and we would embrace one another in raptures of joy. I would repulse a hundred suitors in the manner of Ulysses reclaiming his long-lost Penelope, and marry her, and live happily ever after. I would cross swords with suitors in Hyde Park, and slay them with a hundred strokes. Such were the magic effects of music on my mind.

The absence of music affected my spirits in an opposite direction. She would forsake me. I would turn from her and somehow find another actress, whom although I would not love, but use as a parasite in depending upon her love for me. I would marry her, and then perhaps later destroy her. I would run away and mix with other actresses, all of whom I would treat in the same manner. I would indulge in their sympathy as they talked and fondled me, as I lay prostrate on a bed, an object of deep melancholy or in the agonies of death. I would behave like a madman, and end in misery and ruin.

Sometimes I contemplated renouncing the female sex as a race of seductive sirens or destructive harpies intent on the ruin or tyrannising of men, and I saw myself as a leader for their massacre and extirpation in the cause of peace and happiness. As I suffered these crazy visions of fury, sweat passed over my brow which I needed to wipe away. Sometimes loud or discordant music brought on these visions – tuneless music, cruel to my ear. I would stride furiously up and down the room, involuntarily making vicious stabs at pieces of furniture with my fists, or other violent movements, until my mind became so stirred by fury, that at last I was obliged to turn off the wireless. I would then sit down, and rest mind and body, holding my head in my hands. I preferred my energising moods of anger to those of depression and moroseness, but it was when they both combined that I was reduced to the most abject condition. It was then I was struck by the most violent headaches – a most dangerous condition – for does not Robert Burton in his, *Anatomy of Melancholy*, explain that such a combination results in mania?

Sometimes in my irrational fits of fury I thought of assassinating some great personage, purely for the vanity of alerting the world to my misery. The immediate cause of my unsettled spirits was the unpleasant delay and anxiety in awaiting Miss Dainton's reply to my letter and poem which she must have received by Monday 28th May. At that time I was even stirred to anger against this sweetest of creatures. I had decided boldly early in that week to phone her the following weekend should I not receive her reply. I anticipated her absence from home, but I would ask for her mother and enquire as to whether she had forwarded my letters. I would also enquire of her mother as to whether her daughter would like to see the publication of the ode. That was a sufficient excuse for phoning.

This latest photograph of Miss Dainton in, *The Evening News* was of her dancing with the actor, Robert Beatty. It was sufficient proof that, *Count Your Blessings*, had ended its season, and suggested that she was now out of town, for the picture had been taken at the International Film

Star Ball in Bournemouth. This was distressing, for it demonstrated the hopelessness of letter writing. Other means must be sought in achieving a successful connection. That night I listened to music for about an hour; had a bath, and retired to bed at about ten o'clock to sleep soundly.

2nd **June** – On Saturday morning I awoke at 7.15 and arose at 7.45. I had planned my day. I ate little for breakfast, and afterwards, on suggesting to my mother that I phone Miss Dainton, she expressed her opinion against the idea. "But she hasn't written," I insisted. "I must do something." – "Film stars are such a hoity-toity type of people," she replied. "I should just leave her alone."

Such a comment was very hurtful, for leaving her alone would be impossible. I waited some moments before replying to my mother. Geoffrey Dunstan and my mother were the only confidants with whom I discussed Miss Dainton. With the former I spoke freely about her, but with the latter I was apprehensive and mistrustful. I enjoyed speaking with Geoffrey on the topic, but I loathed to speak with my mother on it – but the latter I could not ignore since I wished to use the phone – and use it in confidence. "When I'd phone, I'd ask to speak with her mother of course," I said at last. "I believe Patricia Dainton is at Bournemouth at the moment." – "And what would you say to her mother?" she asked. – "I'd enquire as to whether she had forwarded my correspondence." – "You'd perhaps never get onto her. These actresses are only interested in strangers if they think they can get money, or some other material advantage." I was too nervous and agitated to continue the discussion and so I dropped the subject.

That day I had planned to fetch my new spectacles from the opticians, Curry & Paxton, in Great Portland Street. They had sent a card on Thursday saying that the glasses were ready for collection. I told my mother that I would leave for them right away. I asked for money for the bus fares, and as she only had ten shillings, she asked me to get some change by buying two sliced loaves from the bakery Scotscakes. Accordingly, I did this (which was one of my weekly jobs), and then I left for the West End with two shillings and sixpence. I had to travel on two buses, the second of which took me to Gt. Portland Street. I was not acquainted with that part of town, and the bus took me past the stop at which I should have descended. However, being a keen and fast walker, I soon found the shop.

[At this point we must break off from the Journal, and relate the drama of how I acquired my first pair of spectacles. It all began with a school medical inspection at which it was found I was seriously short-sighted. – "You'll discover a great difference as soon as you have your first pair of spectacles," explained the inspector. "For a start you'll have no trouble in reading the blackboard."

As soon as this unfortunate news was communicated to my parents, there was uproar in the household. "He can't possibly wear glasses," exclaimed my mother. "It'll spoil his looks entirely, and when he leaves school he'll never have a fair chance of getting a proper girl friend. Nice girls don't like boys with glasses – it makes them look like egg-heads." My father agreed entirely, even if his reasons were slightly different. I was not the sporting type, but at least I looked as if I could be the sporting type as long as I refrained from wearing glasses. If I was landed with the latter, I would really look as I actually was, i.e., a duff athletic type who came last in all the races.]

CHAPTER 15
An Unsuccessful Mission

"Hunger for the unobtainable or the barely obtainable is one of the greatest incitements for heightened desire that humankind knows. Cosy availability and the lambert flame of passionate love are rarely found in combination.

Ronald Conway, *The Rage For Utopia,* Allen & Unwin, 1992, p. 142.

A family crisis over the wearing of spectacles – Details of my daily life and plans for courtship – First visit to Conduit street

It was a tradition on both sides of the family that we had always been a good-looking race of people, few of whom were reduced to wearing spectacles, and it was a humiliation that I was now going to be confronted with a situation to make me look like a bank clerk, or a fossilised absent-minded professor. My grandparents and certain aunts and uncles agreed, and as the subject was discussed, I was looked at in dismay. Ugliness, of all conditions, was unforgivable!

It was decided I should be sent to the top eye specialist in the country in the hope of somehow finding an alternative to wearing spectacles, and one Wednesday afternoon, my father took me along to see an elderly consultant in Harley Street. The waiting room was huge, gloomy, and quiet, but furnished with invaluable antique pieces and priceless ornaments. I was, apparently, the only patient in the building. A timeless quality pervaded the entire place.

Eventually we were shown into the consulting room and the eye specialist was a man of immense charm and wide-ranging culture. Before the examination there was a leisurely conversation about nothing in particular, and he then related several obscure jokes, none of which I comprehended. After a careful examination in the darkened room, with its threadbare Persian carpets and dusty artefacts, there followed another long conversation. Yes, I was short-sighted and the cause was a mystery, particularly in view of its sudden onset. Did I read in bed? I should never read in bed as it induced a particular form of eye strain. Unfortunately there was no alternative to wearing spectacles in view of the degree of my short-sightedness.

A general conversation then followed and I was asked what books I liked to read. "I hope you read worthwhile books," said the specialist. I mentioned several titles, and he then entered into a digression on literary topics, culminating in a story about a Prussian soldier who had a hole in his stomach, the point of which I failed to grasp. Lastly, there was a discussion about fees, and as this was a situation of one leading Consultant facing another, it was decided that fees should be waived.

In view of the drama which led to this decision, I was loathed to be hampered with spectacles, but philosophically accepted the situation which led to this inevitable outcome.]

The Journal continues for 2nd June:- Throughout this day I felt melancholy and disagreeable after my mother had persuaded me it would be unwise to phone Miss Dainton. I had to wait in Curry & Paxton for about 15 minutes before I was attended to, although the place was almost empty. I tried on my glasses, and as they felt comfortable they were satisfactory. I left with a bill and had another long walk so that for economy I could travel home in one bus without changing. As the bus was jogging along, I thought of another strategy in approaching Miss Dainton, and it seemed the only option left. I would take my present accompanied by a note to 16 Conduit Street without prior warning, and there deposit it in the same way and for the same purpose as Mephistopheles and Faust left their casket of jewels on the step of Margarethe's cottage. I might also ask the footman or servant answering the door to speak with her mother, Vivienne Black, on the grounds that the parcel needed "an explanation." With these thoughts I continued my journey in contentment and renewed hope.

On arriving home and putting the new scheme to my mother, she was against that too. "She would most likely never receive the present," said my mother. – "But I would address it to her," I replied. – "It's a pity you should throw away a beautiful thing like that," commented my mother. – "Anyway, I *will* do it," I insisted. – "But what will you do with this actress if you did get to know her? You're not in the film world." – "That's my business," I said perturbed, and hurriedly left the room. I then went to the Public Library to find out about this "Robert Beatty" who had dared to dance with the girl I loved. In the photograph he looked a tall, bulky, thick-headed man – the sort who might be a professional boxer. I discovered he was born in 1909 which meant he was about 42 years of age. This was a pleasant relief for surely Miss Dainton would never be so stupid as to marry someone twice her own age, but nonetheless, the nagging thought still worried me that he was still a bachelor.

I then went to Southwood Bookstore, and was lost in deep meditation. I spent a quarter of an hour there examining Mr. Atkins' collection of books. I saw an excellent edition of Boswell's *Johnson* in 6 volumes, well illustrated. Every few moments I glanced out of the window to see if my bicycle was still there. On leaving the shop and approaching my bike, I discovered it had been replaced by an inferior model. I was seized with panic but acted calmly. A furniture shopkeeper and a responsible looking middle-aged assistant were standing on the pavement chatting to customers adjacent to the Bookstore, and I enquired as to whether they had seen anyone take a bike. They were startled, and one of them remarked, "It's easily done." – "And you say that bike's not yours? Was it better,?" asked the shopkeeper. – "Much better," I replied resentfully. – "It's wicked! You find that kind of thing happens everywhere nowadays," said the shopkeeper.

"Perhaps Mr. Atkins has seen someone take it," suggested the shop's proprietor, as the bookseller was re-entering his store. The dwarf, Mr. Atkins, had been running to and fro between his shop and the newsagents on what errands I have no idea, but he had not seen the bike. At that moment the realisation flashed through my brain that I had not brought my bike with me, for I had walked from Muswell Hill. This was a happy relief but it put me in an awkward situation. I would be thought mad if I excused myself on the grounds of loss of memory, or be thought a thief if I claimed damages on false pretences. – "Someone's stolen his bike," said the assistant to Mr. Atkins, in making matters worse for me. – "I've not seen anyone take a bike," repeated Mr. Atkins. – "That bike's mine," said another man who just came onto the scene. – "I'll go and enquire of the police," I said. – "That's right," said the proprietor of the furniture shop. "The police station's just down the road."

Without further comment, I walked away in the opposite direction. I walked rapidly, increasing my pace towards home, deeply embarrassed as I left the bewildered group which had gathered about me on the opposite pavement. I dared not turn round to see the expression on the faces of those I had left behind. This regrettable absence of memory was due to my pondering on plans for winning the heart of Miss Dainton. My mother received the tale with amusement. I had a large lunch having exercised all morning. In the afternoon, I wrote my note – or more correctly, on account of its length, my letter – to accompany Miss Dainton's present. That took me up to six o'clock, and I made a rough copy.

[In breaking off, once again, from the Journal, I may recount the contents of the letter. After presenting the "humble present," I then enter into a pompous declaration as to what I have *not* given: "I have no such trophies as ostrich feathers to give you, or gold or diamonds, or jewellery of any kind, for these are things of vanity." (The reference to ostrich feathers arose from a recent photograph of Miss Dainton being presented with an ostrich feather by the visiting Australian cricket team. This was a piece of press publicity which greatly irritated me, and I was disgusted by the sight of these grinning and drooling men worshipping at the feet of the woman I loved.) The letter continues: "I present you with a specimen of my own artistic creation, which hopefully at least reflects something of my own personality, and because of this, I hope you will think   better of me in the future."

The letter then continues with the most absurd sentence to appear anywhere in the entire correspondence, for the gift is made *conditional* on my being received into her presence. Hence, despite the depth of my passionate love, and supposedly, the sincerity of this, I could not entirely suppress an underlying commercial instinct which rose to the surface. This was a question of give and take, and a bargain had to be struck. The announcement of this concludes with the words: "I hope you would never be so cruel as to spurn me now. There could be nothing more on earth which would torture my mind. If you cannot read Greek, the bust is of *Homeros*, commonly known to English readers as Homer, the father of poets. It took 6 months to complete as I believe I mentioned in an earlier letter. Perhaps one day you would do me the honour of allowing me to make a bust of yourself.

"The painting, which I also include in this package, I executed 3 years ago, and it does me little justice in view of what I have learned since. I painted it in Swanage, on a hotel roof, whilst spending a summer holiday at the resort. The view looks towards Old Harry Rocks, and the strip of land in the far distance is Bournemouth. Unfortunately, it is somewhat spoilt by the clouds which swept over the sky when I came to paint it. I have recently completed a picture far superior to this in water colour. It is entitled, *Prometheus Chained*, and illustrates Aeschylus's great drama of that name. I should very much like to give that to you. It is quite a large painting, being two feet in length by one in width." [The painting currently hangs in the living room of my younger brother in Bristol.] "I am engaged in a still larger picture of King Lear in the storm, and its title is taken from the quotation, *Off, off you lendings!* [This painting is also now in the possession of my brother.] "One day I should like to paint a portrait of you in oils. It would be a credit to us both. I hope you liked the ode I dedicated to you, and posted in my last letter. I shall be waiting anxiously, and I fear, impatiently for your reply. I love you more than any mortal possibly could, therefore, please act kindly towards me. My gift is surely proof of my affection, and it may serve as a bond between us. I love you forever," &c. There then follows the following P.S.:- "Since you have not replied to my earlier letters, I have without warning had to bring my present to your house in person, for it could not go through the post. Do not interpret this explanation as containing a suggestion of ill intent – for who could entertain such thoughts towards one as beautiful as you?"]

The Journal continues as follows:- I decided to deliver the present the next day, or Sunday afternoon, for it would most likely be the time when Mrs. Black would be found at home. My mother went along with this idea, and a further advantage was that my parents would be visiting Uncle Maurice and Aunt June for tea and possibly supper. As they lived in Upminster, and that was a long journey, my parents would need to leave the house by 2.0 pm. Immediately after they left, I would change into my best suit and then leave myself. I obliged my mother to swear she would never reveal my scheme to any other person – especially not my father, for he would blow up the situation, and make it a talking-point amongst my other relatives.

I ate a comparatively small tea, due to the excitement of the forthcoming events, and at 6.25 pm I listened to *Those Were The Days*. Old dance music always took me into the realm of fantasy, especially the gentle rhythm of waltzes which *always* brought me into the world of love and romance. The programme which ended at 7.15 pm left me unoccupied for the first time that day, and hence the opportunity for my thoughts to wander. The realisation fully dawned on me of the exciting life I created for myself through my affair with Miss Dainton, and shortly this episode must reach a climax. It was then that I first had the idea of setting up this Journal, for it was surely to record something of universal interest which was psychologically unique. In anticipating the possibility of future fame, and having always wanted to record the facts of my early life, were additional reasons for starting such a Journal. My mind was made up.

Accordingly, I ran upstairs to my bedroom, unlocked my tuck box containing all my old school exercise books, manuscripts, and paintings I had completed over the past five years, photographs of Miss Dainton, and other objects, and withdrew my unfinished manuscript, *The Talk of Many Things*, being a book of poetry, for the purpose of my new work. I settled down at my desk and began writing. I did not intend my Journal to be a work of literary value, but only that it record minutely my personal life, so that sometime in the future it might serve as a source for extracting passages for the purpose of a more thoughtful autobiography. I wrote at speed and enjoyed it, and was satisfied with what I produced, but I also found that the Journal was taking on a length greater than anticipated.

By 9.0 pm I had written about ten pages, when my brother burst into the room without knocking with all his rude impertinence. Every time he did this I was taken aback by the shock. – "What do you want,?" I demanded. – "You're wearing your spectacles," he remarked. That evening was the first time I used my spectacles, and although they did not enlarge print when reading, they proved an enormous advantage in distinguishing objects from a distance. – "Yes, of course I'm wearing my spectacles. What do you think they're for,?" I answered peevishly. "Now clear out," I added with a nod of the head. I always told him to leave the room when he entered, since nine times out of ten, he only came to annoy me. "You've got to come downstairs," he said. "We're going to see the Festival lights." – "I can see them any time," I replied. – "But we're all going up in the car." – "I don't want to come. I'm busy," I said, for I disliked such stupid vanities as viewing city lights. – "What are you writing,?" he said looking suspiciously at my Journal. He was always curious about things which were none of his business, and used crafty means for finding things out for himself. – "That's nothing to do with you," I retorted, perhaps a little too sharply, for it would only arouse his suspicion all the more, and he might search for my Journal without my knowing.

Nonetheless, I assented to his suggestion, and that evening we went up to town to visit the Festival of Britain lights. My youngest brother, Oliver (then 6 years old), became very disagreeable, and on our return he dropped off to sleep. The lights were reasonably well arranged, but were vastly overrated. The press was only full of their praise to attract further visitors to the Exhibition, so that undeserving people might fill their pockets. In those days no review could be relied upon as truly objective, as the only purpose was to enrich business interests of one kind or another – and besides, I loathed anything which sought to attract the London mob. The lights of the Battersea Gardens were evidently better than those of the Festival, since there were many more of them and they were coloured. The Festival lights comprised colourless bulbs, and they only marked the boundaries of the Festival area – apart from those which decorated the mystical Skylon. Looking across at the lights from the north bank of the river, the town was no more illuminated than on a cloudless night in full moon.

On approaching the Exhibition, as well as the Battersea Gardens, the pavements were packed with the curious mob, and at ten o'clock there was still a half mile long queue to enter the latter. But by 10.30 pm people were spewing out in their thousands, and large numbers of police were directing the crowds – like sheep-dogs ordering the sheep – and microphones were being used to disperse the visitors to buses or underground stations for their journey home. This, I suppose, is the penalty to be paid for travelling to central London on a Saturday night.

We arrived home at 11.0 pm, and as I was dead tired, I went to bed without a wash. I had earlier intended to have a bath that night in preparation for tomorrow's adventure, but gave up the idea and slept soundly instead.

3rd June – I was rudely awoken on Sunday morning by the piercing and tuneless bell of St. James's church (just opposite the house) summoning the congregation together for the eight o'clock service. I loathed the grim monotonous toll of the church bell, irrespective of whether it struck the hour or otherwise. It had a funereal prison-like tone, and might have summoned devils around its belfry rather than angels. The unknown bell-ringer, who was not too timely with his tugging on the rope, was as ugly to me as the Hunchback of Notre Dame. At night, whilst I lay in bed trying to sleep, I would wait in abject fear for the next hour to toll, and when it did, I pulled the bedclothes over my head, and pressed my fingers into my ears. I enjoyed the bell-ringing of old country churches, for that was amongst the most beautiful of sounds, but who could derive pleasure from this urban din?

It did, however, serve the purpose of driving me from my bed, together with the bright sun shining through my thin curtains, as it had done over the past few days. I jumped into my slippers, which were always carefully placed at the left side of my bed in readiness to receive my feet. I habitually re-wound my clock on the mantelpiece, before drawing back the curtains, and I needed to shade my eyes as the sun flooded the room. There was a cloudless sky – a good omen for the day ahead. Having washed and dressed and read, *The Times Literary Supplement*, which I received every Friday, I stored it in a large cardboard box kept atop the wardrobe. During the weekends I rarely cooked my own breakfast, and on this occasion, I waited an hour before my mother came downstairs, and had it laid on the table, and meanwhile, I perused the latest news in, *The Sunday Express*. The Sunday papers were usually the most entertaining yet useless for political news or hard comment. I did not regret this since I was depressed by the troubles of the world: heavy losses in Korea, rising prices, etc.

After breakfast I went about my usual routine in brushing my teeth, brylcreaming my hair, and the lavatory, all of which was completed in a quarter of an hour. I then made my bed, which I had to do in the weekends as Mrs. Craddock was only employed for five days a week, and in the weekends she had to look after her husband who had been blind all his life. For the rest of the morning until lunchtime at 1.15 pm, I speedily wrote my Journal, although I had not nearly brought it up to date. In the middle of this task I was interrupted by violent shouts from my father calling me downstairs. I threw down my pen apprehensively and went to my parents' bedroom. He gave me a pair of his "old shoes" as he called them, but they were in perfect condition as with all his clothes. They had modishly pointed ends. I put them on, they fitted and felt comfortable, and so I decided to keep them.

Over the past two years I had never accepted any of his old clothes with gratitude, but this was a welcome exception. Apart from these I had only two pairs of lace-ups. The first were a brown pair, expensive, strong and made for hard wear. I had had them for two years, and the soles were worn down, and one of them had almost fallen away. The leather was ruined and stained from the want of polish. The laces were black and broken and un-matching, as they were taken from other pairs. I broke my laces about every three weeks and they became shorter and shorter until they had to be replaced, and sometimes I used string in place of laces. In this footwear I fearlessly went to school with the mud in winter and the dust in Summer, and I only cleaned my shoes for special occasions.

[I break my Journal here to record a recollection which occurred at school at about this time. One afternoon when we were gathered in a half circle, seated on chairs, I was reprimanded by the teacher for giggling and asked to explain my behaviour. "So-and-so is tickling my foot," I answered. – "How can he tickle your foot,?" exclaimed the teacher incredulously, upon which I revealed my soul to be worn through to the naked skin, and of course this was met with laughter. Such was the condition of my clothing in an age of rationing!]

To continue the Journal:- My second pair of shoes were also given me by my father after he had worn them for 26 years, and although they were in sound condition, perhaps the leather was softer than it should have been. This latest pair I had been given were received with gratitude, as I could now deposit my present at 16 Conduit Street dressed as a perfect gentleman, although I would have also preferred a haircut the previous evening, but children under 18 years of age were not allowed to visit the barbers I attended on Saturdays.

We had a delicious salad lunch although my appetite was limited due to the nervousness of the approaching adventure, and my heart began to beat rapidly in the hope that the scheme would proceed smoothly. We finished lunch at 1.45 pm and there was a short interval before my parents left. My mother washed up; my father went upstairs to prepare himself; and my two brothers went into the playroom: the elder to play monotonously on the piano, and the younger to play with his toys. Miss Wall was expected any moment. Later she would get our tea and put Oliver to bed. I went upstairs to take my new suit out of the cupboard ready to change into. On coming down again my father was taking the larger car out of the garage and my mother was changing into her best costume. I went into the lounge and ate an orange. On finishing it, I went into the hall and found my parents were about to leave, and Miss Wall was just arriving, although a little late.

My mother gave instructions to Miss Wall, whilst my father reminded me to lock the back gate at 7.0 pm, and we all said goodbye to my parents. As they left, I ran upstairs, three at a time, to change into my new suit. I looked out of the bedroom window and watched the car slowly backing out of the drive, and my brothers were excitedly waving their hands. When the car had left, which was at 2.0 pm, I carefully changed into my suit. I had shaved that morning, and before furtively going downstairs with the heavy parcel under my arm, feeling like Guy Fawkes depositing yet another barrel of gunpowder beneath the House of Lords, I washed my face and brushed my hair. I had never before looked so smart, and this embarrassed me, for should I be caught smuggling myself from the house, I would undoubtedly arouse suspicion.

On reaching the first floor I encountered Miss Wall. I concealed my embarrassment by smiling and adopting a candid attitude. She stood smiling, admiring my suit, and asked me to come forward to examine it better. "Where are you going this afternoon,?" she enquired. – "Up to town," I replied bluntly. – "Will you be in for tea,?" she asked. – "I expect so," I answered, whilst hoping I should meet Vivienne Black and be invited to tea at Conduit Street. She complimented me on my suit again, and I proudly pointed out the waistcoat. I said goodbye, and took my leave, and to my relief no one was in the hall of the ground floor, but on departing from the front, I saw my brothers playing in the yard with the smaller car.

Strangely to say, although they saw me in my new attire and carrying the parcel, they made no comment. I avoided standing in the bus queue just opposite our house in case my younger brother might come over and question me, and so I walked to the further bus stop by the roundabout where I would anyway be assured a better seat on the bus. The sun was burning hot, and I hoped I should not arrive at Conduit Street in a state of perspiration.

As I travelled in the bus, I pondered on the appearance of Conduit Street. My mother remembered it as a narrow street with night clubs and restaurants, usually patronised by the acting profession. I imagined it as a long straight street of Georgian houses without shops, mostly inhabited by those on the fringes of the aristocracy. And as for a number 16, the door would be answered by a footman or maid in full uniform, and if Vivienne Black was in, I would be ushered into a large drawing room where she would be stretched out on a *chaise longue*, smoking a cigarette through a long holder, and behind would be French windows looking out onto a small but verdant garden. She would be taking her hourly nap after lunch and reading a light novel.

Such were my thoughts during a journey which was slow and frustrated through confusion. Having waited 15 minutes for the first bus I had to change at Archway where I was told to take a 137, but I mounted a 27 and was told to take a 134 to the Dominion, where I should catch another bus for Oxford Street with the intention of dismounting at Bond Street. This annoyed me, for I had just descended from a 134 and I had to wait at the end of a long queue for 20 minutes and had to pay a penny extra for the fare. Several full 134s passed by, packed with Festival visitors. On the second bus I had a most unpleasant ride, for it was stuffy with the heat as the windows were closed, and I was seated beside a rough woman with noisy children. Everyone was wearing summer clothes with rolled up shirt sleeves, and I was oppressed by the smell of sweat from their filthy bodies.

It was a relief to breathe the fresh air on leaving the bus at the Dominion, and the junction which I knew as a crowded area when I visited on Saturday mornings to view the bookshops was now empty apart from a few local residents, and so now there was a strange unfamiliar environment. The empty streets evoked a mood of melancholy. I waited two minutes for a third bus to take me to my final destination, but I became impatient and decided to walk the rest of the way. This gave me more time to finalise those questions I would put to Vivienne Black. It was a long walk, more than half an hour, and when I reached New Bond Street it met my expectations as a place of fashion, but as it was entirely free of traffic, it had a forlorn appearance.

It was another 15 minutes before I reached Conduit Street, and then my heart sank. It had none of the prosperous or lively associations I anticipated for such a street, and indeed, I had to re-read the street name to assure myself I had actually reached my destination. It was a short squalid street on an incline joining two more impressive roads. Everywhere here were ugly placards and commercial business plates, and not a sign of clubs or restaurants – or anything suggesting the stage or screen. The place looked both inhospitable and uninhabitable. On the right side of the street was a bomb site, half of which had been cleared and converted into a car park, and there were a few business premises, and a hideous block of flats at the far end. How could any self-respecting person live in such a dump? I walked up the street, looking for number 16, hoping it would be in one of the better quarters. The numbers were confusing, for they were not odd on one side and even on the other, for those on the right side continued from those on the top left. I walked up and down the street, and suddenly, behold,! Number 16 was in front of me, half way up the hill on the left.

My heart throbbed, but only momentarily, for my spirits sank as I stood before a bleak dirty looking brown door which called for a coat of paint. A new lock had been added to the door which was approached by a pair of grimy steps. Vivienne Black and her daughter evidently lived in a flat, for there were brass business plates at the side of the door:- first floor: Military Tailor; second floor: unspecified; third floor: Leon-Cassel Gerrard, Stage Management. For the fourth floor there was no name plate beneath the bell. Could that be the home of Vivienne Black? I felt most discouraged. Could it be the third floor, for Vivienne Black advertised herself as being involved in "Artistes Representation," and I saw little difference between that and Stage Management? As for the name "Leon-Cassel Gerrard," perhaps he was in partnership with her, or perhaps she had taken over his business.

It was a painful question and I was left in a wretched quandary. On the left, at number 15, was a Habit-Maker, and on the right was a Rolls-Royce automobile showroom – but apparently, still included as 16 Conduit Street. My hopes rose somewhat, and I went round the corner in search of another door, but it only led to a dark and filthy alley. There were no other doors, and so I returned to the first, and after a fearful hesitation at the unfriendliness of the place, I pressed the bell for Leon-Cassell Gerrard, and waited with bated breath. There was no reply. There was a deathly silence, and it looked as if no one had entered or left the building for twenty years past. How could such a beauty as Patricia Dainton enter such a filthy building? I rang several bells, and dawdled for a quarter of an hour, but nothing stirred.

At last I realised there was only one thing to do: I would have to carry the parcel back home with me. My mission had been a failure, and what most tortured my mind was the failure to discover any reference to Vivienne Black. This evoked a nightmare scenario, suggesting she might live a ghost-like existence, or possibly use any number of convenience addresses where mail was forwarded and then on-forwarded again. Oh, that I had never gone there, or had taken the trouble to phone first in ascertaining the correctness of the location – but my mother had advised against it. I would never take *her* advice again.

Sadly, I began my homeward journey, but by a faster route: taking a train from Piccadilly Circus to Tottenham Court Road, but I changed my mind and left at Leicester Square – for the fare was only three halfpence – but it cost me another 1/6d. from Charing Cross road to home on a 134 bus. Had I taken the bus from the Dominion it would only have cost me sixpence halfpenny. It seemed as if I was always miscalculating to my disadvantage! Nonetheless, I had a comfortable seat on top of the bus, as it jogged along, and I surveyed the miserable slums of Camden and Kentish Town, and Tufnell Park. Seated as I was, looking down onto these black and depressing buildings, I recollected there were people in the world worse placed than me, and this somewhat lessened my melancholy.

On arriving home I slid quietly into the house by the back gate which I locked behind me, and then entered the house. It was deadly silent as if no one was in. I stealthily ran up the stairs to my bedroom, put the parcel back onto my bookcase, and changed back into my old suit. On going downstairs again, I went into the lounge and saw my brothers and Miss Wall in the garden. The French windows were open. I ate two oranges and then sat in a chair hidden from the view of the garden, for I was in no mood to socialise. I went into the kitchen and drank five glasses of water, one after the other. The others had already had tea, for there was used crockery lying around, but a place had been laid for me, and so I ate some bread and butter with my beloved marmalade, which I chose above any other spread apart from chocolate or Butter-nut.

Whilst so engaged, Miss Wall came into the kitchen from the back door into the garden, and expressed surprise at my early return, to my slight embarrassment. Before leaving the room, she told me what else I could eat, and where I should put my plate afterwards, and what we were to have for supper, etc., and then my younger brother entered, and began to be noisy and irritating, and I gruffly asked him to leave the room which he refused, and I perceived a crafty smile on his lips. "Where have you been,?" he asked cheekily. – "That's none of your business," I replied. – "Have you been to Pat Dainton's?" I was taken aback by the question. My mother must have revealed my plan, or more probably, he had seen the parcel addressed to Miss Dainton which for several days had been placed on my bookcase, for he was always intruding in my room. I said nothing. "I hear your bike was stolen yesterday," he continued insolently. (My mother must have told him that.) – "No," I replied sharply. – "Well, you thought it had been stolen. And you said you were going to the police about it."

I became apprehensive. My mother was not one to explain things in detail. – "Well, did you go to Pat Dainton's?" he enquired again. I wondered what made him so curious, and then a horrible realisation came over me and I experienced a spasm of sudden anger, but I was too scared to look into his face, or make any gesture in furthering his suspicion. Clearly, he had been searching my drawers and found the Journal, but I was unprepared openly to confront him with the fact. "I don't know what you mean," I only said. – "Did you give her the present?" – "What present?" – "You know, the present." – "I never said I was giving her any present." – "Oh yes you did." – "Get out of the room," I exclaimed, rising from the table. He stood his ground, and after a pause he remarked, "You won't have actresses around you if you treat them like that." I was at boiling point, and at that moment I hated him, and could have thrust my bread knife into his chest, but I could do nothing except surrender to his humiliating remarks. "I can read people's thoughts," he continued. "I can read yours like a book." – "How dare you!" I roared, and then the storm broke, and I poured out the accusations of espionage and trespassing, and reading private papers which were none of his business.

He admitted his guilt, but then resorted to flattery by saying, "It's very good English." – "Clear out," I repeated. – "But tell me, just tell me, did you give her the present? Did you meet Pat Dainton?" – "Clear out at once – and how dare you insult her as 'Pat'!" I hated her beautiful name to be disfigured to the ugly diminutive of "Pat." He persisted for a few more moments, promising not to pass on any information I should divulge, but as I would tell him nothing, he left the room. The discovery of my Journal added to my agonies, and I realised it must now be kept under lock and key in my tuck box. After tea I had intended to listen to music to soothe my spirits, but after the upset, I felt it better to go upstairs and continue my Journal, but on the first landing my brother confronted me again, and I had to push past him and tell him to mind his own business. As I mounted the next flight of stairs he answered his own question by reminding me that my mission had been unsuccessful, as the parcel was back on my bookcase, and he was sorry I had had a spoilt afternoon. I sent him away with some oaths and told him not to prowl around my room again.

CHAPTER 16
A Gift for a Goddess

"Whoever makes great presents expects great presents in
return." (Quisquis magna dedit, voluit sibi magna remitti.)

Martial, *Epigrams*, Bk. V, Ep. Lix, 1.3

Schemes of murder – Am diverted by a Restoration drama – I speak with PD's mother – Second visit to Conduit street and the outcome

Once settled in my room I was too perturbed to do anything constructive, and I was in no frame of mind to continue my Journal. I was tortured alternately by fury and depression, and my grand hopes about Conduit Street had turned into a nightmare. Nothing had gone right that afternoon, and to cap it all, my Journal had been discovered. All my dreams and plans of the previous weeks in meeting Miss Dainton in privacy had fallen through.

There was only one faint possibility left. I would need to concentrate all my energies and trust in the good intent of her mother in accessing the one I loved. Accordingly, I stealthily crept into my parents' bedroom, shut the door firmly, and also the windows, for the net curtains were being blown by the cool evening air – for I needed both privacy and silence from the street outside – and I took up the telephone directory and searched for Vivienne Black.

I sat on my father's bed, took up the receiver and asked for the number. My heart beat fast as I heard the number ring, and I waited some minutes but there was no reply. I laid the directory aside in despair, not daring to take it downstairs again, in fear of meeting my suspicious and over-inquisitive brother, before returning to my room. My mind was in a worse turmoil than before. I had no more patience or energy left for repeating old strategies or designing new ones. On the one hand I was thrown into the depths of despair, but on the other hand I was determined to meet Miss Dainton even if it cost me my life. All this time whilst debating pros and cons in my mind, I was too excited or intolerant to listen to music, and so I paced my room like a caged lion awaiting his keeper for food, but all the while I knew there was no keeper to bring me my Miss Dainton. Wild ponderings were no help to my unsettled mind as I entertained deeds increasingly violent and villainous.

Eventually I decided on the ultimate act of law-breaking. I would set my alarm for 1.0 am that morning, put on my slippers and wrap my body tightly in my dressing gown, take my scout knife with its sharp four inch blade, and French bayonet (which supposedly had been picked up as a souvenir from the field of Sedan), creep downstairs and slaughter the entire family. I would surrender myself to the police later that day as having committed the supreme deed of self-sacrifice in the cause of love, and having been condemned to death for my crime, I would ask for one more concession from the judge, which surely he would not have the cruelty to withhold in the face of my impending death. My dying wish would be a private meeting with Miss Dainton to declare my love, which having been granted, I would die in bliss in the cause of eternal love. And there was one more wish to request: to complete my Journal and the story of my love for the beautiful actress, so that it might be published, and ensure the guarantee of my name for posterity.

In preparation for the awful deed, I took out my scout knife and French bayonet and hid them beneath my pillow and set my alarm for 1.0 am. The clock would be hidden beneath the bedclothes so that its deafening ring could be immediately stifled and not awaken others in the house. Suddenly I heard my brother mounting the stairs towards the landing, and I realised I should be ruined if he caught me with these weapons. I decided to slaughter him as soon as he entered the room, and then my parents on their return from Essex, but I realised that such a change of plan would necessitate the murder of one more person: Miss Wall, a simple and benevolent old woman to whom I was not ill-disposed. But then I hardened my resolution against such sentimental reservations. I waited behind the door for Gavin to enter, when I would plunge my dagger into his heart. Then I became ashamed of my impatience, realising it might upset all my plans, and I momentarily hid the knife beneath the bed.

My brother burst into the room, and I asked what he wanted. "I've got a new idea," he exclaimed. – "What do you mean?" I cried in anger. – "Look here, I can write to Pat Dainton telling her I'm your brother," and at that point I cut him off as I flew into a rage at his interference. "Miss Dainton is my business and no one else's. Now stop being a nuisance and clear out," and with that I slammed the door in his face. I heard him slowly as if sadly descend the stairs. He had come on a good-meaning mission, but what did he know of love or the affairs of the heart, and what sort of letter was he capable of writing which would help advance my friendship with the beloved?

For the next hour and a half, I continued silently pacing my room, still resolved to carry out my original plan that night. Would I ever win my Miss Dainton? I asked myself. There were so many barriers to penetrate, and I must have been amongst the most insignificant of her suitors. I was fearful she might become engaged before I had met her face to face, to win her love. She was beautiful, renowned, and talented, and perhaps for that very reason she was less likely to attach herself to a man in the nearer time-scale. The very number of her suitors, and the confusion of choice, would ensure that possibility. She would need time and leisure before picking out a partner. And another thing: her mother is Scottish, and the Scottish are a cautious race, and if Miss Dainton has inherited that quality, so much the better. God bless her for her caution!

At 7.0 o'clock I went downstairs having secured my Journal under lock and key in the tuck box. I scanned the *Radio Times* for details of the Sunday night drama on TV, and decided to watch Congreve's, *The Way of The World* at 8.20 pm, which was preceded by a film about the Festival of Britain. I had never before seen or read a Restoration drama, and so I looked forward eagerly to the performance, and hoped it would alleviate the pain I had suffered during the day. I told my brother, who was sitting on the verandah reading a book, about the play, and was relieved to find he had ceased to concern himself about Miss Dainton.

We had a disgusting supper that night, although Miss Wall, as usual, was full of herself about what she had prepared, by wringing from us our affirmation we were satisfied with her macaroni cheese pie, but it was little more than a milky mix.

At 8.0 pm I blacked out the lounge and switched on the TV. Miss Wall was upstairs putting Oliver to bed, but she came down later, and before the play began it was announced as "unsuitable" for children due to the "outspoken language of the Restoration dramatists." I tried to coax my brother upstairs, but he refused, but he was un-offended by the language, and probably failed to understand the love strategies of the drama. Later Miss Wall joined us and seemed fascinated by the play, remarking, "Didn't they behave funny in those days." The comedy and the ridiculous characters foolishly in pursuit of love, despite all the impediments placed in their path, and the rational commonsense underpinning the meaningful satire of the story so raised my spirits that I had to discard my plans for later that night. Instead, I decided to ring up Vivienne Black the following evening and more patiently and ingeniously pursue her daughter, more in the spirit of an elegant Restoration suitor in pursuit of love. Accordingly, I went to bed with fresh hopes and a more peaceful mind in awaiting tomorrow's fate.

4th **June** – On Monday I followed my usual monotonous week-day routine. I was violently awoken by the alarm at 6.0 am after a deep night's sleep, and still being dead tired, I had to struggle against falling asleep a second time. Ten minutes later, I stumbled from my bed, putting on my slippers and dressing gown, and went downstairs to wash my hands and face with a sponge, and having gone to the lavatory, I went upstairs to dress. At 6.30 am I prepared my breakfast, and it was the same every day: three slices of toast, fried bread with fried egg, and a mug of Cocoa, and possibly fried tomatoes if these were available. On rare occasions I had grapefruit to begin with, for I was fond of fruit and usually ensured there was a good supply in the house. Breakfast concluded, I piled my plates beside the sink and went upstairs to brush my teeth, etc. We always used free samples from a dental manufacturing company, and at that time I was using Ammi-dent tooth powder – a disgusting concoction. Macleans was my favourite toothpaste whilst I disliked Philips because of its bland taste.

Returning to my bedroom, I put on my shoes and jacket, took the paper from the letter box and read the *Daily Telegraph* until 7.45 am. In preparing to leave for school, I took my bus money from my mother's purse in my parents' bedroom, they being still in bed, and after she ascertained I had a clean handkerchief, I would leave for school having picked up my raincoat on the way out. I caught the 102 bus for Golders Green, usually sitting on the top deck, and on arriving at the bus station at the beginning of the week I would always look out for the photographs of pretty actresses appearing at the Hippodrome. I had formed this habit since seeing pretty photographs of Ann Todd and Mai Zetterling – the latter whom I found especially attractive. I walked up North End road, usually arriving at school about 8.15 am. After roll-call at 9.0 am on Monday we had form hour, followed by the school council, but I rarely attended that as I preferred to work.

During break I told Geoffrey everything which occurred during the weekend concerning Miss Dainton, but I revealed nothing about my personal feelings. As usual, he scorned her! Break over we had English followed by two open Rooms to conclude the morning. At lunch I was sitting at Monty's table for the next fortnight, and the rest of the dinner hour was split between studying Latin and discoursing with Geoffrey about Miss Dainton. In the afternoon I had maths, private work, and work estate, but I felt little inclined towards schoolwork as it was intensely hot, and before the end of the afternoon, I was filled with excited anticipation at the idea of phoning Vivienne Black, and my heart beat rapidly as to how I should conduct myself, and I tried to rehearse the conversation in my mind. I discussed my hopes with Geoffrey Dunston as we walked down the hill again towards the bus station, but he was unsympathetic as he was a misogynist towards all women, but nonetheless, he praised me for my courage.

The bus left for home at 4.15 pm or thereabouts and I was home by 4.35 pm, and having hung my coat on the stand, I ran upstairs to the toilet to urinate. At school I never went to the toilet area or urinals, as I hated public toilets, and since I was at Highgate School, I could never pass water if others were standing around. I then washed my hands, which I always did before eating, and at school we had a hands inspection before being allowed into the dining hall. I changed into my slippers and then went down for tea. In the kitchen I was greeted by Mrs. Craddock, and after I sat down at the table, I ate my usual slices of bread and marmalade and margarine – or butter if there was any, and usually only one cup of tea, or up to five cups if the weather was hot.

That day I had tea on my own, with only the hunchback, Mrs. Craddock, for company, sitting across the table, occasionally trying to make conversation. "Oliver's gone out with Miss Wall," she said. – "Has she,?" I responded. – "They're late returning." – "Yes!" – "I suppose he'll come back covered with ice cream and chocolate, and will need a good wash." – "I expect so," I remarked. Although the feud between Mrs. Craddock and Miss Wall was ongoing, they were always civil to one another when face to face. "Gavin's late today," said Mrs. Craddock. – "Yes," I answered, and at 5.0 o'clock I rose from the table, thanked her for the tea, and took the telephone directory to my parents' bedroom.

It was fortunate that no one else was in the house, for my mother had presumably gone up to town, and my brother was expected back any time. As before, I secured all doors and windows before lifting the receiver and asking for the number. My heart beat rapidly as I heard the number ring. The phone was answered. "Could I speak with Vivienne Black,?" I said, and immediately wondered as to whether I had been impolite in not prefixing her name with "Mrs." – "I'm afraid she's out at the moment," replied a man with a pleasant cultured voice, and I imagined him as a clean-shaven broad-shouldered man but not corpulent. "When will she be in?" I enquired. – "Any time within the next half hour. Can I give her a message?" – "No thank you, my business is confidential." – "Can I give a name?" – "Nigel Corfe."

He repeated my name slowly as if writing it on a slip of paper. "I'll tell her you phoned," he concluded. "Thank you," I replied, and he repeated the parting gesture. When phoning I always allowed the other person to replace the receiver first, and I did it on this occasion too. On phoning my cousin, Michael Brown, some months earlier, after we said our "goodbyes," we both held the receiver in our hands in dead silence for at least two minutes, until he finally said a last "goodbye" before replacing the phone.

Although I had not got through to Vivienne Black, I was elated by my partial success. At least I felt assured that she lived at 16 Conduit street, and that she was not abroad, and that she must have received my letters to pass on to her daughter. This gave me hope. I returned the directory to the lounge, and went to my room to read, which I normally did between 5.0 and 7.0 pm. I decided to wait an hour before ringing Vivienne Black again. By that time my mother had returned and was talking with Miss Wall in the lounge, and I had hardly entered the room, when the latter put me into an embarrassing situation by exclaiming, "I see you haven't got your best suit on today." – "No," I answered blandly. – "You should have seen him yesterday afternoon. He *did* look smart." – "Yes, it does look nice on him," said my mother. – "I don't know where he went, but his hair was brushed back and he had nice new shoes," continued Miss Wall. "I suspect he went to visit his lady friend – I'm not saying he did – but that's what it looked like." – "I don't think he's got a lady friend," said my mother sharply, "but if he keeps himself smart, I expect he will one day."

I could stand the embarrassment no more, especially as Gavin was sitting on the sofa listening intently. I surreptitiously took the directory once again to my parents' bedroom and tried to ring the number again, but this time there was no reply. How could this be? Had her Secretary passed on my message, and was she afraid of answering the phone because of this? I pondered on these things when I was alone in my room. I had a large supper that night, and instead of writing my Journal from 8.0 to 9.0 o'clock, I listened to music before having a bath, and I soon fell asleep in bed although I found the bright street lights did not conduce to a good night's rest.

5th June - On Mondays I usually had my sweet rations, unless my mother happened to be out, which she was the day before. I had a quarter pound allowance per week, and always spent this on two two ounce bars of chocolate. I was not fond of hard fruit sweets (in which my father indulged) always preferring Caleys, Cadburys, or Nestles chocolate amongst other makes. On arriving home from school that day I bought my rations and they usually came to a shilling, which my parents gave. But I was also owed my weekly pocket money which was 1/6d.

At 5.30 pm I rang Vivienne Black on Mayfair 6271, holding the following scribbled note as to what I should say: "Good evening! I believe you are the mother of the actress known as Patricia Dainton. During the past few weeks I've been sending her various letters, and have had no reply. I began to doubt your address as to whether or not it was 16 Conduit Street." My heart throbbed as I heard the number ring, and when the receiver was lifted, I spoke in a hurried and forced tone. "Could I please speak with Vivienne Black," I began. – "Speaking," replied an aristocratic lady, and the firmness of her voice indicated a person of importance. I then began to read my spiel. "Yes," she replied with slow attentiveness in answer to my first question. I then completed my spiel, and there was a short pause. "Well," she began slowly, "all day I've been opening and answering mail." I felt this was somewhat off the point, and was no reply to anything I had said, and although her voice was aristocratic and firm, it was by no means haughty. She spoke slowly yet seemed to lack a natural wit for someone in her elevated position.

Her manner was simple rather than charming, and natural rather than imposing. Her accent, however, was not English, but rather Scottish intermixed with American. I explained that I had a present for her daughter and had visited on Sunday but not found her at home. "Only my office is situated here," she explained. – "I wondered whether I could make an appointment to see you, when I could give you the present to pass onto your daughter?" – "Certainly, would tomorrow do?" (I beamed at the pleasure of my success.) "Yes, I could come tomorrow," I replied. – "In the morning, shall we say at about ten o'clock?" – "I'm afraid I cannot come in the morning. What about the afternoon?" – "Would three o'clock suit you?" – "What about five o'clock or five thirty?" I suggested. – "Alright, yes, I could see you at five thirty." – "Which bell do I ring?" – "Just walk straight in. We're on the second floor."

After polite parting gestures, I replaced the receiver. I was thrilled at my success and at once entertained visions that Patricia Dainton would soon be in my arms receiving my kisses. I ran into the spare room, where my mother was hanging up some clean curtains, and I told her the news. "Do you know what you'll say to her mother?" she only asked. – "I have everything worked out in my head," I replied. I told her I would rush home after school, change quickly, and then take the present up to town. My mother advised against this on the grounds that I would be hungry and worn out, and anyway, could never make it in time. She advised I should go direct from school, and this I decided upon, but it would never have occurred to me because of the curiosity it would arouse on account of my best suit, and because of the strange parcel I would be carrying.

Any feelings of embarrassment I felt would just need to be repressed. I dreaded the questions that Stuart West might come up with, as this boy (who was distantly related to Chaim Weizmann), was curious about anything which seemed unusual, and he might make a fuss amongst the other boys. My mother advised that after school I should take the number 2 bus from Golders Green to Victoria and descend at Selfridges, walk down Oxford Street to Marshall & Snellgrove, and then turn right into New Bond Street. That night I went to bed with a peaceful mind.

6th June – That morning I put on my best suit and left the house without comment from my brother, having collected my bus money of 2/6d, allowing for the extra fares. The previous evening I had neatly re-written out my Ode to Miss Dainton on a large sheet of paper to give to her mother. As I wanted no one at school to see the label attached to the package, I enclosed the latter in newspaper and string.

On leaving the house I was extraordinarily smart, but I feared that by 4.0 o'clock I might appear somewhat untidy, and that my shoes would be dusty, and my hair ruffled. I brought my comb with me, but what I feared most was the heat of the day, and that I might perspire by the time I reached Conduit Street. I decided to keep as much in the shade as possible, for I realised the importance of making the best possible impression on Vivienne Black. But even in the bus queue I became embarrassed, for it seemed as if I encountered malicious looks because of my dandified appearance. As usual I was one of the first to arrive at school, and my present was half hidden under the mackintosh which hung over my arm. I locked the package away in the locker and left it for the day.

Our first lesson that morning was to be biology, where I accordingly set up my desk, but I got out my Latin book and began studying that. I had no sooner opened my *Clarendon Latin Course* and set the book comfortably before me, when my mind wandered off the subject, as it had done so often since the beginning of the Miss Dainton affair. I was over-excited about the forthcoming evening, and imagined falling into a long conversation with Vivienne Black, and that we would adopt an easy and candid manner with one another as a prelude to a long-lasting friendship. We would conduct a congenial discourse on a serious topic, yet both of us would be witty and laugh, and be lost in our loquaciousness.

As I lounged in an armchair opposite VB at the other side of the desk, I would rest my legs on a coffee table as we chain-smoked, filling the room with a grey mist. Her male Secretary might enter momentarily, cast a disapproving glance at me in view of my occupying so much of his employer's time, and then retreat with his tail between his legs, whilst the typists might put their ears to the key hole of another door in curiosity at this strange visitor who was captivating their boss. I would read her my Ode, and then hand her the copy, and when the office was closed she would take me out for tea, and we would part the closest of friends, having been invited to visit her for tea at her residence the following Sunday, where of course I would meet her daughter who by that time would have returned from Bournemouth.

Gradually my schoolmates arrived and set up their desks whilst I tried to make myself as inconspicuous as possible with my nose in a book as if in deep study, and my new spectacles were particularly useful in this respect as they gave me a scholarly look. Some complimented me on my smart and tidy appearance, and I thanked them for the compliment, and fortunately no one asked the reason for my transformation. Geoffrey arrived and I went outside, embarrassed by my attire, and confided in him about my success, but he seemed uninterested, and this annoyed me. I wanted someone to share in my excitement and there was no one else I could approach.

At call-over I saw Stuart for the first time that day, and he had still not put up his desk which meant that he was late. Unsmiling (for he was the serious type) in his squeaky yet dreary voice, as if he had just climbed out of bed, he asked, "Where did you get that from?" – "From Selfridges," I answered, "in the sales." He continued to question me like a customs officer. – "How much was it?" – "Five pounds," I replied casually. – "Call that cheap?" he cried indignantly. "Yes," I said, upon which he called on others for their opinion of the price, and when they agreed with my side of the argument, he shut up. It became a hot day, but by 4.0 o'clock I was not perspiring, and when I left the school with my heavy package I was unnoticed – even by Stuart. I walked down the hill with Geoffrey, and when we parted to my surprise he wished me success. I took a number 2 bus and my heart throbbed all the way to Oxford Street.

On arriving at 16 Conduit Street, I boldly entered the building, and climbed two stairs at a time to the second floor. I stood outside a large mahogany door on which was written: "Vivienne Black, Artistes Management." There was dead silence in the building, and strangely to say, the door was ajar. As there was a bell I rang it and waited for what must have been several minutes without evoking any response. I was nervous but nonetheless pushed the door open, walked into a small waiting room with opaque glass windows looking into a larger office, and closed the door behind me. There were four chairs and everything was dark mahogany.

On a door leading into an inner office appeared the words: "No artistes seen without an appointment," and that door also had a bell and so I rang it. I heard a door slam within, someone walked forward, and the door was opened. A well-groomed middle-aged man in a grey suit with curly hair stood before me. He was broad, not tall, but somewhat corpulent, and he held a fountain pen in his right hand as he waited for me to speak. "I've made an appointment to see Vivienne Black," I began. – "I'm afraid she's out now," he replied, and by his voice I immediately recognised him to be the man with whom I had spoken on the phone – and my guess about his physical appearance had not been so far out. I remained dumb-struck for several seconds whilst the Secretary stood silent. – "When will she be back?," I asked.

It was true I had arrived half an hour early for the appointment, but it was odd she should be absent at that time of the day. There was a longer pause, and at last he replied, "She won't be back today. She was unexpectedly called out to the film studios." – "She was expecting me," I insisted. – "I know. She rang your home to tell you not to come. She was called out at 4.0 o'clock." – "I see," I replied with slow thoughtfulness. "Then I'll ring her tomorrow." – "Alright," he said. We exchanged goodbyes" with a congenial smile, but I initiated the latter gesture, without which I doubt it would have been returned, for he seemed a solemn although not a gloomy or disagreeable person.

After I left I hoped he would speak well of me to his employer, for I had been civil in responding to his cool reserve. Naturally I was disappointed and felt somewhat angry towards Vivienne Black, but perhaps after all it was not her fault for business must have first priority. I slowly walked down the stairs. Conduit Street presented a vast contrast compared with the previous Sunday afternoon, for now it was noisy and filled with traffic.

CHAPTER 17
Gestures of Suicide

"Our torments also may in length of time
Become our elements."

John Milton, *Paradise Lost*, Bk. II, 1, 274.

Preparations for the third visit – I meet Vivienne Black – A new plan followed by a desperate correspondence – Failure of my literary efforts – Attempts at self-injury – Suicide letters

By 6.30 pm I was home, and after a brief tea, my father wanted to take my mother and me next door to the Odeon to see the film, *Toms Brown's Schooldays* (Director: Gordon Parry, 1951), which was attracting much attention. As it was a Wednesday, my father's half day, when he went to town for a haircut or to Cotterills to stock up on dental supplies, he had that day been in the West End with my mother where they had tea in a restaurant, arriving home shortly after me. Gavin would not be taken to the cinema as he would be going with his school at the end of the week.

Immediately on arriving home from town I was met by Miss Wall who told me someone had phoned me that afternoon. "Who,?" I asked. "A young lady called Vivienne Black," answered Miss Wall. As she finished these words, I ran upstairs to hide my parcel once again. I was relieved to learn it was Mrs. Craddock who had answered the phone, for I dreaded the possibility that it could have been my mother, as she might have enticed Vivienne Black into a stupid conversation.

We went to the Odeon at about 7.15 pm and left when the picture house closed at 10.30 pm, when I came home, had a quick wash, and went to bed. We sat in the most expensive seats, the front row of the balcony (for my father was particular about having the best of most things), and although the plot differed somewhat from Thomas Hughes' book, the film was well produced, although I could not possibly have seen the screen clearly without my glasses. It was actually filmed at Rugby School, but Howard Davis, who took the title role, was perhaps a little too tall although then only 12 years of age.

7th June - On returning from school, I phoned Vivienne Black, who answered in person and immediately apologised for my not having received her message. I asked if I could see her on Friday, but she would be out all day, and I then suggested Saturday but her office was never open then, and finally we fixed for noon the following Monday which was my half term. – I was meanwhile progressing well with my painting, *Off, Off, You Lendings*.

9th June – For the greater part of the day I wrote many pages of my Journal, but made slow progress in bringing it up to date, as my life seemed to progress faster than my pen. My Journal was expanding beyond what I had anticipated, e.g., I expected 1st June to take up about ten lines when in fact it occupied over seven pages.

10th June – This morning I worked hard on my Journal and had sufficient patience to continue in the afternoon, but I thought it wiser not to confine myself in my room all day in case I should visit Vivienne Black with a pale complexion. It was a hot and pleasant day and I decided to walk to Hampstead and back across the Heath. I left after lunch, taking my usual route along Muswell Hill road to the Woodman, thus avoiding Highgate Wood with its ugly trees and nasty black soil, with its urban rather than rural environment, and pretentious drinking fountains. (It did after all belong to the Corporation of London.) I then climbed Southwood Lane, a steep but pleasant road, and stopped briefly outside the ancient pair of clinker built cottages on the right, by the corner of The Park.

They were still in disrepair and as sinister as ever, and no one ever emerged or entered the doors, and the walls were covered with ivy and other plants. What legends and stories we junior Highgate schoolboys spun about these mysterious and horrible cottages! Soon I reached Highgate Village and passed beneath the high grim walls of the Senior School, and having passed the graveyard where Coleridge was buried (a fact I gleaned recently from my father), I turned down Hampstead Lane. I passed by the Junior school and then entered Kenwood which I loved, walking by the elegant mansion of Lord Mansfield, one of the great Lord Chancellors of the 18th century, and pondered on the possibility of one day painting the beautiful scenery in oils.

On leaving Kenwood through one of the iron gates through the railings marking the perimeter of the estate, I entered the Heath and soon reached Hampstead which to me was the ideal place in London to reside. I examined the paintings and other art works of the summer exhibition in the High Street, and then returned by the quicker route of Spaniards road above the Heath. As it was a clear day, there was a magnificent view of London, and the dome of St. Paul's towered over the city far below. I passed through the old Toll Gate at the Spaniard's Inn, and was home by 4.30 pm, having estimated my walk at 7 miles.

11th June – It being half term, I did not arise until 8.0 o'clock, but I did not directly dress in my best suit, as I did not wish to arouse the suspicion of my father at the breakfast table. I felt excited, for in four hours I would be in the company of Vivienne Black, and it was another sunny day. Breakfast over, and my daily toilet done with, I greased my hair with brylcream and brushed it flat. I was already pleased with my appearance, and then I shaved, using a new "Personna" hollow ground razor blade which proved most effective for sharpness. The acne which attacked me slightly had diminished over the past week, although I had not regularly applied *Eskamel* which was not a very effective medicament. However, I had used it the previous night and the complaint had worsened rather than decreased.

Over an hour was spent in improving my appearance, which included brushing my shoes and putting on my best suit. I decided to leave home at 11.0 o'clock, and in the meantime I did some shopping for my mother and then listened to some orchestral music on the Light programme, pacing the room to the pleasant tunes. My mother had given me two shillings for the bus fares, and sharp on eleven, I switched off the wireless and picked up my parcel. As I passed through the hall, my mother was gossiping with Vera (the Russian lady) who had called round for a chat, and after a polite exchange, I rushed off.

On reaching Conduit Street my heart again beat with excitement. There was no shade from the sun, as there had been on Wednesday, and on reaching number 16 I climbed two stairs at a time to the second floor, and walked straight into the waiting room where I rang the bell. I heard someone stride to the door, and in a second it was opened. A tall blonde woman with a black dress and a well-powdered yet cracked face stood before me. "Surely this could not be her mother," was my first thought, for she seemed rather ugly. We exchanged smiles, and I was about to ask for Vivienne Black (thank God I did not) when she ushered me into her office and set me down in a deep leather armchair. She cleared various papers on her desk, sat down opposite me, and was apparently engaged in several telephone calls at the same time.

All this occurred within a fraction of a minute. She sat at a large desk with five telephones, three of them in use. Two were in her hands, and one lay on the desk, but she was speaking through none of them, but pressing down the receiver button and making the phones ring. She was clearly used to this activity, for she acted with agility and calm – and not a trace of impatience. In her modish style of behaviour she would take a deep puff from her long cigarette, and blow out a great cloud of smoke which would rise gracefully to the ceiling, but she did not raise her head to blow out this smoke but kept it lowered over the receivers, and I thought this latter a rather vulgar gesture for a person of her status.

She sat in an upright leather chair without arms, and she bent over the desk, one leg over the other. As I sat quietly, I studied her carefully: her black dress was open from the neck down to her breasts, and her chest was well-powdered too, and her skin seemed to be tanned by cosmetics, for it was too dark to be natural, although it added to her attraction. Her hair was flaxen with yellow patches, and she had a large frame but well-proportioned limbs. Her waist was perhaps a little too corpulent, and her arms too thick for a woman, but otherwise her appearance was not objectionable. She was attractive and dignified, but did not have the qualities of a glamour girl. The office had a business-like environment, in that papers were strewn untidily everywhere, and the room seemed in confusion. The furniture was old-fashioned, the carpet dirty and worn, and there was little light, as there were no windows, only a skylight over the desk. Several photos were crudely pinned up on two wooden strips, and three other doors led into other rooms.

Every few moments Miss Black would look up and give me a smile. It was a very beautiful smile – the most charming smile I had ever received, for it was untainted by sentimentality or affectation, but exuded pure affection. I returned the smile, and began to like her better as every minute passed, and in my eyes she was transformed from a painted old hag into a creature of great comfort and human attraction. As I looked at her, I realised it was not skin which met my gaze but a thick coat of grease paint, and I felt tempted to press my finger onto her face to see how deep the paint was.

She spoke softly, and offered me a cigarette which I declined, and then asked me what the weather was like outside. I was so astonished by the question that I gaped stupidly, and so she asked again as to whether it was still "bright." I answered in the affirmative, and must have looked at her as if I doubted her sanity. Could she not see the weather from the skylight? She gave me a beautiful smile, explaining she had been kept in the office all morning. By now I began to recognise the likeness between her and her daughter. For a start, there was the beautiful smile, and I could easily have thrown my arms around her neck and covered her face with kisses.

At last she reached someone on the phone, asking for "a thousand cards for Dainton," and after a short pause, she put down the receiver. Then she got onto someone else whom she addressed as "my pet" (presumably her daughter), and after that she phoned someone called "John" with whom she spoke for about four minutes. She then put down the receiver exclaiming, "Well, at last that's done." I arose from my seat, saying I would cut the string to remove the newspaper from my parcel, but before I had time to retrieve my penknife, she produced a pair of scissors and cut the string herself.

Overcome with shyness, I awkwardly removed the newspaper which she threw away together with the string in a green waste paper bin – similar to those we had at school. I handed her the present and she placed it on an armchair. "Pat will get the present tonight," she said. "I'll give it to her when she comes in this evening." – "Thank you," I responded. – "Pat thought you might like some of these photos," she continued, and she took a pile of about 50 photographs from a drawer and held them before me. She came round to my side of the desk, and standing beside me, began to go through the collection, pointing out those which she thought were particularly well done. "Pat said you could have as many of these photographs as you wanted," she continued. "Most are not very good. That's a good one of her dancing," she said placing it aside. "That's when she went down a coalmine. Most of these were taken in the home." These photos were useful in revealing many of Patricia Dainton's interests: there were photos of her walking in the street arm-in-arm with two boys (never one), of her in a swimming pool, of her in many kinds of costume, and most surprisingly, of her sitting at an easel with an expensive box of paints, a brush in her hand. In all these pictures she was revealed as an innocent and exceedingly happy and virtuous girl.

[Here the Journal comes to an abrupt end.]

The upshot of the day was that I not only returned with a dozen or so press photographs of Miss Dainton, but also a huge mugshot 4' x 3', which I carried home in a cardboard roll. This photograph was hung and displayed in my bedroom for the next 18 months or so. The documentary evidence for what follows is taken from diary entries and surviving correspondence, or copies of letters either sent or withheld.

On Saturday 16th June 1951, it is recorded that I had formulated a "new plan" in approaching Vivienne Black, and I phoned her on Wednesday 20th to be told to phone her on Monday 25th, and on that occasion I was told to ring on Thursday 28th, again without success. I phoned her again on 2nd July when she was out, and then on 4th when I spoke to her and she promised me tickets for the television studios on 7th when Patricia Dainton would be appearing in a short play that Saturday night. The said plan entailed asking her to act as a literary agent in publishing two of my novels, *Anthony Anvil*, and, *James Thornton* – the latter unfinished.

A long rambling letter was sent to her, on Tuesday 10th July. The tone was desperate, even bordering on the impertinent. It began, "During the past few days – or rather for nearly three weeks, I have been trying to make an appointment with you. I quite understand how busy you are in your office and at the studios; yet I think I am also right in assuming you are reluctant to receive me due to the un-revealed mysteriousness of this so-called 'plan,' I wish to discuss with you. You have a perfect right to be hesitant for anyone's suspicions would justifiably be aroused.

"I do not wish to bombard you with persuasive arguments in imploring you to let me see your daughter, as I suspect you think, for that would be insolence. I wish to discuss a plan which is of the utmost importance to me, but has nothing to do with your daughter – or at least, not in the shorter term. You may perhaps suspect that I have formulated this plan to put myself in a more advantageous situation to woo your daughter. It is true the plan only entered my head a month ago, but there are strong arguments in its defence, and I believe you will need very little convincing. I shall bring solid proof in its favour, and that will mean carrying a bulky parcel" [presumably manuscripts] "and I will demonstrate that since my 8th year, my personality has been developing in such a way in preparing me towards such a plan.

"It cannot be put into execution without your advice or assistance, yet it will cause you very little bother. I do not wish to reveal the plan in a letter, as I feel it can only be discussed face-to-face. It is in no way utopian, as you will see, but entails the completion of a task which is no more than a normal occupation.

"Please forgive me for placing that condition on your daughter in receiving my gift, as set down in the letter which accompanied the package. If there was anything else in the letter which you found objectionable then please forgive me. I hope that you and your daughter are not angry with me. When you gave me those beautiful photographs of your daughter, I felt quite guilty about the condition I laid down in my letter. I am obliged to write this letter as I can only phone you after 4.30 pm, and you are usually out at that time. I do not wish to disturb your secretaries, as I fear I have done. May I apologise?

"When I phoned you on Wednesday, you said you would try to obtain a ticket for me to enter the BBC, and see your daughter acting in, *The Inch Man*. I received a garbled message asking me to go to Lime Grove Studios and be there by 7.50 pm, and ask for a ticket in my name. The person who gave me the message" [being my father] "said that a young man had phoned at 11.0 pm last night and spoken in a hurry. When I arrived at the Studios" [which was on Saturday 7th July] "there was no ticket reserved for me. I had travelled unnecessarily half way across London to the wrong location, when I could have walked less than a mile to Alexandra Palace from where the show was televised. However, a kind lady at Lime Grove let me see the show in a private viewing room. I think your daughter acted very well. It was the first time I saw her on stage or screen. I'm endeavouring to uncover the cause of the mishap which occurred. I do not blame you, but I think you should be informed of what happened.

"I enclose a fully addressed and stamped envelope for your immediate and brief reply in fixing an appointment to see you as soon as possible, since if I do not see you by 18th July it may cause me some bother." [This was because I was going on holiday several days later.] "I do not want to be left much longer in a state of suspense, not knowing what future course to take," &c., and then follow a couple of repetitious paragraphs, and I sign off, "Yours sincerely (and may I say affectionately), Nigel Corfe." The letter may indicate that I had some sense of right and wrong *per se*, but it betrays a total ignorance of psychological motives, and reading it for the first time after almost 60 years, I am appalled by its naivety, for from the first line to the last, it can only irritate and annoy. The only explanation giving rise to the attitude of the letter can be found in the fact that I had only been exposed to brute-power relationships without any exposure to the need for tact, diplomacy, or kindness in those situations when gain or benefits are sought.

On Monday 16th July I visited Vivienne Black on the second occasion and left her the intended manuscripts, and on the following Friday the school broke up for the summer holidays. On 8th August I sent Miss Black the following letter: "You have now had my manuscripts for approximately five weeks, and I expect by now they have been returned to you by the readers. I would therefore like to make an appointment with you to hear their opinion." I then pass some self-deprecating remarks about the two novels, supporting this with Edward Gibbon's contention from his autobiography that, "the author is the best judge of his own work." I then declare I am shortly to write a stage play which, "I am fully confident will be far better than anything I have written so far. I have already embarked on a second and more detailed rough draft. I will tell you more about it when we meet." I then declare my hurry to see her, and ask for an "immediate" reply, once again enclosing a stamped addressed postcard in saving her "valuable time."

Almost as a p.s. I added, "I was sorry to hear of your recent illness when I phoned yesterday and you were out. I hope you are now fully recovered to health." The said play was, *The Fatal Conscience*, a historical drama in five acts about the British Army during the 1745-46 Jacobite uprising, a minor character of which I recollect was plagiarised from the comic landlord in Oliver Goldsmith's, *She Stoops To Conquer*. I began writing the play on Friday 31st August 1951, and shortly thereafter returned to school. It was completed after about 6 weeks, and although I met Vivienne Black on several subsequent occasions, she passed me over to her Secretary, or perhaps more correctly, her business partner, Hugh Richardson, who received me and with whom I discussed my various dramatic literary efforts until the end of 1953.

By Saturday 24th May 1952, I must have become sufficiently impatient and desperate to write to Miss Black the following letter: "I still love your daughter as much as ever, and will continue to love her until my dying day. For almost a year I have striven to make myself worthy of her. First I wrote, *The Fatal Conscience,* and it turned out to be an indifferent play despite my diligent improvements. Mr. Richardson gave me very helpful advice, and I then wrote the farce, *No Funeral!*, which was certainly a better effort, and always I had your daughter in mind. The standard was still wanting in reaching the demands of the

London stage, and so I then wrote, *The Capitalist Rivalry*, a short detective thriller. This was certainly better than the two previous contributions, but Mr. Richardson found it unoriginal and the dialogue stilted. I will always be grateful to him for his useful criticism.

"I am now in complete despair, and do not know what to do next, as I have lost my enthusiasm for writing and have writer's block. All this is because of your daughter, and I think of her every day. If you would allow me to meet her just once, I would be forever grateful to you for the privilege. It would also encourage me to write another play, and hopefully, one which would satisfy Mr. Richardson – but I cannot hope to write without the necessary inspiration of seeing your daughter first. If I was to meet her, I would maintain my high spirits, and I promise not to betray a hint of my physical longing for her. If she happened to loathe me, I promise never to worry you or your daughter again.

"Please do not judge or condemn me on account of those long, rash, and eccentric letters I wrote to your daughter last year. I wrote them in a great confusion of feelings, of depression, hope, and happiness, either intermixed or alternating, and this may have led to a form of temporary madness. I'm sorry about that burdensome chunk of clay I presented her as a present. Please let me see her, for then perhaps I might be fired to write a masterpiece. If you let me see her, I'll repay you with anything in my power. If and when I happen to publish anything which is to your liking, I shall dedicate it to you as an eternal memento," &c.

The curious thing about the above and other letters to Vivienne Black is that they assume that the mother is acting as a barrier to meeting the daughter, as if the latter had no opinion or will of her own in the matter. The truth of the situation is that this accusatory stance is intended as discreet prodding in persuading the mother to take pro-active measures in bringing the daughter and the persistent letter writer together.

Over the next few weeks I became increasingly depressed and suicidal, although Hugh Richardson was still considering my latest literary production, and I was bombarding his office with telephone calls. Apparently Vivienne Black was meanwhile expected to go into hospital for treatment of some kind, and illness kept her away from the office. On several occasions during these weeks I resolved on suicide or half-suicide on specified dates usually a week in advance. On two occasions I attempted to stab myself near the heart, in such a way as to cause hospitalisation so that I might call Patricia Dainton to my bedside as I lay near the point of death.

I was inspired to this action by the story of Karl Ludwig Sand after his assassination of the reactionary Kotzebue in 1820, when in horror at his deed in seeing the small daughters of Kotzebue run to their father, he then stabbed himself and lay for days in bed as a hopeless invalid until his death. I took this story from Dumas' *Celebrated Crimes*, the 8 volumes of which I had recently bought from the Southwood Bookstore. Standing by my bedroom I opened my shirt, pulled down the front of my vest, and made stabbing motions at my chest with a dagger. I incurred several scratches but lacked the courage to thrust the knife into my chest. It was fortunate I did not attempt a serious wound, as the margin between injury and death in any chest wound is minimal, and of this I was ignorant at the time – although subconsciously I may have sensed it.

On Tuesday 24th June, I wrote the following suicide letter to Vivienne Black, but fortunately it was never despatched, and I still retain the original and its copy. It read as follows: "Dear Miss Black. – I wrote to you saying I would love your daughter until my dying day, but since you insist I never see her, you have forced me to remove myself from the worst of all possible worlds. I have fled many miles from this accursed metropolis to carry out the deed, to avoid the contempt which arises from attempting to arouse false sentiment, for my corpse will never be found.

"I heard you were ill, and I offered to visit you and bring you flowers, but you have lied to me on so many occasions, that I don't believe your supposed ill-health. I shall kill myself with a knife on a high mountain, overlooking a beautiful panorama, with a photograph of your daughter on my heart. I hope you and your daughter will remember me until death. I expect that you and your daughter will have many more happy and enjoyable years ahead. Please send my best wishes to Mr. Richardson. – Yours very Sincerely, Nigel Corfe. – P.S. I advise you for your conscience sake to destroy this letter as soon as it is read. May the Furies haunt you forever, for you are my murderer."

It is uncertain as to whether the following letter, dated 30th June, to Vivienne Black was despatched or not. I suspect the latter, since had it been received, it may well have been passed to the police or my parents for further action. It reads as follows: "Why have you not replied to my last letter?" [Presumably that of 24th May.] "I wrote protesting that I wanted to see your daughter, through an arrangement of the utmost discretion in avoiding any fuss. I repeat, I shall love your daughter until the very last, yet soon my seemingly unending patience will be stretched to breaking point. For eighteen months I have loved her, and used every reasonable means to arrange a meeting, yet all in vain. Since you absolutely insist on refusing to accept any reasonable terms I propose, you force me to take unreasonable means.

"Please phone me after 4.0 pm on any weekday as soon as possible. If I do not receive a reply by 9.0 pm on Friday 4th July, I shall stab myself between the ribs, in this way morally obliging you to visit my death bed in hospital. It would be far less inconvenient for you to speak with me for ten minutes on the phone, than undertaking the tiresome and time-consuming journey entailed in visiting me in my hospital bed. I am sorry to be obliged to resort to such a violent threat, but what other means do I have left? I am strongly resolved to commit this violent deed, and only you can prevent it. – Yours," &c. "P.S. When you phone me, if anyone else should answer, please do not reveal your name."

Such a letter was clearly motivated by descriptions of the endless death bed scenes I had read about in history, or in romantic novels, or witnessed in so many operas. I then had a romantic notion of the deathbed experience, quite oblivious to the fact in real life of the pain or confusion caused to the subject, or the hypocrisy or pretentious expressions of sorrow of relatives and other hangers-on, whose only real thought is of material benefits to be gained from the nearly deceased.

The most significant aspect of the letter is its reflection of my appalling mental state, and that seemingly, I was approaching a nervous breakdown. Whilst I was not to experience the latter, worse was to follow, but in the next chapter we must record happier events of my life during those stormy years.

CHAPTER 18
Respite with my Grandmother

"Without friends no one would choose to live even if
he had all other goods."

Aristotle, *Nicomachean Ethics*, Bk. VIII, Sec. 1.

My grandmother moves to Bath – My wanderings in the city – Treats and outings – Visits to Hampton Hall – The move to my aunt and uncle – Attitudes to smoking – Character of Uncle Bill

Every Summer throughout my teenage years I stayed with my grandmother in Bath for a fortnight or so, and always enjoyed these holidays. When she sold the family home, Sampford Place, in Melksham in 1946, she rented unfurnished accommodation in Lansdown, high up on the hill on the northern side of Bath, being a short walk from her eldest daughter and son-in-law, Inez and Bill, who resided at 10 Sion Hill.

My last visit to Sampford Place was shortly before the sale of the property to the local council who converted it into a boys' orphanage. Later it became an old people's home which was extended with new buildings stretching across what used to be the kitchen garden. When I visited the home in the 1970s I was appalled to discover that the elegant old staircase with its cast iron banisters and rosewood handrail had been ripped out in the cause of modernity and in creating greater space for other purposes. Meanwhile, the fine old drawing room with large windows at both ends, and housing a magnificent grand piano, had been converted into a dormitory for 20 or so elderly men in the early stages of dementia.

That last visit to Sampford Place was a hurried episode, when my grandmother was disposing pieces of furniture and ornaments for which she would have no room in the flat at Bath. She took me into my grandfather's study and asked me to choose a book. There were many impressive tomes which would shortly pass into the hands of book dealers, and as I did not want to appear greedy, I made what I thought at the time was a modest choice, by choosing Henry M. Stanley's, *My Dark Companions and Their Strange Stories* (1893), with numerous line illustrations, an enlightening book on the myths and legends of tribes in sub-tropical Africa.

My grandmother moved into the impressive house of Lady Cubitt, occupying a spacious flat on the third floor. The house was set well back from the street in a large well-kept garden, bordering meadows on the mountainside. The flat was so large that she sub-let a room to a "respectable" middle aged lady who held a civil service position, and the two would share the sitting room in the evenings, either quietly engaged in needlework, or reading, or listening to dramas or other interesting programmes on the wireless. It might be thought that walking up flights of stairs to a third floor would be too much for someone of her age, but she never complained, as my mother would certainly have done if placed in a similar situation.

During these holidays, to which I always looked forward, I was never for a moment bored. I wandered around the town admiring the architecture, browsed in the many second hand bookshops, where I always found antiquarian works of great interest, and in the mornings, spent much time in the Pump Room, listening to the Palm Court orchestra, drinking the hot spring water every day, and sometimes having a coffee. At that time Bath was not yet the tourist trap which it is today, and there was no charge for entering the Pump Room (which was regarded as a public café as any other), and there was certainly no charge to drink the water from the fountain. With regard to antiquarian books I still recall seeing Goldsmith's *Roman History*, and a 12-volume edition of Johnes' translation of *Froissart's Chronicles*, the latter priced at £12 – an exorbitant amount of money and quite beyond my means. In retrospect I am glad I never contemplated buying the set, since some decades later I bought a fine edition of Lord Berners early Tudor translation, a far livelier work by a man who served in the military under Henry VIII and was better placed to empathise with the experiences of Froissart than the 18th century scholar, Thomas Johnes.

When I was not alone wandering around the antique markets, or exploring the nooks and crannies of Bath, my grandmother took me to visit various relatives. Most often, naturally, we visited Aunt Inez and Uncle Bill. As we strolled along for the first visit, my grandmother reminded me I should always address her son-in-law as "Sir," and of course I always did. I was always afraid of him, for I knew he had a fearful temper, but he always treated me with good humour and a few jokes. I was not obliged, as my father was, to challenge him at Ludo! When we visited Aunt Blanche and Uncle Percy at Bathampton, again my grandmother said I should address Percy as "Sir," as that was polite in addressing any older man, but when I did so, he gently turned to me with the words, "You don't have to call me 'Sir,' I'm your uncle," and so I waived this form of address.

On several occasion I visited Melksham, briefly calling on the Keens to pay them my respects, when my grandmother prepared a delicious jelly pie amongst other culinary delights for the day, for she was an excellent cook. Another person I visited in Melksham at this time was Madeleine Garrett, the mother of Simon (whom I had pushed off the wall many years earlier) and Julia, a god-daughter of my father. I remember dropping in for tea with her, and she had a great interest in history, and enthused over the recent books of Arthur Bryant who was a current historian despised by my English teacher, Ronald Fuller. Shortly thereafter the family moved to a fine house near the centre of Bath.

On other days my grandmother would take me to the cinema, and I remember seeing a film about Queen Elizabeth and the Armada starring Flora Robson, and another taken from a horrific story by Jack London about a ruthless merchant sea captain starring Edward G. Robinson. Most of all she liked to take me to see French films when they were screened, arguing that these reflected a more civilised style of life than the crude products of Hollywood. One of these was Max Ophuls, *La Ronde* (1950), about love and seduction in 19th century Vienna, which she admired for its good taste and subtlety in dealing with an illicit topic. Her penchant for all things French was doubtless partly influenced through her friendship with her French sister-in-law, Lou, the daughter of Edward VII's favourite chef whom he brought over to England, besides being the wife of her favourite brother, Loots.

Although brought up in the Victorian era, she was no prude when it came to artistic creation of any kind, and I remember her enthusiasm over Kathleen Winsor's novel, *Forever Amber*, about the rise to riches of a peasant girl through sexual favours during the reign of Charles II, which was serialised in the press before she purchased the hard back edition of the book. She openly admired the heroine, and perhaps she used the book as a metaphor in suggesting I should guard against developing into a charmless puritan or dullard. She was, however, sensitive about the use of language in these matters, and I remember one Christmas at 105, when the Browns were with us, and we were playing a parlour game, she chided Anne for using the word "Sex," which she said should never be used in polite company, and that one should use the terms "gender" or "male or female" in its place.

I enjoyed talking with my grandmother and her lodger during the evenings after supper about all kinds of topics, and on at least one occasion she made a cryptic remark about my fondness for "socialising with old people." Perhaps she suspected (and rightly) that I was socially wanting, and needed to better develop my social skills amongst my own peers.

There was one topic she broached with unabashed directness, and that was my father. "For goodness sake don't grow up to be like your father," she exclaimed on several occasions. "That would be the ruin of you!" She explained he was a man without charm or personality, who was a bore in company, and aroused the antipathy of all "nice people" of his own age. The fact that he may have been disliked by the older generation also was not really relevant for the success of his social life, since they belonged to the past rather than the future. My aunt Inez, of course, took every opportunity to support my grandmother whenever she touched on this subject.

The Corfes were a "mean-spirited people" with a "vulgar commercial instinct," and hardly fit for mixing socially in good company. I had little hesitation in absorbing these opinions, and assured my mother's relatives I would not grow up "to be like my father." I should note, however, that according to my mother, her father did not share these views. Her father always "admired success," and as a Scotsman – or of immediate Scots descent, he saw little virtue in purely social attributes, and besides, he was of working class origin, and both he and my father were fellow Freemasons.

Quite apart from my own differences with my father, and all I had suffered from him in terms of punishment, I had more respect for the daughter of an Admiral, as a kind and morally upright person and a dutiful servant of the Crown, than for a family which derived its wealth from a chain of chemist shops in Kent. Money-making may have spelt success but it augured little in the formation of good character – or so I thought at the time. Throughout my life I have always had a weakness in overvaluing the idea of medals, titles, and rank, as the recognised and well-deserved rewards for virtue and effort, and have seldom been seduced by the attractions of money if the latter was not linked to fame, honour, or public recognition. All such achievements, of course, should be open to the majority, and have been so on the Continent since the

Napoleonic era. They are, therefore, not incompatible (or should not be) with the ideals of an egalitarian society. The lure of money *per se*, without a noble object for its use, is chiefly attractive to those at the base of society, or those debased persons who prefer Mammon to honour. Such was my prejudice at the time.

It may have been thought that the loss of Sampford Place would have deprived my grandmother from the opportunity of entertaining on a grand scale, but this was not to be. From time to time she held luncheon or dinner parties at fine restaurants in Bath, one of these being at the Hole in the Wall in New Bond Street. I attended several of these parties, when a dozen or so guests were invited, and once I remember meeting a member of the Dunn family, who owned a nationwide chain of men's hat wear shops, and decades later (when men ceased to wear hats) they diversified into selling men's suits. He was a modest self-effacing man of about 40 and was accompanied by a lady friend. At the same party was an elderly musician who deplored my taste for Wagner, and went into full flow in praising the versatility of Mozart.

Most of all I enjoyed our visits to my grandmother's younger sister, Blanche, at Hampton Hall. On arriving, we would settle down to talk in the enormous drawing room with its hundreds of ornaments and artefacts, and as soon as she saw my eyes wandering, she would suggest I go away and "explore," which I eagerly did, and would not be seen again until called by the gong for tea. The house was a treasure trove of rare antiquities which never failed to hold my attention, and I would move from room to room and floor to floor, as if in a museum. My great Uncle, Percy, had his clockmaker's workshop adjacent to the room where 365 watches from all lands and historical epochs were displayed in glass cases, and it was his hobby to keep them in working order.

My father loathed his mother-in-law, partly because of her agnosticism, and he once exclaimed she needed, "a good dose of religion," and he liked her other relatives little better. For example, he referred to Uncles Vaughan and Denys as mere "middle men" and not proper business people. Towards the end of my schooldays, he expressed his strong disdain for Aunt Blanche, on account of her constantly praising my character and promising attributes. She was delighted I was "so interested in everything, and so curious to know more," which was, "so unlike most young people today." In her younger days Blanche had written a history of costume, and so there were many things which engaged us in discussion.

After one such visit in 1952, she wrote to my parents saying how delightful it was that I visited her and Uncle Percy at Hampton Hall, and how "good-mannered" I was, and after some words of praise about my abilities and promise, my father lost his temper, saying she knew nothing at all about my "true character," and that in reality I was "good for nothing." Every Christmas my father, supported by my mother, ridiculed Aunt Blanche for her penny-pinching in recycling Christmas cards from the previous year, as she had no compunction in cutting out old designs and pasting them onto blank card onto which she wrote her greetings. "How does she know we didn't send her this card ourselves last year,?" chuckled my father. – "Because when she prepares them, and before she does the cutting out, she ensures that won't occur," I suggested in reply.

After two or three years at Lady Cubitt's, the lease which Aunt Inez and Uncle Bill had on 10 Sion Hill expired, and so the house would be placed on the market. This posed an embarrassing financial threat, for the couple were almost penniless and dependent on Uncle Bill's old age pension. What was to be done? No one would have suspected their true financial situation in view of the loud noise which my uncle made in the town. He was not merely vociferous but expressed his fury, and succeeded in arousing the enmity of many leading lights on the Council and employees of the local authority, through letters to the papers and protests to the planning authorities – and he was not a man to guard his language. Of course he brought all his authority to bear as a qualified architect in defending the classical purity of the 18th century environment of Britain's most beautiful city.

It was fortunate that my grandmother was able to come to the rescue of her daughter and son-in-law by buying the house for them, and the arrangement was that she would live with them until her death. This was an excellent idea, and it was put into practice, and the outcome was entirely satisfactory. Inez and Bill had their own furnishings and possessions, of course, and these were in as good a taste as those to be found at Sampford Place or Hampton Hall. My grandmother therefore moved into the ground floor of 10 Sion Hill, where she had her own bedroom and sitting room, both of them large, with huge Georgian windows looking out to the back of the building, down onto the sloping garden and then down into the city centre far below. The two rooms were tastefully furnished with all the mid-Victorian pieces, oil paintings, Chinese vases and prints, and intricately carved ivory ornaments, etc., which had originally enriched Sampford Place.

During my annual visits to Bath I still retained the freedom to come and go as I pleased, but the extra bonus was my aunt as a second host, and so additional treats were arranged, such as visits to nearby villages or stately homes, or to restaurants or the theatre. The most extensive outing was a several days' trip to Stratford-on-Avon (but not accompanied by my grandmother, who chose to remain at home) where we saw several Shakespeare productions. On returning from the trip and turning into Sion Hill, a neighbour, being a middle-aged lady driver, almost pranged our car, Aunt Inez being the driver of our vehicle, as Uncle Bill was a non-driver.

This was a serious matter, but it was something which could only be "dealt with" by the man of the family. Nothing was said at the time of the incident, but Bill said he would phone the lady concerned as soon as the front door was closed behind us. He phoned the driver, and what followed was one of the most furious tirades I ever heard, interspersed by the strongest expletives imaginable. At the time I was astonished that such a "respectable" man would even know such words – let alone use them. The call was made in the hall as I sat in my grandmother's living room, but I heard every word. The call ended with his slamming down the receiver. Nothing more was ever said about the episode afterwards.

By this time I had taken up smoking, of which my grandmother fully approved as a social prop towards more elegant behaviour and greater self-confidence in a social gathering, providing I smoked the *right kind* of cigarette. When, one day, I arrived back in the house with a packet of Wills Woodbines, she expressed her strong disapproval, good-humouredly telling me never to bring such a brand into the house again, as they were only smoked by "working class people," and I would soon lose my better friends if I persisted in smoking such a cigarette. The fact that Wills was responsible for financing the main building of Bristol University may not have impressed my grandmother, but I always enjoyed trying new brands and eventually I bought an album (which I still retain) where I pasted the front packets of all the cigarettes I smoked together with my comments on their flavour.

Although I was never a deeply-inhaling smoker, I was what might be described as an intellectual or connoisseur smoker, who at one time was interested in developing a serious literature on the pleasures of smoking in the same way that there exists a literature on wine, or in China, a literature on tea drinking. When I subsequently brought Craven A and then Craven Plain packets back to Sion Hill, my grandmother complained that these were "women's cigarettes," and that I might be thought effeminate if seen smoking such brands. She recommended Capstan or Navy Cut as suitably masculine cigarettes to give me a better image. As stated elsewhere in this memoir, I eventually gave up smoking in May 1963, at the age of 28, on taking a ferry from Helsinki to Lübeck, and I have never smoked a cigarette since.

It was about this time that my grandmother decided to buy herself a television set. This idea was disapproved of by her son-in-law, who thought that such a "contraption was a piece of time-wasting rubbish," but she nonetheless went ahead and bought it to the disgust of Uncle Bill. Inez and Bill took the superior attitude that they were above falling for the sickness of TV-itis, and so my grandmother was left alone in the evenings to watch her programmes which she greatly enjoyed, but the stance of her daughter and son-in-law did not last for long. At 5.0 pm on Sunday afternoons the Brains Trust was transmitted with Bertrand Russell, the falsely titled Prof. C.E.M. Joad (he was in reality a Dr.), Jacob Bronowski, and several others, and this was a programme which Uncle Bill suddenly decided he wanted to watch.

Accordingly, my grandmother held a tea party in her sitting room every Sunday afternoon, although her daughter kindly prepared the mustard cress and egg sandwiches. Aunt Inez often sat with her mother in the evenings, but Uncle Bill never did, as he spent most his time scheming and scribbling in his study upstairs, but at 5.0 o'clock sharp, his enormous form would enter the room, when he would take up his dominant position in an armchair facing the television set, whilst the other three of us sat around apprehensively. What followed was a regular occurrence as one Sunday after another. Uncle Bill would glance with an increasingly disapproving expression at the panel of speakers as the programme progressed. Then he would begin to move uneasily in his chair, the whites of his knuckles showing as he tightened his grip on the rosewood arms.

Aunt Inez and my grandmother looked with greater apprehension towards the man in their midst, expecting an explosion any moment. Uncle Bill's face would redden, and then he would roll his head. Eventually, he could stand no more, and he would burst out, "The man's a bloody fool! He doesn't know what he's talking about!" This was invariably aimed at Prof Bronowski, for whom my uncle had an unremitting loathing. Whilst my grandmother would sit silently, glancing with strong disapproval at her son-in-law, Aunt Inez would laughingly try to calm the situation with, "It's only the television, dear. It'll be over soon." If he loathed one of the panellists so much, why did he not refrain from watching the programme in the first place?

At the time, and for many years afterwards, I could not fathom the probable cause of my uncle's loathing for the eminent professor. I now realise he was nurtured at a time when philosophical idealism was still pre-eminent in Britain, under the influence of such varied men as T.H. Green, Bernard Bosanquet, and particularly, F.H. Bradley; and although he was certainly materialistic in questions of science and religion, as with many people at the time – and still today, he was unable to stomach the "far-fetched" materialistic interpretation which Jacob Bronowski brought to the arts. Hence he regarded the academic as an insolent young whippersnapper, who as a scientist, was intruding into spheres of knowledge in which he had no business and of which he merely had a superficial understanding. These outbursts, it may be noted, occurred some twenty years before the BBC produced Bronowski's outstanding series of television "essays" entitled, *The Ascent of Man*.

My grandmother employed her own cleaner, and after a while, a friendship developed between them, and when she discovered the helper was a keen Whist player, she decided to invite her socially for an afternoon of card playing. When Uncle Bill heard of the proposed visit, he was scandalised, saying that a woman of his mother-in-law's status could not possibly start socialising with a char. If the neighbours or other friends discovered this, they would all be made to look ridiculous. My grandmother stood her ground, insisting she had a right to invite whom she chose into her own rooms, and so Uncle Bill was made to retreat in a sulk.

It is probable that the influence of television had a democratising effect on my grandmother, bearing in mind the snobbish attitude she had earlier adopted towards her in-laws from the 1890s onwards. She had a liking for Wilfred Pickles and his prize-winning programme with its refrain of, "Give him the money, Barney,!" and she attempted to become a participant on his programme, which I thought strange at the time, in view of the modest status of those usually called upon to take part. She sent her CV to Wilfred Pickles, but as I anticipated, she was not invited onto the programme.

During my later visits to Bath I enjoyed regular visits to the Magistrates Courts, listening to the different cases which were heard. There was one case of a middle-aged man who was prosecuted for indecently exposing himself to a 13-year old girl. He had one leg and would massage his stump with ointment in the window of his apartment without any covering over his thighs. When it came to the defence, a clergyman was called into the witness box to vouch for his parishioner as a person of impeccable character, but the problem was that this was not the first time he had been prosecuted for exactly this offence. At one point the Court was cleared so that the girl could be more thoroughly questioned as to what she had seen, and when the public were readmitted, the girl was in tears. When I told my grandmother about the case, she said that that was "typical" of these religious people, and that clergymen were amongst "the worst of all" when it came to sexual peccadilloes.

During these annual holidays I often helped Uncle Bill in the garden, digging or clearing stones from the sub-soil, or tidying the area. I noted in my diary that he was a "slow worker," but he was elderly and somewhat overweight, and as he seemed to have little other exercise, he must have found gardening a heavy chore. On one occasion he proudly showed me a back number of *Punch* in which he, amongst a group of three or four others were portrayed in a cartoon. This must have been in the arts review section of the magazine.

When the holiday came to an end, and I was about to depart, Aunt Inez would say, "Go and knock on Uncle Bill's study door, and say goodbye." I would tentatively knock on the door, and wait for the reply from within. On entering, I would say, "I've come to say goodbye, Sir. Thank you for having me." Uncle Bill swivelled round in his chair from the side of his desk, and looking at me over his bifocals, he would say jokingly, "I hope you don't feel you've been *had*!" The parting words never differed from one year to the next.

We shall return to my relatives in Bath a little later in this memoir, when Aunt Inez together with my grandmother concocted a scheme to remove me from my parents' household, which had it succeeded would undoubtedly have been beneficial to my future prospects and better frame of mind.

CHAPTER 19
The Misery of Home Life

"Art is nothing more than the shadow of humanity."

Henry James, *Lectures: University in Arts*

The rebelliousness of my brother and his expulsion from home – The circumstances in which I and my youngest brother were eventually to break from our parents – Misery for all – The break-up for the foursome – Illness and hypochondria – Friendship with my cousin

During the three or four years leading up to the end of my formal education at the age of 17, home life was incessantly depressing. At about the age of 13 my brother went through an apparently religious phase, that is, he constructed an altar on his chest of drawers with candles, a huge Bible, crucifix, and incense which he burned in a bowl. This scandalised our paternal grandparents, who feared that Gavin "was going over to Rome," and it became the talk of the family, and my grandmother said that something "ought" to be done about it. My father wisely refused to do anything, dismissing it as a passing childish phase. Aunt Joan and the Browns were amused by the episode, and thought Gavin was veering something between eccentricity and going out of his mind. In any event he was making himself unacceptable for socialising in good company.

Gavin had little interest in socialising or for that matter in status in any shape or form. In that way he was different from me, for I feared social ostracism and wanted to conform, and made every effort to be acceptable. Whilst internally I may have been a rebel, externally I presented a front of conservatism and conventionality. Gavin was the opposite, for whilst he seemed to care not a jot what others thought of him, internally he seemed to accept the world for what it was, providing only that he was left to do his own thing. He was never an idealist or utopian, or someone who set out to change the world from a more realistic aspect. His outward rebelliousness, therefore, led him to withdraw from the family as something which was "boring" or surplus to need.

If his religiosity was seen as disturbing, far worse was to come. The high church style altar eventually disappeared, and he then took up the trumpet which caused a serious noise and disturbance in the house. It was decided to divide our residence at 105 Muswell Hill Road into three large self-contained flats, and we would occupy the ground floor flat. We therefore returned temporarily to 196 whilst the building work was carried out, and my grandfather's second surgery (that is, the smaller of the two surgeries) became my brother's bedroom. It was there where he began to play his trumpet to the increasing annoyance of my father, for apart from the disturbance inside the house, it created a strange impression of his "professional premises" to passers-by in the street. What was to be done about it? There was a battle of wills.

But if religiosity or loud music was to cause an upset, even worse was to follow, viz., his association with girls. His relationship with girls was not necessarily of a strictly romantic nature. Whilst we were still living at 105 he met a sorrowful looking waif sitting on a bench by the shops adjacent to the Odeon cinema. He got into conversation with her, listening to her sad story about being an orphan with no proper home of her own. Gavin was so moved that he secretly brought her home, smuggling her into the garden through the back gate. She was a thin, rather tall girl with fair hair. My father was quite put out by the sudden appearance of this vagrant of unknown origin, who might be carrying any kind of disease that he gently called her over, led her out into the street, and firmly bolted the garden gate behind her. My brother repeated the story he had been told, but then nothing more was said about the matter except that "strangers should not be admitted to the house."

One weekend after dark, shortly after we had been re-settled into 196, Miss Wall discovered Gavin sitting on the leather settee in the waiting room with a girl beside him. This was reported to my father, who protested that his professional premises were being abused, and that no one was allowed into the house when my parents were away. During the spring and summer months during this period, our parents were away for most weekends at their new property at Elmer Sands, or else staying at another cottage they bought at Bognor, so they might supervise the building of the two storey White House, a fine brick building, to replace the bungalow, Woodhouse, which was torn down to make room for it.

During these frequent weekend absences, if we were not looked after by Miss Wall, then occasionally Mabs and Bill, or even Uncle Quentin and Aunt Sybel, were called in to take up a supervisory role. None of these four persons enjoyed the task. Bill hated having to look after a crying toddler like Oliver, and even complained about the child's miserable behaviour, and throwing food about, after the return of my parents. My mother thought that such complaining coming as it did from "friends," was poor form. Quin and Syb, on the other hand, did not complain about having to look after three children during their parents' absence, but they gossiped amongst themselves, remarking on tea which was left un-drunk in the pot, and the general wastage in the management of the household. They also thought it was mentally unhealthy that I confined myself in my bedroom for most of the day. It was easy to overhear this moaning, for whilst we children were playing on the upper floors, the elderly couple remained downstairs confronting one another in the kitchen or the lounge.

When my brother's behaviour was deemed to have become intolerable, through his playing the trumpet and associating with "undesirable people," at the age of 15 he was obliged to leave the family home, although by this time he was still attending the Senior School at Highgate. The circumstances of his actually leaving the house fell halfway between his expulsion and his voluntary decision to live elsewhere. When this occurred my Father announced that Gavin was well on the way to a life of "crime" which would besmirch the family name. The "Corfes were a respectable family" who would *never* endanger the family's reputation by law breaking, and it was up to me to maintain the high standards which had always been upheld. No "Corfe" had ever landed up in prison, and every endeavour should be taken to prevent such an occurrence in the future. Even as he said these words, he knew them to be untrue.

My Uncle Maurice had recently "disappeared," leaving behind a mysterious convenience address, which my father chuckled over as a necessary ruse in protecting his own "reputation." It was whispered throughout the family that Maurice was in "jug" as my mother colloquially expressed it with a smile, for some kind of fraud, and this occurred on two or three occasions, and he was always forgiven by my grandfather, who then proceeded to give him financial support for his next business venture which usually failed sooner or later. My father looked askance at my grandfather's gestures, and this was probably the deciding factor in his reluctance to ever give financial support to any business venture of his own sons – not that the latter ever approached him with this in mind – but he did refer from time to time to the "wasted thousands" that my grandfather invested in helping his erring second son.

With regard to Uncle Maurice's involvement with the law, although on the one hand, this was common knowledge, on the other hand, it was a taboo topic for open conversation.

Uncle Maurice was what is sometimes referred to as a "likeable rogue." He was always good-natured and when the family visited him and June and their daughter, Alvis, they always gave the impression of running a profitable business. At one time he had a pig farm, and at another he was managing a large pub in the West country which organised large-scale variety or talent shows. I remember him lugging up heavy crates of beer from the cellar, as meanwhile amateur comedians or singers displayed their artistry on a stage in a crowded hall packed with drinkers sitting at tables. Enjoyment was had by all! Maurice was always a hard worker. At other times they owned various women's clothing shops in Essex. The last time I met Uncle Maurice was in the late 1970s when he visited my home and proceeded to take an intelligent interest in several of my books. He was full of conversation and opinions about life, and his personality was quite opposite to that of my father.

When my brother left home, he moved into the house of a large Irish family, the Kellys, where for a time he slept with one of the younger daughters, at the other end of Muswell Hill Road, which happened to be immediately adjacent to Mr. Partridge's property. Mr. Partridge was scandalised by the arrangement, describing the Kellys as a "disreputable" family, who held noisy parties, and indulged in all kinds of "unconventional behaviour."

Some years later I was to attend several all-night parties there, and the eldest daughter, Eve, who for a time became a fashion model, was to marry Gavin's best friend and school mate, Nick. In their cramped living room there was an enormous oil painting of the Virgin Mary cradling the infant Christ in her arms, and during the all-night parties, all the rooms in the house were packed with boozing guests. On one occasion in the early hours, when the drink ran out, one of the party goers said he could resolve the situation, and left the house with three male companions, returning half an hour later with six crates of beer.

The four had broken into the back of the Woodman, at the top of the road at the corner of Archway, and stolen the beer from the cellar. However, the four youths then found they could not open the bottles which were secured with caps, upon which I took one of the bottles, and as they crowded around, I carefully demonstrated how the bottles could be opened without breaking the glass necks. Eve, meanwhile, began laughing uncontrollably, and later she told me it was the funniest sight she had ever witnessed: a respectably dressed gentleman explaining to a gang of half-witted burglars how to open beer bottles they had stolen but lacked the wit to use for their intended purpose.

When it was discovered that my brother was secretly re-entering our house during the weekends whilst my parents were away, my father took out an injunction against his entering the property, informing Gavin that he would be taken into police custody should he attempt a break-in. Shortly after he was expelled from the house, my father delivered a homily, saying that I, too, should watch my behaviour. He described Gavin as a "tramp" who could put up with any conditions, "cold, hunger, rain, and living in the open," but that I was a much "softer person," who would crack up under such harsh conditions and that therefore I should make every endeavour to "behave properly." I think my father's assumption in contrasting our characters was incorrect. I was no less tough or resilient than my brother, but in different ways.

Whilst it was true that Gavin appeared unconcerned by the deprivations of physical comforts, and on one occasion was even picked up by the police in Cornwell and brought home as an under-age vagrant, he never adapted or extended his vision in such a way as to live in a foreign clime. He was English born and bred, and never enlarged his outlook in embracing other cultures, apart from the influences of his beloved jazz. In later life, he openly admitted that he hated "abroad," as he curiously expressed it. As it happened, I was also to be expelled from the house, some years later, at the age of 23, three years after completing National Service, and my expulsion was accompanied by a great swipe across the face which sent me reeling back against the banisters of the staircase.

The irony of the situation was that I was not directly responsible for the upset. My brother was at that time doing his National Service, and whilst home for the weekend, organised a party which got out of control. I did my utmost in tidying up the house (and fortunately no damage was incurred), but the party was reported by Miss Wall to my father as soon as he returned to the house on Monday. The crisis point was reached when my father found used condoms in his bed, and when my father exclaimed furiously, "What sod's been sleeping in my bed?" I mistook his words to mean, "What socks are these in my bed?" and when I responded, "What socks?" I was struck across the face, presumably for an act of assumed insolence.

Fortunately, I had friends in the Young Conservatives (of which I was then a member), who were kind and helpful, and a week later they transported all my books and other possessions to a rented room in Hornsey Lane, Crouch End. Two years after that, in 1960, not satisfied with any aspect of life in England, in either the spheres of work or social life, I moved abroad for 10 years in finally breaking the umbilical cord and establishing myself as a free and independent human being, and I never looked back.

My youngest brother, Oliver, was to take an even more radical measure. Although my parents realised by this time that the cane was an ineffective instrument in moulding children to their will, and as I remarked earlier, he was never caned, he was nonetheless oppressed and instilled with all kinds of fears about the dangers of living, and it was impressed upon him that his two elder siblings were highly undesirable characters whose company should be avoided at his peril. For some years he was supercilious and critical of his erring two elder brothers, and he became nervous and developed a lifelong stutter, and in the early 60s emigrated to Australia, never to return, apart from occasional visits of two or three months at a time.

After some years the foursome relationship between my parents and Mabs and Bill began to show strains as it was stretched to its limits. It became the hushed discussion topic amongst close relatives, and I remember my grandfather in Ashmount responding to my grandmother with the words, "But you can't tell a man in his forties what to do." My grandmother, as with her eldest son, was struck down with bouts of occasional depression when she would take to her bed for days on end. In addition, she was struck down with King's palsy, losing the use of muscles on one side of her face, and then one afternoon in 1950, whilst the couple were dozing in front of their miserable coal fire, she fell into a sleep and died.

At that time I was in bed with a severe bout of flu, and so could not attend the funeral, but I wanted to rise from my sickbed and view her corpse as it lay in the coffin on the dining room table in Ashmount. When I put this proposition to my father, he responded by saying, "Are you sure it's not morbid curiosity, rather than your wish to pay your last respects, that you make such a request?" As I had never seen a corpse before, it may have been curiosity (without the morbid) but I admitted to neither of these probabilities, and opted to remain in my sickbed.

As soon as the mourning period had passed, my grandfather took on a new lease of life, going on several world cruises, taking his daughter, Joan, as a kind of chaperone. My Aunt Joan said he went quite "wild" during these trips, running up the staircases of the ship two at a time, and chasing after attractive available women. On one occasion, on a ship which stopped at Cape Town, he met a fellow passenger, who like him, had served in South Africa during the Boer War 50 years before. On another trip, he described how Stromboli was spewing forth its smoke and ash, and how pleasant and reassuring it was when the handsome clean-shaven English Captain resumed his command on the bridge after dropping the dirty bearded Italian pilot to return to the harbour in Palermo.

My mother was obviously the first to complain about the foursome arrangement but she felt in no position to force her case, and for the most part she repressed her feelings and felt little inclination to protest. What was said in private between my parents will never be known, but I remember during one particularly miserable Christmas whilst sitting round a meal in the kitchen at 196, my mother bursting into tears after my father exclaiming, "You look nothing like the woman I married. How could a woman change so much?"

At that time, I thought this a stupid remark, firstly, because ageing is a natural process which must be accepted by all; and secondly, my mother had certainly not developed a middle-aged appearance by this time, and was not to do so for many more years. I remember seeing my mother middle-aged for the first time, and that was some 12 years later, after an absence of three years when they visited me in West Berlin where I spent the summer in 1963. Whilst I remained silent at my mother's rebuff at the kitchen table, my brother, Gavin, actually had the courage to confront my father with the words, "Now look what you've done!"

On another occasion when my mother made veiled threats about separation or divorce, my father boldly responded that that was not even an option, as she would be condemned to a life of misery and poverty. As she had no qualifications she had no possibility of improving her lot through work – unless she was prepared to see herself reduced to the level of a charwoman – and such a course could not be allowed, as it would be scandalous, and reflect badly on his professional status. Therefore, she should shut up and accept the life she had created for herself.

One day whilst washing up over the kitchen sink, whilst Gavin and I were sitting at the table engaged in homework, she announced she would be getting a separation, and that we should have to choose either to live with her or our father. Neither of us made any kind of meaningful reply. I had no doubt, however, that if the decision had finally to be made, my brother would choose to live with his mother. I, on the other hand, although I loathed my father and regarded him as an object of terror, decided secretly in my own mind that I would live with him.

There were two reasons for this: firstly, because I put a higher priority on securing my financial future, and realised that money was the most important factor in guaranteeing the material standards of life; and secondly, I instinctively felt that despite all the brutality I incurred, my father had an underlying wish for my success in life, which exceeded the wish-fulfilment he had for his younger sons. The first born was the favourite because he was the first born and heir, and because of all the cultural, traditional, and legal implications inherent in the English right of primogeniture.

As it happened, and as I believe all the family sensed from the beginning, separation or divorce was never seriously considered. The break-up of the foursome-style relationship was to come from another direction. Bill clearly regarded himself as a modern man of the far left who repudiated bourgeois values, and was quite prepared to accept the idea of an open marriage in our fast-changing post-War progressive society. But with the passing of time, the reality of this did not seem such an attractive arrangement. A shared wife may have been an acceptable arrangement for our Celtic forebears in Ancient Britain, but it was not really workable in the Britain of the 20th century.

A shared wife is no proper wife – not even when the other man is paying all the expenses, and chauffeuring all those concerned around the countryside for weekend trips in his impressive Austin Sheerline. The merriment must have begun to wear thin, despite all the 4-star hotels, and the hot meals, and the alcoholic beverages in raising one's spirits, as soon as it was realised that only one couple were having all the fun, whilst the other were not only total opposites in every way conceivable, but were sidelined to little more than admiring the landscape.

The final outcome was that Bill sued for divorce, for reasons and in circumstances of which I am entirely ignorant. All I know is that with the first whiff of divorce, Mabs was dropped like a hot brick. Any suggestion of scandal, or threat to my father's impeccable respectability, was something which needed to be avoided at any cost. After all, he was a pillar of society, not only at the top of his profession in north London, but a longstanding worshipper and sidesman at St. James's church, a prominent member of Rotary, and of course, a keen Freemason rising in the ranks of the mystic fraternity. As soon as the foursome fell apart, nothing more was ever mentioned about Bill or Mabs again. All this occurred whilst I was on National Service between 1954-1956.

Many years later, I was to meet her for the last time one evening in Schmidt's famous German restaurant in Charlotte street – which alas, is no more. She was middle-aged, but just as cheerful, and accompanied by an Indian doctor friend. She asked after various members of the family, and after we parted, I never heard what became of her.

During my final year at school – I left at the end of the summer term in 1952 at the age of 17 – my first priority naturally continued to be the pursuit or courtship of Patricia Dainton. This was to be achieved exclusively through the writing of plays which were read and critically reviewed with the idea of their reaching a sufficient standard for West End production. As soon as I had produced a play which was accepted by a West End theatre, I could then approach the one I loved on a basis of equality without any feelings of inadequacy. However, I realised that time was an important factor. I would need to hurry.

Patricia Dainton was a woman of supreme beauty, and there must have been others courting her attention, and my only hope of success was through a fast-track course to literary competence of a high order. Although I did not realise it at the time, the London theatre of the period was at a low ebb when it came to playwrights who were truly original or innovative in reflecting the changing world around them. In the decade following the Second World War domestic dramas were still being churned out which differed little from projecting the middle class life and values of the 1930s. This may have been a minor reason why I received such kind guidance and encouragement from Hugh Richardson over a two-year period.

During this time, and up until my entering the Army in January 1954, I studied every aspect of the drama, from playwriting and production, to the history of the drama, to reading what were considered the best plays from Aeschylus to Noel Coward. I never missed listening or watching a worthwhile play on the radio or TV, and in addition, I read widely in history, philosophy (mostly ancient), novels and other books of a specific practical nature.

The strain of my obsession with Patricia Dainton ensured that I was living off my nerves, and consequently, I was frequently ill with headaches, as well as the common cold, as often recorded in my diaries. I was also moody, ill-tempered, and almost deranged in my disorganised behaviour in getting onto wrong buses or tube trains, etc. The diary entries are filled with irate exchanges with bus conductors and ticket offices at underground stations, as to what fare should be paid, or as to the correctness of the change given, bearing in mind the complexity of dealing with 20 shillings to the pound and 12 pence to the shilling.

On the other hand, I had a sharp sense of humour (although this is not often revealed in the diaries) and I was an excellent mimic of those in authority, and made school friends and others laugh at my impersonations. In the Army I was to become popular through my mimicry of NCOs and officers who were either unpopular or seen as eccentric, and had comrades in stitches of laughter as we cleaned our kit in the barrack room, or relaxed in the evenings in the NAAFI. Those with whom I socialised or jostled in a general sort of way saw me as an extrovert, as I was a great talker and rarely afraid of expressing a free opinion, although I always regarded myself as an introvert.

But worst of all, I suffered severe hypochondria in anticipating an early death. The disease with which I was most concerned was tuberculosis. How apt it would have been for someone with my artistic temperament to begin coughing blood before dying of consumption! How many aspiring poets and composers had met such a romantic end!

My spare figure and pallid complexion, and constant snuffles during the Winter months were sufficient evidence of poor health. When I went to see Dr. Blackburn in Fortis Green Road, he examined my chest with a stethoscope, and then sent me off for an X-ray to a specialist clinic in the East End Road in Finchley. I remember sitting in the waiting room of this clinic one sunny afternoon, opposite a sad-looking but handsome lady about ten years my senior. She had attractive well-endowed breasts, and I imagined we would both be sent to the same Sanatorium, where we would conduct a passionate love affair for six months before dying in each other's arms. This useless piece of wish-fulfilment was clearly inspired by the 1950 film, *Trio*, which I must have recently seen, being a dramatisation of three Somerset Maugham stories, one of which was, *The Sanatorium*. When I returned to Dr. Blackburn, he reported that I was entirely fit.

Although emotionally I was indissolubly tied to Patricia Dainton, this did not prevent me from seeing attractiveness in other women, or even engaging in brief off the cuff flirtations. My diary entries are full of references to seeing "an attractive blonde" on buses, trains, or in some other public place. But I continued, nonetheless, to retain normal relationships with my relatives amongst this stormy swirl of emotional chaos, and whilst amongst the Browns, I may have been considered odd – and my love for Miss Dainton was kept as no secret – it was my brother, Gavin, who was considered the outcast and total rebel. I still had a close relationship with my cousin, Michael, and there was a lively correspondence between us. None of my letters survive, but several of his sent from Framlingham College are still extant. They are mostly concerned with our aspirations and plans for the future.

The following is dated 19th May 1951:- "Dear Nigel. – Here is the letter I promised to write to you if you remember, at the end of the 'Conjuring Show'" [This refers to a performance to which we were taken by our grandparents.] "Well everything is running smoothly so far. Yesterday we had a General Inspection by a Brigadier, the whole corps turned out, he stopped and talked to me, and then again while we were training. Not long ago we had a Field Day that is the whole corps go to a certain ground and fire Bren guns and rifles, and have mock battles. This went down quite well, but it was very cold and rained practically the whole time. – The other day a barn, containing two pigs and some farm machinery caught fire and about three fire engines turned up to put the fire out. The pigs got away but they could not get the tractors out in time before the roof collapsed, bringing down a big water tank. How are you getting on at school? On June 8th I am running in the Beccles South

Suffolk Championships. Well, Nigel, there is no more news now. Longing to hear from you," etc.

The following letter was sent 17 months later on 19th October 1952, by which time, of course, I had already left school:- "Dear Nigel. – I thought it about time I wrote to you. I hear from my mother and father that you have left your job. They told me when I came home last Wednesday for my interview at Guys." [It was his mother's idea he should study medicine despite the fact of my father insisting that his nephew was "quite unfitted to undergo such a course."] "Unfortunately I did not get in so I am hoping to go back to my original idea of going into the Army for my career. – What are you going to do now? Well, the term has settled in quite well and it does not seem that I have been back a month. I have had many games of rugger and squash in that time.

"Last Thursday we had a full day's corps parade. It was very interesting. We went to a place called Sizewell which is quite near Southwold on the coast. It is very practical for camp manoeuvres as the ground is partially woodland and partially open countryside. I do not think, however, the day would have been half so successful if the weather had not been fine. – I learn that St. James's church looks very beautiful now." [This refers to the roof repairs following the fire-bombing.] Did you go and listen to the Archbishop preaching there? The Play Reading Society tonight are reading, *His Excellency*. I expect you have heard or seen the play before. I know they have made a film of it. – Well that seems to be about all the news. Write if you have time. Give my love to all. I don't know the number of your house" [Probably because of the moves between 105 and 196] "so I am sending this home first. All the best, Yours, Michael."

The following letter is dated 4th March 1953, by which time I had already been entrenched five months in a solicitors' office just off Piccadilly:- "Dear Nigel. – I said I would write to you this term so here is the letter. Well, how are you getting along Nigel old boy with your job? I am looking forward to seeing you next hols when we can have lunch at some café and then go for a walk down the Burlington Arcade. We must make it early on in the hols because I want to get a waistcoat from the Burlington Arcade. It was my birthday not long ago and father said he would put some money towards my getting one. I had some money for my birthday and I think I have enough for a really nice one, so after lunch we will go together and choose it. I have had a marvellous term so far and as it is in athletics, I have been practising hard, and in a few minutes I am going out to do a bit of training.

"I have now fully made up my mind concerning my career. When I leave jolly old Framlingham College, I hope in September or October to take an Examination for the Royal Military Academy of Sandhurst. If I fail this exam, I will still go into the Army in National Service, but will try to get into Sandhurst from there, which I hope is possible. I hope to become an officer in the British Army then for the rest of my life until I have to retire from the service. On the Saturday before last the Head Master hired the cinema in the morning down town. Running that week at the small picture place was, *The Sound Barrier*, and as the College took up the whole place, we had a private showing of this very good and spectacular film. If you have not seen it already I thoroughly recommend you to see it. The main people in the cast are Ralph Richardson, Nigel Patrick and Anne Todd.

"On Monday last we had the steeplechases. The whole school, everybody over fifteen, lined up on one of the fields, there were about 175 of us, when the gun goes off we all charge madly towards a water jump. The race is about 1 ½ miles long. It is actually an Inter-House race. If you come in the first eight out of your house you then run in the Inter-set, which is a race of about 2 to 2 ½ miles long. I came 30 out of the whole race, so I am therefore running for the house in the Inter-set, it is rather a tiring race. Last Wednesday the whole school had a holiday as it was Princess Alice of Athlone's birthday and as she has something to do with the College we had this little 'vacance.' Three of my friends and myself went to Dennington where we had a very good lunch at a very old Inn called the Queen's Head. We had a typical English meal but it was a change from the College.

"On February 14th and 15th Howard and myself went out with mother and father. We all went to see the flood damage at Aldeburgh and at Southwold. It really is amazing what the sea can do. We noticed lots of houses smashed to pieces, and all the flat marshy land beyond the sea wall is now full of sea water, which has ruined it for grazing. Well, Nigel, that seems to be about all. I am looking forward to seeing you and hearing from you. Remember me to your mother and father and Gavin and Oliver. All the best, Yours, Michael." Although I do not remember what I wrote in reply to the other letters, I do remember that I sent him all best wishes for eventually getting into Sandhurst, and that this was currently the finest military academy in the world, only bettered in the near historical past by the officers' cadet college at Potsdam in the Wilhelmine period.

*

The last bedroom which I occupied at 105, i.e., after we returned to the house following its conversion into three self-contained flats, was the small ground floor front room, previously the breakfast room and then the music room with a second radio where I listened to concerts or other programmes of little or no interest to other family members. During fine spring and summer evenings, in my late teenage years, I remember sitting in this room and glancing across the street at a casually dressed good-looking man in his mid-30s, who sat on the steps to the garden entrance of the house opposite. He was always accompanied by a large Alsatian which he stroked affectionately, and the sight of this man filled me with profound sadness.

He was clearly a lodger who rented a room, but he gave the impression of being friendless and lonely. He had a reddish moustache and was well-groomed, and I ascertained he had an educated background. On a warm sunny evening, was there not something better to do than sit by the street on a garden step stroking a dog? A sunny evening is a time for joy not for melancholy, but happiness was never on his countenance. I wondered as to his occupation and past. He had most probably served in the armed services during the War, but he now had the appearance of a man with few relatives and of limited financial means. His own situation, I concluded, was more wretched and miserable than my own. He represented a symbol of all that was depressing in the doom-laden hopelessness of Muswell Hill.

CHAPTER 20
A Violent Crisis Point is Reached

> "O, that a man might know
> The end of this day's business ere it came!
> But it sufficeth that the day will end,
> And then the end is known."

Shakespeare, *Julius Caesar*, Act V, Sc. 1, 1, 123.

My confirmation and what it meant – Discovery of Miss Dainton's marriage – Dull days at stuffy Elmer Sands – A desperate scheme

Towards the end of 1951 it was decided that arrangements should be made for my confirmation. This was not something I welcomed, but I decided not to make a fuss. I would passively undergo the course and then endure the necessary formalities for the sake of peace and quiet. In due time I received an abrupt unsigned undated note from the Vicarage which read as follows:- "Confirmation classes will commence after Evensong next Sunday, March 2nd, in the chapel. Regular and punctual attendance is essential." The communication was post-dated 25th February 1952.

About a dozen of us attended the course, mostly young people from different backgrounds, but two persons stood out: a young Indian who in today's politically correct parlance would be described as having "learning difficulties" and a highly affected woman much older than the rest of us in her mid-thirties. Whilst the first had to be guided by someone who held his hand, the second was only intent on asking stupid and pretentious questions in drawing attention to herself. The group was led by a young curate, the Rev. E.H. Rigler, a short man with a lame leg – or possibly one leg shorter than the other. He reminded me of Richard III as portrayed by Laurence Olivier in the film of that name.

The instruction was aimed at appealing to the lowest intelligence to such a degree that it was insulting to any reasonable being, and that little discussion which was elicited from the group was either facile or absurd. I asked myself, in glancing at the Indian, what was the purpose in obliging someone who would be medically classified as a moron to attend such sessions? I did not suggest to myself he should be denied admittance to the church as a Christian, but that it was hypocrisy to pretend he comprehended anything taught. The crowning intellectual argument of the young curate was, "How can anything be untrue if it has been accepted by leading religious thinkers for almost two thousand years?"

The multitude of falsities and discussion points contained in such a statement are so numerous that it is difficult to know where to begin. I was appalled by the dishonesty entailed in simplifying the principles of the Christian faith, so that it might be accepted as spiritually uplifting to the most ignorant and stupid part of humankind. At the time I appreciated the fact that the deceitful reasoning dished up to the *hoi polloi* comprising young confirmees was quite different from that served to those training for the clergy, but there was no moral justification for simplifying dishonesty of the worst sort in attempting to promote the highest authority of all. My feelings throughout these sessions, therefore, were those of disgust, and because of this, I was not prepared to waste my time, or demean my faculties by attempting to repudiate such obvious absurdities.

At the end of the course arrangements were made for a private meeting with the Rev. E.A. Dunn in his gloomy Vicarage immediately behind the church. After a short wait in an antechamber, I was led into his inner sanctum. After a brief introduction he then asked if I had any "doubts," or any points which I would like explained. I thought for a moment, realising that this was a last chance to give the church an opportunity to explain any obscurities. I then came up with the following question: "Yes, Sir, could you explain the Trinity?" The learned divine looked momentarily perplexed, and then embarked on an apologetic explanation, which from memory went as follows: "That's a difficult question to answer, and I can only explain by giving an analogy," etc., etc., and I thought to myself, here comes the twisted logic.

At the end of his explanation, and sensing that I was still not satisfied, he then took a line which I would interpret as insulting, when he said, "It's really necessary to be trained in theological doctrine to have a proper understanding of the Trinity, and as a humble layman, Christ will not expect you to comprehend all the work of the Fathers in building up the Church." I then thought to myself that Christ has nothing to forgive me on that score, as he knew nothing of theological doctrines which were only invented by fallible and quarrelsome priests centuries after his death. I said nothing more, but then the Rev. E.A. Dunn came in with the inevitable punch-line: "What really matters is faith and nothing more." In other words, in the light of this, the Confirmation sessions could as well be dismissed as a waste of time.

Having disposed of matters concerned with my Confirmation, he then turned to my personal life, asking about my future prospects, and what I had achieved at school. When I revealed to him the truth that I had left school without qualifications and without conventional prospects, within his rigid framework of thinking in accepting all things conventional whilst rejecting the possibility for the extraordinary of any kind, he interpreted this to mean I could only be a simpleton, and therefore must have few hopes or aspirations. "Christ does not discriminate between those of ability and those who have none, and so never live in fear of failure, howsoever humble your position in life. Christ will always have regard for you if you maintain your humility before the cross."

I sat there aghast in my chair, unbelieving at what I heard, incredulous that such insults had been thrown at me. What kind of world did he exist in, in this doom-laden inhospitable ascetic Vicarage? This was a man of God – maybe – but a man without an ounce of human understanding. Did he really assume I had already consigned myself to the dustbin? Did he really believe I had no hope or aspirations for the future? Why had I exposed myself to the humiliation of going through this ghastly pantomime of those Confirmation sessions?

About a week later, on Wednesday 4th June 1952, the Confirmation ceremony was held at St. Andrews Church, Alexandra Park road, presided over by the Bishop of Willesden. I had to take along a little card, framed in red, headed, "Confirmation 1952," which included the words, "You are requested to be at," &c, &c, "at 7.30 o'clock precisely and to bring this card with you," and then in capital letters, "EXAMINED AND PRESENTED BY ME, E.A. Dunn." The dictatorial text was more in the tone of a summons for a man to attend his own execution by firing squad than to attend a celebratory religious function. Put simply, it indicated the Reverend had bad manners.

At the back of the said card was a four paragraph text headed NOTICE, which instructed us as to how we should behave on arriving at the church. As the tone assumed we were either naïve or rebellious, or semi-literate morons, the text was therefore interspersed with insolent phrases, such as: "When you have taken your seat, kneel down and pray. ... While you are waiting, read your Bible, or Prayer-book, or Hymn-book. ... Do not look about you. ... When the Service begins follow every word. ... be ready to answer aloud and earnestly when the Bishop asks you the question. Remember what it means ... When you go up, say fervently a prayer that the Holy Ghost may indeed confirm and strengthen you. ... Come quietly back, and kneel down and pray that you may be faithful unto death. ... Keep kneeling and praying for yourself and others."

As we stood by the altar rail, as priests and deacons in their golden and brilliantly coloured copes moved to and fro with goblets of wine and silver platters of communion wafers, amongst their number, dressed in all his glory as I had never seen him before was Mr. Partridge. He gave me a knowing smile as if to say, "Well, I expect you're a better person now," and as I stood there waiting, I wondered in my own mind as to how many other "small boys" he had abused with false accusations of "touching their private parts" since I had last attended daily tuition at his house six years previously. Later that day at home my parents held a small Sherry party in my honour, and my grandfather gave me a Book of Common Prayer and a book of Sermons printed and published at the start of the century. "I hope you'll read them," said my grandfather referring to the Sermons. I never even bothered to open the cover.

A cynical approach to the principles of religion should not be read into the above paragraphs. I was not atheistic nor even agnostic. I believed in God, but I did not take my beliefs from the superstitious ravings of a primitive people who repudiated the great civilisations of their time, for to a modern man or woman, aspiring to true enlightenment, that would have been an insult to the very *idea* of God. A god who openly promoted genocide, was not merely a false but also a dangerous god, who carried his teachings through the millennia to the present day.

The only moral argument which could possibly be evoked in promoting the dispossession, the persecution, and the indiscriminate massacre of the Palestinian people could only be found through following the teachings of such a god. And belief in such a god was not merely a local issue affecting a small geographical area: it extended to threatening the peace of all the world. The God in which I believed was a being of justice and equity. He could not be found in the ancient scriptures of any particular people or culture, with all their strange perversities and prejudice, but only in the rational and disinterested principles in promoting the good of humankind and the environment of the universe as we find it. All else was deceit and error.

The God in which I believed was more likely to be found in Immanuel Kant's book, *Religion Within The Limits of Reason Alone*, with all its wisdom and intelligence, than in digging up the teachings of the ignorant past. I disdained the Rev. E.A. Dunn because as a small child I had had enough of his weekly tirades for "fighting and smiting," as I made clear in an earlier chapter of this book. This Prebendary of St. Paul's was a true *Old Testament* man, as partially demonstrated by the fact that he is chiefly remembered today for his efforts and success in converting North London Jews to Christianity.

In 2007 I set out my religious views in a book entitled, *Deism and Social Ethics*, which although it may be little known in England, is a best seller in America, where the principles of Deism are still held in serious regard. The fact of the matter, however, is that the majority of European non-conforming church-goers at the present time are in reality already Deists in that they turn a blind eye to the theology and dogmas of the church; accept the singing and ritual for its aesthetic value only; and find comfort in the Christian fellowship as a social bonding mechanism which has little to do with the principles of religion. This is the best that can be hoped for from conventional religion as we find it, although my definition of the deity does give a rational basis for thinking about the nature of the Supreme Being.

*

On 8th July 1952, less than a month before the end of my formal education, I was struck by a bombshell. On phoning Vivienne Black and speaking with Hugh Richardson about my latest dramatic contribution, in the course of the conversation, he casually revealed that Patricia Dainton was now married. At the time I was too shocked to make any comment on the revelation, but later that day, I armed myself with a knife – uncertain of my intent – and took the tube to South Kensington, and loitered for a while in the area without actually identifying his street of residence. I was either undecided what to do, or my courage failed me, for after a while I returned home.

Some days later I was sitting across his office desk, and after expressing surprise and shock at Miss Dainton's marriage, I asked the name of her husband which was given. Hugh Richardson remained calm and matter-of-fact, remarking that it was only to be expected "biologically" that a woman of Miss Dainton's attractiveness should find a husband at an early date and that as her marriage was in the public domain, he was surprised I had not heard about it before. When I started to probe further, he abruptly explained he knew nothing about Miss

Dainton's private life, and that Vivienne Black was merely a business partner and not really a family friend.

For the following two months I entertained murderous and suicidal thoughts, and made feeble attempts at stabbing my chest, incurring nothing more than scratches. On 10th July my father told me not to consort with women of any kind, or even to think of them. I should concentrate on harmless activities like reading books as an antidote to carnal thoughts. I tried to trace the whereabouts or details of the occupation of Miss Dainton's husband from various film and theatre directories, but could find nothing.

Almost nightly I dreamed about the one I loved, and on 14th of July I dreamed about sleeping with the mother and daughter together. During the holiday period, during which I was at Elmer Sands and earlier at Bath (of which more anon), my mind was temporarily taken away from this crisis situation. At Elmer Sands there was fine weather, and I took long walks along the shore as far as Littlehampton in one direction, and occasionally to Bognor Regis in the other. The physical side of life was comfortable, but the social side was appalling, because of all the restrictions as to who it was acceptable or unacceptable to mix with. I was therefore alone if not lonely, because of the enjoyment of my own thoughts and the books I had brought with me from London.

There were the Douglases, an elderly couple who lived in a kind of imitation observation point overlooking the sea, immediately adjacent to our own property with whom it was acceptable to socialise, but he was a disagreeable old codger with whom few wanted to associate. He spent most of the day far out at sea in his little boat catching conger eels. Then there were the Steeles, the head of the household being a solicitor, with whom it was acceptable to socialise, but they only visited occasionally, and when we did meet, it was only for an hour or so for a glass of Sherry. And then an embarrassing episode occurred when my mother suggested we should keep our distance from the Steeles for a month or so.

Late one afternoon our good-natured wire haired dachshund, Woofa, which would "never have harmed a fly" – and had at one time been terrorised by a rabbit, as described in an earlier chapter - returned to the house with a bloated stomach, a smile on her face and wagging her tail, but with tell-tale feathers sticking out of her mouth. The following morning we heard that the Steeles were distraught because a "fox" had eaten one of their chickens. Woofa, therefore, had to be "grounded" in the garden, and not allowed to wander freely as before.

And then there was another family, the Hobbs, with a particularly attractive daughter, with whom we were not allowed to associate – or even to recognise with a daily greeting, and they were messing around with several boats directly on the foreshore opposite our house. They always seemed to be enjoying themselves and they were often accompanied by other friends. But they had the smell of "new money" and all the vulgarity associated with that, and so they were condemned as "common," and as noisy people who tended to show off, and were pretentious.

As I sat alone on the dyke of the stony embankment, I looked longingly at the attractive brunette, envying the other young men who danced around her, but I knew she was forbidden fruit. There was really no one else I was interested in socialising with in the stuffy middle-aged ambience of Elmer Sands. However, it is recorded that on 2nd September 1952, I dreamed of Cynthia (my second love at Swanage), and being told and disappointed at hearing of her marriage. It was her younger sister who gave me the news.

As a teenager, I increasingly began to loathe the attitude of my parents – as usually expressed through my mother – that we were an exclusive family unit, to which the admittance of friends or acquaintants was not really welcome. On countless occasions I had to endure hearing the phrase, "This is only for the family," in response to suggestions of inviting round friends to participate in some special event. These rebuffs were not made out of snobbery in rejecting particular friends, but purely out of dislike for meeting new and sometimes unusual or interesting people. Anyone outside the family circle was regarded as somehow "different," and if not actually "inferior" they were regarded as a nuisance and intrusion into the intimacy of family life.

Just as bad was her attitude to public events, for she complained when tales of disaster, such as earthquakes or war, were screened on TV. – "Why do they have to show us these things?," she moaned. "They're nothing to do with us." I remember on one occasion, following an earthquake in Italy, when cartloads of fleeing women, raising their arms in despair were shown on the newsreel, to which my mother remarked indignantly, "Why do foreigners have to behave like that? British people would never make such a fuss or draw attention to themselves." That may have been true, but I was offended not only by my mother's insensitivity, but more significantly, by her lack of interest in the outside world or wish to comprehend the causes of events. Her insouciance in the face of tragedy filled me with disgust as irresponsible and inhuman, and I could only explain it away as a "typical characteristic" of the British middle classes at that time.

On a more personal level I found no intimacy in our family life – or none that was pleasant. I yearned for company and friends, and during my school day years, it was only natural that I wished to invite them home. I concluded that my parents were inherently unsociable, and indeed, they rarely entertained, except at Christmas. My attitude was increasingly responsive and friendly to all kinds of people, irrespective of class, race, or social background. King Alfred's was advantageous in this respect because of the many nationalities attending the school, and I remember boating in Regent's Park on Saturday mornings with two Egyptian boys from a diplomatic family. I once met several IRA members in the Bald Faced Stag in East Finchley, and I remember that after a few rounds of drinks, we turned to an interesting discussion of Plato and Aristotle.

When I later told my father what interesting Irishmen I had met in a pub, he was appalled, and getting hot under the collar, he exclaimed, "I hope you didn't give them our address." – "No," I answered. It should be borne in mind that this occurred some 15 years before the era of troubles which began in 1968. I could only see my parents as being narrow-minded and provincial, and intolerably dull in refusing to leave the insulated bubble in which they chose to exist. After all, I could never have discussed Plato or Aristotle with my parents. As home life was intolerably depressing and oppressive, I saw this as a living death. In these respects, my brothers received the same impression, and it became a life-long point of comment between the three of us.

This is not to suggest my parents were opposed to free thought or free speech, but their belief in freedom was purely abstract. My father was rather awed when seeing young people arguing or discussing the issues of the day. He admired them for their initiative and intelligence, without having any notion of the opinions they actually held. He believed rather in the principles of freedom than the practice. The same may be applied to his attitude to politics. Although always ultra-conservative, he once attended a public meeting addressed by Aneurin Bevan, and returned with immense praise for his powers of oratory, and whilst full of admiration for the man, was opposed to his views.

On my return to London my thoughts were again directed as to a strategy in winning the love of Patricia Dainton. Her marriage was no bar to my discouragement or sense of right to her possession, for no man could love her with such an intensity of passion, and I felt that this gave me a moral right transcending all the false and artificial conventions of the law. It was often said that the law was an "ass," and this must be truly so if it acted as a barrier in forbidding the consequences of love. I resolved on a duel to settle the issue, and as firearms were not easily obtainable, it would need to be a fight to the death with swords. On 26th September I read an article in the *Penny Cyclopaedia* on duelling to be informed of the customary formalities necessary. This, as stated in an earlier chapter, was a reference work in some 33 volumes, published by the Society for the Diffusion of Useful Knowledge in the 1830s, which I had bought from King Alfred's School when it was removed from their library as surplus to requirements.

On 4th October 1952, opposite Edgware Road tube station, in the road of that name, I passed by what then would be described as a large corner junk shop, but if it offered the same merchandise today, would more properly be described as an Antiques Emporium, and I noted that they had swords priced at £1.00 each. The shop was closed, but I noted the contents with satisfaction, and it contributed to hardening the practical aspect of the plot I was hatching.

Later that day in the Library, in researching the rules and etiquette of duelling in preparation for the episode ahead, I was momentarily alarmed with the disturbing information that killing a man in a duel in English law was an offence equated with murder in all respects. I decided to dismiss such a legal snag from my mind on the grounds that the power of love transcended any other authority. Two days later I arose early and left for the shop in Edgware Road, where I bought a pair of vicious looking Moroccan sabres decorated with tassels. They were wrapped in brown paper, and if questioned about the parcel when arriving home, I would explain it contained timber for making picture frames, as I had already discussed this with regard to my own paintings.

On arriving home unseen, I went to my room and unwrapped the parcel. I tore off the tassels and threw them away, and then drew the swords from their scabbards and lovingly cleaned the blades with paraffin. The blades could have been sharper for greater effectiveness in sooner drawing blood, but I would have to be contented with how they were. Lastly, I re-wrapped the parcel in readiness for taking them to Hugh Richardson's flat first thing tomorrow morning. My plan was to hold Hugh Richardson and his wife at sword point, forcing them to phone Miss Dainton's husband, telling him to make his way to the flat within the next few minutes – or at least, within the hour. I realised, of course, that preliminary phone calls might need to be made to Vivienne Black, or others, before finally tracking down the person concerned.

If Miss Dainton's husband failed to reach the flat for any reason, then Mr. and Mrs. Richardson would be slaughtered in cold blood. Speed was the essence in ensuring the success of the plan. I realised the fallibility of the scheme, but I had no other alternative, if I was to win the heart of Patricia Dainton, and prevent her further defilement by someone who was unworthy of her. Of course there was the possibility of the police becoming involved, followed by a siege of the premises, in which event I was prepared to suffer a noble death, through cowardly gunfire if it came to it, in the cause of transcendent love.

That afternoon I attended a special function at King Alfred School, possibly arranged for those who had left the school the previous term. I was surprised by the warmth of the reception by school friends, as well as teachers, who enquired as to my aspirations and future, and I reciprocated in no less a friendly manner. I had an enjoyable time socialising in the library, and at 4.0 o'clock I met my intellectual hero, Ronald Fuller, who took me aside and advised that I seek suitable training and employment in a museum, which he thought was an environment ideal for my temperament and abilities. He was so persuasive that I almost thought of abandoning the scheme I had hatched for tomorrow morning, but realising that I had already invested £2 in my project, and loathing the idea of wasting money under any circumstances, I realised there could be no turning back.

The following morning, 7th October, I rose at 4.45 am, had two mugs of coffee, shaved, dressed in my best suit, and quietly left the house with the package under my arm. It was a fine morning and I walked all the way to Hampstead underground station, admiring the beautiful sunrise over Hampstead Heath. At the station I refused the offer of a return fare for obvious reasons: knowing either that I would return in triumph with the one I loved, or else be slaughtered in the courageous attempt. I therefore took a single ticket to South Kensington.

At the time I may have recollected the beautiful Pre-Raphaelite painting I had first seen in the *Magazine of Art* as a 6-year old, of the brave knight replacing his sword into its scabbard as his rival lay dead at his feet, and behind them stood the beauty with her long flaxen hair, ready to throw herself into the arms of her victorious hero. This was the deserved reward for true heroism, for the consummation of lasting love and possession could only be achieved through the shedding of blood. This reactive aggression at the experience of frustrated love may indeed seem abnormal or extreme, but it should be remembered it fulfils the natural instincts of most animal species of the higher order, for what does the stag do during the rutting season, or the lion or the tiger when placed in a similar situation? It may be that I was endowed with testosterone somewhat above the average, but all of us differ in our hormonal make up.

It took me some time to find Drayton Gardens, for there were few people in the streets to ask at that early hour in the morning. At last I found the apartment block, and as I climbed to the second floor, I opened the top of my package to expose the hilts of the swords. I rang the doorbell and gripped one of the hilts. It was about 7.0 in the morning. After a protracted wait (which was not unexpected) the door was opened by a woman in a dressing gown. As I tightened my grip on the sword hilt, she took in her breath and raised her hand to her throat in a defensive gesture of horror. "I've come to see Mr. Richardson," I only exclaimed. – "It's very early, and this is a strictly private address," replied the woman who was just approaching middle age. "I'll go and ask him," and she shut the door without even asking my name.

After another protracted wait she returned, but her manner was quite transformed, for she was calm and friendly. "Could you phone Mr. Richardson later today at the office after ten o'clock?" I was so taken aback by her cool reassurance that I only replied, "Yes," and with that, I left the building. I had humiliated myself through cowardice, and as I travelled home, I fell into a mood of melancholy and despair.

On arriving home, Miss Wall became angry with me for allowing my breakfast to get cold, adding, "Where have you been at this time in the morning, and leaving the house without telling anyone?" She noted I had brought something into the house (the swords were already hidden in my room by this time), and as to whether I had "sold something," or was something "on my mind?" Minutes later my father arrived on the scene, reprimanding me for leaving the house at an ungodly hour, and obviously for "an immoral purpose." Later that morning, in despair, I made futile attempts at stabbing myself.

CHAPTER 21
The Problem of my Future

"The future is a world limited by ourselves; in it we discover only what concerns us and, sometimes by chance, what interests those whom we love the most."

Maurice Maeterlinck, *Jayzelle*, Act I

The collapse of my school work – School reports – Career advice from teachers and relatives – My father vetoes my preferences – The "nice" man at the Youth Employment Bureau

At this stage in the narrative it is necessary to turn back some six to nine months, in glancing at the prospects of my formal education. The turmoil of the Patricia Dainton affair was to prove disastrous for almost every aspect of my schooling, and certainly with regard to achieving any kind of worthwhile qualifications. My fate in this regard was not necessarily sealed in the early months of this affair, say between April to June 1951, for I clearly remember cherishing thoughts of going up to Oxford to study political science, with Patricia Dainton at my side as a loving and supporting wife, and then going on to take a PhD as a resident in a college, and eventually producing a scholarly 3-volume work on the necessary principles in achieving a just and equitable society. Such an intellectual ambition, however, was not to be achieved for almost another 60 years.

But such practical aspirations as I had at that time, did not last for long, for with the strains and stress of frustrated love, my schoolwork fell apart, with the consequence that my ambitions became increasingly utopian and unrealisable. I suffered from exhaustion, and in the afternoon fell asleep in the library, my head resting in my arms on my exercise books. The school was therefore obliged to write to my parents, informing them that my progress in all subjects had so deteriorated that it would be useless my attempting to take the General Certificate of Education. The letter then suggested that I seemed to be showing symptoms of illness, and that it might be advisable that I be sent to a psychologist.

My father snorted over the breakfast table at this suggestion, dismissing the idea of psychology as a "load of nonsense." He then turned angrily to me and said, "Do you masturbate?" I denied that I did, irrespective of the truth of the answer. He then delivered a lecture on masturbation, declaring it was almost invariably the reason for academic failure. I sat there embarrassed and said nothing. In a later letter to my parents, the school offered the option of my either leaving the KAS at the end of the present term, when the examinations were to be taken, or staying on an extra term until I was 17. My father gave me the choice, and I opted to stay on for the extra term to benefit from the lessons in English and History.

Clearly I was on the verge of some kind of nervous breakdown due to the strains and uncertainty entailed in my courtship of Patricia Dainton, and the psychological causation and manifestations of this, and not due to the occasional physical act of what was once described as "self-abuse," or in good old Biblical terms, Onanism – see *Genesis* 38:9. If there was any conflict in the interpretation of human nature between science and the Bible, my father, of course, would always opt for the latter. On not a single occasion did he ever question me (or any other person for that matter in so far as I know) on my happiness or unhappiness with life in general. As he repudiated entirely secular notions in influencing contentment or moral purpose, his sole recipe for easing discontent was church-going. My diary entries during teenage years are filled with references urging me to attend church on Sunday mornings. He was not able to enforce his will in this respect, and indeed, I was filled with disgust at the church services I attended at St. James's because of the way in which they insulted the intelligence and relied on the deceit of arousing falsely-based emotions.

It would be useful to draw on my school reports during my time at King Alfred's in presenting a more objective portrayal of my academic strengths and weaknesses, and up-turns and down-turns, and general behaviour. The first is the Report for the Christmas term of 1950:

English:- "He has worked very hard indeed this term and steadily improves. His essays are always interesting, but he must try to make them simpler, and to say what he means as clearly and concisely as he can." –R. Fuller. *History*:- "Nigel has worked hard and well in the main. He is apt to be diffuse, and should concentrate on getting essentials clear." – F.C. Johnson. *Geography*:- "He has done a few satisfactory stages, but is not regular enough in giving in his stages to be marked." – B.H. Montgomery. *Mathematics*:- "He has done very little and appears as uninterested as ever." H.V. Kemp. *Biology*:- "Improving slowly." – Miss March. *Art*:- "His concentration and tenacity is excellent. He is gradually acquiring more skill." V. Mitchell. *Woodwork*:- Very enthusiastic. Satisfactory." – D.R. Thomas. *Physical Training*:- "Somewhat erratic in performance and behaviour!" – P.H. Haselden. *Form Report*:- "Nigel is a very keen and helpful member of the form, though sometimes inclined to be dictatorial. He can usually be depended on to provide original and stimulating ideas in form discussions." – Miss Marsh. *Head's Report*:- "Nigel has enthusiasm and infinite patience for his favourite subjects, and is always ready to take part in discussions, but in mathematics and science he makes little or no progress." H.M.E. Barber.

The second Report is for the Spring term of 1950: *English*:- "Shows great enthusiasm and is an immensely keen worker. His essays are always carefully thought out and full of promise." – R. Fuller. *History*:- "A conscientious and industrious worker." F.C. Johnson. *Geography*:- "Very poor. He has made no attempt to cope with the written work this term." – B.H. Montgomery. *Mathematics*:- "No consistent effort – work extremely untidy." – H.V. Kemp. *Biology*:- "Nigel tries hard, but is very slow." – Miss Marsh. *French*:- Fairly good." – R.C. Johnson. *Art*:- "His work has been painstaking when he has not been distracted, which happens too easily." – V. Mitchell. *Music*:- "Is very cooperative in the group and shows interest." – J. Trygvason (The future father-in-law of Vladimir Ashkenazy). *Woodwork*:- "Satisfactory progress." – D.R. Thomas. *Printing*:- "Very keen." – F.C. Johnson. *Physical Training*:- "Always willing and cooperative." – P.H. Haselden. *Form Report*:- "Nigel is at present neglecting all academic work except English and History, without thought for the future, but in other respects has had a calmer and happier term." – Miss Marsh *Head's Report*:- "Nigel has now overcome the preliminary settling down difficulties and has made a place for himself in the new environment. He plays his part in various constructive activities, but his work is too specialised. If he expects to take the School Certificate Examination he will have to broaden his approach." – H.M.E. Barber.

The third Report is for the Summer term of 1950: *English*:- "Nigel is a great reader and full of enthusiasm, and his written work shows promise. When he has developed more discrimination, he should do very well indeed." – R. Fuller. *History*:- He works enthusiastically, expressing himself well and showing great interest in the subject." – F.C. Johnson. *Geography*:- "He has done some work but has not given his stages in regularly nor made much effort to complete and correct stages which I had rejected." – B.H. Montgomery. *Mathematics*:- "He has done very little this term." – H.V. Kemp. *Biology*:- "Nigel has little idea of relevance in his work, but he tries hard." – Miss Marsh. *Art*:- "Shows great interest and works well." – V. Mitchell. *Music*:- "Very satisfactory." – J. Trygvason. *Woodwork*:- "Satisfactory. A good worker." – D.R. Thomas. *Form Report*:- "Nigel's behaviour has been much steadier this term: in fact, he now seems to have settled down, both in his work and social activities. His contributions in form are somewhat erratic, but much more rational than hitherto – I wish I could say the same of his mathematics." – Miss Marsh. *Head's Report*:- "On the whole Nigel has made useful progress this term, but he must endeavour not to become too one-sided." B.H. Montgomery.

The fourth extant Report is for the Spring term of 1951: *English*:- "Nigel is a very conscientious worker and shows endless patience and enthusiasm over essays – but they are still too turgid and diffuse. He must try to be more simple in his writing." – R. Fuller. *History*:- "Nigel gives plenty of time and care to his history, though his interest in the subject is in general rather personal and fanciful." – F.C. Johnson. *Geography*:- "He shows great interest in the lessons but his written work is not given in regularly. He should ask me to give him more help." – B.H. Montgomery. *Mathematics*:- "No interest – no work done." – H.V. Kemp. *Biology*:- "Nigel has managed to achieve very little this term." – Miss Marsh. *Art*:- Nigel has an intelligently questioning attitude and his draughtsmanship is sure and strong." – V. Mitchell. *Dramatic Work*:- "Made a start and should persevere." – Mrs. Soskin. *Woodwork*:- "Satisfactory in all stages." – D.R. Thomas. *Physical Training*:- "I have seen very little of Nigel this term.! – P.H. Haselden. *Form Report*:- "Nigel always has his own opinion, and voices it with great confidence. He is a leading spirit in the form, and most cooperative." – Miss Marsh. *Head's Report*:- "Nigel continues to do well in his rather limited field. He is gaining confidence all the time." – H.M.E. Barber.

The fifth Report is for the Summer term of 1951: *English*:- "Nigel is a great reader and is very interested in this subject. His essays are original and he takes endless trouble over them. He will do very well if he can learn to be more simple and lucid." – R. Fuller. *History*:- "Nigel takes an interest in his work, but finds it hard to sort out and present ideas clearly." – F,C, Johnson. *Geography*:- "He has made a great effort to work conscientiously through the stages this term but I still wish he would consult me more freely about his work and so avoid many mistakes." – B.H. Montgomery. *Mathematics*:- "He has revised some elementary work on his own this term." – H.V. Kemp. *Biology*:- Nigel has tried hard this term, but his grasp of the subject is very limited." – Miss Marsh. *Art*:- "Nigel's painting, which was very good last term, has developed into really original and talented work. His approach is freer and more imaginative now. An excellent term's work." – V. Mitchell. *Woodwork*:- His work could be better, but he makes up for it by showing interest." – D.R. Thomas. *Games*:- "Tennis: very fair." – P.H. Haselden. *Form Report*:- "Nigel takes a great interest in form affairs and is always reliable and eager to help. I think he is making marked progress." – Miss Marsh. *Head's Report*:- "Nigel has unusual gifts in certain directions, and serious limitations in others. He has made the most of the opportunities we can give him to develop in his own way." – B.H. Montgomery.

The sixth Report is for the Autumn term of 1951: *English*:- "Nigel's written work is always interesting and original but his test results are very poor. He should curb his facility a little." – R. Fuller. *History*:- "Nigel has shown an improvement in his written work, but he still needs to express himself more clearly. A fair term's work." – F.C. Johnson. *Biology*:- "Nigel finds it difficult to distinguish between fact and phantasy, which is a disadvantage in a scientific subject." – Miss Marsh. *Art*:- "Nigel's work in preparation for examination is not nearly so good as the work he does unhampered by conditions. The latter is always imaginative, sensitively drawn, and beautiful in colour." – V. Mitchell. *Debating*:- "Nigel's contributions to debates have been most interesting and original." – H.M.E. Barber. *Form & Head's Report*:- "Nigel is studious and determined and he has done much interesting work in certain limited fields. It is useless to pretend, however, that he has made much progress along the lines required for examination purposes. As a member of the community he has an original contribution to make and he has been generally helpful." – B.H. Montgomery.

The seventh Report is for the Spring term of 1952: *English*:- "Very promising. He is an omnivorous reader, full of enthusiasm, and his compositions are interesting and original; but his habit of wandering off the point, or never reaching it, makes him a deplorable examinee." – R. Fuller. *History*:- "Nigel has written one or two interesting stages, but in general he finds it difficult to distinguish between significant and insignificant facts. Not a very satisfactory term." – R.J. Handford. *Biology*:- "There is not much point in his continuing with this subject." – Miss Marsh. *Art*:- "Nigel has seemed to live in a dream world all this term. His conversation and observations have been fascinating and his drawing almost non-existent." V. Mitchell. *Debating*:- "Nigel is always willing to speak on any subject, and he usually has something interesting and unusual to say." – H.M.E. Barber. *Physical Training*:- "No attendance." – P.H. Haselden. *Form & Head's Report*:- "Nigel makes an interesting and original contribution to the life of the community. He reads widely but his intelligence is confined to particular channels and he has shown himself quite unable to cope with specific work for examination purposes. Next term we will provide him with special work which is suited to his abilities." – B.H. Montgomery.

The eighth and last Report is for the Summer term of 1952: *English*:- "Nigel has worked well this term, and shows great interest in this subject." – R. Fuller. *History*:- "Nigel's written work has shown rather more discrimination his term." – R.J. Handford. *Geography*:- "He has worked conscientiously and his stages are more lucid and concise – although still untidily written." F.C. Johnson. *Biology*:- He has suddenly taken on interest in one or two special topics and produced some good work." – Miss Marsh. *Art*:- "Nigel has emerged from his dream world once or twice this term, and has produced a few good paintings but he has seemed far away most of the time." V. Mitchell. *Current Affairs*:- "Nigel has strong views, argues them powerfully, and often has good authorities to quote." – H.M.E. Barber. *Physical Training*:- "No attendance." P.H. Haselden. *Games*:- "Tennis: He has not appeared often but seems to enjoy playing." – P.H. Haselden. *Form & Head's Report*:- "Nigel has had a successful last term. Freed from the worry of an approaching examination he has developed new interests and made good progress in his work. His interest and work in the library have been of great value and he often surprises me by the range of his knowledge. In his own specialised way he has considerable ability and I very much hope he will find an occupation where his gifts can be fully needed." – B.H. Montgomery.

It has been necessary to record the differing opinions and feelings of my various teachers as to my character, abilities, and the possibilities for my future, over a several years' period, to give greater credence to this memoir, and in explaining (if not justifying) my attitudes and aspirations in the immediate future leading up to my entry into the Army. I was clearly perceived as a problem, but I nonetheless retained the goodwill and all the help that my teachers were able to give me at the time. Mr. H.V. Kemp, my mathematics master, for example, attempted to interest me in the history of mathematics, and lent me a book on this subject, in his attempt to encourage my greater interest and understanding of such an important discipline.

As I may have clarified in an earlier chapter, I never broached the question of the Patricia Dainton affair at school except to a single confidant, Geoffrey Dunston; and I never discussed my difficult home environment except in an open class situation during Art lessons with

Mrs. V. Mitchell, our teacher, and others sitting around. On those occasions, the topic usually circulated around the strictness of my father and the oppression of home life, and that is what I believe Mrs. Mitchell was referring to when she wrote, "His conversation and observations have been fascinating." I remember her asking the year of my father's birth, and her surprise that he had not been born during the earlier epoch of the Victorian period. She felt that his attitudes were unreasonable and anachronistic.

The teachers must have met together to discuss the options for my future, and how they might handle me in view of the difficulties they confronted. Once in the middle of the school day, a group of four inspectors came into our classroom and after moving around the desks, stopped and questioned me for several minutes. I immediately sensed I had been identified in advance for their specific attention, and towards the end of their interview, their leader said in a matter of fact tone, "It may well be that in later life, you have something important to say." As soon as they departed, this left me thinking, and I realised they must have approached me because of the contradictory situation I presented to the school. Whilst on the one hand I tended towards being a deep-thinking intellectual with a knowledge-base above my years who should be guided towards an Oxbridge education, on the other hand, I had become a hopeless examinee.

As my schooldays drew towards a close, I encountered expressed concern and tentative advice from several quarters as to the direction I should take in the future. Hetty Barber, the Head mistress (and mother of the Jazz musician, Chris Barber), suggested that as I wished to be a writer, I should just write, in exploring and finding my own strengths, and on another occasion, she suggested I should seek a position in the British Museum when I would find myself in a congenial environment. Miss Gallant, my father's nurse (or what would nowadays be described as a dental assistant), urged me to take on any kind of "respectable" employment, and not be influenced as to whether it was congenial or not, as "work is not supposed to be enjoyable" and that "pain and unpleasantness was a natural part of life." I felt that such advice was most unhelpful.

My great Uncle Quentin advised me to go into banking, but I told him I did not want to spend the rest of my life sitting on a high stool entering figures into a thick leather bound ledger. He tried to explain that banking was a little more than that, but at the time I did not understand the gist of what he was trying to say. On several occasions I met Quin and Syb in their miniscule one-room flat at Russell Court in Woburn Place, just off Russell Square, and Quin and I would go for a walk and visit second hand bookshops in Charing Cross Road, and discuss my future, before returning to the flat for a cup of tea.

They were a penurious but contented couple, and besides being an amusing buffoon on appropriate occasions, he was always an interesting conversationalist with strong ideas. His politics were left of centre and he loathed America, and was always critical of their foreign policy, and with regard to domestic policy, he believe that government should rule in such a way as to ensure that all had the opportunity for employment. As I have noted in earlier chapters, they were good friends of my parents, as his free professional advice in the spheres of surveying and house purchasing was always called upon when my father contemplated buying a new property. Once my father contemplated buying a house in Westminster, close to the Houses of Parliament, but finally the idea was dropped when Quentin discovered that the property had what was technically described as a "dirty freehold."

As the couple had minimum assets for daily expenditure they spent the greater part of their leisure time visiting the Royal Courts of Justice in The Strand, or else the Central Criminal Courts in the Old Bailey, and they regaled us with endless interesting stories about major trials and curious facts they picked up about the ambiguities of the law. They knew the leading barristers by reputation, and had their favourites who created dramatic tension in the Courts through devilishly clever cross-questioning or impressive oratory, and they planned their trips in the same way that a keen theatre goer would follow his chosen stars of stage or screen. Their lively interest in the world about them ensured they never used the excuse of poverty in old age to depress their spirits. How different Uncle Quentin was from his sister, my paternal grandmother!

A little later in the year, by which time I had already experienced some unfortunate job mishaps, I received the following letter from my ever-helpful Aunt Inez, dated 4th November 1952. "My dear Nigel. – In case you haven't noticed the enclosed advertisement from *The Times* of today I am sending it to you as Uncle Bill and I think it might be just what you are looking for! In any case even if you are in a job I should write and find out about it. It sounds almost too good to be true but there must be something in it. Write *at once*, and make your letter short, people in business haven't time to wade through rigmarole! Just say, 'in reply to your advertisement in *The Times* of Nov. 4th I intend to make books my career. I am 17 years of age, educated at …English Literature and history being my chief studies. I should be grateful if you will grant me an interview. – Yours faithfully' – commencing 'Dear Sir,' of course! And if they do want you for an interview you must try and get time off from your present job, if any??

"If nothing comes of this I should read the adverts in *The Times* if I were you, Personal columns as well as sits. Vacant, all sorts of things crop up from time to time. No more now as I am in a hurry to catch the post. Wish we had seen this earlier in the day, but never mind perhaps it will not be too late. Yours affectionately." The letter was accompanied by the following P.S:- "Granny suggests you ask Miss Gallant (?) to type the letter for you and you just sign it. She says you'll *never* get an interview with your handwriting. Show the advert and this letter to Miss G., and I am sure she will help you with it." The following was the text of the advertisement: "CAREER IN THE BOOK TRADE – Important group of Publishers and Booksellers in Central London are prepared to engage young men and women interested to work with books. Previous experience not essential. Congenial working conditions with canteen facilities. Five-day week, 14 days holiday with pay. Starting salary for those accepted, male £325 pa, female £250 pa. Excellent opportunities for those wishing to make books their career. – Write at once to Box A.41, The Times, E.C.4."

Shortly after leaving school I attended an evening social event for seniors, and those who had recently left, and towards the end of the evening, the Art mistress, Mrs. Mitchell, who was an attractive young divorcee of 26, approached me, saying, "I think I've stayed here long enough. Would you like to come home for a coffee?" Naturally, I immediately sensed that this was a sexual invitation, and I was happy to accept the offer, but I wanted to socialise a little longer at the party, and in my foolishness and ignorance, I expressed this preference, not realising at the time that in such circumstances, a woman rarely repeats such a proposition.

When I searched around for Mrs. Mitchell a little later, I was told she had already left with another boy of whom it was said had an incestuous relationship with his sister. I could have kicked myself in my frustration and disappointment. Had I allowed myself to be seduced, it would have done wonders for my state of mind and mental stability, and as I had already left the school, Mrs. Mitchell could not be said to have compromised herself with regard to unethical conduct with pupils.

Concerning my own views on my employment prospects, I had little idea in which direction to concentrate my efforts, and when I did express an inclination, it was sure to be opposed by my parents. For example, I thought that a career in some sphere of art might resolve the issue, but towards the end of my last term at school, my father burst into my bedroom one evening, and hot under the collar, began spluttering incoherently about the "impossibility" of anything to do with art "as there was no money in it." The fact that my father was to reverse his opinion on this within the next couple of months is another story.

I then contemplated a career in journalism, this having been suggested to me, and it was even discussed around the dinner table, but several weeks later after the incident described above, my father again burst into my room in a similar fashion, saying he had lunched with his fellow Rotarian and editor of the *Hornsey Journal* that afternoon, who explained that a "career in journalism had no future whatsoever." And besides, it was certainly no career for the son of a dental consultant. It was an appalling trade which entailed "waiting around in the rain all day for celebrities who never appeared," or, "boozing in pubs with colleagues who did nothing but exchange gossip amongst themselves."

It was finally decided that my only course was to visit the Youth Employment Bureau of the Labour Exchange, which I seem to recollect was towards the bottom of Alexandra Park Road. Here I was closeted away in a small room with a short white-haired man in his late fifties with gold-framed spectacles. He asked me many questions, some of which were curiously out of place, and I found him over-friendly. He sent me off to several interviews for unsuitable positions, and every time I returned to his office, he interviewed me along a different track of questioning with the idea of investigating a new source of employment. It occurred to me he was wasting my time – not to mention his own – but as a novice in the matter of job-seeking, it was not for me to comment.

He had become increasingly personal, and one day he asked my religion and what church I attended, and I dutifully answered. He then came out with the words, "May I kiss you?" I was petrified out of my wits by this horrific suggestion, and in my dazed condition, I could only come out with, "Where?" – "On the cheek," he replied. "I suppose so," I only responded, for I felt dazed and imprisoned and completely within his control. He came round from behind his desk, and asked me to stand up. I stood to attention, my hands pressed to my sides, shivering in horror as he kissed me once on the cheek.

On returning to his desk, he became quite exuberant, saying he would like to introduce me to his wife at the Methodist Church in Muswell Hill next Sunday. That was the church he always attended, and he was sure I would like his wife. He would wait for me at the church entrance and we would sit in one of the back pews. I verbally assented without, of course, having the slightest intention of associating with this paedophile. When I returned to the Labour Exchange about a week later, he took my absence the previous Sunday in a bad frame of mind, saying that he and his wife had waited half an hour for me after the church service had ended in case I had mistaken the time. I made no attempt at an apology, and he then sent me off for another interview in Regent Street, which happened to be with a lingerie wholesaler, and if I interpreted this as a cynical gesture of retaliation, then I suppose that is what it was.

The last that I heard from this objectionable public servant was an undated scrappily typed letter on a half sheet of quarto paper, headed Youth Employment Bureau, post dated 9th February 1953, which read as follows: "Dear Corfe. – It is now about 4 ½ months since you started work and we are wondering how you are getting on. We would like you to keep in touch with us and if there is any assistance we can give about employment, we shall be pleased to do so. If you would call at the Bureau to tell us about your job or to talk over any employment problems, then we should be pleased to see you on Friday evening between 5 pm and 7 pm, or on Saturday morning between 10 am. and 11 am. If you are unable to call perhaps you would care to write or telephone. If your parents or guardian would like to accompany you, we should be pleased to welcome them. – Yours sincerely," &c.

In those far-off innocent days, the term paedophilia had no meaning for the general public, but clearly there were those with the guile and unending patience to pursue their nefarious ends through ingenious means. And by such means they succeeded discreetly in covering their tracks. I laughed at the curiously foxy hypocrisy of the letter, and filed it away with my other correspondence as an unusual memento.

CHAPTER 22
My Bath Relatives versus my Parents

"A family is but too often a commonwealth of
    malignants."

Alexander Pope, *Thoughts on Various Subjects*

Visit to Bath – The au pair Barbara – Our intellectual friendship – Aunt Inez suggests a stay in Germany – Plans are formulated – My parents opposition – My father's rudeness to Barbara – My Aunt's secret letter – Am forced into employment with T.G. Williams Ltd. – Am relieved to be sacked – My mother takes me to an interview

My annual holiday in Bath which in 1952 comprised the last two weeks of August, was to culminate in proposed arrangements which might have transformed my life, and would certainly have lifted me out of the oppressive Patricia Dainton episode which had now dragged on for 16 months and was to last for the same period again. Instead, the outcome of the holiday was to lead to dashed hopes, and considerable acrimony between two sides of the family.

For almost a year Aunt Inez and Uncle Bill had employed a German au pair called, Barbara, from Ludwigshafen, Germany. She was a tall, well-built girl, in her early twenties, handsome rather than pretty. Aunt Inez and Bill showed her around the area, taking her to stately homes and other places of historical or cultural interest, and if they travelled away from home, they always took her with them, and she even accompanied them when they visited Elmer Sands.

My parents disliked the idea of this "foreigner" tagging along with their relatives. She was an extra expense – and besides she was supposed to be a servant not a friend. When the three were taken out for a meal at Elmer Sands, my father objected having to pay for a "German woman," although of course he could say nothing about it at the time, except maintain a glum silence and ignore the unwelcome guest. My mother said that her sister had had her "head turned" by the au pair, and that she was spoiling her and treating her as an equal. It was ridiculous that this girl had to be "in" on everything, and overhear everything her employers and their friends happened to say.

Eventually my mother excused her sister on the grounds that as she had no children of her own, this "German woman" had become a "daughter substitute." When this was recognised, Aunt Inez became a subject for pity rather than straightforward annoyance. It was a tragedy she never had any children of her own – she would have been such a good mother, although it was uncertain, in my mother's opinion, as to how good a father Bill might have been. Her sister's attitude to the au pair was therefore excused on account of her natural motherly instinct.

When I left for Bath my mother jokingly warned me not to disgrace myself with my aunt and uncle by getting up to any "high jinks" with the au pair. My father said nothing. The time at Bath was as enjoyable as ever, and in the evenings, Aunt Inez, Barbara and I, sat with my grandmother in her living room, engaged in lively conversation – Uncle Bill always remaining in his study (except on Sunday afternoons) where he had "work" to do, although no one knew exactly what that work consisted of. Barbara was the first German I had ever met, and as I was deeply curious about the culture and characteristics of her country, every evening the conversation turned to comparisons between our two countries, and to the life and prospects of contemporary Germany.

She gave her first impressions of England, saying how surprised she was that everyone talked about the weather as soon as they met in the street, and how stupid she thought this was. It may have been that as Bath was situated in a mountainous area, it received more rain than most places, and that it was only natural people should express their hopes or exasperation over the weather. She spoke about the poverty and hard conditions in post-War Germany, and how the people had been reduced to eating potato peel. When I repeated this to my family at home, some weeks later, in the presence of Mabs and Bill, the latter who was no less anti-German than my father because of his far left sympathies, scoffed with the remark, "Well, I wonder who ate the potatoes then?"

She came from the French Zone of Germany, and the industrial city of Ludwigshafen was situated on the left bank of the Rhine, on the zonal frontier, and she described the vengeful spirit of the French occupation forces which contrasted sharply with that of the British and Americans. "That's typical of people who never lifted a finger to fight in the War," remarked Aunt Inez. Barbara explained how she often crossed over the bridge into Mannheim, in the American Zone, purchased essential foodstuffs, and re-crossed the bridge with her black market goods after ogling the French soldiers, who smiled or wolf-whistled, and let her pass freely without question or search. We laughed at her guile in these daring adventures. She said her heart was often in her mouth as she approached the bridge, and that it was her long silky brown hair which did the trick. She always held our sympathy whatever story she told.

Aunt Inez was pleased to see I had struck up such a good friendship with Barbara, for we both had much to say. After some days, when it turned 9.30 in the evening, my grandmother and Aunt Inez said they were retiring for the night. "But you two sit up as long as you like," insisted Aunt Inez, and this became the procedure thereafter, as Barbara and I sat up until 11.0 or 12.0 in deep conversation before finally retiring. Although I believe these relatives did not expect us to have any physical contact, I do believe they hoped for some kind of romantic feelings to develop between us in ensuring a longer term relationship, and some months later Aunt Inez spoke in such a way as if to indicate her belief that his had actually occurred.

The truth, however, is very much more mundane. There was never a romantic connection between us. Our relationship – certainly from my part – was purely intellectual. I admired and respected her as a person, and I valued her friendship, but I could never have considered her as a "girl friend." She was not really my type. She was too large and muscular, and besides was about five years my senior – although Patricia Dainton was also around the same age. I preferred women more feminine and petite. Nonetheless, we had many enjoyable evenings together. We exchanged views on our parents, and when I told her about my father, she said that hers, too, was strict and penny-pinching. She also complained about her mother.

Shortly after the War, she and her school friends began listening to music put out by AFN (American Forces Network) Frankfurt, and one day her mother broke into the room, and ordered the children to turn off the wireless, and they were forbidden to listen to such "decadent music" again. A year or two later Barbara explained she came to appreciate her mother's gesture, for had they continued to tune into AFN Frankfurt, their aesthetic ear would have been corrupted, and they could not have wholly appreciated the great classics of German music.

She described the charisma of Hitler through the experience of her elder sister, who as a young schoolgirl before the War had waited with classmates for hours in the streets, when the Führer came to visit Mannheim, and of the overwhelming spiritual experience she had undergone through seeing him in the flesh. "That was the effect he had on people," she concluded. "We had such hope in the future." Towards the end of the War her brother had the privilege of being enlisted into a crack fighting division of the SS, and was sent to the Eastern front. On being captured by the Russians, he was sent to a prison camp with appalling conditions, and due to severe malnutrition he went temporarily blind, and it was only due to the humanity and decency of comrades, who ensured that he was not denied his rations in the scramble for a subsistence diet, that his life was saved. On eventually reaching home, a year after the War ended, he decided to make a life-long study of philosophy and was entered into a university.

This led us to discuss German philosophy, and she told me about Schopenhauer and Nietzsche, and their not very complimentary ideas about women. We never touched on the more important philosophies of Kant or Hegel, and possibly, she might have had difficulty in outlining their doctrines; but we did discuss Goethe, and the poets, Herder and Klopstock, and of course the renowned translators of Shakespeare, Wieland, Schlegel and Tieck.

One afternoon whilst we were all together, Aunt Inez casually remarked that it might be a good idea if I could visit Germany, in view of my interest in the country. I enthusiastically accepted the idea, and to our surprise, this was immediately taken up by Barbara who said it was quite practical and she knew of family friends who had a boy of my own age with whom perhaps I could stay. No sooner had the three of us spoken, than the idea was formulated into a plan. I said I would buy a text book the following day, and Barbara said I would need to stay in the country for at least six months if I was to learn the language properly.

The following day Barbara wrote off to her friends regarding their taking in an English lodger as a family member for six months, and Aunt Inez sent off a short note to my parents. The proposition was an excellent idea, as a period abroad would give me greater time to sort out the question of my eventual career. It would fulfil all the benefits of what we now describe as a "gap year." I bought a German text book, which I immediately began to study, and I practised my pronunciation in front of Barbara, who corrected my errors, and said I was following the phonetic symbols with remarkable accuracy. A spirit of optimism and hope with regard to my future suffused the household, and all of us seemed to gain a "spring in our step," and later that day I overheard my grandmother in the kitchen exclaim to her daughter, "Anything to get the boy out of that dreadful environment!"

That evening when we were together in the sitting room, whilst Barbara was absent in the town centre attending her weekly social at an au pairs club, my grandmother began to praise Germany and German values, upon which Aunt Inez laughed out loud, exclaiming, "You're getting quite pro-German in your old age – you should watch out,!" and we all laughed together. My grandmother probably recollected that there had been an era of warmth and friendship between the two countries before the First World War, when her own husband had acted as a German interpreter in communicating with German Naval officers, and my grandfather may well have been on one of the British battleships which attended the Kiel Week Festivities in June 1914.

On the day the British departed, their German officer friends declared, "Friends today, friends tomorrow, Friends forever!" Within six weeks the bloodiest catastrophe in world history was to be launched, through a series of absurd misunderstandings, following an even more ridiculous quarrel over a terrorist incident in an obscure part of the Balkans. The fault did not lie with Germany, and in the light of contemporary research, the guilt for the criminality and military incompetence which followed, is to be cast equally on all the major European powers of the time.

During my last evening in Bath, as the four of us sat in my grandmother's living room, it was understood between us that the German visit was "on," and only final details needed to be settled. My Aunt Inez urged me to "behave well" in the country, and to always remember that as an Englishman I was representing my country, and to behave like an Englishman and inspire others to follow my example. On Friday 29th August I arrived back in London and lost no time in outlining the proposals for a stay in Germany. Quin and Syb were staying at the time, and when I began to outline the cultural importance of Germany as a European state, I received little sympathy. My father dismissed Barbara as a "German spy," whilst Uncle Quentin, who had served on the Western front in the First World War, said that a "German was only best when dead." My father recollected that a group of Germans had once visited Muswell Hill in the 1930s, and that obviously their only motive was to "spy out the land below" in preparation for the bombing of the city, upon which Uncle Quentin said that in another twenty years the Germans would be bombing Britain again, if the Americans kept pumping in this "wretched Marshall Aid."

The following day we left for a late-in-the-season week's seaside holiday at Elmer Sands. Meanwhile, I kept up a correspondence with

Aunt Inez, and on 5th September I received a post card from her saying she had seen my school friend, Richard Thomas, acting the part of Fleance in *Macbeth* at the Theatre Royal. At first my parents maintained a dumb silence with regard to my visiting Germany, but my father meanwhile became moody and constantly lost his temper over all kinds of trivial matters during our ten-day holiday.

As there was a problem with accommodation at the family with whom it was proposed I should stay, a firm offer was made by another family, with "von" in front of their name, situated in the nearby town of Neustadt, in the heart of the wine growing area. Neustadt would anyway be a far more pleasant place to stay than the smoky industrial city of Ludwigshafen. It would be a privilege to stay with a family with the title of "von," but when I tried to convey this to my father he was unimpressed. I then drew up a paper, headed, "Advantages of going to Ludwigshafen or Neustadt," and presented it to my parents.

The listed points were as follows:- "1. In England my weekly cost for existence is between £2 10s. to £3, and if I went to Germany the cost would be about a third of that, thus only £1 would be enough to keep me, plus 5 shillings for pocket money. 2. It would broaden my mind. 3. It would enable me to learn and read German literature, thus adding to my cultural assets. 4. Mere's (i.e. my mother's) monthly allowance would be the same for less work and thus would give her more spare time and less worry generally. 5. The opportunity is exceptional and I would be staying with excellent people. Thus you are worrying about paying £1 5s. a week to have an excellent education, and surely that same amount is good for having me out of the way. The only disadvantage of going to Neustadt is that you would need to pay the return fare."

In response to this pressure, my parents delivered a firm "No" to any idea of visiting Germany, and the same was communicated to my relatives in Bath. The idea was dismissed as entirely impractical. Whilst my father's motives may have been driven by an anti-German instinct, my mother's were somewhat different. Noting how susceptible I was to female charm, she anticipated I might well return with a German "Frau," or at least with some kind of romantic fixture. In a bankrupt impoverished country like Germany, an "English husband" would be a wonderful catch for any "Fräulein" with a head on her shoulders. I would find myself surrounded by pretty girls in no time – like bees around a honey pot – and I could not be trusted to resist their advances. There was little I could say in answer to these predictions, as I would welcome any such advances, and treasure any Fräulein with whom I developed a loving relationship.

On 9th I was back in London, and on 10th I received the following telegram:- "Barbara arriving Paddington two forty Thursday. Dakers," –

that is, the next day. Barbara had completed her year's stay in England, and was returning home, and arrangements had been made for her to stay overnight with us, before I would escort her to Victoria station the following morning. My parents were reluctant to receive her, but could not very well refuse such a request from close relatives, and so they expressed their mood with an offhand manner and dumb rudeness. She was to blame for all the upset in the family.

The following afternoon Barbara and I found ourselves in the sitting room discussing German music. When my father returned from the surgery after work, without acknowledging Barbara's presence, he came out with the remark that it would be preferable if I "went to live in Russia instead." These words were not intended in the sense they might be understood by the readers of this book. He was not saying, "you should get a dose of Soviet Communism to bring you to your senses," but the complete opposite. Stuck as he still was in the mindset of 1941-42, he was trying to compliment the Russians in insulting their wartime enemy.

He admired the brutality and wholesale robbery by the Russians of all technical equipment and machinery in their occupied territory, and went along with my grandfather's notion that the Western allies were "fools" in not further reducing the Western half of the country to a state of total misery and starvation. After the surrender we should have pursued a policy of systematic extermination and not been satisfied with mere surrender. In the words of my grandfather, we had repeated all the same mistakes in 1945 as in 1918. Such views, reflecting the Morgenthau Plan, were nonsense of course, since they took no cognisance of history, economics, power politics, or the social influences of human nature. I believe that my parents and grandparents had been listening to too many sermons by that ignorant cleric, the Rev. E.A. Dunn, and too many *Old Testament* Bible readings exhorting "fighting and smiting," and had had their heads turned in the process. How else is one to explain this virulent hatred?

If, on the other hand, one is to take a more generous approach, it might be appreciated that my father was 12 years old when the First World War ended, and when he awoke in the middle of the night (after what was supposedly a good dream), he cried out, "The Kaiser's abdicated, the Kaiser's abdicated!" In the Second World War he lived for six years in daily fear of having his house bombed flat, and for at least two of those years, of having his family killed as well. As he was always a highly strung man, I suppose these must be taken as exonerating circumstances in explaining if not excusing his hatred. Within the next 20 years, however, his attitude was to change. With the passing of time, he admitted there were "good and bad in all countries," and he could never have anticipated that two decades later he would have a German daughter-in-law – and from Prussian Junker stock.

As we sat in the sitting room, Barbara offered me one of her Du Maurier cigarettes, upon which my father said I should not smoke more than one cigarette a day. He was in a bad mood and went to bed at 9.30 pm, and for the hell of it, Barbara and I chain-smoked until we retired about an hour later.

The following morning I took Barbara to Victoria station, and as we travelled by bus on the top deck, she handed me a "secret letter" from Aunt Inez. It expressed her deep frustration and disappointment at my parents' unreasonable rejection of the plans we had formulated for my visit to Germany, and went on to explain my parents had always turned down every suggestion she had proposed in advancing my future. The letter ended with the request that it be destroyed as soon as read and the pieces handed to Barbara. As we sat in the train in Victoria station, Barbara reminded me of my aunt's request, and I took out the letter, tore it into small pieces, and handed the latter to her.

The only time when we were to briefly meet again was five years later, on the first occasion of my going abroad, when I toured Germany for a fortnight. By then she was married, and I spent a day in Mannheim, where she met me at the station, and took me to her home in Ludwigshafen where I dined with the married couple. My father was shocked I had written to a married woman, expecting to meet her again after such a long absence, remarking that I was entering dangerous waters and should not be surprised if her husband challenged me to a duel. "That's what they do in that country," he said. "They're very jealous of foreigners interfering with their women." That was the rubbish which he pretended to believe.

On returning home from Victoria station, in the realisation that all my hopes had been dashed, I was told that my only course was to follow the "friendly advice" of the man at the Labour Exchange, and set about getting myself a proper job. I fell into a deep depression, and what shortly transpired were those near-violent events described in chapter 20. I was thrown back into the bottomless pit from whence I had climbed and almost made my escape. I had no idea and little interest in what menial employment I would be forced to take up.

The situation was not helped by my father's sarcasm. One evening over the dinner table, he suggested it would do me good if I became a Verger, adding, "You'd look good following a procession in a black gown, carrying a staff with a silver knob. At least you'd be mixing with respectable company for the rest of your life." Surely he understood by now my disgust at churchgoing – or was this something he could never comprehend?

I felt humiliated in the realisation that with any job I accepted, I would find myself amongst people whom I despised and with whom I had little in common. I was deeply interested in literature, history, and philosophy, to a degree far transcending that of the ordinary man or woman on the Clapham omnibus, and where was I likely to find such congenial company in a commercial office? It is probable that the only congenial environment in which I could appropriately find myself at that time was Oxbridge, or possibly, the UCL with its founding and traditionally maintained more agnostic environment. The only other alternative would have been to take up the offer of a medium to long stay in Germany, where the totally new environment and the obligation to achieve fluency in a foreign language would have assured a complete break from the psychological baggage of my former life, and where I could have found myself, and developed my own personality.

I could then have returned to Britain afresh, a mature person, either settling into further education or into appropriate employment with a future. But the opportunity had been thrown away, and in their ignorance, my parents had made the wrong decision as ever – motivated as they were by their package of foolish prejudices. Instead, what now was to be my fate? Eventually, I refused to attend any more interviews, until my parents dragged me – almost physically, to places for prospective employment.

The first occasion on which this happened was when my father took me to the commercial artists, T.G. Williams Ltd., of 73 Hatton Garden, E.C.1. Before we left, he obliged me to make up a portfolio of my artwork which he carried under his arm. When we arrived at the firm, we were spoken to through a hatch in a window, by the MD, as we stood in a small entrance. My father opened the portfolio and began laying out the paintings on a counter by the hatch. I could see that the director of the company was not overly impressed, but my father began selling my artistic abilities to my acute embarrassment. What did he know about art? I had a low opinion of my technical skill as a draughtsman, and I found this presentation of my third rate work deeply shaming. And besides, only two months earlier I had been told by this man there was no future in art. What, therefore, was he doing now? My father's persuasion, however, must have been effective, for the outcome was that I was told to come in and start work next Monday at 9.0 am. And everything had been discussed and concluded without my even needing to open my mouth. The job interview had been performed by proxy.

Dutifully, I began work on Monday 15th September 1952. The previous evening I had been given ten shillings for fares and food to last the week. Dreading the day ahead, I left the house at five past eight, and as I sat in the tube from Highgate, I felt intensely disagreeable, and I must have worn an especially nasty expression, for I was stared at with disapproval, and as a woman got up to leave at one of the stations, she turned to me with the sardonic remark, "I can see you're a perfect gentleman!" On arriving at Hatton Garden, I had forgotten where the company was situated, and so I walked up and down the street several times, and was 15 minutes late. The standard working day was from 8.30 am to 6.0 pm, but as a trainee I was only expected to work from 9.0 am to 5.0 pm. I handed in my insurance card to the cashier and one of the directors, Mr. A.E. Ilett, and within minutes I had begun work. I found myself washing endless jars and palettes. I felt profoundly humiliated. What had I done to deserve this punishment,? I asked myself.

At five past ten I was asked to deliver a packet to a nearby firm of engravers situated in the *Daily Worker* building. I left the block and began searching for my destination. Soon I was lost. When I stopped a passer-by and asked for the *Daily Worker* building, he looked at me suspiciously and passed on. Clearly he had labelled me a Communist to whom he would not stoop to give an answer. I then asked a policeman, who deigned not even to look at me, whilst saying I was in the wrong end of the street. He, too, thought I was a "political undesirable." I've had enough of this for one morning, I thought to myself, I'm going to take a break, and I walked into a Lyons Tea House and had a coffee and cake. I sat there for an hour or more, watching the world go by, as patrons came and went. Eventually, I decided to take another stab at delivering the packet. This done, I had to make my way back to T.G. Williams Ltd., but again I was lost, and then encountered a man in the street, who with a grin on his face, said the police were looking for me.

At last I found my way back to the firm, and was immediately bombarded by the four directors, who asked where the "hell" I had been and what had happened. I calmly replied that as I had left at the back of the building instead of the front, I had become disoriented and lost my way. They accepted the explanation, and my immediate boss went into a sulk, and left me idle and alone sitting on a chair. At 1.15 pm I went to the Express Restaurant for lunch, sitting opposite two Germans, and on returning to the firm, I was questioned by the manager as to whether I had heard of James Walker watches, and the names of other manufacturers for whom they designed packaging material, and by my answers, he could see I had little interest in commercial art.

I was then shown the Grant projector in action, and invited to look through one of their catalogues. Later, I made tea for the artists and was congratulated on the "very good cuppa" I had brewed. I was asked if I always wore glasses, and they then discovered I had not even registered in my mind the name of the firm I was supposedly working for. The day ended with looking at different styles of lettering, having read an appropriate chapter in a book on commercial art. I left at 5.0 pm, feeling bad-tempered and with a splitting headache, and this was worsened by a 2 ½ hour journey home.

During the following days I was engaged in lettering or painting in the same, including the following phrases: "The Coronation," "Gas Company," "Xenophon and Zeno," "Oil and electricity," "Water Jar," and, "The Vines." On one day I lunched at Gamages for 3/11d., on another at the Tavistock for 2/8d., both beyond my means, and I sought out cheaper places to eat but with little success. As we sat bent over our work one morning, the manager said, "You know, you can earn a lot of money through commercial art," but I was not impressed by this intended encouragement.

During the second week I must have been more relaxed, for I was drawn into more general conversation, and asked to bring in my tempera painting of King Lear. When I did this, colleagues crowded around, and one exclaimed, "This is futuristic stuff," and they began to laugh, but I did not take offence, for I appreciated that the narrow perspective of a commercial artist to his trade was necessarily quite different from the layman's approach to art in general. The discussion then turned to Picasso and other contemporary artists who were dismissed as "rubbish," and again, as my views on art were not in alignment with accepted trends, I did not find this offensive, and so I said nothing.

Nonetheless, despite this relaxation, I was not making progress, and engaged in horseplay, and placed a beetle in the tea of one of the younger members of the team. I followed instructions with obedience, and most the time was drawing or painting to order, but my mind was elsewhere. It was not that I despised the people I was with, it was simply we had nothing in common. They were understanding, and helped me as best they could, and tried to integrate me into the company, but I was unresponsive. They were conscientious hard-working people, employed in a vital industry in supporting Britain's productive manufacturing base, and I must have tested their patience to its limits.

In retrospect I am surprised I was not fired on the first day. That was a time when employment protection was almost non-existent, and had I behaved in such a way towards the close of the 20th century, I am sure I would have been fired justifiably much sooner, despite all the Employment Protection Acts. The difference, of course, was that the 1950s was an era of under-employment, and all labour skills were highly valued, whilst in today's world it is not uncommon for 200 people to be chasing a single low-status job. When Gavin's school friend, Seaton, visited the house, I regaled them both with mocking impersonations of my work colleagues, and had them in stitches of laughter.

On the Saturday following my second week, my father received the following letter, dated September 26th:- "Dear Mr. Corfe. – I am very sorry to inform you that in our opinion it would not be wise to continue training your son in commercial Art. From our own long experience and knowledge we think that he would not make a success at this trade and would be wasting his time and ours to keep him any longer. We should therefore like him to terminate his trial with us next week-end October 3rd and suggest that he tries an alternative trade. If you wish for further information regarding same we shall be glad to speak to you regarding it. – Yours faithfully, T.G. Williams Artists Ltd., J. Cook, Secretary." I was relieved at the receipt of this letter, and my last week with the company was the least unpleasant of the three.

With the prospect of my leaving colleagues became more sympathetic and friendly – even familiar in trying to tease out my inner thoughts and ideas for the future. When it was revealed that I did not "mix with girls" the manager seemed stunned, and shaking his head, exclaimed that that "was a very bad situation." During the lunch hours I visited nearby second hand bookshops, and attended open air meetings at Lincoln's Inn Fields, contenting myself with bars of chocolate instead of 3-course meals. On Tuesday 30th September I attended a talk on "Nature and Nurture," standing beside a Divorce Court Judge who had Chambers within the Inner Temple, with whom I chatted.

As a consequence I was late back at the studio, not arriving there until 2.20 pm. On the following day I attended a talk by a Catholic speaker, who threatened to call the police in ejecting a heckler from the crowd. The heckler, who was a Quaker, became violent and pushed the Catholic off his platform, and began haranguing the crowd on the evils of the Vatican, upon which he in turn was removed by the police, and the Catholic resumed his place. He then embarked on a life-confession, saying he had once been a Fascist until finally reclaimed by Christ. On the following day there was no speaker at Lincoln's Inn Fields, but some years later, in the second half of the 50s, I was to spend almost every lunch hour listening to the speakers at Lincoln's Inn, and afterwards, a group of us, mostly middle-aged or elderly men, and a student or two from the nearby LSE, would adjourn to a Lyons Restaurant and continue our discussion for another hour or two.

On returning to work I spent the afternoon sweeping the office and studio, having sprayed the floor with water to prevent flying dust. On the last day, shortly before 5.0 o'clock, Mr. J. Cook gave me my week's wages, and that for the following week also, in lieu of a fortnight's notice, and I shook hands amicably with all the staff. Then Mr. Curtis, the manager, gave me the following parting advice, saying, "Before you get another job, see you get some good adolescent interests like sport and women." This was good advice, but I would choose to forego the "sport."

The second occasion on which I was taken by my parents to a place of prospective employment occurred on Monday 20th October, some 2 ½ weeks after leaving T.G. Williams. An appointment had been arranged for me to attend the West End Juvenile Employment Bureau, and my mother was to take me there. At breakfast that day my father was in a foul mood, saying I was to take the first job I was offered, irrespective of whether I wanted it or not. The previous two weeks had been profoundly depressing, and my mood veered between the suicidal and murderous with every day that passed. On one day I had contemplated poisoning the entire family by putting eye drops from the medicine cabinet into a cake, but I was frustrated in my plan when my mother put the cake into the oven before I had had an opportunity to pour liquid into the mixture.

On other days I was to pull all the curtains in the house, and wander around with a Zulu club, in readiness for beating its inhabitants to death. No one seemed to remark on this eccentric behaviour, and no one even seemed to sense I was in a violent mood. My mother casually remarked that the curtains need not be pulled until darkness came, but that was all. The calm and sense of normality experienced by everyone except myself infuriated me all the more. On several occasions I found myself standing behind my mother when she bent down over some task, and I could have dashed her brains out with a single blow of the club, but every time I was overcome by cowardice.

After some days, she casually remarked, "Why are you walking around with that? You don't need a walking stick – there's nothing wrong with your legs." A walking stick indeed! What insult was that? Was she so ignorant she could not recognise I was carrying a deadly military weapon of an African tribe? Some time later – I do not know how long, my father was to keep this club constantly by his bedside, almost until the day of his death. I do not know what originally drew him to do this, but it became a kind of secret joke, or subject of laughter between we three brothers, that he had a paranoid fear of burglars, and that he needed to keep this weapon in readiness for a break-in.

The highlight event (if it can be described as such) in the several weeks leading up to the 20th October, was the visit of Dr. Fisher, Archbishop of Canterbury to St. James's Church on 12th October. It had not been my intention to attend this event, but there was such a fuss about the forthcoming visit, that my curiosity got the better of me, and I decided to go along. My father, who as a sidesman, was somehow involved in organising the event, said that as I had not already obtained a ticket, I would need to queue early outside the church, as this was a ticket only event. I had been standing since 5.30 pm for half an hour in the rain, when suddenly the Browns and Uncle Maurice arrived all the way from Totteridge, and as they said they had a spare ticket, they took me with them into the church.

As the seats were numbered, I was separated from my relatives and placed between two ugly girls, with a "luscious blonde" seated in view not far away. Four people in the pew in front of me were removed from their places by sidesmen after an irate exchange, as their tickets were not in order, and another group was directed there instead. The Archbishop's sermon was entitled the Great Vocation, and he began by saying he was breaking the rule in making a parochial visit, and turning towards the Rev. E.A. Dunn, he added, "but this is a rather personal visit." On returning home my father was furious I had been given a ticket by other members of the family who knew nothing about my "obstreperous" behaviour and "disloyalty to the family," and that I should now concentrate my efforts on getting into the Army at 17 ½. When I then began watching a TV play about Germany, he switched it off, and sent me to bed at 9.0 o'clock.

When my mother and I sat before the adviser at the West End Juvenile Employment Bureau, on the afternoon of 20th October, I became irritated when she began to talk me down, by expatiating on my inexperience and lack of qualifications. Everything she said was negative. What was to be achieved by that? Nonetheless, I was identified for a job which was thought might suit me. This was as a clerk at a solicitors' office at 2 Old Burlington Street, just at the back of the Royal Academy. An interview was arranged immediately, and we were sent off to the address. On arrival, I pleaded with my mother that she remain outside the building, as I knew that anything she said would be counterproductive.

She assented to this suggestion, and began loitering on the opposite pavement, and was lucky not to be beaten up during my absence, for she was trespassing on the exclusive patch of a particularly elegant prostitute in her mid-thirties. She was saved from such a fate, however, by the presence of mind of the Commissionaire at the solicitors, who kindly invited her to sit down on a chair inside the building. Moments before I had been led up a broad staircase, into a large consulting room of the Managing Partner, Mr. Young, of the firm, Young, Jackson, Beard & King (sols.) Commissioners for Oaths.

CHAPTER 23
I enter the Legal World

"Reason is the life of the law; nay, the Common law itself
is nothing but reason ... The Law, which is perfection of
reason."

Sir Edward Coke, *Institutes*, Pt. 1

An upstairs downstairs world of gossip – The varied staff – A question of class
consciousness – How a legal mindset was to be of benefit in the future – My interest
in jurisprudence

In this huge high-ceilinged room, its walls lined with ancient musty-smelling leather bound Statutes, and Halsbury's Laws of England, and a threadbare Turkish carpet beneath my feet, I found myself seated before a spacious desk, on the other side of which sat a lively curiously sandy-haired man of uncertain age with gold-framed spectacles. He wore a pin-striped suit, had elegant gestures, and during that first interview conveyed the impression of being a man with perfect manners. This was a world in which I had never found myself before, but at once I sensed there was something congenial in the legal environment.

He outlined what the job involved, explaining that the work was very basic, filing, carrying trays of letters to and fro, taking documents to be stamped for Duty at the Registry Office, and even carrying cups of tea up to the partners, their associates and secretaries. It was work not really matching my aspirations and abilities. He was reluctant to employ me. It was really suited to a Secondary Modern boy with minimal qualifications, and besides, the firm did not really have an opening for someone hoping to be an Articled Clerk. I replied I was still interested in the position and that the post would give me some perspective of the legal profession.

He asked my age, and then concluded I must only be looking for something to fill in the 15 months or so before I was called up for National Service. He pondered silently for a few moments, and then agreed to take me on, adding that in due course another firm might be found to take me on as an Articled Clerk. I happily agreed to this possibility. He said it might be useful if I went to typing school, but that I should forget it as soon as I qualified so as to guard against being "used" as a typist. He outlined the terms of employment: £3. 0s. 0d. a week; hours 10.0 am to 5.30 pm, and alternate Saturdays until 1.0 pm; and a fortnight's paid holiday per year.

Satisfied with the arrangement, I left the room and was surprised to encounter my mother sitting downstairs, and we went off in an optimistic mood to a Lyons Corner House and a bun and coffee. I spoke with some brightness about the prospects of a legal career, and when we left the restaurant, my mother went home, whilst I went to Foyles and browsed around the bookshop. I could not have anticipated that I was about to enter an "upstairs downstairs" world, and that I was to be in the "downstairs." It was to be a world of foul language and boredom, of long periods of idleness, and of petty and often malicious gossip about the partners on the upper floors. The partners, meanwhile, were quite oblivious to the fact of how their lives and interests, their quirks, and most personal daily habits, were closely scrutinised almost every hour or minute of the day.

The outer office or post room, where the switchboard was situated, festered with distracting gossip, and this was supplied by down at heel clerks from the upper floors, with a chip on their shoulder or a score to settle. The clients who visited the office fared even worse, for whilst on the one hand, they were always received with civility and polite smiles, their personalities, their faults, their eccentricity, or their lunatic behaviour, was analysed, discussed, and laughed about on every floor of the building. In a profession which more than any other marked its correspondence, "Strictly Private and Confidential," nothing was confidential, and even the tea boy came to know the most sordid or secret details of the regulars who stepped across the threshold of Young, Jackson, Beard & King.

On the following Monday, 27th October, I began my "legal career" as a solicitors' dog-body, arriving at their offices in good time at ten to ten. My immediate boss was the immaculately uniformed Sergeant-Major Short of the Corps of Commissionaires. His name belied the reality, for he was a huge man, tall and heavily built, elderly, sometimes moody and depressed, but basically good-natured and humane. As I was to realise shortly after entering the Army, the colourful patch sewn onto his lower sleeve, indicated that he had once been a Warrant Officer 1st class, or a Regimental Sergeant-Major.

He was the King of the switchboard, and the first thing I learned was how to operate it, and as to who and who not to put through to the partners, and as to the personal quirks of the latter as to whom they *never* wished to speak to. S-M Short sat in a large leather dilapidated swivel armchair in front of a huge table sufficient to hold the day's post, with the switchboard behind him. I sat at another large table nearby with an ancient typewriter. This outer office was a gloomy place which always needed artificial lighting, for the window looked out onto a small closed courtyard beneath a five storey building. S-M Short was partly deaf and in the evening of his life, but sometimes he became lively, and came out with tales about the wonderful days of his service in India many years before.

As one of my main tasks would be to collect letters from the secretaries for signing by the partners or articled clerks, and then later collect them from the latter for folding, inserting into envelopes, and sticking on stamps in the outer office or post room, I needed to be introduced to all the 25 or so staff in the building. This task was undertaken by the young articled clerk, Mr. Clarke, who shared an office with others on the 4th floor.

On the ground floor, in front of the outer office, facing the street, was the waiting room which also doubled as the office of the articled clerk, Mr. E.A. Andrews. He was an elderly diminutive man with a large bald head and red face, who worked part time. He had come from humble beginnings in the East End of London, and had worked for the company since the start of the century. He lived on his nerves, and although he was always good-humoured and pleasant to colleagues, he swore like a trooper over clients who were "mad," "bad," or, "insufferable," and he often had us in fits of laughter when he broke out into a torrent of foul language. He chose to type his own letters on his ancient Oliver typewriter and as with several other old hands in the firm, his index fingers were deformed out of joint after decades of two-finger typing. As a door connected his office with the post room, he was often in the latter, when he would gossip or give instructions that some time-wasting "bloody" client or other on the phone should not be put through to him.

He had done service in the First World War, and "gone over the top," saying they were so heavily drugged, "they didn't know what they were doing." All he could remember is that they charged forward regardless as shells whistled past them, both in front and behind, in a smoke-filled environment. No one could see where they were going, nor hope to identify the enemy.

If Mr. E.A. Andrews could be described as originating from a working class background, he had a son, Mr. D.C. Andrews, who was a qualified solicitor and partner of the firm. But if Mr. D.C. Andrews was middle class in his manners and propriety – and he was – his qualifications as a fully-fledged solicitor did not mean he was a social equal of the two leading partners, Mr. Young or Mr. Adams. Just as light years of social differences seemed to exist between father and son, so the go-ahead successful younger man, remained very much the social inferior of his two colleagues of approximately the same age. Mr. D.C. Andrews gave the impression of being a lonely man in the partnership. He was often moody or depressed, or even sometimes bad-tempered with secretaries or underling clerks. He handled the clients with "new money," such as Sam Leapman with his chain of mens' outfitters throughout London and the provinces, or with those people who happened to walk off the street, whilst those clients whose families had been connected with the firm for generations were reserved for the more senior partners.

Mr. Young and Mr. Adams may be described as belonging to the lower-upper classes, in that they were descended from the younger branches of the nobility, and on the walls of their offices hung prints of their 17th or 18th century ancestors. These were people who may have cherished their coats of arms, but when it came to titles, they could never hope to inherit anything more grand than, "The Mr. Honourable this," or, "The Mrs. Honourable that." Such is the limiting tendency of the English law of primogeniture, which if it has helped preserve the mystique and the aristocratic coin of privilege in Britain through exclusivity; its absence on the Continent has debased the coin of all noble titles through the quantity of their number, so that a Count or a Duke – or even a Prince or Princess – is little distinguishable from the common lot of humanity.

What distinguished Messrs Young and Adams from the rest of the staff was their studied aloofness and air of social superiority, a certain freedom of spirit, and their generous and constant expenditure on leisure pursuits. "They go out every night to the theatre, or a boxing match, or a ball," exclaimed S-M Short in a disapproving tone on one occasion. "They never stay at home. We're always ordering tickets for something or other for them."

There was one other room of significance on the ground floor, and that was at the back of the building, and this was the office of the senior partner, Mr. Jenkins, who rarely visited the firm. He had qualified as a solicitor before the close of the 19th century and was already in his nineties. During my 15 months with the company, he never visited the office more than three or four times, and he would always notify his intention in advance, when there would be a great scurrying and panic in preparation for his presence. Particular papers, documents, or accounts had to be prepared and piled on his desk, and a coal fire had to be lit in advance. As I never came to see him physically, he always remained for me a ghostly figure. His custom was to arrive by taxi, and S-M Short would rush out into the street, and lending his arm, would assist the elderly man into the safety of his inner sanctum.

The closest I came to know him was by the sound of his footsteps shuffling along the stone floor of the passageway outside. No one was allowed to disturb him during his three of four hours at his desk – not even to bring him a cup of tea. After his work was done, he departed as mysteriously as he had arrived, a taxi having been called in advance. His room was the gloomiest office I have ever seen. It was the largest room in the building, the walls painted a dark green, and as there was no window, the place was lit by a skylight over the desk, and on the latter I remember a lamp with a green shade. The fact that the room was unused and empty for the greater part of the time may have endued it with a tomb-like atmosphere. It had never been decorated since Queen Victoria sat on the throne, and since there was a general ruling it was out of bounds, it was regarded rather in the light of a sacred chamber hidden in the recesses of an ancient Egyptian temple.

On the first floor was situated Mr. Young's office (already described), and nearby a rather smaller room, being the office of Mr. Adams. On a higher mezzanine floor was the cramped typing office of the longest serving secretary, Miss Arberry. She had already worked for the company 33 years, and was known for her nervous disposition and general incompetence, and was often in some kind of tizzy and petty trouble with the senior partners. As with many women of her age at that time, she suffered from severe stomach pains – supposedly indigestion – for which she had her prescribed bottles of medicine. She had many stories to tell about the partners and others who had worked for the firm over the years.

On the next floor, Mr. D.C. Andrews had a dingy office overlooking the bleak view at the back of the building. In an adjacent room three secretaries sat over their noisy typewriters, and often they were disagreeable if they felt under pressure. On the floor above them was the Cashier's department. This room was shared by three men: Mr. Legge, an articled clerk in his forties, and a great purveyor of juicy gossip; Mr. Clarke, who despite his young looks had already been married nine years; and the bumbling middle-aged Mr. Pope, the firm's cashier. Mr. Pope, a thin bespectacled man with thinning hair, was one of those people who was always cheerful in his misery, that is, he customarily expressed the deepest pessimism on all manner of matters with a cheerful countenance and a joke.

Mr. Young referred to him as an "incompetent old fool" – and even addressed him in such terms. I was to have almost daily contact with Mr. Pope, as he needed to give me cash advances for bus fares to the Inns of Court in delivering documents or to Somerset House for searches into births, marriages, or deaths, or to the Registry Office or elsewhere for the stamping of deeds. He had a kindly attitude towards me, and would ask from time to time, "Do you have a girl friend, Corfe?" and to my negative reply, he would respond, "The girls will get you, Corfe, the girls will get you in the end! You watch out!" as if this was the most dreadful fate which could befall a man. This seemed to suggest he must have had a dreadful home-life as a hen-pecked husband.

On the top floor was situated Mr. Peverett, an articled clerk who had worked for the firm since the start of the century. He typed his own letters and had achieved his own deformed index fingers over the years, but he did have an elderly female assistant. He was a lively man despite his age, full of good humour and interesting stories about his early years at the firm. When he was first employed he had to keep fires lit in every room in the building, but his main task was to open the carriage doors of clients as they arrived at the office. "You should have seen the people who passed through the doors in those days," he said impressively. "Dukes and duchesses by the dozen! You don't get that class of people any more – just stuck up snobs with 'Honourable' fixed to the front of their names. This firm's seen better days, I can tell you. There was money around in those days, but not any more. When I started out, I made more money from the tips of clients as I helped them out of their hansom cabs than I did from my salary."

Adjacent to Mr. Peverett's office was a small room occupied by a little man called Mr. Salmon. No one knew exactly what he did – he was a kind of legal jack-of-all-trades, and he attended to his own correspondence. He tended to be secretive and reclusive, but when Mr. Pope was off sick, he took over the Cashier's job. He had a friendly cheery manner, but he remained a bit of a mystery. "Whatever he does, he must make money," explained S-M short in a discreet undertone. "He's Jewish, and they don't work for nothing!"

Whilst Mr. Clarke introduced me to all the staff in the morning, in the afternoon Mr. Young showed me the strong room in the basement of the building. Here all the deeds were kept, either in strong boxes or on shelves, in a dusty poorly lit area, and I was to spend many hours over the next 15 months in this underworld, searching for documents which had never been touched by the hand of man for decades or even generations. Once, at the bottom of one of the several boxes of the Du Pré family (a leading client of the firm) I discovered a complete suit of chain mail, and if it was not for the rust and dirt I would have tried it on – despite its great weight. Was it really necessary for Knights to be weighed down by so much steel?

On the following day, a strange American couple arrived, and after I placed them in the waiting room there were loud voices and they began to quarrel violently. Minutes later I took them to see Mr. Young, and subsequently I learned they had taken an Oath several days earlier, and failed to understand the meaning of this. They were the first of many extraordinary people I was to encounter. Later that day I developed stomach pains after licking and sealing hundreds of envelopes and affixing postage stamps. The last hour of the day was always hectic in getting the post out on time, and henceforward I was only to use a wetted porcelain roller for adhesive purposes. Several times a week there were registered letters to be despatched, and these called for sealing wax and the use of the firm's official seal in pressing the hot wax onto the backs of the envelopes.

On the third day I took a casket of priceless jewels to Hemmings at 28 Conduit Street, and it was impressed upon me that this was an especially important errand only entrusted to someone of the highest integrity, but for much of the day I was already becoming bored as there was little to do for most of the time. Mr. Peverett suggested I should begin to practice typewriting, and I embarked on this with keenness, whilst the Sergeant-Major looked on jealously, mumbling under his breath that it should not be the task of men to type.

Shortly thereafter I investigated the possibility of Touch Typing classes, as I did not want to end up with deformed index fingers. I signed up for such a course held at the Tollington Secondary school in Muswell Hill. At first we practised finger exercises on paper cards, and followed dictation, first with sight and then blindfolded. Later we progressed in actually using typewriters, and very soon I became quite proficient. I have always wondered why touch typing is not taught today, when it is important for far many more people than earlier because of computer use, and because blind typing with the use of ten fingers is much faster than two fingers can ever be.

Classes were twice weekly, and on one occasion the school's headmaster paid us a visit, and somehow he got onto the topic of psychology. He was a bespectacled dyspeptic man and told us a story about an especially bright but problematic pupil who was sent to a psychologist and diagnosed as mentally ill, and then promptly died of a brain tumour six months later. He then indulged himself in a rant against psychology, saying that all psychologists should be strung up by their necks in the national interest. At the time his attitude struck me as a piece of typical *Muswell Hill twisted logic*, and it transpired that he belonged to the same Rotary club as my father.

Later in the week, one afternoon, I was taken by Mr. Young to the Inns of Court, the Land Registry office, and to a Judge in Chambers with regard to a forthcoming court case. He adopted a friendly and lively manner, trying to engage me in small talk – but I was not used to the civilised custom of small talk – and in my inexperience and naivety, I began to feel grossly inadequate and then ridiculous. Eventually there was little he could say, and I felt ever-more embarrassed with every lame response I attempted. What did he think of me? I knew I had made an appalling impression, and by the time we returned to the office, I felt deeply humiliated. I knew he had endeavoured his best to strike up an easy-going or friendly relationship. He was a good and well-intended man, but I saw none of this and because of the intensity of my feelings at the time, I began to form an intense dislike.

The blame, of course, lay entirely in my own inadequacy. On re-entering the building, I went into the post room, whilst he leaped up the stairs, three at a time, and into his office. As soon as I heard the door close behind him, I heard a peel of laughter, and assuming that I was the object of his ridicule, my dislike was turning into hatred. The explanation which I found at the time was that all this was the upshot of class differences. I had never found myself in such a situation before. If I stemmed from the upper-middle class, then he originated from the lower-upper class, and there was a mighty gulf which separated us from our perspectives of the world. Both of us were proud of our class distinctions as otherwise the *awareness* of these differences would never have occurred.

Such class differences did really exist. They were manifested through the free or extravagant expenditure of the lower-upper class, whilst the middle classes concentrated on saving and investing, and only expended to the extent of maintaining their status or keeping up appearances. My father understood this when he criticised the Browns for "living above their status." However, the tectonic plates of the class system were about to shift, and all such values would soon be discarded throughout all sectors of society with the rise of the new consumerism. But such class resentment as I had at that time need never have been manifested in such intensity if it was not for the inadequacy of my own personality – and such feelings were most un-English.

Etiquette and manners in Britain had smoothed the path for an easy relationship between all the classes, but these were qualities I lacked. I had neither tact nor diplomacy. The only quality or value I understood was the expression of *candid truth*, and this was poison to anyone who hoped to progress in society or freely enjoy the benefits of an open world. My feelings were un-English because hatred between the middle and upper classes was something unknown in England. Such feelings had only existed in Continental Europe – most notably in France and Germany, during the 18th and first half of the 19th centuries, which had given rise to revolutions and the toppling of regimes. It was only with the gradual emergence of 19th century nationalism in the second half of that century that conflict between the middle and upper classes diminished to insignificance. Nonetheless, these were my feelings at the time, generated by my own narrow background and ignorance of life. At the same time I began to form a slightly lesser dislike for Mr. Adams.

Some days later, on Friday 31st October, whilst collecting the out-tray of signed letters in Mr. Young's office – and I was only in his room for several seconds – he was in conversation with Mr. Adams, and I overheard the first say, "I think he's a fool," and the other answered, "I don't think he's that," and Mr. Young said, "But it shocks me." Although the two men showed no embarrassment over my fleeting presence, instinctively I felt that once again I was the subject of their discussion.

On that day I also received my first pay slip for £2 16s. 7d., 3/5d. being deducted for tax and insurance. My total savings were now £4 5s. 7d.

The free tongue and mocking humour of Mr. Young, irrespective of whether it was aimed at me or others, became increasingly unsettling, for I was made to feel all the more vulnerable, and realised the need to guard my every word and gesture. When in his office, he had few inhibitions of speech in the presence of subordinates, as if the latter were deaf to anything he said. I was constantly in and out of his room (as well as that of the other partners), fetching or delivering mail, and during the most fleeting visit it was impossible not to overhear what was said. Once, whilst in the presence of Mr. Adams, he exclaimed, "But really, didn't you notice the way he was glancing at her across the table last night?" – "No, I didn't," responded his partner. – "He wouldn't even speak with her all the evening. Mind you, I think he's quite a decent chap and all that."

On another occasion he was on the phone, and I caught the words: "And it was gone half past twelve at night, and I was standing by the window in my pyjamas, shouting to him, but he wouldn't answer," and he followed this anecdote with a burst of laughter. These were men who enjoyed life to the full. They were good, confident, free, natural, and easy, without fears or complexes, and I envied – even hated them for their happiness. My self-destroying envy was similar to that of the Arch Fiend, as he secretly viewed the happiness of Adam and Eve in Paradise before planning their destruction, as so vividly described by the genius of Milton in his psychologically penetrating political epic. My home environment, with its oppressive religious background, had been so appalling that I had never known before that such freedom and joy was humanly possible in the real world. I had only sensed such feelings and behaviour through the world of fiction which at least served some purpose in widening my world horizon.

Early one morning the following week, as S-M Short and I sat idly in the outer office, we heard footsteps slowly descending the staircase in the hallway. "That's Mr. Adams on his way to the toilet," explained the Sergeant-Major in an undertone. (There was a ground floor toilet just outside Mr. Jenkins' office.) "He'll be sitting there for the next half hour, so there's no sense in putting any calls through to him. It's the same every day. I don't know how a man can put up with such constipation!" Nothing went unobserved. Later in the day on collecting mail from his office, I caught him on the phone putting money on a horse. When I remarked on this to my work colleague, he replied that Mr. Adams was addicted to the turf, and that sometimes he was asked to go outside and pay money to a bookie.

As so much of my work entailed delivering and collecting documents from barristers' Chambers, within the next few months I was to know every nook and cranny of Gray's Inn, Lincoln's Inn, and the Temple, and to absorb the spirit and physical environment of the legal world. I was also a frequent visitor to Bush House, when I often carried huge amounts of cash for the stamping of duty on deeds. Within my first fortnight at the firm I asked Mr. Young to recommend an introductory text on English law. He had to think for a while, and then he recommended W.M. Geldart's classic, *Elements of English Law*, published in the Home University Library, and I bought, read, and absorbed this with interest. Soon after, I obtained and read Philip S. James's, *Introduction to English Law*, published by Butterworth. When Mr. Young saw me with the second book, he said he had known F.S. James of the Inner Temple at College, and that he was a "very dull man," and that probably his book was dull as well.

These books in conjunction with talking with colleagues, and listening to gossip, and observing what went on in the office, was to give me a sound understanding of the law, and what comprised the law and what did not. I quickly learned to see through all the myths and common misapprehensions which ordinary people had concerning the operations of the law, and to view the world from a legal perspective. The law was not about right and wrong *per se*, and even less was it about morality. Those ordinary mortals who went through life imagining the law as these things fell into all kinds of booby-traps in their innocence as soon as they became embroiled in a legal situation.

The law is essentially a game or a puzzle which has to be played out according to a complex set of rules. It is set down in *written* language which has to be referred to, but even that written language is subject to differing interpretations, and in the right circumstances the clever lawyer may even succeed surprisingly in turning established law upside down. To enjoy the use of the law one must enjoy the use of language. In later life my experience and limited knowledge of the law was put to useful practice on several occasions – and with no cost to myself.

Many years later as the UK director of a freight forwarding and shipping container enterprise, wholly owned by a German company, the latter over-expanded and was bankrupted overnight. When chaos ensued in a dozen countries, I seized the initiative as best I could in salvaging the remains of the UK operation. I was sued by a major trading organisation, but unwilling to pay a penny in legal fees. Fortunately, I knew how to draw on Statutes and other legal books, and I prepared a lengthy legal defence based on an array of differing points. My first point was based on a clause which I interpreted as having an opposite meaning to what was originally intended.

When I visited the Judge in Chambers, who was to try the case, first I charmed him to be sympathetic to my case as a David standing up to a Goliath, and then I presented my argument. He understood the meaning at once and accepted my interpretation. When the case came to court I was confronted by two prosecution barristers, and there followed two hours for the presentation and initial discussion. When it then came to consider the first point of my defence, the Judge gave his interpretation of the clause, and the case immediately collapsed with all costs to the prosecution, and to the disgrace of the aggrieved corporation. I was disappointed at being denied the opportunity to present the other points in my arsenal to the open court, as I felt them to be equally convincing. Even if I had lost the case, I would not have been personally out of pocket, as I was covered by limited liability and my share ownership was negligible, but I enjoyed the legal challenge and the game of law.

Despite any untoward personal misfortunes I may have felt during my time at Young, Jackson, Beard & King, I am nonetheless indebted to them in that I have never need fear the circumlocutions or costs of the law. In later life I was to become deeply interested in jurisprudence, or the philosophy of the law, rather than in the law as it stood, for the former entails an essential study of the social sciences for anyone seriously intent on achieving a better society for humankind worldwide. But jurisprudence comprises a realm of knowledge for which practising lawyers have little time or inclination unless they happen to be steered towards the world of politics. As Leslie Stephen observed more than a century ago, "English barristers and law students were serenely indifferent to the 'philosophy of law.' They had quite enough to do in acquiring familiarity with the technicalities of English practice." [*]

CHAPTER 24
My Life in the West End

"The only really educated men are self-educated."

Jesse Lee Bennett, *Culture & A Liberal Education*

My continuing literary efforts – Theatre going – A Philosophy course – Strange visitors to the office – The Sergeant-Major loses his job – The arrival of Mr. Dawes – The Coronation – Love for a waitress

During these 15 months leading up to January 1954, I remained an omnivorous reader, but mostly books confined to political philosophy, or the theatre and theatre production. I spent much

---

[*] Leslie Stephen, *The English Utilitarians*, Duckworth & Co., 1900, Vol. III, p. 318.

time reading in the outer office, which was looked upon with askance by the Sergeant-Major and other colleagues, but was nonetheless tolerated, firstly, because it was more acceptable than doing nothing, and secondly, because the books I tended to read were regarded as educational and hence beneficial to my future. I was fortunate in being surrounded by people who had some consideration for my welfare.

My first priority naturally remained producing an acceptable play for the West End theatre, although my feelings for Patricia Dainton began to wax and wane. I was now uncertain as to what my purpose was in wanting to be a dramatist. If Patricia Dainton could not be a wife, then perhaps she could be a friend. I once dreamed of reading an article by the journalist, Godfrey Winn, in *The Woman's Own*, that Patricia Dainton was unloved by her husband, and my hopes rose, only to be dashed on awakening to the real world. I wrote four plays in this period following *The Fatal Conscience*. They were, *No Funeral!*, a farce, 1952, *The Capitalist Rivalry*, a detective thriller, 1952, and finally, *The Ardent Suitors*, 1953.

When Hugh Richardson learned I had entered a solicitors' office, he commiserated rather than congratulated me, saying he had studied law at Cambridge but subsequently found the profession most uncongenial to his temperament. I badgered him constantly with phone calls, but rather than feeling gratitude at his endless patience, diary entries record annoyance at being asked to phone back at some later date. I phoned him at both the office and at home, and eventually his wife explained he was no longer living at that address, and she gave me another number which was the home of his mother in Lancaster Gate. It seemed that his life, too, was being thrown into some kind of turmoil through the possibility of separation or divorce, but I betrayed no sympathy – possibly, because his situation was none of my business, and I was too absorbed with my own interests and anxieties.

On Thursday nights I regularly visited the West End theatre to see a play. After work I went to Cadburys in Regent Street when I invariably supped on hot chocolate, an assortment of chocolate biscuits, and a chocolate ice cream with hot chocolate sauce, all beautifully served on fine crockery with heavy silver plated cutlery, by waitresses in traditional uniform. Apart from the food itself none of these serving style luxuries are available today – or what approaches them is merely a pastiche or poor imitation of what really existed in an earlier epoch.

On 12th March 1953 I saw one of the greatest dramatic performances of my life at the Arts Theatre, with Wilfred Lawson and Beatrix Lehman in Strindberg's, *The Father*. I found this a profoundly moving drama of the quarrel and rising hatred between the army Captain and his wife as to their daughter's education, and the ingenuity and evil of the wife in driving her husband mad. I found the final scene, when the wife and the father's mother gently coax the Captain into a straitjacket which they secure, truly horrific.

This was human nature in the raw, bereft of all the artificial falsities of the complacent Panglossian outlook which typified the London theatre at that time. Shortly thereafter I read many of his plays, and obtained Elizabeth Sprigge's excellent biography of the great Swedish writer. I was already an ardent fan of Ibsen and Checkhov, and several years later I was to become an enthusiast of Ingmar Bergman – the greatest of all film directors – with their haunting aesthetic beauty, their subtle almost hidden irony, and their revelation of the tortured soul in its many different aspects. One never tires of Bergman in the same way one never tires of Shakespeare, for always there are new perspectives to discover in the characters and events of his films.

During this first Winter I joined an evening class on Philosophy held by the School of Economic Science, at that time situated in Suffolk Place behind the Haymarket. It comprised a course of 12 lectures I had first seen advertised on the underground, and now 60 years later, in the 21st century, the same school is still holding a similar course of lectures and still advertised on the underground, although I have no doubt the content and lecturers have changed.

Life in the outer office remained as dull and dreary as ever, only enlivened by the constant supply of gossip. I learned that Mr. Young owned a farm near Lewes and that he had a flat in Victoria. One afternoon Miss Arberry came into the post room with her letters, and having time on her hands, she told us about her terrible War experiences in the office. Once they had to leave the building when 1,000 lb. bomb fell on the Regent Palace Hotel, and how they sheltered next door in the vaults of the Royal Bank of Scotland and in the cellars of Austin Reeds. For several years the windows of her office were boarded over, and the constant exposure to electric light damaged her eyes, and how she had a nervous breakdown for two months, and how dreadful it was at home, just off the Old Kent road where the bombing was incessant.

I must have conveyed a dejected impression, for that was my interpretation of Mr. D.C. Andrews statement when one late December afternoon, he turned to me ironically as I collected his letters, with the words, "What will you be doing this evening Corfe? I suppose you'll be taking your girl friend to the *Palais de dance*!" On the 22nd of that month it was announced at short notice that Mr. Jenkins would be in the office, and it was S-M Short's task to light his coal fire. No sooner had he done this than the room was smoked out as the chimney would not draw, and there was panic and angry words, from different directions, until the problem was corrected.

By January 1953, it was the Sergeant-Major who was becoming depressed, and in front of me to Mr. Legge, and nodding in my direction, he had cause to exclaim, "You won't get anything out of him – not even a kind look." This must have been a reference to my reserve and obsession with my own thoughts, or because I occasionally returned with snacks from the town without offering to share what I ate.

On 16th January a strange drunken woman came onto the phone, saying she wanted some train tickets from Mr. Young who was unavailable at the time. Mr. Clarke was called downstairs, exclaiming it was Mrs. Pickering, saying that she was supposedly "off the bottle by now." He went out into the street to see if she was using any of the nearby telephone boxes, as she had been asked not to visit the office in a drunken state. When Mr. Young became available he explained she permanently occupied a room in a well known West End hotel, and that it was the role of the firm to pay her hotel expenses but otherwise to keep her financially on a tight leash.

When Mr. Peverett came down later that afternoon, he explained she had once been a great beauty at the turn of the century, and had been a mistress of Edward VII. "You should have seen her in her heyday," he exclaimed. "She used to turn up at the office in a carriage with six horses. She had everything a woman could want!" Over the following months she was a frequent visitor, and sat waiting in the post room to see Mr. Young. She was a large woman and quite friendly, and asked after my interests, but she was regarded as a problem by the firm which had taken over the responsibility for her care from her family.

On 22nd of March a "strange looking" middle aged man visited the office who happened to be Sir Leigh Ashton (1897-1983), the director of the Victoria and Albert Museum. He had recently married, but his wife refused to consummate the marriage, and so he found himself in the awkward predicament of having to sue for an annulment. I read the pitiful details of his case which had to be drawn up for consideration in a judge's Chambers with interest, but it struck me as an absurdity that a grown man had been so naïve as to place himself in such a situation. What kind of relationship did he have with this woman before the marriage? Was the question of sex never discussed? If that's what he wanted, then why didn't he take the precaution of leading her to bed before the marriage? Perhaps his prospective wife regarded him as so ugly that no man would expect sex from a woman in the first place.[*]

---

[*] By the time of Sir Leigh Ashton's death in 1983, the following facts were already public knowledge: firstly that he had entered into a marriage of convenience in 1952, and secondly that he was homosexual. In the legal papers drawn up for the annulment of his marriage neither of these facts were referred to or even suggested.

There was a tall good-looking well-dressed young man, a Mr. Honourable Somebody-or-other, who frequently visited the office. He spoke little and had a vacant expression as he sat silently in the outer office. After he had gone upstairs to see Mr. Young on one occasion, Mr. E.A. Andrews burst through the door from his adjoining office, and confided to us that the young man was as "mad as a hatter. You could never imagine the amount of money his family spend on psychoanalysts in trying to treat his illness." On 12th October 1953 the American film star, Yolande Donlan, made an hysterical phone call, demanding to see Mr.Adams, as her flat had been broken into by the vendor, and she had no idea of her rights in this foreign country.

When the Sergeant-Major came into the office on 28th January, he exclaimed in a solemn undertone, "Well, the bad boy is to be hanged today." There had been riots outside Wandsworth prison that morning, for although Bentley was "for the drop," he had not fired the fatal shot which killed the policeman, but he had urged on his under-age accomplice, who escaped with a life sentence. 1953 was to mark the death of several celebrities and notorieties.

On 17th February it was announced that Mr. Jenkins was dead, and a hushed environment fell over the office. Miss Arberry said she had served him for 33 years, and that he had had a foul temper. Mr. Adams' mother had been his client, and she recollected what "a sweet little boy her son had been," when she brought him along to the office in his Eton uniform. Mr. E.A. Andrews was the first to don a black tie, but within two days it was announced that Mr. Jenkins' office was to be re-decorated and many of its contents thrown out. It was the end of an era, and there seemed an impatience to mark the change, and ensure that no ghosts of the curmudgeonly old man would haunt the building. The following week the partners and the elderly articled clerks finally saw him off by attending his funeral.

As I returned to the office from Bush House on 4th March, the loud-mouthed newsvendor at the corner of Vigo and Regent streets, who was usually shouting, "Blood and murder, blood and murder! Read all about it,!" was on this occasion hailing the public with, "Jolly good news: Stalin gravely ill. May have only 48 hours to live!" On passing the news to S-M Short, as soon as I was inside the building, he retorted, "I hope the bloody bastards start a revolution as soon as he's gone." – "It may be a good chance to start war if they do," I hazarded to put in. Mr. D.C. Andrews coolly remarked, "It'll be interesting to see what happens."

On 23rd March 1953 I awoke to learn that Queen Mary had died, and on my way to work, I bought a black tie at Austin Reed's for 5/6d., but on arriving at work, I found that only the partners were wearing black ties. Later than day the Sergeant-Major and I were asked to read through a document which had been copied to check for errors. I was to do the reading, and my colleague was to stop me if he found a discrepancy. Half way through the task, he blurted out, "You read just like a bloody clergyman. You should try going into the church."

By this time Mr. Young had a girl friend, a tall proud woman with a snobbish manner, called Miss McGregor. She took an intense dislike to me, possibly because she could not always be put through to Mr. Young when she phoned, for she was very impatient. When she sat in the outer office, she would talk to S-M Short whilst ignoring me entirely. One day on 1st May 1953, when I connected her to her friend, before I had had an opportunity to replace the receiver, she exclaimed, "Haven't you got rid of that wretch yet?" This increased my resentment and dislike of Mr. Young, as clearly I had become a topic of conversation between them.

On 13th May the outer office received a shot out of the blue. S-M Short was called up by phone to Mr. Young's office "right away," having no idea as to the reason why. Ten minutes later, he came down the stairs again, very despondent. "I've been sacked," he said. – "Whatever for?" I replied astonished. – "They say I'm deaf and too old." The news spread round the office like wildfire. When the elderly Mr. E.A. Andrews came through the door of his connecting office, he exclaimed, "Disgusting! These people don't have any principles. This firm's going down the drain, and so you're better out of it anyway."

Everywhere he received sympathy, and there was talk about the "nasty people" who ran the firm. Within two days, however, the Corps of Commissionaires had found him another placement, and he left on 15th. "It's somewhere with a brighter atmosphere and better pay," he said. Everyone wished him luck, and when I shook his hand, he said sadly, "You'll be all right, son, when you're in the Army. You'll have a life of your own then, with people of your own age." I was now in charge of the outer office, and my first task was to reorganise the stationery cupboard.

My autonomous control of the outer office did not last for long, for a week later S-M Short's place was taken by a Mr. Dawes. Mr. Dawes had previously worked for the firm, as a member of the Corps of Commissionaires, but he was tired of wearing a uniform and all the ritual belonging to a semi-military organisation of superannuated men who still had a hankering for rank and reluctance for returning to full civilian life. He therefore returned in the guise of a nondescript civilian in a very ordinary grey suit. I immediately ascertained that his services must have been secured before the dismissal of his predecessor.

Mr. Dawes was an intelligent man, but entirely without initiative for bettering his lot in life. He was basically lazy, and slouched back in his predecessor's leather armed chair, chain smoking from first thing in the morning until his departure in the evening. The office therefore became an area of impenetrable grey smoke during the day, as several ash trays lying around filled up to their brim towards evening. He had an easy and relaxed manner, and not only ingratiated himself with the partners, but had a remarkable facility for drawing out information about themselves which S-M Short had never possessed.

The office therefore became a greater centre of gossip about the private lives of the partners than it had ever been before. In the War he had served with the Ghurkas in Burma, for whom he had a low opinion, maintaining they were overrated by a lot of myth and rubbish as to their gallantry. He also had a low opinion of army life, saying it made men "lazy" and did nothing for their character. His advice to me, therefore, was that I should try to avoid National Service if at all possible.

About three weeks later on 2nd June, the office as with most others was closed to celebrate the Coronation. Gavin and I spent most of the day in front of the TV set from 10.15 am onwards, watching the proceedings: the Queen's departure from the Palace and arrival at Westminster Abbey, followed by the Coronation Service which concluded at 1.50 pm when the Queen and her entourage went into St. Edward's chapel. We broke for a lunch of sardine, egg, cheese, and tomato sandwiches, prepared by Miss Wall, who was with us for much of the time, as our parents were away at Elmer Sands, and then back to the TV when we saw the Queen depart from the Abbey at 2.20 pm, followed by the great procession, including Churchill wearing the gown of a Viscount, the Sultan of Zanzibar (who received much applause), and the Queen of Tonga, the only other monarch of the British Empire, who dwarfed the guardsmen who accompanied her.

Gavin and I shouted and cheered, and sang the National Anthem, and it was curious to see the Duke of Cornwall bang excitedly on the window of his carriage, in pointing out his mother's coach to Princess Anne, and finally we saw the carriages return to Buckingham Palace at 5.0 pm, and forty minutes later, the appearance of the Royal Family on the balcony. Shortly thereafter, the crowd broke through the police cordon and mobbed the railings of the Palace, one man crying out, "Long live the Queen!" There was a fly past, but this seemed of little interest to Prince Charles as he took his mother's wrist, and pointed to the surging masses moving forward down the Mall.

The following day, Mr. Salmon told several of us in the outer office how he had been wandering around the back streets of the West End, the previous evening, and witnessed the most disgraceful scenes. There was fighting between two gangs in Wimpole street, and not enough police to control them, and as soon as he had made a quick get-away, he next saw drunks putting their hands up ladies' skirts and generally behaving in a disorderly manner.

On 10th June I had a long political conversation with Mr. Dawes on the future of the Empire, and the prospects of territories approaching independence in the not too distant future. He was pessimistic with regard to their achieving democracy, arguing they would soon collapse into anarchy, and that material standards would decline rather than improve. Although by today's standards his opinions would be judged politically incorrect, he had a percipience which matched his predictions in many parts of the world.

We then began discussing the personalities of the partners, and his descriptions and assessment of Messrs Young and Adams agreed with mine entirely. They were men who adopted superiority above others and readily ridiculed those they considered socially inferior. "That's the Eton culture they've been brought up with," he explained. They couldn't think any differently. They were certainly not to be trusted. "In this place it's best to keep your head down, do what you're told, and nothing more," he concluded. His attitude was typical of an ex-serviceman from the ranks. Just show a friendly face to keep the officers "sweet", but volunteer for nothing!

Some months later, on returning to the office after an errand towards lunch time, Mr. Dawes met me with the words, "Your brother just called in." – "I hardly think so," I replied, "both my brothers are at school." – "Anyway, he looked just like you. He'll call back." The visitor, it transpired, was Michael Brown, who called on the spur of the moment so that we might lunch together. When he returned, I introduced him to Mr. Dawes, and they had a friendly chat together. When we left for lunch Michael remarked, "That's a very nice man," and we lunched at Stewarts Restaurant for 5/6d., where we both had a Guinness. Afterwards, we smoked a cigar and strolled down the Burlington Arcade, looking into Michael's favourite clothing stores, and eventually, I helped him choose a flashy waistcoat. That was on 14th September and in several days he was due to join the Army.

As the days passed I became increasingly depressed and demoralised by the work environment, and by the 21st I even contemplated handing in my notice. Life had become so pointless! I then decided against handing in my notice since it would be financially disadvantageous, and I thought it would be a better idea to murder Messrs Young and Adams. Whilst Mr. Adams had recently acquired a girl friend, Mr. Young had actually married Miss McGregor, and whilst I envied the first for his happiness, I feared the second all the more as I anticipated the possibility of his increasing dislike. But how could such a double murder be undertaken? It could easily be achieved by putting Jeypine in their tea, for this poison was free for the taking from any of the toilets. On reflection, I thought this might not be entirely advisable because of the smell of the chemical – for there was no way of ridding the scent of perfume.

I then thought that the use of carbolic acid would be a better idea, and I imagined the two gentlemen running downstairs in agony and gasping for water. I would be prosecuted for murder and found guilty, but saved from the death penalty on the grounds of insanity, and sent to Broadmoor. But on realising I had no idea how to obtain carbolic acid I was obliged to give up that idea also, and to continue tolerating the two men as I had done until now. The fact that I had thought such thoughts suddenly relieved my manic depression, and I was surprised to discover I was already in a better frame of mind. A great weight had been lifted from my shoulders.

During these months of confinement within this legal milieu, when I engaged in the most menial and humdrum tasks, feeling that my status was little better than that of a serf, I imagined experiencing my liberation through witnessing and participating in a great revolutionary breakdown of the existing order. These political thoughts were not imagined through a great movement of the left, for I always had, and would continue to disdain any politics which called for class conflict. My vague imaginings were rather for a great bloodletting, along the lines of the Reign of Terror, in calling into being an era of social justice and reconstruction benefiting all humanity. Such thoughts were nourished by the long winter, and the dark evenings towards the end of the working day, as I hurried up and down the five storeys of the building in the rush to get the post out on time. At that time I nurtured the commonly-held romantic view of the French Revolution and its violence, and had little understanding of the complex attitudes dividing French society and the sheer ugliness and hatreds which were the underlying reality of existence.

During the lunch hour I ate in all kinds of places, and whilst I usually tried to have a 3-course lunch (which was customary in those days) I also tried to save money. According to my diary entries, I always had a haircut at Austin Reeds during this period, although I cannot remember a single occasion of having gone there. I generally had the best and cheapest sit-down lunches at crowded nearby pubs. One such place was the Duke of York where I saw a particularly beautiful waitress, and although she wore a gold ring, I decided to court her. She had blonde hair and I admired her lovely cravat, and the way the other waitresses called her "dear" and brushed down her back when I entered. I first saw her on 5th October 1953, and left an especially generous tip of 6d. for which she said, "Thank you."

Within two days I learned her name was Pauline, and several old men had the habit of calling her "darling," which I found annoying. She soon obsessed my thoughts, and I decided to write her a letter – as the best and most discreet way of making an initial approach – when I would invite her to the theatre. I also decided to compose and include an ode with the letter. By 6th October I realised what "a good wife she would make" and I also ascertained she had already spoken about me to the other waitresses, who gossiped together about the various patrons of the establishment. On 7th I was the first to arrive in the dining room (which was advantageous), and Pauline was seated on a chair looking up at an electrician on a ladder mending a light.

Without even requesting it, she immediately served me a glass of water, and it struck me how sensitive and considerate it was to think of such a gesture. Perhaps her love for me was as great as mine for her. I noted that "she looked so young and sweet," but our intimacy progressed no further that day. At the end of the meal, a tall old man of about 60 jokingly asked if he needn't pay for his lunch, at which Pauline was put out, and an older waitress intervened, saying he *had* to pay the bill. The old man, addressing Pauline, then said, "Then I won't take you out tomorrow night," and there was laughter all round.

By the 8th I had drafted my love letter and completed the Ode in five verses, and these I typed out in the office. The following day I made several alterations to the poem and re-typed it, and sealed the completed contributions in an envelope, which I took along to the Duke of York's at lunch time. But I became apprehensive and my courage failed me, and I sensed that Pauline's kindness towards me was patronising rather than the expression of genuine love. What was I to do? I quickly smoked through a cigarette, and then hurriedly left after leaving my usual tip, but I was angry with myself for my lack of determination.

On the 13th I noted that Pauline tended to smile behind the backs of all the young men, and although I found this disconcerting, I realised that my feelings or irritation would just have to be repressed. I carried the precious envelope in my breast pocket for a fortnight before my courage was sufficiently stirred to deliver the letter. Finally on the 22nd October, having finished lunch and paid my bill, I rose from the table, having removed the envelope from my pocket, and advanced towards the hatch where the waitresses tended to gather. But Pauline was nowhere to be seen. As she had disappeared into the kitchen, I was obliged to tell one of the other waitresses about my missive.

When she emerged, her colleague exclaimed, "Here's a young gentleman to see you," upon which I said, "Here's a letter for you. You can give me a reply tomorrow." Pauline looked me straight in the face with the most pleasant and candid smile, receiving the letter without betraying any emotion or surprise. She only answered, "A reply? All right! Thank you!" It was clear she was taken aback, and to save her any more embarrassment, I made a hurried exit from the pub. In the doorway to the street, I lit up a cigarette, and once beyond the window view of the Duke of York's, I rapidly made my way through Hanover square, back to the office in the highest spirits, almost unbelieving in the success of my mission.

The text of the letter was as follows:- "Dear Waitress. – Please take no offence against my simple lines. If I offend you, remember, you would think better of them, had you thought otherwise. I am so fond of you, and some night, I would like to take you to the theatre. If I have seemed dull, it is only because I have been frightened of you. Please give me a reply tomorrow, when I come to lunch. I have enclosed an envelope and a sheet of notepaper. If you are married or engaged, forgive me, or if you think indifferently towards me, please give either excuse and all will be forgotten. Whatever your answer, I shall understand. Your answer is final. If you seal the envelope, I promise not to open it until I've left the restaurant. – Yours sincerely," &c.

As a love letter, of course, it was no less ineffective and off-putting as those earlier letters addressed to Patricia Dainton some 15 months before. And towards the close, it became absurdly conspiratorial. The following is the enclosed Augustan-style poem, or Ode addressed to a Beautiful Waitress:-

I

Did ever Venus mould a form so fair,
Or bring to earth such beauty clear?
When did the world last bring to life
A damsel of such heavenly rife?
Oh, never never has it seen,
Such beauty of Angelic sheen!

II

She walks, and seems at once to be
A flaming fire of beauty free.
A thousand on her turn their eyes,
Their hearts are struck, an arrow flies;
Shot from Cupid's immortal bow,
Their hearts with love do overflow:

III

"Oh fairest maiden most sublime,
Most beauteous perfect of all time,
If thou wert only mine," they cry,
Then sink away in melancholy to pine.
Could ever lady be so wondrous great,
With beauty so, that none can imitate?

IV

Her hair is of the thread of flaxen silk;

Her eyes do sparkle; her jewels the ilk;
The forehead high, her face alight;
Her chin well made; and she is wholly bright.
She stands with classic grace above,
And walks with dignity, thus winning love.
                    V
Oh hearken all, come here and list,
Come judge this beauty, I insist!
Surely all of you agree and say,
That she's the greatest beauty of today:
Most lovely, most virginal and fair,
With brightest smile, and graceful air.
With gentle and celestial fame,
She rises with a greater name.
So long live Miss ..., praise her,
And send her love and happiness everywhere.

I was in such high spirits on returning to the office, that I remained exuberantly loquacious for the rest of the afternoon. This was manifested by the fact of my being engaged in a lively conversation with the typist, Miss Allen, for half an hour on recent drama productions on the London stage and TV. I was pleasant and friendly – even obliging, to the other secretaries when I collected their letters, and not a cross word passed my lips, nor a gloomy glance my countenance, for the duration of the afternoon. I could hardly believe my good fortune! When Mr. E.A. Andrews asked me to get his Ronson lighter repaired, I walked all the way to the Strand and back (so great was my energy), and on my return, I could tell him the cost would be 8/9d., and that it would be ready to fetch in three weeks time.

At noon the following day, I left again for the Duke of York's. As Pauline placed a bowl of mulligatawny soup before me, she bent over and whispered in my ear, "Thank you for the invitation, but I'm married." – "I see," I only replied, and I showed no emotion. I did not bother to read the paper I had brought with me, and neither did I give her a second glance throughout the meal. She had not even bothered to write me a little note, although I had supplied the wherewithal for such a purpose. As I went up to pay the bill, I heard one of the waitresses say to another, "She didn't even know what it was until last night." When I left the usual tip, Pauline exclaimed, "Bye, bye," but I was too dumbstruck to reply. I have never returned to the Duke of York's from that day till this.

There were other occurrences during that eventful October. I was surprised to learn there was a feud which had lasted decades between the two oldest employees of the firm, viz., Messrs. E.A. Andrews and

Peverett. I was shocked when the former began to attack the reputation of the latter to Mr. Young, one afternoon, as we all stood in the post room. Mr. E.A. Andrews contended that his rival had hated Mr. Jenkins "like poison," and had circulated his opinion throughout the office that, "Mr. Jenkins was the most selfish and envious man he had ever met."

On the 21st it was announced that Mr. Adams was engaged, and Mr. Dawes, of course, was the first to know. He had already received prior notice of the event and he showed me the announcement in the *Daily Telegraph*. Soon the secretaries were congratulating their employer, but because of my own disappointments in love and feelings of envy, I ungenerously chose to keep a distance, and concentrate on the business of the office.

CHAPTER 25
Old School Friends and Others

"It redoubleth joys and cutteth griefs in halfs."

Sir Francis Bacon, *Essays: Of Friendship*

The Browns' new residence – A KAS function – Gilbert Harding – Passion for Miss Dainton revived – Attempts at the cure of pipe smoking – End of the PD affair – Assessments for military fitness – Osbourn and his Jewish girl friend – A spiritualist meeting – An evening with Richard Martin – Geoffrey Dunston and our doomed friendship – My grandfather's second marriage

During those 15 months leading up to January 1954 I had, of course, another life beyond the legal world of Young, Jackson, Beard & King, and towards the end of this period, there was a crescendo of differing emotions and contradictory events as if much had to be crammed into a small space of time, before a new start in life. And that new start was to be my conscription in the Army.

Towards the end of February 1953, my Uncle Harold's best friend, Graham, who had been an officer in the Navy during the War, was married to a German lady from Hamburg, and Harold had gone over to Germany for the wedding. I had met Graham on several occasions at family events, and wondered what my father thought of his youngest brother's best friend fraternising with and then marrying one of the "enemy." On the 21st February we all received pieces of the wedding cake which my father deigned to accept, but it was too late by then for him to reverse any decisions with regard to my visiting Germany.

In any event, he remained in a moody and depressed state during most of this period and on a bright warm day on 24th May, we made a first visit to the Brown's fine new residence in Harpenden, to which they had recently moved from Totteridge. My Uncle Dick was now a Regional Director for Frigidaire, and enjoying success, and the family were often entertaining generously on an elaborate scale with black tie dances and parties. At one such event, after my Aunt Joan had become friendly with Terry Thomas, whom she had met whilst escorting my grandfather on a world cruise, the film and TV comedian had also been invited, but he did not appear – and my mother remarked that it would not have been proper had he done so.

On this particular afternoon my father behaved oddly, sitting on the verandah in a deckchair in the heat in his overcoat, either talking to no one or making silly or outrageous statements. When his sister light-heartedly remarked on this to my mother, the latter replied, "Felix has just been awful lately!" – "Do you think he's going mental?" asked Joan in a joking fashion. "Who knows?" answered my mother. - "Perhaps he's going soft in the brain," chuckled my aunt. On other days he would lie in bed and sulk, and it was only when Mabs and Bill were around that he perked up.

On the 13th of June I joined a small crowd listening to a Communist speaker standing outside Findlater's wine store opposite the Presbyterian Church in Prince's Avenue, Muswell Hill, who was calling for a demonstration against the hanging of the Rosenbergs which was to take place next Thursday. Some weeks earlier, I had met my old friend, Osbourn, heckling a Communist speaker at the same place, and later he turned to me with the words that, "this country's finished" and he was thinking of emigrating to America where he thought there were better chances for the future. I had not met him for years, and he seemed politically naïve and immature.

On the 4th July I attended an event at King Alfred's meeting many of the teachers and old school friends. Mrs. Munro, an American teacher and pacifist, advised me to go to prison for 6 months rather than be conscripted, as she felt the former option would be more noble and courageous. I saw several attractive women who were parents, and then I spoke with my old sparring partner of the debating society, Raphael Samuels, who was now at Balliol studying Bede, and he regretted he no longer had time for general reading. He had spent the Coronation day drinking to the future of the Second British Republic.

On the 10th of the same month, after collecting my new glasses from Curry and Paxton, and passing by the BBC in Langham Place, I caught sight of a tall man with a fat belly and dirty baggy grey trousers, a squirrel red sports jacket and cigar end in his mouth, as he hailed a taxi. As there was something familiar about his appearance, I stared at him in amazement, upon which he smiled at me in return, and on entering and driving off in the taxi, he pulled down the window, leaned his body out of the vehicle and waved at me cheerfully. It was none other than the great TV personality, Gilbert Harding, of the panel game, *What's My Line?* About a year earlier he had met my cousin, Anne, at a party, and being drunk at the time, he had confronted her with the statement that she was "flat breasted."

The following day I went to Palmers Green Labour Exchange to register for the Army. I was met by a man with a savage temper, dressed entirely in black. He accused me of causing extra work by signing on late, saying that a solicitor's clerk should know better. He then picked up an enormous placard, 3 feet high by 4 feet across, and placed it on his desk. It read that I was liable to a fine not exceeding £5 in addition to imprisonment. The gesture was so absurd – it was like a sketch from a pantomime – that I did not know whether to laugh out loud or guffaw in contempt.

On returning from my annual holiday in Bath towards the end of August, I was oppressed by two factors, firstly, at having to return to "the worst of all cities" – or at least to the stuffy stuck-up milieu of Muswell Hill, for that was its reputation, to the point of ridicule, in the eyes of many throughout the capital. The hypocrisy of its people, with their thought-numbing religiosity, and the rigidity of their views, condemned the place to a zombie-like existence. One could hardly breathe the air for the morgue-like dullness of the place. Those were my thoughts at the time.

The second factor was that for some inexplicable reason, my passion for Patricia Dainton was suddenly revived. For some days I dreamed about her night after night. I awoke on the 26th August having dreamed about her for the greater part of the night. We went through a great panorama of time together, and I found myself writing letters to her from the middle of the 18th century onwards, and always we were re-born, and in our transmigrations we were thrown together, but always she would marry the same man, and I would be disappointed in love. In this E.T.A. Hoffmann-like fashion I was doomed to eternal torture and misery.

Eventually I turned to pipe-smoking to assuage my wounded feelings, for I had heard that the comforts of the pipe are a cure for all kinds of melancholy. Michael had recently brought me back a pipe from a skiing holiday in Interlaken. I had not tried it before, as it had laid six months in a drawer, and so on the 29th, I filled it with tobacco and lit it up. After 50 minutes it went out, and on emptying the pipe I found the tobacco had not been entirely exhausted. I re-filled and relit the pipe, and it went with gusto, and I happily blew out great clouds of smoke in triumph. But then I had a stomach upset, and to cure this I drank several glasses of water, but I felt worse, and so I lay down on the bed, propping myself up with high pillows. Finally, I was violently sick.

This was a gross humiliation. Not to be defeated, some days later I relit the pipe again, but again I was struck down by illness, a severe headache followed by vomiting. This was a situation which could not be tolerated. My father smoked his pipe all day during the weekends and never suffered any ill effects. To fail as a pipe-smoker would be unmanly, as all the most tranquil and self-possessed men were pipe-smokers – for that was the purpose of a pipe. Why, then, did I have a problem with this helpful item? I concluded it was a question of "practice makes perfect," and so I tried the pipe again and again, always allowing for reasonable intervals between one attempt and the next, but always it left me ill. Eventually, I gave up the practice of pipe-smoking, and kept Michael's gift as both a souvenir and evidence that I had indeed once smoked a pipe.

By the 2nd of September I had achieved sufficient equanimity to resolve that Patricia Dainton should be consigned to the past, and that instead, I would marry any beautiful woman, but these feelings were reversed on 26th on seeing a photo of my beloved once again in the *Daily Mail*, together with others, on the occasion of the last night of the London production of *Lucky Boy*. The end of the Patricia Dainton episode, however, was not finally to reach a close until January of the following year, about a week before I was to report for military service. On 16th of that month, Gavin came wantonly into my room, with a smile on his face, exclaiming, "Do you know that Patricia Dainton is to have a baby?" I turned on him savagely, telling him not to "talk nonsense," and I pushed him out of the room.

As he said nothing more, I assumed he was trying to hurt my feelings with an invention of his idle imagination. I forgot the matter, but later in the day I read in the paper that this indeed was true. It transpired that she was married to Norman Williams, formerly an actor and now a TV producer, and that shortly he was off to the USA on a 7-month assignment. Patricia was due to have her baby in July, and on Wednesday she was to leave her sweet little house in South Kensington and move to her in-laws in Cheshire until the new arrival. On the return of her husband from America he would then have at least six films lined up for her in which to perform. At last I finally realised there was little sense or possibility in pursuing the friendship.

By 8.0 am on 31st August 1953 I had to be at the Army Centre, where I spent most the day with a crowd of other prospective recruits undergoing tests or just waiting around. First we were sent upstairs for an intelligence test, and after more waiting, during which we were given two encouraging pamphlets to read on Army life, we were conducted into another room and asked to piss into vases and fill them to the brim. As one boy was unable to do this, he was given water to drink and then shut behind an iron door to try again. Then the colour of our eyes were examined, and after this we were asked to remove our clothes, and doctors' fingers were pushed into peculiar places and we were asked to cough. By this time I was beginning to feel nervous, although the clerks and medical staff were civil and discreet.

Then I was examined by a Sir Henry Somebody-or-other, and when he learned I was a writer of plays, he suggested I take up journalism. My stomach was examined and then he became worried about my back, and so I was examined by other doctors for several opinions. My back was X-rayed, and finally I was taken upstairs to fill in a long form, before being interviewed by a Colonel who suggested that clerking would be my best occupation in the Army. As I ended the afternoon by looking around the Roman collection in the British Museum, the Army Centre must have been in the Bloomsbury area. On the 1st of October I was called in for a second series of X-rays on my back, after which I was told that despite a past injury everything seemed to be fine. This gave me some concern, for I had hoped to be excused military service on medical grounds.

A fortnight later, on 16th, my brother offered me a helping hand by saying that my old school friend, Osbourn, knew a good way for avoiding conscription. It was suggested I phone him that night and ask for "Dick," as I had only known him by his surname. When I got through, we had a long conversation. He hoped that for my sake I had failed the medical, but if not I should take to chewing tobacco to bring on heart palpitations. It was still not too late, for if I chewed tobacco for a week and then went to my GP, he would certify me as having a weak heart and I would be guaranteed exemption. He said he was fed up with Highgate, and that it was a "dump" like all other schools, and he wanted to leave at the end of the term.

He said he still regularly got into trouble, mostly with Bennett as an accomplice, and when he wrote a vulgar poem for a junior boy who was caught with it, who then sneaked on the author, he was taken to the Headmaster, "Holy-holy Bell," who lectured to him on sex. Osbourn had used his ingenuity in skipping games and PT for three years, and Bell would be furious if he found out, but as the school was so inefficiently run that possibility was unlikely. He described how Bennett had stuck a stiletto into another boy's behind, and to save the skin of his friend, Osbourn had lent him his penknife to say that that had been the weapon, as otherwise he would have been expelled if a stiletto had been involved. He then said he had seduced a 15-year old girl whilst on holiday that year, and feared the consequences of the incident being brought to court.

However, he still met her occasionally in Putney and they carried on a secret correspondence.

She was a Jewess, but hated the fact, although she looked every inch a gentile. "I'm damned fond of the girl," he said, but he would refrain from elopement and hoped to marry her in three or four years if they hadn't meanwhile drifted apart. She was not the type "to turn whore." It was remarkable that the leading anti-Semite of his year group at Highgate Junior School five years earlier now found himself in this curious situation. I went along with all he said for the sake of our former friendship, whilst being shocked by the puerile and empty environment in which he seemed to exist at Highgate Senior School. There seemed a huge gulf between the intellectual poverty of this renowned institution, purportedly run by a religious bigot, compared with the rich academic life at King Alfred's which I had left some 15 months before.

What would have been my fate had I been accepted by the Senior School? I never bothered with the tobacco chewing for fear it might actually harm my health for the longer term. Osbourn subsequently fell ill, and was to die in his mid-twenties. Did he anyway die through maintaining the habit of chewing tobacco in avoiding National Service?

On the 28th October I was again summoned for a back inspection, this time at the Orthopaedic Ward of the North Middlesex Hospital in Edmonton. It was a depressing place with semi-paralysed people lying about on trolleys, and after undressing and undergoing several examinations by doctors who were pleasant and good-humoured, I was X-rayed once again. On the 23rd November I went to Dr. Blackburn, complaining of severe chest pains, and after an examination, he said I had scoliosis of the spine in that it was bent both ways, and that this was probably due to an early childhood form of rickets, or else lack of calcium.

On telling my mother about the diagnosis, she was outraged, as she had always endeavoured to ensure I lay in a cot with a flat mattress. It was arranged I should see Dr. Batchelor, the Orthopaedic Surgeon at Guys. The consultation with Br. Batchelor took place on the 12th December at his premises in 78 Harley Street, and after an examination and an intended confirmation from the result of the previous examination at the North Middlesex Hospital, he expressed the opinion that I would be fit for the service. This seemed to finalise the matter, and destined the course of my future.

One Sunday in October (11th) Gavin promised "a spot of fun," if I should join him and a group of his cronies from school to attend a Spiritualist meeting that evening at the Athenaeum. As I thought this might put a bit of "lightness" into the life of Muswell Hill, I decided to go along, and we were joined by Seaton, Nick Bills and Brian Law – the latter whose misdemeanours were soon to involve him in a troubled future. The service began with hymns, which were mocked by false words by my companions, and then a cockney woman with a gipsy shawl took over as chairwoman. Seaton began giggling, and had his face in a handkerchief for most of the time, and Brian Law followed suit. Later Nick pointed to the floor, exclaiming there were spiders, in an attempt to frighten some old women nearby, and when the event concluded with a demonstration of clairvoyance, for once there was silence in our corner, as we were curious to see some ghostly phenomena or other remarkable occurrence, but nothing happened out of the ordinary.

When the collection plate was passed around, Brian Law pilfered 6d., but said afterwards that if we had dropped the plate we could have gained more by "helping to rescue the coins from the floor." I was dismayed by the behaviour of my brother's friends, but nonetheless, I was not going to lose the opportunity for a rational argument with those who had attempted to organise this psychic trickery. I therefore found myself in an argument with a man on thought, mind, and matter, and the theory of atoms not supporting the practice of spiritualism. Once outside the building, Brian pointed out a "comfortable wench" who was being paraded up and down the street by two boys, and whom he thought he might seduce, and then we broke up as a group and went our separate ways.

One weekday whilst on my way to get deeds stamped, I passed by the Princes Theatre, and met my old class mate, Richard Thomas – or Richard Martin, as he was now professionally known. It was the 6th November and he was queuing for tickets for friends for the Stratford Company's production of, *Anthony and Cleopatra*. I told him I had obtained my ticket earlier in the day. He had become somewhat pimply, and his hair was untidy, all the result of the rakish actor's existence I concluded. He was interested in my critique of the Stratford *Lear* I had recently seen, and I argued it would make a great film if sufficient imagination was used with the right scenic effects. We discussed the old school, and I told him I was awaiting call-up papers and the question over my spine. "That was probably due to your jousting outside the Geography block, all those years ago," he chuckled, and we laughed over the fooling around during that first term at school. I was not going to tell him about the Woodbridge episode. We agreed to lunch together later in the week, and as I left he cried, "Don't get too bored in the office."

On the 19th I arrived early in the evening at the Princes Theatre to see the performance, bringing my father's opera glasses, and I stood near the stage door watching the actors arrive, and nearby was a long queue for the gallery. I saw Marius Goring arrive in a duffel coat, but he was unrecognised by the crowd, and others arrived, usually dressed as nondescriptly as they could. There was a queue entertainer with an enamel tray which he smoked with a chemical flame before drawing sketches and erasing them, one after another, and then he delivered several Shakespearian soliloquies which he satirised at the end. He said he had read *Hard Times* 30 years ago, and had been hard up ever since. He then sang an operatic aria which he called *My Madonna*, explaining that the Madonna was a prostitute picked off the streets of Paris, and there was general laughter, before he went round with a hat collecting pennies.

On reaching me, he exclaimed, "How's life with you,?" and patting me on the shoulder and turning to the crowd, he cried, "We're all Shakespearian lovers." Then an accordionist arrived, and on receiving a slap on the back, I turned round to see Richard Martin. He was surprised I had bought such an expensive seat at 8/6d. in the stalls, assuring me I would have an excellent view from row 11. He then asked me to come round to the Stage door after the show when we would then all go off together with the rest of the cast for a meal.

After the performance I asked the doorkeeper for Richard Martin, and was told to go to the top floor Room 12. On the way up, I saw the well-built black-skinned Alexas, an attendant of Cleopatra, knocking on a dressing room door, exclaiming, "Can I come in, darling?" Room 12 was crowded with a dozen or so men, who had minor parts in the production, removing grease paint from their faces, and noisily chatting. I congratulated Richard on an excellent production, saying I was particularly pleased with the way Lepidus was portrayed. On his mirror were photos of his 16-year old girl friend who was leaving school next term and destined to be an actress. She lived in Stratford, but happily she was coming to London tomorrow.

There was much crude talk amongst his free living but hard-up acting associates, and when they were ready, a crowd of us left for a nearby restaurant, and the noise and rowdiness of our group dominated the room, but was nonetheless good-naturedly tolerated by the general manager, Demos, who took our orders. One of the actors, a particularly fat boy, carrying a copy of *The Idiot*, was cheerfully lifted by four others over the table and placed in his squashed-up seat by the wall. I told Richard how impressed I had been by *The Father* at the Arts Theatre, and then the group joked and told obscene stories for much of the meal. "I don't expect you understand all this theatrical talk," said Richard towards the end of the evening. "Oh yes, I do," I responded. "I've read my Shakespeare. See *Hamlet*, or, *The Midsummer Night's Dream*, for example. Actors today behave just as they did in the Elizabethan era." Finally, he insisted on paying for my meal as I was "his guest," and the bill came to 5/-.

During this period I attended several Old Alfredian events, one being the AGM which was chaired by Paul Davis, the elder brother of my literary friend, Jonathan. I became exuberant, over self-confident, and spoke out of turn during these proceedings, and several times needed to be called to order. I complained the association did not hold enough events, and when it did, there was insufficient drink available. This was challenged by Paul Davis, who stood in for Hetty Barber, the Headmistress, who was ill, and he reminded me that my friend Geoffrey Dunston, had become so drunk after 17 glasses of punch at an event earlier in the year, that he had to be carried home.

And the two who made themselves responsible for this were also drunk, and all three collapsed on Hampstead Heath, and Geoffrey never reached home until 3.0 am in the morning. Later, I came up with some more constructive suggestions, and these were voted on and accepted, and after the meeting closed, a party of us adjourned to the kitchen where we drank Sherry and became more garrulous. At one point I must have spoken with some bravado about the fine people who stepped across the threshold of our office, for Anthea Ionides, the elder sister of my classmate, Penelope, took me to task by saying that in her school she taught the sons of dukes and earls, and that at the Victoria & Albert Museum, there was an exhibition of Ionides family portraits. Her family were indeed high-born Greeks whose connections with this country as diplomats, merchants, and patrons of the arts, were traceable to the start of the 19th century.

From time to time, I continued to meet Geoffrey Dunstan, but our friendship was doomed to fall apart for reasons given below. He came to tea on the 21st November, and was liked by my parents because of his conventional, if not rigid, attitude to life. Naturally, our first topics of conversation were news about life at King Alfred's. I was shocked to hear that Jonathan Davis had now given up studying literature entirely. This was because he had recently achieved 96% in an examination for higher mathematics, and so all his energies were to be directed to the sciences. At first I felt this was a betrayal in view of his extensive knowledge and love of literature and the other arts, but then I realised the sciences should always be given a preference for study if the aptitude was there for these more difficult subjects.

Geoffrey then told me about his own troubles, and that he was fed-up with school and looked forward to leaving. He said he had had a major row with John Handford, the history master, with whom he was always arguing, describing him as an "almost undisguised Communist." Handford had been urging Geoffrey to attend his Philosophy classes, and finally, after an exchange of insults, Handford threatened to prevent him from attending theological college unless he showed up at the Philosophy classes. At that point, Geoffrey complained to Mrs. Barber, and John Handford was forced to apologise. I expressed sympathy for my friend, but I had my reservations.

It was commonly known that John Handford was a Marxist, and possibly he was a Communist too, but nonetheless, he was a scholarly teacher with a broad view of the world. He was probably more concerned with his pupil's sense of rationality than in safeguarding his reputation as a teacher. Were all Handford's teachings as a historian in conveying a materialistic perspective of the world to be undone after three years in a theological college? I could sympathise with the aims of the teacher to turn the pupil's interest in another direction. Geoffrey was not only turning into a bigot, but into something worse than that – he was turning into a prig.

Our friendship was first formed as we had identified ourselves as Christians in a sea of agnosticism – even atheism, amongst our peers. There were also many Jewish pupils in our midst, but the majority were liberal, free thinking, and sceptical, with little time for religion. It was also a very international environment, and at first, Geoffrey and I, as two rather typical English boys may have felt ourselves to be in an isolated situation. But my Christianity was little more than a badge of identity, as something which I accepted at face value unthinkingly as a moral good, for I had no other ethical compass at the time, and because of this, for the first two terms or so, I was prepared to flaunt my Christianity in a careless and possibly vulgar fashion.

Later, Geoffrey became someone against whom I bounced ideas, and then a privileged confidant as soon as the Patricia Dainton affair developed. But I remained the dominant partner, and I interested him in certain specialised spheres of literature, such as the writings of the 18th century historians. When he bought the Works of Dr. Robertson from Foyles, on my recommendation, and brought several of the volumes to school, he was ridiculed by Ronald Fuller, who had time for Gibbon and Hume, but few other historians of the period.

Fuller, whose tastes were strictly literary, had a high regard for such "thrilling" 19th century historians as Froude, Macaulay, Motley and Prescott, and these were writers I read in due course, although in later life, as a more scientific historian, I formed a higher regard for their contemporaries, Grote, Lecky, and S.R. Gardiner – not to mention their equally reputable colleagues in Continental Europe. Regarding the 18th century historians, Fuller may have held the common opinion of scholars of his era, but time has changed that situation, and I rather think my opinions then have now been vindicated.

For example, Adam Ferguson's *History of the Progress & Termination of the Roman Republic* (1782), has recently been resurrected and recognised as a work of major value, whilst two of the works of his fellow Scott, Dr. William Robertson, viz., his *History of Scotland* (1759), and even more, his *History of the Reign of the Emperor Charles V* (1769), are still amongst the most readable and well-balanced works on their subjects for the general reader. But the views of Ronald Fuller were to prevail over both of us in the shorter term, for soon before I entered the Army, I sold several of the valuable 18th century historical works I had then acquired,   amongst these being, Rollins *Ancient History*, Mitford's *Greece*, and Nathaniel Hook's *History of the Roman Republic* – although it is only the latter work which I should be interested in re-acquiring today.

As Geoffrey and I rarely discussed questions of religion, I did not realise he was hit with the religious bug, and similarly he may have been unaware of my own religious views, as I only presented a false front in maintaining the conventions and keeping the peace. I did sense, however, that he was beginning to become insufferable.

On that afternoon in November, after we had had a long conversation in my room, we went downstairs and joined the family, where we met Uncle Quentin and Sybel. When I announced that Geoffrey was now the Head boy of the school, the old man took him by the hand exclaiming, "Let me congratulate you, my dear boy. And where do you live?" – "In Hampstead Garden Suburb," replied my friend, somewhat overwhelmed by my uncle's manner, for he had recently moved there from Woodford. – "The most beautiful spot in London," responded Quentin. Geoffrey then explained he was to study at a theological college situated between Golders Green and Swiss Cottage, and that the boarding of the students was compulsory. Uncle Quentin again congratulated my friend, saying what a fine thing it was to be a clergyman, but by now it was with irony, for he clearly had his tongue in his cheek.

The following day as I was quietly reading the *Radio Times* in the lounge and my mother was stoking the fire, she turned to me and said, "I've got a secret to tell you – but don't tell anyone else." – "What's that?" I asked my curiosity aroused. – "Grandpa's probably going to marry again." – "To whom?" – "To the lady who lives in the flat below." My grandfather had recently built a 3-storey block of flats on a bomb site in Queens Avenue, sold Ashmount, and moved into the middle flat with his youngest son, Harold, who had now chosen, since returning from the War, to be known by his middle name of Martin. I did not know why my mother wanted to keep this matter a secret, and I asked myself as to whether it was a fact or merely a rumour. Some moments later I left the lounge for an adjoining room to listen to a concert, and my immediate response to this prospect of marriage cheered my spirits, for my grandfather had been hen-pecked by his first wife, and I wished him happiness.

When later in the evening I confronted my mother for more information, she replied without cynicism or anger in her voice, that this was "bad news." – "Why?" I asked. She explained that the lady in the flat below was a 46-year old wealthy widow, who had a 19-year old daughter who shared the flat, and that my grandfather would seek to marry her off to her fiancé at the earliest opportunity and finance the young couple to ensure this. Then, on his decease, which could not be many years ahead, all his money would be left to his wife's family.

I was deeply shocked by these sentiments, not only because I thought them selfish, but because I felt the younger generation should never need to think about living on a future inheritance. I was, of course, sufficiently naïve at the time to have no understanding of the threat of those family conflicts arising from matters of inheritance when a grandparent marries a much younger spouse – or any spouse. As it was, my grandfather lived another 12 years until the age of 85, and on his passing, there was a short but acrimonious legal conflict, the outcome of which ensured the greater part of the inheritance passed to the Corfe family.

CHAPTER 26
An Ending and a New Beginning

"He that flies from his own family has far to travel."
(Longe fuit, quisquis suos fugit.)

Petronius, *Satyricon*, Sec. 43.

How I ended my employment – A party at KAS – My *Apology* – Final parting – Christmas 1953 – Letters of thanks and good wishes – I join the Army

The absurd episode which led to the end of my employment with Young, Jackson, Beard & King, must now be related. On the 11th of December I arose at 8.15 am, and left for work in a hurry, but on reaching Tufnell Park I was alarmed at realising I had left my glasses behind. Cursing and confused I returned to Highgate station, and on reaching the barrier and explaining my predicament to the inspector, he asked as to whether or not I wished to re-use my ticket. Thoughtlessly, I replied, "No, I'm too much in a rush. I'll have to take a taxi to work," upon which he crushed the ticket in his hand, and I walked home through the Woods.

My mother was angry to see me return, but not as angry as I was with my forgetfulness, and so I retrieved my glasses from atop the bookcase, and left the house again. I thought it might be expeditious to take a steam train from Cranley Gardens to Finsbury Park or King's Cross, but the man at the ticket office was so dilatory and absorbed in his time table charts, that I left before he had time to reply.

Walking towards Highgate and then towards Archway, and hailing several taxis, all of which were occupied, I looked at my watch and discovered it was already 10.15 am. On the spur of the moment, I resolved not to go to work – or ever again. I began to relax, and slowed my pace as I walked towards Kentish and Camden Town and then Regent's Park. It was foggy and by now there was little chance that the mist would clear. I decided that if questioned as to my actions – for the office was bound to phone home in enquiring after my whereabouts – I should say I had fallen into a kind of coma and temporarily lost my memory. I sat down on a seat opposite the Zoo and watched an eagle trying to escape from its enclosure. It struck me that this bird was a metaphor for my own condition, and I recollected Milton's eagle, "mewing her mighty youth, and kindling her undazzled eyes at the full mid-day beam," as described in his great pamphlet, *Areopagitica*, in its appeal for freedom.

I walked through the spacious park, seeing several policemen, and I wondered if and when they would be sent out to search for me as soon as the partners in Old Burlington Street became desperate at my absence. Eventually I walked down Park Lane and had a 3/6d. lunch at Lyons, and there was a mad young bearded artist there who tried to engage me in conversation. I sat long and smoked, and wondered whether I should go back to the office and set fire to the place. I left the restaurant at 1.0 pm and walked through Belgrave Square and along Victoria Embankment, and sat and watched the barges pass by. I then walked to the City and took a train from Cannon Street to Highgate for 10d., changing at Charing Cross, and then I took a bus from the Woodman to my home.

Stealthily, I entered the house at 3.0 pm, when I heard my mother call out for the three of us by name. I was about to go upstairs, but went into the lounge, and stupidly exclaimed, "I sort of fell into a sleep walk as I went to Highgate station." My mother sternly looked me up and down, and then I added, I was "fed up" with the firm, and had no intention of returning. She said Mr. D.C. Andrews had phoned half an hour ago to enquire as to whether I was ill. After an argumentative exchange, it was agreed she would not tell my father providing I kept my job until after Christmas. I went to my room and my brother brought me a cup of tea and a slice of roast beef, asking me to keep out of the way until the time when I normally arrived home after work. I heard my father enter the house and I felt a spasm of terror in case he might discover my whereabouts.

At 6.0 pm my mother rang the fire bell which was used as a gong in calling the family to the dinner table, and during the meal, there was a tense silence and few words spoken, as if something was wrong but no one knew what. That evening I went to an Old Alfredians' get-together, and there was much merriment as the supposedly medieval-style mulled wine began to flow, and I became pleasantly tipsy and garrulous. In quoting Beaumont and Fletcher, one of the guests expatiated on the "joys of the vine," and even Geoffrey Dunston dropped his guard when he and Freddy Herzog turned off the lights by removing the fuses, and then they squirted and chased the dancing couples with a soda siphon, crying, "Let's have the girls on the floor." Later I spoke with Julie Heyting, an attractive girl, who said she saw me nearly every day walking through Highgate Wood, and I was surprised when she said that Richard Martin was to leave the Stratford Theatre Company, as he was tired of bit parts, and wanted to join a smaller repertory group where he had a greater opportunity for more serious roles. At the end of the evening I helped wash up as we sang songs, and later I took the bus home with Geoffrey and several others.

The following day I went to the office as usual, and began pottering about filing the flimsies and tidying the stationery cupboard, when Miss Allen came down and ironically remarked, "I thought you had committed suicide, or got murdered or something yesterday," and that the office had been left in chaos, and that Miss Arberry had even wept over the task in attending to folding and sticking down the mail. I had been cursed to high heaven because of my absence. After Mr. Adams had fetched his newspaper and gone to the toilet for half an hour, he returned to his room, and ringing down to me, said sternly, "Put the switchboard through to me, and come and see me immediately."

This is it! I said to myself, and leaped up the stairs to his room. I found Mr. Adams standing by his desk, and I was asked to explain myself. This was an invitation to talk all day if I was to *really explain myself*. What could I do? I could only hope to explain myself in the crudest and most simplistic fashion in such a hurried business environment. I admitted I was resentful, and feared the anger that would be aroused if I was more than half an hour late, and that I, too, was angry. "Angry with who,?" asked Mr. Adams. "With the firm," I answered. – "That's impertinent," responded Mr. Adams. – "But it's true, Sir," I insisted. – "Didn't you think of your mother, and how worried she would be at learning of your disappearance?" I had no reply to that. "I suppose you know, Corfe," he concluded, "that we can't keep you after this behaviour." I then turned tack by saying I quite understood his attitude and was sympathetic with his decision, upon which he said I would leave after Christmas. Finally, I requested permission to prepare and write a

written *Apology* to explain my behaviour the previous day. "You may do
so, but it won't alter our decision," replied Mr. Adams. "That is entirely
understood, Sir," I assured him.

On returning to the post room, I drew out a bundle of lined
foolscap paper, normally used for preparing deeds in longhand, from the
stationery cupboard, and embarked on this lengthy task. The *Apology* was
never to be completed, but I worked on it for several weeks, and could
never have anticipated it would have extended to book length had I
worked on it to completion. The document, therefore, was never
presented to the partners, and possibly this was fortunate, for the lengthy
fragment which exists, could not have hoped to win me sympathy or
understanding as a desirable employee. The document is that of a hypersensitive person, offended by every gesture of a rebuff, and wallowing in
self-pity and humility as a mistreated dogs-body. The revelation of the
document could therefore only have made me more ridiculous and
contemptible in the eyes of the partners and my other work associates,
and possibly, I was even aware of this at the time of writing.

Below the title, "Apology For My Behaviour on Friday 11th
December 1953," written in red ink, are the following introductory lines:-
"Addressed to Mr. Adams, and at his will, to be lent to the other partners
of Young, Jackson, Beard & King (sols.), and to whomsoever he pleases,
providing only it is for the purpose of serious study and reflection. On no
account, without my permission, must this paper be shown, or any
passage quoted directly or indirectly, to any of my relatives or friends
(apart from members of the firm) whilst I am living. This paper was
written with the permission of Mr. Adams, and is his property, and must
be kept safely away from intruders, and may be burned when he chooses,
after I have left the company." The above suggests I must have attached
an exaggerated importance to the *Apology* as something of general
interest.

Then follows the main body of the document written in black ink:-
"Sir. – The intention of this paper is not that you repeal your dismissal,
for I admit that my rudeness to you on 12th was irremediable – I have not
the impertinence to doubt that – but at least I can attempt to justify my
behaviour, so that I may be seen in a proper light, and when I need a
reference, be given one that is just to myself and true to my future
prospective employers.

"I am appealing to you as an employer and a man of feeling. I hope
you will be patient and hear me through. I have much to say, and
everything will be directed to the point of this apology. The explanation
for my behaviour does not lend itself to simplicity. It is often intricate
and complex, but nonetheless valid in every point. I intend to tell the
truth, the whole truth, and nothing but the truth, about my experiences at

the firm, together with my feelings and opinions which eventually led me to act as I did on 11th. You must excuse any self-criticism, or laying bare my soul, which is not intended as exhibitionism or seeming arrogance towards the firm, for since this essay needs to be a confession to relieve my own conscience, and may I say, to partly satisfy your own curiosity, it must necessarily reveal unpleasant truths."

The document then describes the consequences of my leaving my glasses at home, and every detail of my feelings throughout the day, including the glorious *Schadenfreude* on realising the frustration and chaos in the office of the various employees – particularly the secretaries – at my absence. I was now being avenged on Misses Youatt and Allen, and others in the typists' department, for their occasional rudeness, and petty conflicts in which I had become involved, usually towards the end of the day in the rush to get out the post. There were then references to the privileges extended to those who had resorted to using taxis on various occasions, and how they had always obtained petty cash in covering such expenses, but how could I, a humble tea boy, hope to enjoy such rights?

Then I defended my good reputation by saying that in all my schooldays I had never played truant. Then I began to list and analyse all the examples of injustice and humiliation I had suffered during my 15 months with the firm. As Mr. Adams had stated that my anger with the firm was "impertinence," I felt the need to describe and analyse this anger down to the finest detail, but in the same breath I criticised the anger of the partners towards me on the grounds that anger in a lawyer was "unbecoming and unprofessional." I described my changing attitude to the firm, and of course, I described at length my feelings of class inferiority before Messrs Young and Adams. And so the document went on and on. Eventually the writing ground to a halt when I realised the document could be put to no practical use. At that point the *Apology* was placed in a brown envelope, and hidden away where it remained unseen for almost 60 years.

As the day of my dismissal was a Saturday, and a quiet half-day in the office, I left shortly before 1.0 pm, returning at the required time the following Monday. By this time Mr. Dawes had returned from his week's holiday. I spent most of the day writing my *Apology* which task was accepted as engaging in the firm's business. Miss Allen thought my *Apology* was a good idea, when she brought down some letters for the post, and saw me scribbling away at a great rate. Mr. Dawes stood over me, and asked tentatively, "Do you think you'll finish it today?" – "It'll take a week or two," I replied. – "You'll have a book by the time you're finished," said Mr. Dawes. – "It's not intended to be that," I put in defensively.

On Tuesday the 15th, my father called in at the office to enquire into the circumstances of my dismissal, he having made a prior appointment with Mr. Adams. They were closeted together for half an hour, and I wondered what could be occupying them so much time. I felt my father had no right to intervene in this way, and I felt embarrassed, and he left quietly without my seeing him. The following day at breakfast I asked point blank what had been discussed. My father said I had not put my heart into the job and that I was inefficient and forgetful, and that I had bought 100 ½ d. instead of 100 2 ½ d. stamps, and that I resented being reprimanded, and that although quite intelligent, I was unsuited for an office job, and that they had only kept me on as I was expected to be conscripted in the very near future.

On obtaining petty cash from Mr. Pope on the 21st, he turned to me with his usual smile, saying in his sad tone of voice, "Don't worry about your un-success here. Just keep your eyes open. I think you'll find your place. I think there's a stroke of genius somewhere inside you." At least someone held a positive opinion! My last day with the firm was on Christmas Eve. In the morning I was sent on the errand of fetching Mr. E.A. Andrews' repaired Ronson lighter from the Strand, and I lunched nearby in The George, opposite the Central Courts of Justice, on turkey, ham, chestnut stuffing, sprouts, and roast potatoes, followed by grapefruit, Christmas pudding and mince tarts with brandy sauce, washed down by coffee and a pint of Guinness.

Back at the office I found that Mr. Dawes had been quarrelling with the typists again – despite the festive season. He got on no better with the minor office staff than I did, usually entailing an exchange of words over their failure to put references on correspondence so that letters could not be properly filed, or because of their failure to complete their work in time to meet the post, and all that was involved in hot-sealing or preparing important or registered documents. By the early afternoon I was already receiving the well wishes of colleagues before they left for the Christmas break. I did not say goodbye to Mr. Young, as he had left early whilst I was still in town, and he had to take his wife, who had bronchitis, down to the country.

Mr. Adams left at 3.0 pm, and coming into the outer office he said, "Well, Corfe, I hope you get on very well wherever you go, and if you go into the Army and enjoy it as much as I did, you'll certainly have a good time." Mr. Legge gave me some sweets as a parting gesture, and I was sent on a last errand to get train tickets for Miss Youatt, and when I finally left the office at 3.45. pm, it was warm and sunny, and all the prostitutes were already off the streets. As it was the festive season, I bought a small box of cigars and smoked one on the tube as I made my way home.

That night I dreamed that Mr. Adams asked me what I wanted to do with my life, and taking the words out of my mouth, he said, "You'd rather have time for leisure," to which I assented, and he then added, "and you'd like to run a farm – be a squire – a man of means, and have equal time for work and leisure," to which I keenly replied, "Yes, and only labour on the land two days out of seven. If I had the money, I'd buy a farm." – "You're a man after my own heart," responded Mr. Adams. "Like me, you prefer leisure to work." I felt pleased and uplifted by this common feeling between us.

I visited the office on two further occasions: the first was on the 3rd January 1954, when I was warmly welcomed by Mr. Dawes, and I then went around the office wishing all the staff a happy and prosperous New Year, which was cheerfully reciprocated, and on returning to the post room, I asked Mr. Dawes if I might have two minutes of Mr. Adams' time. He rang up to the latter's office, and then turning to me said, "Go straight up." I explained I had not yet completed my *Apology*, and that on its completion I would only send it to him if I needed a reference. We then exchanged hearty good wishes, and I departed. I felt that perhaps he had a greater understanding of my needs than my parents could ever hope to have.

The second visit occurred about six months later, when I was in Army uniform, and I went around the office talking with most members of the staff, regaling them with stories of Army life. After leaving the Army, and passing by 2 Old Burlington Street some 2 ½ years later, I was surprised to note the firm was no longer there. I consulted the solicitors' Yearbook and several other directories and could find no trace of their existence. I had therefore to conclude that the partnership had been dissolved, and as the names of the three partners so commonly occurred in works of reference, it would have been an un-worthwhile time-consuming task to attempt tracing their present whereabouts.

That Christmas in 1953, on going to church, I took along a volume of Gibbon, discreetly wrapped in a black paper cover, which I read during the repetitive and interminable prayers and throughout the brain-numbing ritual. I thought it was a particularly suitable and healthy antidote to anything preached from the pulpit. On New Year's Day I formed the resolution to adopt a self-regarding Epicureanism as to my outward demeanour, and a stoical disdain of all pests and anxieties in as good a humour as I could muster. On the 6th January my call up papers finally arrived. I was to report to Devizes in Wiltshire on the 21st of the month, and I was glad my training was to take me to the West country.

On the 17th January, my father tried to persuade me, in company with my youngest brother, Oliver, to join them on a walk in the West End. I gently declined the offer, knowing it would only lead to another moral lecture, and so he left alone with Oliver, taking the tube. During my several last Sundays at home he tried to persuade me to accompany him to the Morning Service, but I firmly refused. Far from finding church-going spiritually uplifting, I found it the reverse of this.

It was soul-destroying on account of its sheep-like prostrations, its repudiation of intelligent or critical thought, its projection of blind obedience as a virtue in itself, its exploitation of stupidity in turning reason into unreason, and most of all, its falsity and myth-making deceit on a scale which was not merely disgusting but outrageously obscene. If I wished to experience spiritual fulfilment in regard to religion, and to *seriously* contemplate the true meaning of God, or the nature of existence, then I would turn to a Russian novel, preferably Tolstoy or Dostoevsky, or Dickens' *A Christmas Carol*, or Bergman's film, *Wild Strawberries*, where psychological reality was brought in direct contact with questions of the cosmos. This is where the power of true religion is to be found for the man or woman who wants to be free of ignorance or superstition.

This is not to suggest I was or am against all churchgoing, for I appreciate the aesthetic beauty of religious music and ritual as an appropriate environment for contemplation and gathering one's thoughts. As a nearby resident of Cambridge, which I have cause to visit frequently, I have often taken foreign visitors or other friends to the Daily Evensong (most beautiful of the Anglican services) at King's College Chapel. It is the evangelical (in the sense in which this word is historically understood in the English speaking world in contrast to the Continental usage in differentiating the Lutheran from the Calvinistic theologies) and overtly proselytising Christianity – especially that of the dissenting churches – which is so distasteful and objectionable.

My father may have begun to feel lonely with my impending absence, but he was not a man one could talk to on any matters of the heart, and although he may never have come to recognise the fact, he maintained a rigid mindset until the end despite a gradual move towards more liberal views.

Almost until the day of my joining the Army, I kept up an on-going communication with Hugh Richardson on my playwriting, but I relinquished any such ambitions on joining the service. As Patricia Dainton was now consigned to the past, there was little further reason for involving myself in theatrical life. At the beginning of January I received the following letter from Hugh Richardson, dated the 29th December, and sent from Flat 27, 100 Lancaster Gate:- "Dear Nigel Corfe. – Thank you very much for your delightful present – I'm *extremely* fond of cigars. I also appreciated very much your thought in sending it. I'm sorry the Army are keeping you hanging about like this. It is most unsettling not to know what your future is going to be. I'm rather busy at the moment but if you'll give me a ring on Thursday week (about 10.0 o'clock) we can arrange to meet. Forgive my haste. Once again *very* many thanks for the cigars, yours sincerely," &c.

Some days later I received the following letter dated the 4th January from my Aunt Inez:- "My dear Nigel. – Thank you very much for the lovely calendar. I have hung him in our dining room and he looks very handsome. I am afraid I have been rather a long time writing to you but I thought I would wait until I had some news, as we had a very 'quiet' Christmas and there was nothing to tell you about that! You all seem to have had a wonderful day at the Browns. The Bath Assembly this year is being based on 'Wood, the architect' and is largely in the hands of the Bath group of Architects of which Uncle Bill is a leading light, and he has undertaken to write a short history of Wood's work. It is the bi-centenary of his death, and with his usual thoroughness he has found out quite a lot of things that have never been published so far!

"One thing in particular that he designed was a mansion for Williams Brydges, cousin to the Duke of Chandos, near Hereford. So on Friday we went to Hereford and Uncle Bill having previously written to the head librarian at the County Library he was shewn (and lent) masses of letters written between 1720-25 about this house. Most interesting! We stayed the night and on Saturday morning went to the place where the mansion was, but unfortunately, the family having fallen on bad times they had to sell it about two years ago and it was then pulled down!! There is still a little of if there and the tiny church is intact with box pews and wonderful carvings behind the altar, which Wood mentions in one of his letters saying that he had found an Italian who would do the work and that he would bring him up from Bath and instruct him in what he was required to do.

"No one has ever heard of this before, so we are very excited at having discovered it, and I think we shall probably go there again to take some photographs of the church to illustrate the book. It has always been taken for granted that Wood worked only in Bath and nearby, but we have discovered that he also did some work near Cardiff, so expect that we shall be off there one day soon in our little old car! I wonder if you have got your call up papers yet, and where you will go for training. I had a card from Barbara for Xmas but no letter. I shall be writing to her soon. I am coming up for Crufts in February and I hope (!) staying at 105, so if you have 'gone for a soldier' as a maid of ours used to say, I shall not see you then. Yours affectionately," &c.

On the 19th January I went to Paddington and secured my rail ticket, and early in the morning two days later, my father drove me to the station with my suitcase in which was packed the 5th of the 12 volume set of Gibbon's, *Decline and Fall of the Roman Empire*, and I left on the train for Devizes to start a new period in my life. And to mark this point, I was to be known thenceforward by my first name of Robert.

***

Epilogue

As this memoir brings the life of the author almost up to the age of 18 ½, readers will ask themselves, what became of him after this date, and perhaps more significantly, how was his relationship resolved eventually with his parents, and what became of his brothers? On demobilisation he decided to embark on a commercial career, but if this was to be successful in terms of eventual promotion, he realised that learning to drive would be essential.

I was penurious, as with most ex-National Servicemen, on returning to civvy street, and my father was reluctant to pay for driving lessons, but nonetheless he agreed. By this time, my cousins, Michael and Howard (against whom I tended to measure most of my achievements), were not only proficient drivers, but had their own cars which they used for both pleasure and work. It can therefore be appreciated that I was keen to follow in their footsteps, whilst my father was equally keen to crush any such aspirations as socially undesirable. As he was footing the bill for the driving lessons, he felt entitled to harass the driving instructor in monitoring my progress. One evening, after the first few lessons, he burst into my room, hot under the collar, blustering about the hopelessness of my becoming a qualified driver. "You'll never learn to drive and that's what Mr. So-and-so says," he began.

On regaining his cool, he became more rational and persuasive, saying, "There's nothing to be ashamed of in not being able to drive. There are lots of people who can't drive. Driving is a highly specialised skill and it needs a very particular kind of ability. And besides, it would be intolerable if everyone wanted to drive – and there are quite enough people on the roads as it is." He was especially proud of his own driving skills as he had passed the Advanced Drivers Test some years earlier. He rarely drove more than 40 miles per hour and never over 50, and loathed to be overtaken on dual carriageways by what he described as "road hogs," and these he sometimes threatened to "punch on the nose" for speeding if he had had the opportunity.

The lessons were therefore curtailed, and when I did take my driving test, it was to be in Finland more than a decade later. I had no problems with any subsequent instructor, and eventually I was to drive around on business throughout Continental Europe in major conurbations without difficulty or incident. I believe the real reason my father terminated the driving lessons was that he thought my first motive for car use was for a social purpose, and admittedly, this was partly true, and he was still intent I should have no association with women.

He also intensified his objection to my socialising with my cousins, the Browns, firstly on the grounds they were living "beyond their means," and secondly because they were anyway above my "social status." As happy well-balanced people, they enjoyed life to the full, and joy was something he despised as corrupting and immoral. I ignored his behests in this regard, but it was my mother who then stepped in, and successfully contrived to break up my friendship with Michael. This occurred through a petty incident, the facts of which were distorted and blown out of proportion. I dined with Michael one evening in the West End, and was left to settle the bill, and whilst he was a reasonably paid executive on the managerial ladder of Frigidaire, I had humbler employment, and felt somewhat aggrieved.

On casually (and foolishly) remarking on the incident to my mother, unbeknown to me, she contacted my Aunt Joan, creating a great drama out of the episode of how one cousin had financially exploited another. Joan confronted and reprimanded her son and that was the end of the friendship, and although I nonetheless attended several formal functions at the house, I was hardly a welcome guest. Most hurtful was the fact that I had been excluded from the guest list at Michael's Wedding several weeks later – and although I attended as an uninvited guest at the insistence of my parents, I felt myself to be an unseen ghost amongst my relatives and the great festivities. At subsequent formal functions, I was often partnered with the ugliest girls, and on one occasion when I spent the greater part of the evening with a Swedish beauty, at the close of the proceedings, she was partnered off by my Aunt with another man to take her home, and that was the greatest humiliation I ever endured at the hands of any relative.

At that point in my life, I realised there was no alternative but to leave England forever and find true love in Continental Europe. Accordingly, I spent a year in West Germany and nine years in Scandinavia, where I was able to enjoy untrammelled pleasure and freedom for the first time in my life. This untrammelled pleasure, it should be noted, was not experienced through seeking a hedonistic lifestyle, but rather was incidental to the adventure in seeking a stable and permanent relationship. I worked first as a language teacher, and then as a freelance journalist contributing to the major newspapers, journals, and magazines of the country in which I resided.

On returning to England, I embarked once again on a commercial career, when a German friend of long-standing appointed me as a company director, and later I worked in senior management in a manufacturing environment in marketing and export sales, and finally as a management consultant in promoting the prosperity of SMEs. In the Thatcherite era, with the economic attack on home-based productivity, I engaged in intensive socio-economic research, especially in relationship to the health of British industry, and soon became politically active. In addition, over a period of 30 years, I became active in several other spheres of public life, and in 1987 established the Campaign for Industry, which although it failed as a political movement, achieved invaluable work in laying the foundations for socially-wealth creating industrial regeneration.

After leaving the Army, therefore, my parents became an even greater hindrance to my progress than they had been during my early childhood or teenage years. Hence their influence was almost wholly malign, and this necessitated that I should become a self-made person through my own efforts in developing a sense of objective rationality. The main fault of my parents was not merely selfishness, and meanness of spirit, but the meanness of their purse when they were blessed with the financial wherewithal.

This brings to mind the words of that best and wisest of men, Sir Francis Bacon, who wrote in his essay, *Of Parents and Children*, more than 400 years ago, "The illiberality of parents in allowance towards their children is an harmful error, makes them base, acquaints them with shifts, makes them sort with mean company, and makes them surfeit more when they come to plenty." If the above remarks seem severe towards my parents, or arouse the suspicion that perhaps only one person was so adversely affected, then perhaps we should also turn to the stories of my brothers.

If my parents succeeded in alienating me from my cousin and close friend, Michael, and diminishing my reputation in the eyes of his family, that was the limit of harm they achieved in the broader family circle. My two brothers were less fortunate. Due to the malicious talk of my parents, and subtler stratagems to exclude, they eventually succeeded in alienating both Gavin and Oliver from almost all their relatives, on the grounds they were unfit for mixing in good company. Gavin, on account of his rebellious ways, was referred to by my Aunt Joan as a "Communist," which was quite untrue, since not only was he apolitical, but rather conservative in his views when these were drawn out.

On leaving school, he had a succession of varied jobs, including working for several music publishers, and on marrying in 1963, my father kindly paid for his honeymoon, comprising a first class ticket from Victoria Station to Dorking, and one night in a 3-Star hotel. He subsequently worked for the Hospital Saving Association, which he eventually loathed, and shortly after his promotion and move to Yorkshire, he suffered a nervous breakdown requiring hospitalisation for several months. His wife, who had care of their two small children, concealed the problem from the rest of the family (knowing her in-laws were unlikely to be of much help), and on his recovery, he studied for a teaching degree, and a year or so following his graduation, qualified as an

MA. His teaching career progressed rapidly, culminating in Head of English at a leading feeder school to Harrow, and a Headship of a Preparatory school in Highgate. In his mid-70s, he is still in heavy demand as a supply teacher to schools and the prison service in Bristol where he has lived for 15 years. He still excels as a musician on the trumpet and piano and plays occasionally for various bands.

My youngest brother, Oliver, felt obliged to leave the country almost as soon as he reached his 20s. As with his siblings, he found home life insufferable, and he felt lonely and alienated from the rest of humanity. His first wish was to become a motor mechanic, but he found English class consciousness discriminatory, and he was mocked and ragged because of his cultural background. In Australia he bummed around, and found he was not entirely welcome amongst snobbishly inclined relatives, before disappearing entirely for three years and no one knew whether he was dead or alive.

On re-emerging, he wrote a novel entitled, *The Seagull Rider*, which had some success, vividly describing with humour his loneliness and search for a girl friend as a recent immigrant down-under. Interestingly, he described his parents as a working class couple, and in reflecting on the matter, I feel he was obliged to portray them in this way, as otherwise the degree of their ignorance would hardly be credible, or else he would have needed to write a far too complex psychological novel about an unusually eccentric pair. Truth, then, is indeed stranger than fiction, or rather, there comes a point when the facts of life are so perverse that they defy fictionalisation.

He then settled in Adelaide, and decided to set up a bakery. Over a period of several years and working sixteen hours a day, he built up a team and a prosperous business, eventually obtaining contracts to supply the University and other colleges in Adelaide. On meeting his future wife, who had been a student at the University, he sold the business for a handsome profit, and became a civil servant, so as to work civilised hours, and fulfil the obligations of a normal married life. They had two children and now are grandparents, and live a leisurely life in a spacious property in Stirling in the Adelaide Hills, having acquired a Rolls Royce (amongst other vehicles) and a number of interesting friends in the neighbourhood.

This returns us to the question posed at the start of the Epilogue: how was our relationship eventually resolved with our parents? I should be remiss if I failed to note that on achieving senior management status, my father actually said he was "proud of me," although I rather think my mother nudged him towards this. He was also proud of the achievements of his other two sons. It would also be remiss if I failed to note that he assisted those two of us resident in the UK financially, after our marriages, with regard to mortgage down payments, although this was not asked for by either of us, and he also assisted with other major payments from time to time – usually on hearing we had entered into hire purchase agreements, something of which he disapproved on principle on the grounds of excessive interest charges. In addition he assisted Oliver with regard to his university studies in accountancy in Melbourne in the late 60s.

These benefits aside, we three brothers continued to regard our parents and our childhood past with sardonic humour. There was no other way in which our sanity could be maintained. Meanwhile, my wife, and that of my brother Gavin (who chose to use his middle name, Russell, on completing military service) disliked their in-laws, and rarely missed an opportunity in expressing their exasperation or disdain. At the same time, my parents criticised our wives for numberless petty reasons. Oliver's wife escaped such an abrasive situation since they lived on the other side of the globe.

These difficulties apart, the relationship with our parents for the last 30 years of their lives was entirely correct. There were no resentments or bad feelings, providing past memories were forgotten, or repressed, and a cheerful front was presented for the sake of good form. At the same time, a wholesome distance was kept, and in this way disputes or quarrels were kept at bay. They were always made welcome in our homes, and return hospitality was gratefully received. Nothing controversial was discussed – irrespective of whether it was in the private or public spheres of life - and if they expressed an opinion on any matter, such as the need for the return of hanging or flogging, then we generally indicated assent, although this passive response stuck in our throats, and was a subject for lively indignation after we parted. There was always an exchange of smiles and comfortable platitudes, and these attitudes and false fronts not only induced a deathly boredom, but a profound feeling of depression, as the last ounce of life was squeezed out of this stage-like performance. The unpleasantness was compounded by the fact that sometimes our wives accused us (falsely or otherwise) of too readily going along with our parents' prejudices.

After the death of my father, we took good care of my mother. For several years, every month, I made the long journey to her sheltered accommodation on the South coast, when I stayed for three of four days and cooked her meals, and entertained her throughout the day. For the first time in my experience – she was now in her mid and late 80s – she opened up by becoming very loquacious, and many stories recorded in this book are taken from that period. At noon before lunch, she insisted on our having a Sherry, and at 6.0 pm, before dinner, she would have a Whiskey whilst I preferred a glass of wine. She was glad to have such "good sons," and said she was envied by others in the home, some of whom were hardly ever visited by relatives.

With the deterioration of her health on reaching 90, and her failure to be bothered to prepare proper meals, Russ and I arranged for her transfer to a nursing home in Bristol, just five minutes walk from his flat. With such close proximity, my brother visited her almost daily, taking her to the local pub, and I continued to visit her in Bristol about every six weeks, as I had been entrusted with the power of attorney and needed to monitor her financial affairs. On one occasion the three of us visited the cinema and saw, *Titanic*, and afterwards I congratulated her on not once falling asleep during the performance, to which she replied, "You could hardly fall asleep, it was so loud."

It was then that she came out with her own personal story on the aftermath of the *Titanic's* sinking as related in the first chapter of this book. On other occasions on visiting her either at her sheltered accommodation on the South coast or in Bristol, I took her to the nursing home in Bath to visit her eldest sister, Inez, whose mental faculties had greatly deteriorated. Once when leaving my aunt, after she described how she had a "pet dog in the back garden" and that her "parents were coming to fetch her for an outing that very afternoon," my mother cheerfully remarked, "She seems happier now than she ever was in her younger days." On another occasion when leaving my aunt when she was clearly in a worse mental condition, my mother commented, "I can hardly believe it's my own sister. She never even recognised us."

When Aunt Inez finally died at the age of 99, and I arranged the funeral, I ensured that the Union Flag be draped over her coffin as was her right as an ex-servicewoman who had been a lifelong activist in the British Legion amongst several other charitable organisations. As the honorary secretary of the Women's Section of the Bath branch of the association, on the Golden Jubilee of the Legion, she had been a guest at a Buckingham Palace garden party held in 1971. My mother, on the other hand, lived to be 93, and her middle sister, Joan lived to be 96.

The question may be asked as to whether there was to be any forgiveness between my father and his three sons. This is an impossible question to answer. What is forgiveness? It is the easiest thing in the world to declare as such, but a declaration in itself is meaningless. If a person asks for forgiveness, it is naturally a polite and humane gesture to grant their wish, irrespective of personal feelings. True forgiveness, however, usually follows an apology, but not even that is a guarantee of its true intent. Forgiveness which is genuine usually follows insults, rebuffs, or accidental or intentional petty injuries between relatives and friends normally enjoying good relationships, for then an exchange of good intentions can re-join their friendship, and the offence may be mutually forgotten.

But the situation regarding the rift between my father and his sons was something quite different. Where can grounds for the establishment of forgiveness be found? The thrashings with all their pain created an irreconcilable situation. As they were given as punishment, the man who wielded the cane is hardly likely to apologise for what he thought was the administration of justice – especially as the cane was used in fulfilling the will of God. If, since then, the man has changed his perspective of justice and the nature of punishment, there nonetheless still remain slim grounds for forgiveness, for the memory of the pain and the mental hurt is everlasting. Howsoever he should attempt to formulate an apology, it would only elicit a burst of laughter at the absurdity of attempting a reconciliation. My mind was made up at eight years old, as a rational decision one winter's evening in the West End of London, and I would be unlikely to change it even in the evening of my life.

There is only one course I can see towards the final reconciliation between we three sons and the spirit of our father, and that is through returning to those remarks in the final paragraphs of the Prologue to this book. Blame must be cast on the false beliefs of the age in which he was nurtured at the start of the 20th century – beliefs which led to the unleashing of conflict and destruction on a scale never experienced in the entire history of humankind. These beliefs stemmed from the bigotry, deceit, and hypocritical values of organised religion, irrespective of whether we point the accusing finger at such an atrocious clergyman, as the Rev. E.A. Dunn in Muswell Hill; or a Georgian Orthodox monk in Eastern Europe who ruled his country for 30 years and slaughtered 25 million of his own people; or a Roman Catholic foreigner in another country, who embarked on the systematic genocide of a race, which might have been suggested by the tribal god of its victims.

The war against reason and the civilised values of the Enlightenment was the hallmark of the 20th century. All men and women are the victims of their environment, and the ideas and education in which they are nurtured; and hence, unknowingly, they are used as the instruments of evil. Only through the study of ethical philosophy, linked to the science of psychology and the sociology of humankind, is it possible to transcend the imprisoning bonds of ignorance. But few people have endeavoured to study these most important subjects of all in attempting to achieve a sound and stable society.

My father was therefore condemned to living a life of ignorance, whereby the ingenuity of religious authority interpreted the good as the bad and the bad as the good, and where black and white was arbitrarily transposed at will. Men and women are told to look into their hearts, or use their conscience, in identifying the good, but this instrument of religious teachers is the greatest deception of all. No one is in a position to trust his feelings in judging right and wrong, because feelings are subjective and always self-regarding, and moreover, injuries or offence or personal incapacities of one kind or another, too often lead to false ideas on questions of justice or right decision-making. Hence, the tranquil mind alone, in conjunction with relevant spheres of knowledge, is fit for ascertaining questions of good or bad.

Consequently, for all these reasons, and because of the helplessness of the majority in understanding what constitutes the ethical life, I believe my father should be forgiven all his sins and misdemeanours. It is also necessary for the good of the soul that children should forgive their parents for injuries received, and this justifies the custom of ancestor worship, for we are what our parents made us, for good or ill. In the homes of Chinese friends in the Far East, I have admired their ancestral shrines, and the momentary daily obeisance and the lighting of joss sticks. Hence in the West, the emphasis is more likely to be placed on genetic factors and DNA, and our thanks to our forebears for good health, intelligence, and an equable frame of mind.

It should also be borne in mind, as inferred in the Prologue of this book, that most individuals occupy different spheres of existence, most notably private and public lives which are separate from one another. If my father failed as a likeable or good person in his private life, this could not be said of his professional career or public image within the church or Freemasonry. As a dental consultant he was apparently held in high regard, being often the recipient of gifts by grateful patients whose pain or ailments he successfully relieved. As his patient I never experienced fear or pain whilst seated in the dental chair. If our Judaeo-Christian culture puts the values of private life above those of the public, it should be remembered that the reverse of this pertained in the classical world. And who is in a position to give a final judgement as to which is the better attitude?

In describing so vividly the split in the personal relationship between my father and I, and the fact that no real reconciliation was ever achieved, it may be asked as to whether the writing of this memoir left me with a sense of guilt or wrongdoing? The writing of this memoir, or more specifically, this *Confession*, had to be undertaken whatever the consequences in the striving for understanding and truth – even if the latter could never be attained in any final sense. In answer to the question, on the conscious level I am guilt-free, for I have rationalised the psychological circumstances entailed, and revealed to my own satisfaction that all involved in the drama are free from blame as in different ways they were victims of forces beyond their control.

In answering the question on the unconscious level, however, I am not quite so sure. Only the revelations of our dreams can unfold such deeper truths. Some months after completing this memoir, and after winning the assent of my brothers to the verity of the account, and after incorporating without demur their suggested amendments and corrections, I had a strangely unpleasant dream. The dream took place in the present but it included, as so often in dreams, the participation of those who had long been dead. I felt alone and friendless in the world, and was struggling in vain along city streets to reach those loved ones who were avoiding my company, and I knew not where they were. Eventually I reached a house where a family meeting had been called behind my back, and of which I was supposed to be ignorant. It was held at the invitation and in the house of my great Aunt Ruth, and as I arrived, the meeting had ended and the guests were preparing to make their departure.

As I entered the hallway, the guests were slowly descending a spiral wrought iron staircase from the floor above, their expressions mixed with sadness and anger. First was my father, followed by my brothers, and then my own children, and several other younger members of the family. I felt that my presence was an embarrassment and unwelcome, as no one glanced at me as I stood silently by, and I felt offended and depressed by their response. As my father approached the front door, he turned to me, and without a trace of irony or resentment but with stoical resignation, he gently exclaimed, in a manner I had never known him speak before, "You don't recognise me, do you?" His meaning was not that I failed to recognise his identity, but that I failed to recognise his existence as a human being. Despite the coolness of his manner the statement was clearly intended as a reproach.

I was taken aback by these disarming words for I realised he was confirming the total break in our relationship, and that this matter had brought about the family meeting. In this realisation, and in the face of such finality, I replied in the only way I could in such impossible circumstances, calmly enunciating the words, "No, I don't know who you are." And as those words passed my lips, I awoke with a sense of discomfort and pangs of guilt. In real life, on only one occasion had he come so close to making such a gesture, and that was in 1953, following the Archbishop of Canterbury's visit to St. James's Church, when he branded me as being "disloyal to the family," as described in Chapter 22 of this book. On that occasion he was enraged by the fact that other relatives had given me a ticket to attend the church service led by the Archbishop.

Although on several occasions my mother indicated her husband had mellowed in old age, I doubt the reality of this. Shortly before his death, whilst still at home, he had pulled a plastic bag over his head, in an act of either feigned or intended violence. Did he not realise that suicide was a sin mortal to the soul? On his death bed, several days before his decease through cancer at the age of 83, his violence and anger returned in all its fury. On the visit of his sister – possibly the only woman he really loved – he turned his rage on her younger son, Howard, who had acted as chauffeur – showering him with a torrent of abuse.

When I arrived with my mother several days later, he threatened to cut me out of his will on the suspicion I had been made "redundant." This was during the Thatcherite era during the collapse of manufacturing industry. I was resentful of this threat, since I was more careful in money matters than either of my brothers, whilst Russ had always had the reputation of being a spendthrift. He shouted at me that my brother, Russ, was to have my share of the inheritance. I had indeed been made redundant some days earlier. As I no longer had a company car, my mother ensured that I park my personal vehicle well away from the sight of his hospital window. The secret was well kept, and he never discovered the truth.

A week later he was dead, and I travelled to the South coast to arrange the funeral. Before his death he had been transferred to a hospice, and I visited the room in which he died on 1st May 1990. It was low-ceilinged and the bed was facing the window, and the most beautiful view imaginable for a dying man of goodwill, for it looked out onto a cherry tree in full white blossom in brilliant sunshine. Did he die in peace or in the nightmare hell of wreaking vengeance on the world? No one will ever know for he died alone and unloved, and that is the most demonstrable assurance of the final descent that any person may rationally accept, irrespective of religious belief. It is almost a certainty that his Christian religion and all his churchgoing brought him little consolation at the end.

My mother excused the hysterical outbursts of his final days as symptoms of illness, but I rather doubt the accuracy of her conclusion. They were too much in character with the life he had led. At the reception following the cremation when his ashes (as requested) were thrown to the four winds, there were approximately forty people present, and I met the president of his Masonic lodge, who owned a chain of clothing shops, and was astonished when he described how "good" my father had been "in training the young people in the mystic art," for I could scarcely imagine him befriending the younger generation in any sphere of activity.

If this Freemason was really speaking the truth, then it only confirmed the depth of loathing and contempt he must have had for his sons. We then spoke of other matters, and as he happened to be an old Highgate boy, I mentioned several teachers, including the Latin master,

Mr. Markham. "Did he teach you?" exclaimed the Freemason, astonished. "I didn't like him. He was a nasty piece of work. Quite sadistic with the boys!"

*

Lightning Source UK Ltd.
Milton Keynes UK
UKOW040214110712

195751UK00002B/65/P